RAMBLES I
GLASGOW

Descriptive, Historical, and Traditional

By Hugh Macdonald

with a new introduction and notes by K C Murdarasi

RUTHERGLEN CHURCH

First published 1854.
Twenty-first century edition (paperback)
published 2023 by Hephaestion Press.

9781916490932

Cover design by Hanna Herrmann.
Cover photograph courtesy of GerryBlaikie.com

For Faither.

INTRODUCTION TO THE 21ˢᵗ CENTURY EDITION

By K C Murdarasi

"Antiquary, poet, botanist, topographer, tradesman, songster and litterateur, rolled in one."

This is how the friends of Hugh MacDonald described him shortly after his untimely death. Although his name may be unfamiliar now, MacDonald was a 'well kent' Glasgow character, who was remembered fondly by his large circle of friends and acquaintances. The journalist and poet was held in sufficient respect that memorial fountains were built in his honour on Gleniffer Braes and Glasgow Green, and one of the gates of the Green is also named after him.

It was from the inscription at this gate, while researching another book about Glasgow, that I first became aware of Hugh MacDonald. After reading his *Rambles* for myself, I too started to feel a great fondness for this son of Glasgow, just as his earlier readers had, and it seemed to me that it is only fair to MacDonald, and to Glasgow, that his work should be made available to a new generation of readers.

Hugh MacDonald was born in Bridgeton, Glasgow, in 1817, one of eleven children born to poor Highland immigrants to the city. Although he had to leave school to begin his career in the Barrowfield cotton printing works at the age of nine, he had a deep love of literature and learning. He started writing poetry when he was only about 11 years old and later became a member of the City Club, a literary gathering that met in the Bank Tavern on Trongate, as well as of scientific and archaeological societies. Largely self-educated, MacDonald was a great reader who loved to keep up to date with the latest books.

MacDonald married twice, both times to girls from Rutherglen. His first wife, Agnes, died in childbirth within a year of their marriage. According to Agnes' wish, MacDonald married the bridesmaid from their wedding, Alison, with whom he had five children.

Introduction

After collecting some savings from his work, MacDonald made a brief foray into commerce, running a grocer's shop. The venture failed, according to his friends because he was "guileless even to a fault", giving credit to anyone who asked for it, and MacDonald lost everything. He found work in a block-printing works in Paisley, and for the first few weeks he had to travel from Bridgeton to Paisley and back on foot every day, until he was able to find accommodation there.

However, MacDonald's fortunes changed when his literary talent was recognised. He initially wrote poetry for the radical paper, the *Chartist Circular*, but after he wrote an impassioned letter to the *Glasgow Citizen* in defence of Robert Burns in 1848, the editor, James Hedderwick, persuaded MacDonald to turn his literary talents to writing for that newspaper. MacDonald became a regular columnist and eventually sub-editor. *Noms de plume* were common among journalists at that time, and MacDonald wrote under the penname Caleb.

MacDonald soon combined his love of history, poetry and the natural world in a series of articles about his wanders in the countryside around Glasgow. These were published in the *Citizen* over three years under the name Caleb, and in 1854 they were collected into a book, *Rambles Round Glasgow*. The book was very well received, and MacDonald followed it up in 1857 with another travelogue, *Days at the Coast*, this time covering the scenery and tourist destinations on the Firth of Clyde. He went on to work for both the *Glasgow Sentinel* and the *Glasgow Times*, before dying in 1860 at the age of only 43. He is buried in the Southern Necropolis.

MacDonald was never a wealthy man, and left only a £100 life assurance policy to provide for his large family. His many friends and admirers set up a fund for the bereaved family, including money raised by bringing out an edition of MacDonald's poetry, and the impressive total came to more than £900.

Hugh MacDonald is now little known, even in his native Glasgow. Although his books went through several editions, both are now sadly out of print. This new edition has been released to make

Hugh MacDonald's charming observations more widely available to the people of Glasgow and farther afield.

Since it was first published, the value of *Rambles Round Glasgow* has changed. While it originally aimed to show readers the delights of nature and history that lay near their city, now it shows us a city that has changed dramatically, in some cases beyond recognition. Kenmuir, subject of chapter two, is now mostly covered by the M8 and an industrial zone. Monklands canal has also disappeared beneath the motorway. The 'villages' of Tollcross and Parkhead, Crossmyloof and Cathcart have become suburbs of Glasgow. The "dreary moorlands beyond Kilbride" are now the Whitelee wind farm, where modern ramblers wander the extensive paths between turbines that can be seen from the centre of Glasgow. Only Glasgow Green and Kelvingrove park are fairly unchanged. Despite this, readers familiar with the areas where MacDonald rambled will no doubt recognise certain features despite so much change – the landowners' estates that are now public parks; the old roads in and out of Glasgow that retain their routes and, in some cases,

Introduction

their names; and a number of beautiful buildings that survived twentieth-century Glasgow's notorious passion for demolition.

The Glasgow that MacDonald rambled around was very different from ours in more ways than just the physical. It was an era of industrial growth and terrible poverty. Child labour was commonplace, and large families lived in single rooms in the filthy wynds off High Street. The smoke of factories choked the air and the docks of the Clyde bustled with cargo being loaded and unloaded. It was an era of change and ferment. There was public agitation for voting reform and slum clearance. There were working men's clubs, societies of learning and public libraries that allowed social mobility on a scale that had not been seen before. Travel was also opening up to ordinary people. The railways were expanding across the country, and MacDonald used some of the new railway lines for his farther-flung rambles, as well as the steamers that chugged up and down the Clyde almost like buses.

MacDonald's own interest in social and political issues is clear from the comments he makes as he rambles, taking in game laws, poverty and pollution. Although he moved on from writing for Chartist papers, he retained his democratic sympathies, calling the 1832 Reform Act a "great moral victory". He sympathised outspokenly with the Covenanters, and appreciated the romantic tragedy of Mary Queen of Scots.

Like many Victorians, MacDonald was an advocate of progress, and despite his love of beauty he by no means thought that the productive should be impeded by the picturesque. Of course, the greater part of Glasgow's expansion was still to come, and we can only wonder what MacDonald would have thought of the sprawling metropolis that his native city has become. We can be sure, though, with his warm heart and constant optimism, that he would have found much to praise.

A NOTE ABOUT THIS EDITION

This book is based on the text of the third edition of *Rambles Around Glasgow*, from 1860. When *Rambles* ran to a second edition,

MacDonald included extra material and added notes (indicated in this edition by square brackets) which were "freely introduced wherever they were thought necessary." A 1910 edition added further notes and an introduction by Rev. G H. Morrison, the minister of Wellington Church in Glasgow's west end. As a further century has passed since then, many more notes seem necessary, and so they have been fairly "freely introduced" in this edition. These mostly take the form of further information about the people MacDonald mentions, and updates about the state of buildings and locations that he picks out for attention.

In addition, I have tried to reference his innumerable quotations, where possible. MacDonald had a great love of poetry, and his particular favourites seem to have been: Sir Walter Scott; Shakespeare; the Romantic poets in general; the Paisley poet Robert Tannahill and Glasgow's great Thomas Campbell; and, above all, Robert Burns, of whose poetry he was a tireless supporter. MacDonald was a keen reader of *Blackwood's Magazine*, where many of the poems were originally published. These quotations are obviously from memory most of the time, which, while impressive, often leads to misquotation. In most cases I have been able to track down the lines he intended, and where the misquote is slight I have not pointed it out. In other cases, it makes the identification of the poem harder, and in those cases the notes will indicate a best guess. Sometimes the words MacDonald puts in quotation marks are simply common sayings or slang expressions, for which there is no literary reference. In other cases, I have failed altogether to find the reference, and if any reader knows the source of an unreferenced quotation, I would be glad to hear about it! The dates given for quotations are generally of the first publication, but for some poems they are the dates they were originally written.

Although MacDonald wrote the *Rambles* in English, he throws in some Scots words for colour, and many of his numerous quotations are taken from authors who wrote in Scots. To avoid drowning the reader in footnotes, I have only provided translations of Scots words that I think may be particularly unfamiliar and left untranslated the words that are (in my judgement) better known. Readers who speak no Scots may find it useful to consult the free online *Dictionary of the Scots Language* (dsl.ac.uk). MacDonald also uses Latin words and phrases, as was normal in the nineteenth century. As most twenty-first century readers are probably not familiar with Latin, I have provided a translation of all but the most well-known expressions, as well as definitions of some English words that have become more obscure with the passage of time.

The chapters were originally intended to be read individually, and have no particular order, so the same footnotes are repeated in different chapters, where necessary, so that the reader can dip in and out at will.

"Of a truth we live in a marvellous age."

Image of Hugh MacDonald from the memorial fountain on Glasgow Green.

I t is almost unnecessary to mention that the series of articles of which the present volume is composed were originally published, with the signature of "Caleb" attached to them, in the columns of the *Glasgow Citizen* newspaper, where they appeared at intervals during the course of three successive years. The Rambles were written with the intention of conveying to the readers of that journal some knowledge of the principal landscape features of the country within a circle of from eight to ten miles round Glasgow, with a *resumé* of the Historical, Biographical, and Traditional associations of the various localities included within the scope we have indicated. The district of which Glasgow is the centre, while it possesses many scenes of richest Lowland beauty, and presents many glimpses of the stern and wild in Highland landscape, is peculiarly fertile in reminiscences of a historical nature. In the latter respect, indeed, it is excelled by few localities in Scotland, — a circumstance of which many of our citizens seem to have been hitherto almost unconscious. There is a story told of a gentleman who, having boasted that he had travelled far to see a celebrated landscape on the Continent, was put to the blush by being compelled to own that he had never visited a scene of superior loveliness which was situated upon his own estate, and near which he had spent the greater portion of his life. The error of this individual, however, is one of which too many are guilty. We have thousands amongst ourselves who can boast of their familiarity with the wonders of other lands, yet who have never traced the windings of the Clyde, the Cart, or the Kelvin, and who have never dreamed of visiting the stately ruins of Bothwell, or of penetrating that sanctum of Gothic magnificence, the crypt of our own venerable Cathedral! To such parties we would say, that admiration, like charity, should begin at home; and that there are many things of beauty and of interest to be met with in the course of a brief ramble among the environs of our own city.

To those who may desire to familiarize themselves with the topographical features, the historical associations, and the antiquarian remains of the country round Glasgow, the present volume will, it is hoped, prove in some respects a useful companion and guide. The information which it embodies is the harvest of many a pleasant excursion through woods and fields, of many a delightful research among curious old tomes and chronicles of the past. Its composition was, in truth, a labour of love. During the peregrinations to which it led many valued friendships, many genial acquaintanceships were formed; and the best wish which we can frame for the readers who may honour us by following in our footsteps is, that they may everywhere experience as much civility, as much kindness, and as much hospitality as fell to our own share. Should such be the case, reader and author will alike have pleasure in the remembrance of RAMBLES ROUND GLASGOW.

H. M'D.

92 JOHN STREET, BRIDGETON,
    July 26, 1854.

No. I. The Public Green

Few towns can boast such a spacious and beautiful public park as the Green of Glasgow, with its wide-spreading lawns, its picturesque groups of trees, its far-winding walks, its numerous delicious springs, and, above all, its rich command of scenery. The "lungs of London"[1] may exceed it in extent of surface and in artificial adornment, but in beauty of situation and variety of prospect, our own Green certainly surpasses any of the street-girt metropolitan breathing-places. The Green of Glasgow lies to the south-east of the city, on the north bank of the Clyde, which, in a fine bold sweep, forms its southern boundary. It embraces in all about 140 imperial acres,[2] and is surrounded by a carriage-drive two and a-half miles in length, besides being intersected in every direction by gravelled walks, overhung in some instances by the foliage of stately trees, which forms a pleasant screen from the noon-day sun or the pelting shower; while every here and there seats have been erected for the convenience of the weary lounger. At what period the nucleus of this handsome park first became the property of the community cannot now be ascertained; but it is supposed to have formed part of a grant which was made by James the Second of Scotland to a certain William Turnbull, Lord of Provan and Bishop of Glasgow,[3] on the 20th of April, 1450. In the document conferring the gift, the pious monarch declares that, "for the praise of Almighty God, and of the glorious Virgin Mary, and the blessed Kentigern, patron and confessor of the Church of Glasgow, and for the love which we bear to the Reverend Father in Christ, William, present Bishop in said Church, we have given to the said Bishop and his successors for ever, the City of Glasgow, Barony of Glasgow, and lands commonly called the Bishop's Forest, with their pertinents in woods, plains, meadows, marshes, pasturages," &c., &c. This, it will be admitted, was a right royal gift. To build a bridge or a church was, in the "good old times,"

---

[1] Primarily Hyde Park, Green Park and St James's Park. The phrase was first attributed to William Pitt the Elder (1708 – 1778).

[2] More precisely, 136 acres or 55 hectares.

[3] d.1454, founder of the University of Glasgow.

1

reckoned a pretty safe passport with St. Peter;[4] and it is to be hoped that such a handsome donation as the above would win for the regal donor (a mere boy, by the by!) the especial favour of Mother Church, and secure for him after death a rapid passage through the dreary labyrinths of purgatory. If the Green, however, was included in the pious grant of the unfortunate James, who was subsequently killed at the siege of Roxburgh by the bursting of a cannon, it was at all events originally of much smaller dimensions than it is in our day. From time to time, with praiseworthy spirit, the authorities, as the city increased in extent, secured adjacent portions of territory, until in 1792, by the purchase of the Fleshers' Haugh from Patrick Bell, Esq. of Cowcaddens, the Green ultimately attained its present size. The improvement of these spacious grounds has also been effected in a gradual manner. At no very distant date they were traversed by the Redclaith Gott, or Camlachie Burn, as it is now called, and also by the Molendinar rivulet; while, from the lowness of the banks at certain places, they were liable to be overflowed by every spate in the river; and even at spring-tides, pools and islands were occasionally formed on their surface. From the period of the Revolution until the present time, a succession of improvements on the Green have been effectively carried out. The landward boundary is protected by walls and railings – banks have been formed to restrain the incursions of the river – moist places have been drained – the Molendinar and Camlachie burns have been arched over, and are now conveyed by invisible channels to the Clyde – hollows have been filled up – inequalities have been levelled – trees have been planted – and enclosures have been formed; while the general aspect has been greatly ameliorated and beautified. Among the more prominent benefactors of the Green in times past, were Provosts Peter and George Murdoch,[5] the latter of whom formed the fine serpentine walks, bordered with shrubbery, which are still remembered by the old inhabitants, but which were removed in consequence of certain abuses to which they were occasionally liable.

---

[4] St Peter, in Christian tradition, holds the keys to Heaven.
[5] Peter Murdoch, sugar merchant, was Provost 1730 – 1732. George Murdoch, probably his nephew, was Provost 1754–1756 and 1766–1768.

In our own day the late Dr. Clelland[6] distinguished himself by his attention to the amenities of the Green: under his auspices the splendid carriage-drive was formed, and many other improvements effected. More recently, Councillor Moir[7] has deservedly gained golden opinions by his exertions in the same field; and when his projected ameliorations are completed, the Green will undoubtedly present an appearance vastly superior to what has hitherto been witnessed, and which will challenge comparison with that of any public park in the empire.

In defence of their privileges the craftsmen of Glasgow have ever been honourably distinguished. It was to their public-spirited resistance to the iconoclastic fury of the Reformation that we are indebted for the preservation of our beautiful Cathedral. The same determined spirit has been evoked on several occasions in defence of the Green. In 1744 the Provost and Magistrates were desirous of selling a portion of it, and were only dissuaded from the act by the clamorous opposition which the proposal excited. On various subsequent occasions encroachments on the Green have been attempted, and in some instances even to a certain extent effected; but such has invariably been the indignation excited by invasions of this nature, that they have generally proved abortive. Many of our readers will remember the outburst of popular feeling which occurred a few years since,[8] on the erection of a theatre upon the vacant space opposite the public Jail, and also the vigorous opposition with which the proposal to carry a railway over a portion of the Green was received.[9] It is but fair, however, to mention, that our civic authorities, notwithstanding the occasional exceptions alluded to, have generally proved faithful guardians of the public park, and have expended, with

---

[6] Dr James Cleland (1770 – 1840), a superintendent of public works responsible for several improvement projects.

[7] James Moir (1806 – 1880), tea merchant and radical councillor who championed the interests of the east-end working class.

[8] In 1844. There was a petition for the removal of the City Theatre but it burned down that same year.

[9] Proposed in 1847 by the Glasgow, Airdrie and Monkland Junction Railway Company.

an ungrudging liberality, the large sums originally required for its extension, and subsequently for its improvement and embellishment. In the hands of our present enlightened and public-spirited Magistracy and Council, the citizens have happily nothing to fear with regard to the preservation of such a valuable privilege as the Green; but were it otherwise, we have the utmost confidence that our modern craftsmen are not unworthy of their ancestors, and like them are possessed

> "Of hearts resolved, and hands prepared,
> The blessings they enjoy to guard,"[10]

and that any violation of the popular territory would assuredly be met with an uncompromising resistance.

Having thus glanced, in a cursory manner, at the origin and gradual increase and improvement of the Glasgow Green, let us now indulge ourselves with a leisurely stroll within its precincts. It is a beautiful day in this merriest month of the year,[11] and issuing from the sweltering and bustling streets, the verdure even of the much-trodden sward brings a pleasing sense of freshness to the eye of him who, long "in populous city pent,"[12] has yearned to see the bright livery of woods and fields. The welcome sunshine, penetrating even into wynds and vennels, with its golden invitation from on high, has called forth their wan and filthy inhabitants in swarms. In the vicinity of the Saltmarket, where we have made our *entrée*, the Green is all alive with squalid groups, the children of misery and vice. Beguiled by the radiance of the summer noon, they have sneaked forth, for a brief interval, from their reeky and noisome haunts, to breathe for a time the comparatively "caller air." Unfortunate females, with faces of triple brass hiding hearts of unutterable woe – sleeping girls, who might be mistaken for lifeless bundles of rags – down-looking scoundrels, with felony stamped on every feature – owlish-looking knaves, minions of the moon,[13] skulking half-ashamed at their own appearance in the eye of

---

[10] From 'Ode to Leven Water' by Tobias Smollett (1721–1771).
[11] That is, May. From the traditional ballad 'Robin Hood Rescuing Three Squires'.
[12] From book 9 of 'Paradise Lost' (1667) by John Milton.
[13] A reference to Shakespeare's *Henry IV* I.ii.

day; and, alas! poor little tattered and hungry-looking children, with precocious lines of care upon their old-mannish features, tumbling about on the brown and sapless herbage. The veriest dregs of Glasgow society, indeed, seem congregated here. At one place a band of juvenile pickpockets are absorbed in a game at pitch-and-toss;[14] at a short distance a motley crew are engaged putting the stone, or endeavouring to outstrip each other in a leaping bout, while oaths and idiot laughter mark the progress of their play.

You must not confound these parties with what are called the lower orders of our city. There is a deep within a deep in the social scale: to compare even the humblest working man with such wretches, would be in truth a wicked libel. The industrious poor are now at their various useful, and therefore honourable occupations, and the heterogeneous crowd before you are the idle, the vicious, and the miserable, – the very vermin, in short, of our civilization. Poor wretches! let us not grudge them the limited portion of the Green where they invariably herd, let us not take from misery its few hours of sunshine. If a Burns could be "wae to think upon yon den,"[15] when musing on the author of evil and his fearful doom, surely we may spare a little of our sympathy for the poor erring outcasts of our own race. Their dens, in the bowels of the town, are the veriest hells upon earth. Sin and misery are truly synonymous terms, and bitter, indeed, is the wierd[16] which the idle, the dissolute, and the dishonest even in this life must dree.[17] We know not where a lesson of honesty and industry could be more effectually learned than amidst the haunts of indolence and crime.

Leaving this somewhat unsightly portion of the Green behind (and fortunately it is of limited extent), a walk of a few hundred yards by the margin of the Clyde brings us to the obelisk erected by the citizens to the memory of England's great naval hero. This plain and withal rather inelegant structure was raised by public subscription in

---

[14] A simple gambling game played by throwing and tossing coins.
[15] From 'Address to the Deil' (1786).
[16] destiny
[17] dread

1806, while the popular enthusiasm excited by the victory of Trafalgar and the glorious death of Nelson was still at its height. It is constructed of freestone, and is in elevation about 144 feet. On the 5th of August, 1810, the upper portion of this massive monument was shattered by lightning, during a violent thunder-storm. The damage was soon repaired, but the track of the electric fluid is still visible on the scarred sides of the structure. The green sloping banks in the vicinity of Nelson's Monument, during the summer months, are generally covered with the snowy produce of the washing-tub, and present an appearance of great cheerfulness and animation. Countless groups of wives, lasses, and bairns are scattered about, in every variety of attitude, among the acres of bleaching linen. If sermons are occasionally found in stones,[18] good practical homilies might certainly be drawn from the varied contents of the crowded bleaching-green. The character and condition of countless families may be read with unerring certainty in their display of textile hieroglyphics. The tidy housewife and the dirty drab are here distinguishable at a glance. Every little cluster tells its own tale. Here we have plenty, cleanliness, and comfort; there poverty, filth, and misery. This neatly patched but spotless shirt tells of thrift combined with indigence; that dingy and tattered sheet, of untidiness allied to waste. Here we have honest poverty striving to keep up appearances; there wretchedness and want, careless of character or name. That smart-handed and strapping maiden may well glance with pride at the dazzling result of her morning's toil; while this languid slattern, in "the garish eye of day,"[19] exhibits, perhaps unconsciously, her shortcomings and her shame. Bachelors of the operative class, in their benedictive[20] researches, should really pay occasional visits to the bleaching-green. The character of a sweetheart, we can assure them, may be learned more effectually there than either at kirk or market.

---

[18] A reference to Shakespeare's *As You Like It* II.i
[19] From 'Il Penseroso' (1632) by John Milton.
[20] Relating to marrying, especially for one who has long been single.

Passing Arn's Well, which is famed for the quality of its water,[21] and which received its name from a group of alder (*Scottice*, "arn") trees, which formerly graced the spot, we arrive at the Humane Society House. A numerous fleet of gigs and jolly-boats are either moored or moving about on the breast of the Clyde at this spot. Of late years numerous public works have sprung up on the south side of the stream here; and as many hundreds of the operatives engaged in them reside in Calton and Bridgeton, it has been found advisable to erect an elegant suspension bridge at the spot, for the convenience of foot-passengers. Previously to the erection of this structure, the only means of transit was by ferry-boats, which in times of spate, and indeed at all seasons, were anything but convenient or safe. It is principally to the exertions of ex-bailie Harvey[22] that the public are indebted for the superior accommodation afforded by the handsome bridge which now spans the Clyde at this place, and which also lends such a fine additional feature to the neighbouring landscape. He it was who first broached the idea at the Council Board, and who subsequently got the Bill authorizing its erection carried through Parliament. The structure was completed and thrown open to the public in the autumn of 1855. A moderate pontage is charged from passengers; and it is satisfactory to add, that even as a mercantile speculation it is likely to prove a decided benefit to the Corporation. All honour then, say we, to Mr. Harvey; and may his name, as has been proposed, be associated with the graceful and most useful structure which we unquestionably owe to his public-spirited exertions.[23] The bank immediately above and below the Humane Society House, which is peculiarly rich in springs, has been greatly improved of late under the superintendence of the Green Committee. An artificial embankment has been formed and covered with turf; while walks have been tastefully laid off; and, as in the case at several other places, a clump of trees and shrubbery has been planted, and an enclosure formed for its protection. These gentlemen certainly deserve the gratitude of their fellow-citizens for

---

[21] This well was closed c.1870.
[22] Alexander Harvey (1799 – 1876).
[23] This is St Andrew's Bridge, which is still in use.

their ceaseless efforts to improve and beautify the Green. We are doubtful, however, as to the degree of success which may attend their sylvan experiments. While the fine rugged old elms and stately beeches are yearly perishing in scores under the baneful influences of smoke, how can we expect that tender young plants in such a situation will thrive? Never, we verily believe, were trees so shockingly maltreated — so stifled with carbonic exhalations — so begrimed with soot — as those in that unfortunate middle compartment. Our ever-extending manufactures threaten indeed their speedy extinction. The westling winds bring suffocation to them from the Nursery mills; the Orient blasts come laden with death from the Bridgeton factories; while the stormy north sweeps down on their devoted heads with the congregated vapours of the city's ten thousand chimneys. "Of a' the airts[24] the wind can blaw,"[25] these really ill-fated trees have only reason to love the south. It alone has the slightest compassion upon them; while its visitations in our climate are unfortunately as rare almost as those of Tom Campbell's angels.[26] No wonder they have a doleful, black, and melancholy look; no wonder they are dying off year by year, and threatening soon to leave our once well wooded park a dreary untimbered waste. It was a part of Wordsworth's poetical creed that plants have a sort of sentient existence, and that they really enjoy the sunshine and the shower. We confess, in a certain degree, to a similar belief, and consider it almost a species of cruelty to plant these poor juvenile forestlings where their stern old seniors are unable to keep their position. Let us first do our spiriting with the vomitories of smoke. Let Jukes,[27] or some other enemy of the atmosphere-defiling demon, wrest their dusky plumes, their leaf-destroying vapours, from the tall chimneys, and then let us dibble in our saplings at every spare

---

[24] points of the compass
[25] Title of a song by Robert Burns, 1788.
[26] Thomas Campbell (1777-1844), poet who wrote *The Pleasures of Hope*:
    "What though my winged hours of bliss have been,
    Like angel visits, few and far between;"
[27] Inventor of 'smoke consuming apparatus' to reduce smoke output and increase furnace efficiency.

nook. Until the "nuisance" is at least in some measure abated, we are persuaded that tree culture in the Green will prove to be labour in vain.

It is a fact not generally known, that it was in Glasgow Green, near the site of the Humane Society House, that the idea of his great improvement on the steam-engine first flashed upon the mind of the immortal James Watt.[28] The great engineer was at that period philosophical instrument maker to the University. In this capacity a small working model of Newcomen's atmospheric engine was sent to him for repair by Professor Anderson. While the machine was still in his possession for this purpose he went out alone, on a Sunday afternoon, to take his customary walk on the Green. His mind was naturally enough directed to the contemplation of the principles upon which the engine which he had been repairing was constructed, and just as he was passing Arn's Well, the happy thought struck him, that by condensing the steam in a separate vessel, instead of in the cylinder, as it had hitherto been done, an immense saving of fuel might be effected. Had Watt been an ancient Greek he would probably, on such an occasion, have rushed across the Green, shouting "Eureka! Eureka!"[29] but canny Scot as he was, and probably in wholesome dread of the Kirk Session,[30] he pursued his leisurely thoughtful walk, and (according to his own account of the matter, as related to a highly respectable gentleman of this city, who is still amongst us) had fully mastered the details of his grand discovery before returning home. Immediately thereafter, in concert with his apprentice, Mr. John Gardner,[31] who was subsequently for many years a mathematical instrument maker in this city, he constructed a model of the steam-engine according to his new and improved method. This wrought admirably. The first experiment on a large scale took place at a coal mine near the Carron Ironworks,[32] when his expectations were fully justified, and he was induced to take out a patent for saving steam and

---

[28] (1736 – 1819)
[29] Archimedes (c.287 – 212/211 BC) supposedly exclaimed 'Eureka!' after discovering the method of calculating volume using water displacement.
[30] Lowest court of the Church of Scotland.
[31] (1773-1799) He founded Gardner and Co, manufacturers of scientific insturments.
[32] Near Falkirk.

fuel in fire-engines." Such was the origin of that mighty power which has since done so much for the advancement of modern civilization. Of the authenticity of the preceding statement there can be no doubt, as we have it directly from the gentleman to whom Watt himself communicated the circumstance. May we not be proud of such an association in connection with our beautiful Green? We have hinted that Watt may have had the fear of the Kirk-Session before his eyes during his memorable Sunday ramble. Nor in those days would the fear have been altogether groundless. A remnant of the old Puritan spirit still actuated our local authorities, and Sunday-walking, especially during the hours of Divine service, was reckoned a punishable offence. A band of functionaries, termed "Compurgators," were employed to perambulate the streets and public walks during "kirk hours" on Sundays, in order to compel "stravaigers" either to go to church, or to betake themselves to their homes. Those who refused compliance were at once taken into custody. This system continued in force to a period subsequent to the middle of the last century, when Mr. Peter Blackburn (grandfather of Mr. Blackburn of Killearn)[33] was placed in durance vile[34] for walking in the Green on Sunday! This public-spirited gentleman immediately raised an action against the authorities for such an unwarrantable interference with the liberty of the subject. The case was finally decided in his favour in the Court of Session, and the system of course speedily fell into desuetude.

The "Round Seat" is a favourite resting-place with the loungers of the Green. The Clyde here takes an abrupt bend at Peat-Bog point, and sweeps in a fine semi- circular curve round the low-lying Fleshers' Haugh. It was on this spacious tree-dotted haugh or holm that Prince Charles Edward, the "young Chevalier" of Scottish song, reviewed his troops on the occasion of his unwelcome visit to Glasgow, in the winter of 1745-6. Among the Whigs of Glasgow the Chevalier had few friends. Accordingly, when returning from England he arrived at our

---

[33] Also called Peter Blackburn (1811 – 1870), a Conservative MP. His father, John Blackburn, made his fortune in Jamaica and his grandfather, Peter Blackburn, was a merchant in Glasgow.

[34] imprisonment

city on his way to the Highlands, he determined to make the most of the wealthy enemy. The Highlanders, after their lengthened and bootless campaign, were in a most necessitous condition. Their tartans were nearly worn out, while many of them were without brogues, bonnets, or shirts. On their way to the city every individual they met was speedily divested of shoes and other articles of dress. Notwithstanding such wind-falls, they presented a most miserable appearance. But Glasgow "saw another sight" (and paid for it too) before their departure. Charles, without ceremony, at once took up his residence at the best house in the city,[35] and adopted the necessary measures for refitting his army. The Magistrates were compelled to officiate as clothiers, to the tune of 12,000 shirts, 6,000 cloth coats, 6,000 pairs of shoes, 6,000 pairs of stockings, 6,000 waistcoats, and an equal number of bonnets. "My conscience!" what would Bailie Nicol Jarvie[36] say to such an act of extortion? Whatever the honest Bailie may have said, the described articles had to be produced, and it was in the pride of these borrowed plumes that the review we have mentioned was held. "We marched out (says one of Charlie's English followers, in a manuscript journal) with drums beating, colours flying, bagpipes playing, and all the marks of a triumphant army, to the appointed ground, attended by multitudes of people who had come from all parts to see us, and especially the ladies, who, though formerly much against us, were now changed by the sight of the Prince into the most enthusiastic loyalty." During the review Charles stood under a thorn-tree, on the declivity which forms the north-western boundary of the Fleshers' Haugh, about 100 yards east of the "round seat." One of the citizens, then a boy, many years afterwards said, "I managed to get so near him that I could have touched him with my hand, and the impression which he made upon my mind shall never fade as long as I live. He had a princely aspect, and its interest was much heightened by the dejection which appeared in his pale fair countenance and downcast eye. He evidently wanted confidence in his cause, and

---

[35] Shawfield Mansion, which stood at the south end of what is now Glassford Street.
[36] A character in Sir Walter Scott's *Rob Roy*.

11

seemed to have a melancholy foreboding of that disaster which soon
after ruined the hopes of his family for ever."

The Chevalier and his devoted Highlanders passed away. Their
after fate, as everyone knows, forms one of the darkest themes in
Scottish story.[37] In the contemplation of their subsequent misfortunes,
their faults and failings are forgotten; and now that the unfortunate
Chevalier's name and memory have become "such stuff as dreams are
made of,"[38] every heart thrills in sympathy with the pathetic lyrical
expression of our townsman Glen,—

"Oh waes me for Prince Charlie!"[39]

The old thorn, "Prince Charlie's Tree," as it was called, continued to
be pointed out until recently, when somehow or other it disappeared.
Latterly it had a blasted and decaying appearance, and was protected
by a wooden railing. We have heard it rumoured, whether truly or not
we cannot say, that this venerable and interesting relic was destroyed
some four or five years ago by a band of mischievous scoundrels
during a Queen's birth-day riot. We should not be surprised to learn,
however, that some sacrilegious antiquary has the old stump snugly
deposited among his "auld nick-nackets." As unlikely things have
happened ere now among the disciples of Grose.[40] If our friend Mr.
Moir will forgive our apparent inconsistency, we would entreat him,
when next he takes the planter's spade in hand, to let us have a
successor to the "Chevalier's thorn." Such a spot should certainly not
be permitted to remain unmarked.

Great alterations have been effected on the Fleshers' Haugh
within the memory of persons still living. We remember, in our own
boyish days, a fine spring, called the "Ladle Well," on the northern
declivity, with a considerable ditch or marsh in its vicinity. The well
and marsh, however, have long disappeared, the water of both being

[37] Bonnie Prince Charlie's forces were defeated at Culloden in 1746, ending his campaign to take the British throne.
[38] From Shakespeare's *The Tempest* IV.i.
[39] From 'Wae's Me For Chairlie' by Will Glen of Glasgow (1789-1826).
[40] The antiquarian Francis Grose, 1731-1791, author of *The Antiquities of Scotland*.

now conveyed away by a covered drain, while the grass waves green on *terra firma* where the lasses of Brigtown came to fill their cans, and adventurous urchins, miscalculating their leaping powers – as we from sad experience can testify – were often plunged to the waist in mud. Few of our readers will be prepared to learn that within the past sixty years there was a printfield[41] on the Flesher's Haugh. Such, however, was the case; and we have conversed with a respectable old man who served his apprenticeship in the establishment, which was somewhere about the locality of Dominie's Hole. At that period there was a cart-road across what is now called King's Park. [42]

Proceeding towards the east, along the brow of the Fleshers' Haugh, the most picturesque portion of the Green comes gradually into view. Fine belts and clumps of trees, among which are numerous handsome specimens of the elm, the beech, the saugh,[43] and the ash, diversify and adorn the scene. The foliage here assumes a freshness and beauty not unworthy of a more rural locality. The various shades of green which characterize the woodlands of early summer are now seen in perfection, and produce an extremely pleasing effect; while the wide-spreading lawns and gently sloping banks are spangled with the daisy, the dandelion, and the buttercup. Some of our readers may smile when we mention the botany of Glasgow Green; but we can assure them that, in spite of the ceaseless trampling to which it is subjected, a considerable variety of wild plants may be found by the attentive observer within its precincts. An acquaintance of ours in one season collected not less than sixty species within its boundaries, and we believe that the real number is considerably beyond what he obtained. Among the plants indigenous to the Green, we may mention the shamrock, which the Irish Catholics of our city gather on Saint Patrick's Day; and the mystic yarrow, which the girls of Bridgeton and Calton in hundreds come forth to pluck as a love-charm, between the gloamin' and the mirk of May eve. On the evening of the 30th April

---

[41] A business that printed and bleached cotton fabrics.
[42] Not Kings Park in the southside of Glasgow, but the part of Glasgow Green near King's Drive. It was originally part of the Barrowfield estate and was named after Deacon John King, from whom it was purchased in 1773.
[43] willow

the Green is generally crowded with groups of yarrow seekers. For the benefit of our fair readers, some of whom may wish to test the virtues of the yarrow on future May eves, we may mention the *modus operandi*, as we had it from a bouncing Dublin girl who was out on a recent occasion. On coming to a spot where the desired plant is growing, the maiden kneels, and while gathering a sprig of the dewy foliage, repeats the following rhyme:

"Yarrow, yarrow, here I seek thee,
Here I have thee found;
In the name of my true love
I pluck thee from the ground.
As Joseph dreamed of Mary,
And took her for his bride,
So in a dream I wish to see
My true love by my side."

The yarrow thus taken is placed under the pillow of the maiden as she retires to sleep, when, according to the *freit*,[44] the shadowy form of the future husband is sure to make its appearance during the slumbers of the night. This rather poetical superstition is diffused over the rural districts of the Three Kingdoms; but it is certainly curious to find it lingering in such a matter-of-fact community as ours.

The student of mankind will find much to engage his attention and excite his interest in a stroll round the Green. In the hurry and bustle of the town men lose their individuality. Face succeeds face with such rapidity that one has not time to speculate on the "strang matters" with which they are one and all legibly marked. It is different here, where you have leisure to decipher, as it were, the lines which time and care have traced on the human face divine. Here you have the octogenarian, garrulous of other days, willing to unfold for your gratification, as you rest on the bench by his side, the experiences of a lengthened pilgrimage; there the ancient soldier, who will "never, never march again,"[45] yet who is eager for a good listener to whom he

---

[44] superstition
[45] From a traditional song, 'The Retired Soldier'.

14

may fight his battles o'er again. That pale-faced youth, muffled to the chin, and shivering in the very smile of summer, needs not to give audible utterance to his sad story. Long, lingering, and painful disease is plainly written on his wofully shrunken face and drooping form, while the shadow of an early death even now hangs darkly over him. Poor fellow! what a depth of meaning is in his bright blue eyes, as he lingers to gaze upon the flower-gathering children! Yet is his fate almost enviable when compared with that of yonder wan-faced and scantily clad weaver, who, with downcast eyes, and hands hung listlessly behind him, moves slowly, as if he were counting his steps athwart the sward. "'Tis want that makes his cheeks so pale;"[46] and it requires no wizard to tell that a wife and numerous little ones are dependent upon his exertions for bread, while there is no web in the loom. Alas! for the unwilling idler. This lackadaisical spark, with shirt-collar *a la* Byron, and arms akimbo, now moving with rapid stride and anon in rapt pause, pulling forth his richly gilt memorandum-book, and hurriedly pencilling its pages, can belong but to one tribe. Air, gesture, gait, at once proclaim the aspirant to poetic honours. We could not be more sure of the fact, indeed, although we met him in the poet's corner of a newspaper. Perverse fortune may have doomed him to the counter, but it is quite evident that in his own estimation he has a destiny infinitely above yard-sticks.

But we must move on. From the bank which overlooks the Clyde, at the south-eastern extremity of the Green, a prospect of great extent and beauty is obtained. To the left, over Rutherglen Bridge, in the distance, is seen the elegant spire of Cambuslang, with the towering heights of Dychmont. In front, half hidden amidst trees and gentle undulations, Shawfield and Rutherglen are seen, while the finely-wooded braes of Cathkin swell pleasantly to the horizon, and the mansions of Blairbeth and Castlemilk enliven the middle-distance, which is also studded with villas and cottages innumerable. To the right are Little Govan[47], Camphill, and Langside — the latter the scene of the unfortunate Mary's final overthrow. Indeed, the movements

---

[46] From 'The Orphan Boy's Tale' by Amelia Opie.
[47] Govanhill.

preliminary to that decisive engagement may be better comprehended when they are described with relation to our present position, than if we were even standing on the field where the battle occurred. Here we see at a glance the ground traversed by the hostile armies, and the system on which the movements were conducted which terminated in the conflict at Langside. Marching from Hamilton with the intention of proceeding to Dumbarton by the north-east side of Glasgow, the Queen's troops were confronted at Dalmarnock ford by the army of the Regent Murray, which was drawn up in order of battle in the vicinity of Barrowfield. Desirous of avoiding the impending engagement, Mary's adherents altered their route, and, passing by Rutherglen and Hangingshaw, endeavoured to accomplish their purpose of reaching Dumbarton by a forced march to the south-west of the city. Their course, however, was necessarily a circuitous one, and Murray having become aware of the alteration in their plans, at once pushed across the Green, forded the Clyde, and as we can here see, from the relative position of the places we have mentioned, was, without difficulty, able to intercept them in their progress. Thus out-manœuvred, Mary's generals saw there was nothing for it but either to risk an engagement or make an inglorious retreat to Hamilton. The former alternative was adopted, and the result, as everyone knows, was their total defeat and dispersion.[48]

But to return to the Green itself. At the foot of the bank on which we are standing, and within a few yards of each other, are two fine cool crystalline springs, which, although so near each other, possess very opposite qualities.[49] The one, locally denominated "Robin's Well," is famous for bleaching purposes, and for the dilution of "gude Scots' drink;" while the other, being moderately impregnated with a solution of ferruginous matter, is strictly avoided alike by the washerwoman and the connoisseur of punch. A few yards farther down the stream, beneath a group of stately trees, are the Springboards, and Dominie's Hole (so called from a dominie or teacher having been

---

[48] Mary Queen of Scots was defeated at the Battle of Langside in 1568. For a full account see pp109 – 110.
[49] These wells have both disappeared.

drowned there), the usual bathing-places of the amphibious east-end citizens, when, to use the words of Wilson, the quaint old author of "The Clyde," –

> "The summer's heat drives frequent to the pool
> The active youth, their glowing limbs to cool;
> They dive, and distant far emerge again,
> Or easy float along the liquid plain,
> While curling waves around their bodies twine,
> Through which their limbs like polished marble shine;
> Now with strong arms they strive against the tide,
> Now oaring swiftly, with the current glide."[50]

Many hundreds of people, indeed, bathe here daily during the sultry months, and, in spite of every precaution, few seasons, unfortunately, pass in which several lives are not lost at this part of the river. Life-buoys are suspended on the bank, that assistance in emergencies may be at once rendered. Boards have also been erected by the authorities at conspicuous points, on which, for the benefit of intending bathers, the depth of the river at various places is legibly inscribed.[51]

Pursuing our walk, which now tends city-ward, by "Allan's Pen"[52] and the fine belt of plantation which borders the south-east side of the Green, we are struck at every step by the improvements which have recently been effected. New walks, to the extent of several miles, have been formed within the past year or two, wherever, by the "old brown lines" of footpath, the public had manifested a desire to pass. The sward, at the same time, has been protected at the more exposed points by enclosures of wooden railing, and the result is, that never, within the memory of the "oldest inhabitant," has there been such an unbroken expanse of verdure on the Green as during the present season. At the same time there has been "ample scope and verge enough"[53] left for all kinds of recreative amusements. Cricket,

---

[50] 1764, by John Wilson best known for the tragedy 'Earl Douglas'.

[51] These aids were removed in 1877, and swimming here largely came to an end.

[52] A short-lived tunnel, or pend, constructed in the late eighteenth century by merchant Alexander Allan of Newhall.

[53] From 'The Bard' (1757) by Thomas Gray.

rounders, and football, the sports most popular here, are now practised as extensively as at any former period.[54] On Saturday afternoons, when the mills and public works are stopped, King's Park presents a most cheerful and animating spectacle, with its numerous groups of youthful operatives, after the toils of the week, all earnestly engaged in these healthful and exciting games. In former times the Celtic "shinty" was a favourite pastime during the winter months with the juvenility of our city. Of late years it seems to have fallen almost into desuetude. The same may be said of golf, which we remember in our boyhood seeing frequently practised by elderly gentlemen on the Green. There seems, indeed, to be a fashion in recreation as in things of greater moment. Shinty and golf, however, are both exceedingly injurious to the turf, and, considering the amenities of the Green, it is probable that the fastidious may rejoice in their discontinuance.

Previously to the general flitting of the merchant princes of Glasgow "towards the setting sun," the Green was the favourite haunt of the wealth and fashion of the city. It was here the pride and beauty of the aristocratic Charlotte Street and St. Andrew's Square loved most to congregate, "when summer days were fine."[55] These time-honoured elms, so gaunt and woe-begone, could they speak, might tell of days when the proud Virginian merchant, with his long scarlet cloak and bushy wig, passed haughtily beneath their shade, and the gaucy[56] bailie with his long queue, "That down his back did flow,"[57] went "shug shuggin"[58] past in all the pomposity of civic importance. The readers of *Rob Roy* will remember Frank Osbaldistone's Sunday evening walk in the Green, previous to his midnight meeting with the bold outlaw. This very elm, for aught we know, may have been the identical one behind which the lover of Diana Vernon ensconced himself when he heard, through the darkness, the voice of Andrew Fairservice. Be that as it may, the more fashionable classes of Glasgow have long ceased

[54] Both Glasgow Rangers (1872) and Glasgow Celtic (1887) first formed on Glasgow Green.
[55] From 'Auld Lang Syne'.
[56] well dressed and well fed
[57] From 'Captain Paton's Lament' (1819) by John Gibson Lockhart – see p426.
[58] From *The Life of Mansie Wauch* (1828) by David Macbeth Moir.

habitually to frequent the parlieus of the Green; and it is only when the attraction of a review, a regatta, or some extraordinary spectacle occurs, that it is revisited by glimpses of its former glory.

During the wars of Napoleon,[59] when our shores were threatened with foreign invasion, numerous bands of volunteers, in daily exercise upon the Green, manifested the loyalty and patriotism of Glasgow. It was on the same field that the sympathies of our citizens in the cause of political reform were, from time to time, expressed in multitudinous assemblage. No one who witnessed the monster meetings of the Reform epoch, when the population of our city, in the strength of a united purpose, came forth in their thousands to demand their political rights, can ever forget the grandeur and impressiveness of the spectacle. To the achievement of the great moral victory of 1832[60] (for in its fruits, which are not yet all reaped, it has indeed been great), the magnificent meetings of Glasgow Green must have contributed in no limited degree. Peace has her victories as well as war, and the battle-field where corruption has been overcome, although all undewed with the red rain, should ever be regarded as hallowed ground. All honour then to our noble Green; and should

"Malice domestic or foreign levy"[61]

ever again call for similar exertions, may our citizens, as in days of yore, be prepared to answer the call of duty, and may they long preserve intact these spacious grounds as a fair field for the manifestation of their loyalty and patriotism.

Passing the Washing-house, and in front of Monteith Row – a handsome range of edifices, but erected on a clipping from the Green and within the "stately wall" mentioned by old M'Ure[62] – we make our

---

[59] 1803 – 1815

[60] The Reform Act 1832, which granted parliamentary seats to the new industrial cities. MacDonald was a supporter of the Chartist movement which sought to make the political system more democratic.

[61] From Shakespeare's *Macbeth*, III.ii.

[62] John McUre, author of *The History of Glasgow* (1736)

exit at the London Street "winnles,"[63] and soon find ourselves in "the heart o' the town."

---

[63] windlass or stile

No. II. Carmyle and Kenmuir

The denizen of the populous and dinsome city is apt to look with envy on the condition of those who "live, move, and have their being"[1] among the woods and fields, who have familiar intercourse with the free winds, and are at all times and seasons surrounded with the ever-varying shows and forms of Nature. Yet to us it appears extremely doubtful whether we of the city are not, after all, more keenly alive to the beauties of the country than our brethren of the rural districts. Familiarity, if it does not in all cases beget contempt, is almost certain to engender more or less of indifference. The man who has green leaves and bright petals ever unfolded before his eyes, and the music of bird and stream ever ringing in his ears, must of necessity become less sensible of their cheerful influences than he who only occasionally, and after considerable intervals, has the privilege of participating in such enjoyments. The clerk doomed to the irksome desk, and the operative confined to the workshop, enjoy, we doubt not, on their holidays, a more intense feeling of the beautiful in nature than the farmer who is daily among the waving grain, or the lord of the soil who can roam at will, wherever whim or caprice may lead. Under such circumstances, the excursionist from the crowded city feels that to him indeed,

> "The meanest flower that decks the vale,
> The simplest note that swells the gale,
> The common earth, the air, the skies,
> Appear an opening paradise."[2]

Some such thoughts as these suggest themselves to our mind as, leaving the bustling streets, we take our way up the Clyde to Carmyle and Kenmuir. Leaving the precincts of the Green at Allan's Pen, we speedily find ourselves at Rutherglen Bridge. This structure,

---

[1] Acts 17.28
[2] From 'Ode on the Pleasure arising from Vicissitude' by Thomas Gray (1716-1771).

21

which was erected in 1776, connects the city by its south-eastern boundary with Rutherglen and the adjacent towns and villages. It is a narrow and rather high-backed affair, barely affording scope for a couple of sour-milk carts to pass each other in safety; and must be rather trying to the nerves of outside passengers on the omnibuses which now cross it at frequent intervals, as the slightest collision with any passing body would infallibly send them "right slick" into the water. The municipality, with praiseworthy spirit, is now setting its other bridges in order, and we really think that something might be done to render this one more safe and commodious.[3] Passing the extensive dye-works of Messrs. Henry Monteith & Co. at Barrowfield, and those of Messrs. Bartholomew at Dalmarnock, we next come, about a quarter of a mile farther up, to the fine mansion of the late Dr. Cleghorn,[4] embowered in trees, and situated on a gentle acclivity on the south bank of the river.[5] Nearly opposite this are the works of the Cranston-hill Water Company, surrounded by a strong earthen embankment, which effectually conceals and preserves from encroachment the various reservoirs and filters of the establishment. The Clyde, it is said, was formerly navigable to this point, and Rutherglen, which here forms a fine feature in the landscape, with its beautiful new spire, still boasts a quay for the accommodation of that commerce which has long deserted her. Not a single cock-boat has she now to countenance the effigy of a ship in her burghal coat of arms. We have the authority of Dr. Ure,[6] the historian of the burgh, however, for saying that up till a comparatively recent period coal gabberts[7] of considerable burthen plied almost every day, from the quay of Rutherglen to Greenock, with cargoes of the "diamond."

Passing Dalmarnock Bridge, an elegant structure of timber,[8] and following the windings of the river, we shortly arrive at the

---

[3] The bridge was eventually replaced with the current version in 1896.
[4] Robert Cleghorn (c.1755 – 1821), doctor and chemist.
[5] Shawfield House, which was absorbed into Shawfield Chemical Works and then demolished in the 1960s.
[6] Rev. David Ure, author of *A History of Rutherglen and East Kilbride* (1793).
[7] barges
[8] Replaced by a stone and iron bridge in 1890.

II. Carmyle and Kenmuir

Glasgow Water-works, the mighty engines of which are employed night and day, like a great heart, in propelling the crystal fluid throughout the miles and miles of pipes that extend through the labyrinths of the city. (These extensive works will soon be completely superseded and rendered useless, as the Corporation is about to supply the citizens with the limpid waters of Loch-Katrine.) The Clyde in the vicinity of the works has recently made sad havoc on the bank. A considerable portion of the soil has been carried away, trees have been undermined and levelled, and the path has, indeed, been rendered all but impassable. To make matters worse, a neighbouring proprietor, who would seem to be somewhat of a churl, has driven a pallisade of stobs[9] along the front of his property, close almost to the water-edge, so that passengers have considerable difficulty in getting along. Fortunately the lordship of this gentleman is not of very great extent, and his forbidden territory is soon left behind.

The famous "Harvie's Dyke" next attracts our attention. This wall, as is well known, was erected about thirty years ago by Thomas Harvie, then proprietor of Westthorn, for the purpose of blocking up the footpath along the margin of the Clyde, from Glasgow to Carmyle, which had previously been in possession of the public from time immemorial. Great indignation was of course excited at the time by this encroachment upon popular rights. Indignant articles, letters, and pasquinades appeared in the local journals, until at length, in the summer of 1823, the ire of the citizens was roused to such a degree, that a numerous party, principally composed of weavers and other operatives from Bridgeton and Parkhead, armed with pickaxes and crow-bars, laid siege to the obnoxious barrier, and levelled it with the dust. Passing afterwards in triumph to the opposite extremity of the Westthorn estate, which was likewise defended by a strong wooden pallisade, they continued the work of destruction by setting it on fire.

While engaged in this patriotic though certainly illegal operation, intelligence was brought to the excited crowd that a party of dragoons who had been sent for were approaching, when an immediate dispersion ensued. Several of the ringleaders were afterwards

---

[9] stakes

apprehended, and sentenced to various periods of imprisonment for their share in the transaction. The wall was speedily rebuilt, and for several years thereafter the thoroughfare was completely suspended. Thanks, however, to the public spirit of certain gentlemen connected with the city, among whom were the late Mr. George Rodger of Barrowfield Printworks, "Sandie Rodger" the poet,[10] and Mr. Adam Ferrie, now in Canada, the warfare was resumed in the courts of law. Subscriptions in support of the popular cause were liberally furnished by all classes of citizens; and, after a lengthened litigation, the case was finally terminated by a decision of the House of Lords in favour of the right of passage. The estate has now passed into other hands, and the present proprietor, with praiseworthy liberality, permits the people to enjoy without let or hindrance the beautiful bank by which the arable portion of his land is encompassed.

The scenery around Westthorn is of the most delightful description. The bank, sloping gently to the river, is clothed with fine plantations, the haunts of birds innumerable, which as we pass are joyously piping their most mellifluous strains. The swallow and the more rare sandpiper are flitting over the stream (which in its windings here rivals the linky Forth), haply disturbed by the wading angler, who, as usual, on the Clyde, is threshing the water in vain. Nor is the background less fair, as from almost every point fine views are obtained of the richly-wooded braes of Cathkin or the green slopes of Dychmont, with the spires of Rutherglen and Cambuslang lending beauty to the middle distance. Immediately above the lands of Westthorn, is Dalbeth, the finely-situated mansion of which is now occupied as a conventual establishment in connection with the Romish Church.[11] Morning, noon, and evening, the rambler by the river-side hears the tinkling of bells at this spot, warning the sisterhood to their frequently recurring exercises of devotion. The curious may also, on a sunny forenoon, espy the veiled forms of the nuns, walking with measured pace on the green sward in front of the edifice, or lingering

---

[10] Alexander 'Sandy' Rodger, 1784-1846.
[11] This building became Dalbeth Reformatory School and was eventually demolished in 1996.

in pensive attitudes in the shadow of the surrounding trees. In this quiet and secluded locality there is nothing to disturb the contemplations of the fair devotees more harsh than the murmurings of the Clyde or the songs of the summer birds among the rustling foliage. They seem, indeed, to live a peaceful and a harmless life in their beautiful solitude, yet to our presbyterian prejudices a nunnery seems anything but a pleasant feature in a Scottish landscape. A small chapel has recently been erected in connection with the establishment; and a cemetery for the reception of deceased Catholics has been formed in the neighbourhood.

In the bed of the stream at this place there was for many years a numerous colony of the large fresh-water mussel. In seasons of drought we have seen these bivalves exposed in myriads. Some of the shells contained pearls of considerable value; and we have known a Cambuslang weaver, to realize a couple of pounds by the sale of a forenoon's gathering. A friend of ours, on one occasion, picked up a shell here which was thickly studded with small pearls. None of them, however, were very pure, and we suspect this is the case with the greater portion of those found in the Clyde. Be this as it may, their pearl-bearing character has proved fatal to the poor mussels, which are now nearly extirpated. Small particles of native gold have also been found in the sands opposite Dalbeth.

About half-a-mile farther up we arrive at the Clyde Iron works, associated with the respected name of the late Mr. Colin Dunlop, formerly one of the representatives of Glasgow in Parliament.[12] They are merrily blazing as we pass. The nightly glare of these smelting furnaces is familiar to every denizen of Sanct Mungo's; many it lights home when "owre late out at e'en,"[13] and to many it serves all the purposes of a barometer, as, immediately before rain, from a very obvious cause, its brilliancy is materially increased. As an ingenious and witty poet of the west observed, in certain humorous verses addressed to the late proprietor of this extensive establishment,

---

[12] (1775 – 1837), he represented Glasgow as an MP from 1835 – 1836.
[13] From 'The Gloamyng Buchte' (1824) by James Telfer.

"The moon does fu' weel when the moon's in the lift,
But oh, the loose limmer[14] takes mony a shift,
Whiles here and whiles there, and whiles under a hap[15]
But yours is the steady licht, Colin Dulap!

"Na, mair – like true friendship, the murker the nicht,
The mair you let out your vast columns o' licht;
When sackcloth and sadness the heavens enwrap
'Tis then you're maist kind to us, Colin Dulap!" [16]

An elegant iron bridge erected by the proprietor of the works spans the Clyde at this point,[17] and is principally used for the transmission of coal and minerals, for smelting purposes, from Eastfield, which lies about half-a-mile southward, and is famed for the abundance and quality of its carboniferous productions. The ordinary traffic across the river, however, is at the "Bogle-hole" ford, a short distance farther up, where not only horses and carts, but men, and occasionally bonnie lasses even, with their drapery high kilted, may be seen in langsyne fashion wading from bank to bank through the amber waters. On passing the bridge we would advise our botanical friends to follow our example, and keep a sharp look out for the wild flowers which here spring forth on bank and brae in the most charming profusion. For a couple of miles or so above this, the Clyde is fringed with beautiful trees of every variety, and at this season (May) of every shade of green; while at every step the landscape assumes new features of loveliness, and every sunny nook has its own floral decorations. Among the saughs[18] at the water edge lurks the graceful meadow rue (*thalictrum flavum*); the broad leaved waterburs (*petasites vulgaris*) wave on the alluvial flats; while the dog violet, the primrose, cowslip, white saxifrage (*saxifraga granulate*) starworts of several species, and

---

[14] rogue
[15] cover
[16] From 'Colin Dulap' (1897) by Alexander Rodger.
[17] It was replaced in 1897 with the current steel railway bridge. The piers of the old bridge can still be seen just west of the current bridge.
[18] willows

countless other things of bloom and of fragrance peep from the verdant banks, or cluster in sweet groups round the mossy stems of the overshadowing trees. After a delightful sylvan walk or saunter of about an hour's duration from the "Bogle-hole," we arrive at the village or clachan – for we are puzzled to say which is its proper designation – of Carmyle, with its old-fashioned meal-mills and dinsome dams, over which the foamy Clyde incessantly pours, as if murmuring with its voice of many waters at the restriction attempted to be placed on its liberty. Imagine some score or so of houses — pleasant though humble dwelling-places every one — straggling upward from the river-side, intermingled with garden-plots and trees, and a picture of the little community is before you — the inhabitants, as we learn, being principally millers, cartwrights, sawyers, and such like. There is at present only a couple of places where refreshment for the weary rambler may be obtained; and in one of these, with the reader's leave, we shall "take our ease" for a short time, and discuss a thimbleful of the landlord's Glenlivet and a "crumpie farl" of the goodwife's cake, with a slice of prime cheese from Mr. Drew's dairy,[19] which is hard by, and the produce of which has deservedly attained a more than local fame.

On visiting Carmyle for the first time, a goodly number of years since, we were conducted to a waste spot in the vicinity, which in bygone days was the scene of a melancholy tragedy. The story, as told to us, was briefly as follows: In the olden time there lived — the one at Carmyle, the other at Kenmuir — two young men who had been from boyhood bosom friends. Similar in tastes and dispositions, nothing ever happened to mar the harmony of their intercourse; and, in weal or in woe, they seemed destined to continue all in all to each other throughout life. At length, however, a stranger maiden came to reside in the village, and, as fate would have it, the youths fell simultaneously in love with her. The friends were rivals. One was preferred; the other of course rejected. The unfortunate suitor, from an affectionate friend,

---

[19] Lawrence Drew (d.1884) who became a famous breeder of Clydesdale horses.

became all at once — "such power has slighted love"[20] — transformed into the most bitter of enemies. Meeting by accident one day at the spot alluded to, angry words passed between the two who lately would have died for each other. Swords were ultimately drawn, and one fell mortally wounded. Filled with remorse at what, in his blind passion, he had done, the other in a fit of anguish laid violent hands upon himself, and both were found lying dead among the summer flowers, which were stained with their mingled life-blood. What afterwards befell the fair and innocent cause of all their woe, tradition sayeth not; but the friends, who had been so unfortunately and fatally estranged, were laid by their mourning relatives at peace in one grave, dug at the place where they fell, which has ever since been known as the "Bluidy Neuk." A ferruginous spring in the neighbourhood was long looked upon with horror by the good folks of the village, who saw in the red oxydized earth around it a mysterious connection with the blood which had there been shed. An old lady who was born in Carmyle informed us that the spot was reckoned "no canny," and that in her youth he would have been considered a bold individual who would have ventured there alone after nightfall. So regardless of such matters, however, have modern agriculturists become, that within the last few years the plough has been driven over the spot, and at the time of our visit there is a fine fresh braird waving green over the "Bluidy Neuk."

The walk from Carmyle to Kenmuir bank, which is about three-quarters of a mile higher up the stream, is of the most pleasing description. Both banks of the river are clothed with dense masses of foliage, which are now tinted with the rich variety of shades which

---

[20] Possibly a misquote of the acrostic poem 'Jealousy' from Charles Freeman's *The Lover's New Guide* (1780):
> "Joined for life why should I vex?
> Ever charming is the sex.
> All the powers of love are theirs,
> Love, and all its tender cares.
> Oft of slighted love I deem;
> Useless find I all my dream:
> Surely all my doubts are vain;
> Ye winds, I yield them back again."

renders the woods of early summer almost equal in picturesque effect to those of the fall. The intensely fresh green of the beech — the leaves with "silver lining" of the saugh — the almost olive-hued elm — the leafy luxuriance of the lady-birch — the golden budded oak — the bird-cherry or geen, one mass of snowy bloom, with the mourning robes of the pine, insensibly intermingling and softly blending one with another, produce altogether an effect which the painter may admire, but must in vain attempt to imitate. The attentive ornithologist may here see occasionally that curious and amusing bird the creeper (*certhia familiaris*), climbing the trees perpendicularly; the sandpiper dabbling on the brown sand, or flying with its peculiar cry across the stream; or the lone water ousel sitting on a projecting stone among the gurgling waves, and quietly watching for the minnows and sticklebacks, which form its ordinary prey.

Kenmuir bank is a steep acclivity which rises directly from the margin of the Clyde to the height of some sixty or seventy feet. It is a wild and bosky[21] scene, covered with a picturesque profusion of timber, and is the *habitat* of flowers innumerable. The weaver herbalists of Camlachie and Parkhead find it a perfect storehouse of medicinal rarities; and on Sundays they may be seen in sickly groups prying into every green recess in search of plants which old Culpepper[22] would have loved for their rare qualities, or carrying them home in odorous bundles, confident of having obtained a mastery over "all the ills that flesh is heir to."[23] The botanist may also occasionally be seen lurking here, vasculum[24] in hand, or on bended knee examining the structure of some strange flower. But even the mere general lover of flowers will here find much to reward his attention. At present the May-flower (*caltha palustris*), the wild hyacinth, the craw-flower of Tannahill,[25] the red campion (*lychnis dioica*), the odorous woodruff (*asperula oderata*), the globe-flower or lucken gowan (*trollius*

---

[21] wooded
[22] Nicholas Culpepper (1616 – 1654), English botanist and herbalist.
[23] From Shakespeare's *Hamlet* III.i.
[24] A stiff metal container usually used for collecting botanical samples.
[25] Robert Tannahill (1774 – 1810), poet.

europeus), and many others are in full bloom, and so thickly strewn that even as the poet says,

"You cannot see the grass for flowers."[26]

At the foot of the bank, near its upper extremity, there is a fine spring, which is known by the name of the "Marriage Well," from a couple of curiously united trees which rise at its side and fling their shadows over its breast.[27] To this spot, in other days, came wedding parties, on the day after marriage, to drink of the crystal water, and, in a cup of the mountain-dew, to pledge long life and happiness to the loving pair whom, on the previous day, old Hymen[28] had made one in the bands which death alone can sever. After imbibing a draught of the sacred fluid from the cup of Diogenes,[29] we rest a brief space on the margin of the well, and while we are listening to its faint trickling voice, let us recall a name or two from the many with which it is associated in our memory. Many, indeed, have been the friends with whom we have here held communion sweet. Most gentle and single-minded of botanists was our old and venerable companion, poor Tom Murphy, who, for many and many a year, made loving pilgrimage to Kenmuir. Well he knew each floral inhabitant that lent its odour to the green gloamin' of this tangled nook. From earliest spring to latest autumn he knew their times and seasons. It was his pride to busk[30] with stranger beauties the haunts of his love. Many a germ and many a root he brought from distant glens and lonely burnsides to enrich this fairy spot with their bloom. Flowers of his planting are still here, but the good old man will return no more for ever —

"By Kenmuir steep, or sweet Carmyle,
Or Blantyre's auld monk-haunted pile,
A-wooing Flora's early smile.

---

[26] From 'The Two Voices' (1842) by Alfred Lord Tennyson
[27] Traces of the Marriage Well still remain, but it is now next to Daldowie Water Treatment Works, and not very romantic.
[28] Greek god of marriage
[29] That is, with cupped hands.
[30] dress

Nae mair he'll tread;
Nature's lone pilgrim's left his toil —
Tom Murphy's dead."[31]

Here also came poor George Allan, one of the Harvie's Dyke heroes,[32] to spend his summer Sundays after the irksome toils of the week. He also was a botanist in a humble way. With the long-winded and crabbed names of the science he had but a limited acquaintance. Yet well he knew the majority of our indigenous plants by their good old Saxon names, the most musical of all, and deep was his knowledge of their medicinal virtues, real or imaginary. With all that Gerarde[33] or Culpepper taught he was perfectly familiar, and he loved to tell of the planets by which the various herbs were influenced, and the mystic hours in which each kind required to be gathered. Many a time and oft we have met him, with a group of delighted auditors, expounding, in green and flowery nooks of the Clyde, his wondrous lore. On one occasion (a Sacramental Fast-day) we found him criticising the exquisite song of "The Posie," by the bard of Coila.[34] "I'll no deny," he said, "that, as a thing of fancy and sentiment, Burns' lilt is no sae far wrang; but then he has jumilt the flowers of spring, summer, and hairst[35] a' into ae bab,[36] a thing that's clean contrar' to nature. Ye'll never find the primrose, the firstling o' the year (as Burns ca's it, although it's no the firstling), in the same walk as the budding rose; and yet our favourite poet bauldy said he wad gather them together and twine them wi' ither flowers a' to be a posie to his ain dear May. Tak' my word for't," he continued, "Rab was nae botanist, or he wadna ha'e made sic a mistak'; but if ye'll jist be quiet for a wee, I'll sing ye a genuine botanical sang, written by a friend o' mine,[37] and ye'll no think it the less sweet, I opine, because the mavis and the laverock, as ye hear, are chanting the accompaniments." With these preliminary

---

[31] From 'Elegy on the Death of Thomas Murphy' by MacDonald himself.
[32] See pp23 – 24.
[33] John Gerarde (c. 1545–1612), English herbalist.
[34] 1792, by Robert Burns, 'the bard of Coila'.
[35] harvest
[36] bunch of flowers
[37] This poem is actually by MacDonald himself.

remarks, and after wetting his whistle by a draught from a small pocket flask, he made the echoes of Kenmuir ring with the following, which he sung to the old Gaelic air, "I am asleep, do not waken me:"

"When spring frae the blue lift in beauty comes smiling,
And stern icy winter gangs frowning away;
While blythe sings the mavis the bright hours beguiling,
And woods a' are busking in leafy array;
Coltsfoot and celandine
Wee gowden starnies shine.
And sweetly the primrose and violet blow;
Forth over hill and glen,
Far frae the haunts of men,
Joyously wandering, we flower-lovers go.

"When sweet simmer's smile sets the braes a' a-blooming,
And swallows return frae their haunts o'er the sea,
While rosebud and hawthorn their dens are perfuming,
And speedwells are bright, as a fair maiden's e'e;
Kingcups and daisies fair
Spangle our meadows rare
Lilies are glancing where clear streamlets flow;
Forth over hill and glen,
Far frae the haunts of men,
Joyously wandering, we flower-lovers go.

"When sere-leaved decay o'er the woodlands is stealing,
And bell-flowers are waving their pennons of blue;
While hairst a' her treasures in rich fields revealing
Brings plenty and joy to the blythe reapers view;
Clamb'ring o'er bank and brae
Schoolboys are wandering gay,
Plundering the hazel, the bramble, and sloe;
Forth over hill and glen,
Far frae the haunts of men,
Joyously wandering, we flower-lovers go.

"Though winter in storms o'er the dark earth is flying,
And flowers smile nae mair on the cauld cheerless day,
Yet nature has charms 'mong the lone woods lying,
Dear to the soul which delights in her sway;
O'er ruin's crumbling wall
Green hangs the ivy pall,
Rich coral gems deck the rude holly bough
Where over hills and glen,
Far frae the haunts of men,
Joyously wandering, we flower-lovers go."

"We grudge not the worldling his pomp, power, and pleasure,
Tho' nameless and poor, down life's rough course we steer,
Each field-path and hedgerow to us yields a treasure,
And ours are the beauties encircling the year;
Bird, beast, and flowery lea,
Rock, stream, and leafy tree,
Rich tendrills of love round our hearts seem to throw,
When forth over hill and glen,
Far frae the haunts of men,
Joyously wandering, we flower-lovers go."

Poor Allan concluded his song amidst the plaudits of his humble compeers. Many springs and many summers have passed since last we saw him at Kenmuir. He is now a tenant of the narrow house. The flowers he loved so well return with the returning seasons, but never again shall he rejoice in the beauty of their presence. Numerous, indeed, are the forms and faces which haunt our fancy as we linger by the Marriage Well —

"Memories grow around it thick as flowers."[38]

---

[38] From 'A Life Drama' (1852) by Alexander Smith.

But some have died at home among their own people; some on distant shores have found a stranger's grave; and among those who are still in the land of the living, time and chance have wrought a sad dispersion.

Ascending to the brow of the bank, a prospect of great beauty meets our gaze. Far below, the Clyde is seen between the ivied trunks which bristle the steep, quivering in a sunny ripple, or stretching in wandering loveliness around the green tree-studded haughs of Daldowie on the one hand, and towards the wood-fringed banks of Carmyle on the other. That spacious mansion to the left, couching upon its own verdant lawn, is the residence of Mr. M'Call of Daldowie, and certainly a more desirable place of abode it would be difficult to imagine.[39] In the middle distance, in the same direction, the red tower of Bothwell Church meets the eye — the Castle is lost in foliage;[40] while, far beyond and faintly visible on the horizon, looms the dim form of Tintoc, the conical giant of the Upper Ward. To the right Cambuslang is sleeping in the sun, with the Dychmont and Cathkin hills forming a fine background to the picture which it presents. Turning to the right about, we behold, over a level and fertile expanse, thickly dotted with houses, the mighty cloud of smoke, which ever indicates the city of our habitation, with the dark outline of the old Cathedral, "St. Rollox Lum,"[41] and other prominent features of Sanct Mungo's town peering duskily through the veil. In the distance to the right, the range of the Campsie Fells is seen stretching from Kilsyth to Dungoyne, while the Kilpatrick braes form the horizontal line to the left, and through the gap of the Lennox, Benlomond shows his ample shoulders and snow enveloped brow. Of a truth, sweet Kenmuir! thou commandest a magnificent panorama; and we have often marvelled that, lying within the scope of a forenoon's walk from yon vast maze of industry, thou hast not won at least a hundred pilgrims for each one who has hitherto come to thy shrine.

---

[39] This mansion was demolished in the mid-twentieth century.

[40] Both the church (begun in Norman times, expanded in the 14th century) and the castle (begun in the 13th century, expanded in the 14th) survive to this day.

[41] Chimney of the St Rollox Chemical Works in Sighthill, also known as 'Tennant's stalk'. It was once the largest chemical works in the world. The chimney was demolished in 1922 and the plant closed in the 1960s.

II. Carmyle and Kenmuir

As this is the turning point of our ramble, it now remains for us to decide whether we shall retrace our steps by the margin of the Clyde, a distance we should imagine of some six or seven miles, or by making an inland cut to the Glasgow and Hamilton road, find our way home by a route of about half that length. As the day is somewhat advanced, and ourselves somewhat tired withal, we conclude that the latter course is on the whole the most advisable. Striking therefore into a footpath through the green corn, we speedily find Her Majesty's highway, and passing through Tollcross and Parkhead (commonplace villages both), arrive once more, in about an hour and a-half from the time we leave Kenmuir, at the comfortable fireside from whence, some half-dozen of hours previously, we had taken our start. Recalling our ramble, we exclaim with Wordsworth, —

> "How fair appears the rural scene,
> For thou, O Clyde, hast ever been
> Beneficent as strong;
> Pleased in refreshing dews to steep
> The little trembling flowers that peep
> Thy shelving rocks among!"[42]

---

[42] 'Composed at Cora Linn', 1820.

The boy-life of town and country are often compared, when conclusions are generally drawn very much to the disadvantage of the former. On the one hand, we are shown narrow lanes and filthy closes, noisome streets and evil influences without number; on the other, are enchantingly depicted green fields and sunny braes, clear gushing streams, and the sweet fellowship of birds and flowers. In the one picture there is a sad predominance of shadow; in the other there is a decided "excess of bright."[1] "What a dreary waste," we have heard remarked, "must be the memory of a town-bred man!" He has no langsyne recollections of paidlins in the burn, or gowan-gatherings on the bloomy braes; he cannot boast an old acquaintance in the belted bee, nor tell of joyous associations linked with the wild bird's song. Now, while admitting that there is too much truth in the contrast thus presented to us, we feel convinced, after looking "on this picture and on that,"[2] that the condemnation of town "raising," as Jonathan might call it,[3] has been by far too sweeping. Nor are we prejudiced in the matter either way, having been ourselves, as we may say, neither a town nor a country boy, but a partaker to a considerable extent in the character of both — our early home having been in a suburban situation.

> "Stone walls do not a prison make,"[4]

nor does a residence in the city necessarily imply confinement within its boundaries. Town boys are continually making raids into the surrounding country. They know well when the first flowers begin to blow, and when the birds commence to build their nests. There are but few schoolboys, for instance, even in the very heart of our own wide-spreading town, who do not know the season when the blaeberry assumes the purple die of ripeness, or who could not guide you where

---

[1] From book 3 of 'Paradise Lost' (1667) by John Milton.
[2] From Shakespeare's *Hamlet* III.iv.
[3] Possibly an allusion to Jonathan Swift's 'A Modest Proposal' (1729).
[4] From 'To Althea, from Prison' (1642) by Richard Lovelace.

the blackboyd hangs in autumn its jetty fruit. Every individual accustomed to walk in the outskirts of our city must have observed numerous bands of these tiny adventurers going or returning from their devious expeditions, loaded with

> "Scarlet hips and stony haws,
> Or blushing crabs, or berries that emboss
> The bramble, black as jet, or sloes austere;
> Hard fare! but such as boyish appetite
> Disdains not."[5]

So strong indeed, and so general, is this rambling propensity in the boyhood of our city, that we know of spots even at five or six miles' distance from the Cross, which, in the time of nests, and at the period when the wild fruit is ripe, are perfectly thronged with the little pale-faced vagabonds. To gamekeepers and farmers far and wide these outpourings of urban juvenility are peculiarly vexatious, from their destructive effects on woods and fences; yet the lover of his kind will look with a charitable eye on their occasional depredations, and the philosopher will even see a wise provision of Nature in the yearning which prompts the young heart to leave its city home and wander forth to taste the freshness and beauty of the green fields. Grudge not, therefore, we say to our country friends, the little townling his harvest of hips and baws.[6] The evil he causes in the collection of it cannot be of material consequence to you, while the sweet memories which he insensibly gleans along with the ruddy fruit, and the healing influences which the merest contact with nature produces on the spirit, are of immense importance to him, and may render him, in his after-life, amidst the irksomeness and the temptations of the crowded haunt of men, both a happier and a purer being. Dreary indeed must be the memory of the man whose boyhood has been entirely spent in the verdureless mazes of the city; but we would fain hope, and indeed feel persuaded, that there are comparatively few who have been so utterly unfortunate.

---

[5] From book 1 of 'The Task' (1785) by William Cowper.

[6] elderberries

It was in our own haw-gathering and bird-nesting days that we first visited Cambuslang and its romantic environs, in a ramble to which we now solicit the company of our readers. We have a decided antipathy to direct roads, and generally when business is out of the question, instead of proceeding in a straight line to our destination, endeavour if possible to reach it by some species of zig-zag or circumbendibus. In accordance with this penchant for the eccentric, we determine to make our way to Cambuslang along the south bank of the Clyde, which is perhaps a mile or two longer than the ordinary way, but which compensates for extra length by a considerably greater degree of beauty. Leaving the city by the suburb of Bridgeton, we cross the river by the elegant timber bridge at Dalmarnock,[7] which leads to the coalpit of Farme. From the vicinity of the bridge a fine view is obtained of the ancient and castellated mansion of Farme, the seat of James Farie, Esq.,[8] which, half seen within its girdle of trees, is situated a few hundred yards to the south of the road.[9] The period in which this edifice was erected is unknown, but from its architectural features it is evidently of great antiquity.[10] In recent times considerable additions have been made to it, but as these have been studiously kept subordinate to the old fabric, and are in strict harmony with its characteristics, it still preserves its original air of hoary eild, and is altogether one of the most complete models of the baronial dwelling-place of other days in the West of Scotland.

In 1792 the proprietor of that day had occasion to make some alterations in the interior of the house. In one room a ceiling of stucco was removed, when another of wood was discovered, with a number of curious inscriptions upon it, generally inculcating the practice of temperance and morality. These were written in the old English character, and were evidently of very ancient date. One of them contains a lesson which may be studied with advantage even in our

---

[7] Replaced by a stone and iron bridge in 1890.

[8] 1800 – 1876

[9] The mansion was demolished in the 1960s.

[10] It was probably built in the 15th or 16th century on the remains of an older castle, and expanded in the following centuries

own more civilized though perhaps not more sincere age. It is as follows:

> "Fair speech in presence,
> With good report in absence,
> And manners even to fellowship
> Obtains great reverence."
> "Written in the year 1325."[11]

The estate of Farme is principally composed of an extensive and fertile haugh, which stretches out into a kind of peninsula formed by a bold sweep of the Clyde. It is said to have been for a considerable period a private property of the royal Stuarts. It afterwards passed through various hands; a family named Crawford held possession of it for many years; and about 1645 it belonged to Sir Walter Stewart of Minto. Ultimately, however, it fell into the possession of the Hamilton family, from whom it was purchased by the grandfather of the present proprietor. About a hundred yards above Dalmarnock Bridge we leave the course of the Clyde, and by a road which cuts right across a sort of isthmus, after a walk of a quarter of a-mile or so, arrive again on the bank, at a point some two miles farther up the stream. At this place there is a fine row of trees on either side of the way, the leafy boughs of which meeting and intertwining overhead, form a shady arch, through which in a picturesque vista is seen the village of Cambuslang, with its elegant church spire relieved against the green brow of the Dychmont. Proceeding along Clyde, we soon arrive at the verdant margin of the estate of Hamilton Farme, which consists of rich alluvial meadows, at present bearing splendid cereal coverings, and protected from the ravages of the river in its occasional "spates" by lengthened lines of embankment, which for solidity and strength would do credit even to a Dutch landscape. Opposite the promontory of Westthorn, a small streamlet called "Hamilton Farme Burn" runs into the Clyde. We would recommend our botanical friends to trace its meanderings for a

---

[11] The original quote is "FAIRE SPEICHE IN PRESENCE WITH GUID REPORT IN ABSENCE AND MANERS ENTO FELLOWSCHEP OBTAIN GRAIT REURENCE".

short distance. Running through an almost level tract of land, there is little to engage the attention of the rambler in its appearance; yet to the student of vegetation its fertile banks will abundantly repay a careful investigation. We find the white convolvulus (*convolvulus sepium*), the woody nightshade (*solanum dulcamara*), common valerian (*valeriana officinalis*) two species of willow-herb, and a numerous variety of others. The channel seems to be a favourite haunt of the graceful wagtail tribe, and we well remember some half-dozen years ago having discovered the nest of a pair of kingfishers in a hole in one of the banks. This beautiful bird is well known to be exceedingly rare in the country round Glasgow, and even in Scotland. We therefore prided ourselves very much on our discovery, and anticipated great pleasure in watching its motions and habits. But, alas!

> "The best laid schemes of mice and men
> Gang aft agley." [12]

Some colliers in the neighbourhood had also observed the glittering plumage of the poor birds, and "on deadly thoughts intent" were speedily out in pursuit of them. For several weeks there was a constant series of lurking sports men hovering about. We never learned whether they had actually managed to kill the poor things or not, but we know that the nest was shortly afterwards deserted, and that the kingfisher has not again appeared at the spot. We are sorry to say that a similar course of extermination seems to be pursued wherever a rare bird makes its appearance amongst us. Every now and again we see triumphant paragraphs in provincial newspapers narrating the destruction of ornithological curiosities as if it were a matter on which we should congratulate ourselves that these innocent and beautiful creatures are thus prevented from brightening with their presence our woods and fields. We have no sympathy with these ruthless collectors of specimens, and would much rather hear of one living addition to our country's *fauna* than of twenty names added to the catalogue of a museum. Many well-meaning people complain of our game-laws, and

---

[12] From 'To a Mouse' (1785) by Robert Burns.

it must be admitted that in various respects they are productive of evil; but we feel persuaded that, were they once abolished, a very brief period indeed would see the utter extinction of many species of wild animals which at present enliven and adorn our rural landscapes. The hare would not much longer be seen "hirplin' doon the furr,"[13] the glittering pheasant would speedily be banished from the greenwood, and the evening call of the partridge among the dewy corn would, ere a few years were gone, glad no more the ear of the gloamin' wanderer. In France, where there are no restrictions on the destruction of "vermin," as friend Bright[14] calls the protected animals, there is now no vermin to kill; they have all disappeared, and you may travel for days in that country and scarcely see or hear a solitary bird. The same thing has occurred in the more densely populated States of America. There every man has a gun, and unbounded liberty to use it. The result of this system, however, has been that the *feræ naturæ*[15] have been almost totally extirpated. A friend of ours, who travelled lately through a considerable portion of the New England States, assures us that he has wandered about for weeks without seeing a single bird, unless perhaps an occasional crow, the shyness of which abundantly manifested its acute perception of the danger which continually impended over it in the deadly Yankee rifle. Surely this is a consummation which no individual of taste would wish to see effected in our own land. Even the most zealous foe of class legislation, we should imagine, rather than see our woods and meadows altogether deprived of their beautiful feathered inhabitants, would willingly give up his use of gunship, and admit that in such a case the end was an ample justification of the means.

Passing along the green banks of Hamilton Farme, a pleasant walk of about a mile and a-half brings us to Rosebank, the seat of the late David Dale, Esq.[16] The house is plain and somewhat old-

---

[13] From 'The Holy Fair' (1786) by Robert Burns.

[14] John Bright M.P. (1811 – 1889), radical politician. Most famous for opposing the Corn Laws, he also spoke against game laws.

[15] things wild by nature

[16] Rosebank was demolished in the 1930s. Its grounds had been used by Clyde Iron Works as a slag heap.

fashioned, telling of times when architectural taste had not attained such a respectable level among Glasgow merchants as it has in our own day. The situation, however — a sloping bank which rises gradually from the winding Clyde — is truly delicious, while the house is perfectly embowered among its fine old trees and spacious gardens. The property of Rosebank is now, as we understand, in the possession of the Caledonian Railway Company; and the place has altogether a somewhat dreary and neglected aspect. (More recently some kind of public work has been erected immediately adjacent. This adjunct, we need scarcely remark, does not by any means tend to increase the amenity of the locality.) David Dale, as is well known, was one of the most eminent and most venerated merchants of our city during the last century. He was born of humble parentage at Stewarton, in Ayrshire, about the year 1739, and was for some time engaged as herd-boy to a farmer in that neighbourhood. He afterwards served an apprenticeship to the weaving trade in Paisley, from whence he removed to Hamilton, where he wrought for some time at the loom in the capacity of journey man. From this humble beginning, Mr. Dale gradually raised himself by his industry and perseverance, to the condition of a merchant prince in the manufacturing capital of the west. He was the founder of the extensive cotton-works at Lanark and Blantyre, in both of which places, but more especially the former, he made abundant provision for the physical, moral, and religious improvement of his operatives. Thither he transplanted also, from time to time, numerous orphans and other poor children from the city, instilling into them habits of industry, and attending faithfully to their educational necessities. He was thus instrumental in preserving many from the contamination of those vices which ever lurk in the recesses of our large towns, and which find such a plenteous and dark harvest among the unfortunate children of neglect. In his latter days he became a magistrate in our city, in which character, as well as in that of employer, he gained golden opinions from all classes of men., Among the working people he was generally known as "the benevolent bailie." Mr. Dale died in 1806, leaving behind him a princely fortune to be divided among his five daughters, and a name which is still, after the lapse of half-a-century, venerated among his townsmen.

Immediately adjacent to Rosebank are the house and fine grounds of Morriston, the property of John Bain, Esq. The house is a plain quadrangular edifice of considerable extent.[17] It is situated on a gentle eminence, about three hundred yards from the river; the space in front, with the exception of a small patch of green sward, being at present under cultivation. Everything about the place has an exceedingly tasteful and tidy appearance. The hedgerows are neatly trimmed, while the various kinds of crop are unusually luxuriant, and bear evident symptoms of attention and care. Altogether, we should imagine, from appearances around his domicile, that Mr. Bain must have the phrenological bump of "order" pretty largely developed. On the bank of the Clyde below the house we find the snakeweed (*polygonum bistorta*), the yellow goat's-beard, and a profusion of the white convolvulus.

At the eastern extremity of the Morriston estate the Kirk burn of Cambuslang falls into the Clyde, at a spot called "the Thief's Ford," and at which, according to tradition, Mary Queen of Scots crossed the river in her flight from Langside.[18] This little streamlet has its origin at Easterhill, on the borders of Carmunnock, about two miles and a-half to the south. From its devious tendencies, however, it has in reality a much longer course to travel than this distance would seem to indicate. It is indeed the very model of a Scottish burn, and does not seem to know its own mind two consecutive minutes. To it might well be applied the verses in which our poor friend, Peter Still, the late Buchan poet, has so exquisitely described the wayward character of a nameless north country rivulet, —

> "Mark the wee bit nameless burnie
> Jumpin' – joukin' – slidin' slee,

---

[17] This mansion no longer survives. It was located where the present-day Mansion Street lies.

[18] According to the 1910 edition of *Rambles Round Glasgow*, this is a mistake and Mary did not pass this way. It is named for the time a son of the Duke of Hamilton stole valuables from the Rector of Cambuslang and returned by the ford.

Deck'd wi' flowers at ilka turnie,
Shaded wi' the willow tree.

"Whiles it seems to sink in terra,
Whiles it seems to lose its way,
Whiles it seems o'ercome wi' sorrow
Shrinkin' frae the licht of day.

"Whiles it seems fu' blythe and rantin',
Whiles it seems to turn again
Backward to its flowery fountain,
Laith to lea' the lovely glen."[19]

Partly by the meanderings of the burn, and partly by a flower-fringed road, we now proceed towards the village of Cambuslang, which lies about half-a-mile to the south of the Clyde at this point. On the one side of this way are the fertile lands of Morriston, on the other the finely-wooded grounds of Westburn.[20] On the one hand neatness and order, on the other neglect and comparative desolation. The estate of Westburn is the property of John Graham, Esq., of Craigallion,[21] who, not being a resident on the spot, has apparently left it very much for several years to the freedom of its own will, or in other words, to "hang as it grows." The pleasure grounds, which have at one period been of the most elegant description, and which are still very beautiful, are overrun with weeds, while the fine old trees are sadly in lack of a tasteful pruning. The burn also, which winds in picturesque curves through the park, is, in some places nearly choked with sedges and rushes, among which one could almost fancy it was murmuring over better days.

Cambuslang is rather a cluster of villages than one united township. It is divided into two portions by a deep ravine, down which the waters of the burn pursue their course towards the Clyde. On the

---

[19] From the poem 'Robin and Mary' (1845).
[20] Westburn house was demolished but Cambuslang Golf Course stands on its estate.
[21] John Graham Barns-Graham of Lymekilns and Fereneze (1798 – 1875), Liberal politician. He had several estates in different parts of Glasgow.

south-eastern side are Kirkhill, Vicarton,[22] and Sauchiebog; on the other, Bushiehill, Silverbank, and Westcoats. From the elevated and uneven nature of the ground on which it is built, Cambuslang presents from many points of view a highly romantic appearance. It has no pretension to architectural elegance, the houses being, with very few exceptions, of the plainest description. Most of them, however, have kail-yards attached to them; and we are pleased to see, that besides the necessary kitchen vegetables, a considerable proportion have small plots devoted to the culture of flowers. The population is principally composed of weavers and colliers, with a sprinkling of masons and agricultural labourers.

Near Sauchiebog, where we enter the village, and immediately on the edge of the ravine or glen, we are shown the place where a chapel, dedicated to the Virgin Mary, once stood. This edifice, which was founded and endowed in 1379, by William Monypenny, rector of Cambuslang, has long been removed, not the slightest vestige of it being now in existence. Four acres of land, which were attached to the establishment, are still, however, called "the Chapel Croft." The railway from Glasgow to Hamilton passes almost over the site of the chapel. We would recommend ramblers, at least such of them as are not overly dainty about the brilliancy of their boots, to take the bed of the burn at this place, and follow its course to the vicinity of the church, which lies about the third of a mile farther up. This is our route, and although we have considerable difficulty in making our way, by leaping from stone to stone, we are amply repaid for our labour by the wild beauty of the scenery. The sides of the ravine are of the most rugged and tangled description. In some places they are quite precipitous, and from fifty to sixty feet in height, being composed of stratified rocks of sandstone and shale, which will be found well worthy of the attention of the geological student. The vegetation also is unusually profuse. Among the more remarkable specimens are the enchanter's night shade (*circæa lutetiana*), fool's parsley (*æthusa cynapium*), hemlock, woodsage, and a variety of our most handsome indigenous grasses, among which are the elegant single-flowered

---

[22] Or Vicarlands.

melic grass, and the graceful *aira cæspitosa*. There are several fine springs in the glen, at which groups of girls from the village, with their water pitchers, are generally congregated, lending an additional charm to the landscape, which is altogether of the most picturesque nature. One of these springs, called "the Borgie well," is famous for the quality of its water, which, it is jocularly said, has a deteriorating influence on the wits of those who habitually use it. Those who drink of the "Borgie," we were informed by a gash old fellow who once helped us to a draught of it, are sure to turn "half-daft," and will never leave Cambuslang if they can help it.[23] However this may be, we can assure such of our readers as may venture to taste it that they will find a bicker of it a treat of no ordinary kind, more especially if they have threaded the mazes of the glen, as we have been doing, under the vertical radiance of a July sun.

The parish church of Cambuslang is finely situated on a natural terrace which rises to a considerable height above the burn, which meanders in graceful curves around its base. A more beautiful site for the "house of God" cannot well be imagined, and we really think that the burying-ground, with its fine old elms and quiet secluded aspect, is one of the most pleasing specimens of the "country church-yard". which we have ever witnessed. It recalls to our minds the picture which Gray has so exquisitely drawn, and we cannot refrain, while resting on one of the unassuming headstones, from repeating to ourselves his inimitable lines, –

> "Beneath these rugged elms, the yew-tree's shade,
> Where heaves the turf in many a mouldering heap,
> Each in his narrow cell for ever laid,
> The rude forefathers of the hamlet sleep."[24]

We find nothing remarkable among the gravestones. They are generally of the plainest and most unpretending description, being

---

[23] This well is now dried up. An old rhyme said:
  "A drink o' the Borgie, a taste o' the weed,
  Sets all the Cam'slang folks wrang in the heid."
[24] From 'An Elegy Written in a Country Church Yard' (1751) by Thomas Gray.

perhaps in this respect more truly appropriate to the quiet "city of the dead" than the monumental pomp now so common in our fashionable cemeteries. Pride is surely sadly out of place in the church-yard.

The church of Cambuslang is an exceedingly elegant structure of modern erection, forming with its beautiful spire a fine feature in the landscape for miles around.[25] In the vicinity of the church is a manse, a handsome building surrounded by an extensive and tastefully-arranged garden, and the parish school, a commodious and tidy-looking establishment. Besides this, we understand there is another large school-house in the village, so that there seems to be no lack of provision for the educational wants of the juvenile population.

A little to the east of the church there is a spacious natural amphitheatre, formed on the green side of the ravine which we have previously described.[26] This was the scene of an extraordinary religious excitement in 1742. Mr. M'Culloch,[27] then minister of the parish, was in the habit, for a considerable time previously, of conducting public worship in this beautiful spot, and so effectual were his ministrations that crowds began to flock from all parts of the surrounding country to hear him, under the impression that a special outpouring of the Divine Spirit had there been vouchsafed. Many who had hitherto been indifferent to religious matters became inspired with the greatest devotional zeal and enthusiasm. Meetings for prayer and praise were for a considerable time held daily, and symptoms of an extraordinary kind began to be manifested. In the New Statistical Account we find the following description of this curious affair, which is known as "the Cambuslang wark."

"The first prominent effects of these multiplied services occurred on the 8th of February. Soon after, the sacrament was given twice in the space of five weeks, on the 11th of July and on the 15th of August. Mr. Whitfield[28] had arrived from England in June, and many of the most popular preachers of the day hastened to join him at

---

[25] Cambuslang Old Parish Church, built 1841, has been converted into a nursery.
[26] There is a memorial cairn in Cambuslang Park on the site of the preaching braes.
[27] William M'Culloch (1691 – 1771).
[28] George Whitfield (1714 – 1770), revivalist preacher and early Methodist, famous for his powerful voice.

Cambuslang – such as Messrs. Willison of Dundee, Webster of Edinburgh, M'Knight of Irvine, M'Laurin of Glasgow, Currie of Kinglassie, &c. The sacrament on the 15th August was very numerously attended. One tent was placed at the lower extremity of the amphitheatre above alluded to, near the joining of the two rivulets, and here the sacrament was administered. A second tent was erected in the church-yard, and a third in a green field a little to the west of the first tent. Each of these was attended with great congregations, and it has been estimated that not less than 30,000 people attended on that occasion. Four ministers preached on the Fast-day, four on Saturday, fourteen or fifteen on Sunday, and five on Monday. There were 25 tables, about 120 at each, in all 3,000 communicants. Many of these came from Glasgow, about 200 from Edinburgh, as many from Kilmarnock and from Irvine and Stewarton, and also some from England and Ireland. The 'Cambuslang wark' continued for six months, from 8th February to 15th August, 1742. The number of persons converted at this period cannot be ascertained. Mr. M'Culloch, in a letter to Mr. Robb, dated 30th April, 1751, rates them at 400, of which number 70 were inhabitants of Cambuslang." – A couple of old hawthorn trees near the margin of the burn are pointed out as marking the position where Whitfield, the famous preacher, stood on this occasion, and marvellous stories are told of his powerful voice, which according to tradition was heard for miles around. In 1842, the centenary of the strange occurrence we have described, sermons were preached on this spot; and more recently the echoes of the glen have been awakened by the potent eloquence of Chalmers, [29] who preached here (on what special occasion we do not recollect) to an immense auditory. By all accounts the Cambuslang people would be nothing the worse of another revival. We are assured they are anything but a kirk-going people now-a-days. The parish minister has too often to complain of indifferently filled pews; while a large Dissenting meeting-house, at the west end of the village, has actually been closed for lack of support.

---

[29] Thomas Chalmers (1780 – 1847), anti-poverty activist and one of the founders of the Free Church of Scotland.

III. Cambuslang and Dychmont

While we linger at this place, groups of happy boys are paidlin' in the burn which flows sweetly past. Two ambitious urchins are seated among the branches of the old thorn trees, plucking the green baws and shouting in very lightsomeness of heart – a fair-haired lassie is herding cattle on the preaching brae – and the place altogether has an air of peaceful and tranquil beauty, in the highest degree pleasing, and forcibly suggesting a contrast with the wild scenes of enthusiasm which it witnessed in the past, and which busy fancy endeavours to recall.

South of the village of Cambuslang, the ground gradually rises through a succession of gentle undulations to the hills of Turnlaw and Dychmont, the latter of which was long used by our Druidical forefathers as a station for their blazing beltane[30] fires. Towards this fine hill, which is about a mile and a-half or so from Kirkhill, we now proceed by a very pleasant path, passing Cairns and Gilbertfield. The old castellated house of Gilbertfield stands in a commanding situation near the foot of Dychmont. It is a picturesque old edifice, with peaked gables and a couple of small turrets. There are several armorial carvings over the windows, and it appears to have been erected in 1607, as that date is still distinctly legible on the eastern wall. Gilbertfield, to the sentimental rambler, is rendered a place of more than ordinary interest from its associations with the memory of Lieut. William Hamilton, a Scottish poet of some distinction, who resided within its walls for many years. He was a contemporary and correspondent of the celebrated Allan Ramsay, who says, in a rhyming epistle which he addressed to Hamilton –

"When I begoud first to converse,
And could your 'Airdrie whins'[31] rehearse,
Where bonny Heck[32] ran fast and fierce,
    It warmed my breast;
Then emulation did me pierce

---

[30] May Day, a pagan festival.
[31] complaints
[32] Greyhound in Hamilton's 'The Last Dying Words of Bonny Heck' (c.1700-1710)

Whilk since ne'er ceast."[33]

In another stanza of the same production, Ramsay expresses his admiration of Hamilton's poetical effusions, in a style of verse which is certainly more remarkable for strength than elegance. We give it as a curiosity, –

> "May I be licket wi' a bittle
> Gin of your numbers I think little;
> Ye're never raggit, shan,[34] nor kittle,[35]
>   But blythe and gabby,
> And hit the spirit to a tittle
>   Of standart Habby."[36]

Some of our readers, we dare say, will be of opinion that the inspired wigmaker richly deserved a severe thumping with the "bittle" aforesaid, for perpetrating such a "raggit, shan, and kittle" piece of flattery. In the common editions of Ramsay's works three epistles by Hamilton are generally to be found, wherein honest Allan is freely repaid in kind, and those who choose to study the "claw me, claw you" style of criticism, will find capital specimens in their jingling correspondence. Several compositions by Hamilton, of considerable merit, are to be found in all collections of old Scottish poetry. Of these, an Elegy on Habby Simson,[37] the famous piper of Kilbarchan, is generally considered the best. From a line in this curious production, it would appear that it was formerly customary in Scotland to have a bagpiper playing to the reapers while they were engaged on the harvest

---

[33] From *Familiar Epistles* (1719)

[34] shabby

[35] unreliable

[36] These lines are written in standard Habbie, a verse form popular in 18th century Scots poetry, with rhyming scheme AAABAB. Named after the piper Habby Simpson – see below.

[37] 'The Life and Death of the Piper of Kilbarchan' was actually written in 1640 by Robert Sempill of Beltrees. Hamilton of Gilberfield wrote a mock elegy based on Sempill's poem called 'The Last Dying Words of Bonny Heck' in 1706. Habby Simson lived c.1550-1620.

field. In lamenting the loss of Habby, with his skirting pipes, the author says,

> "Wha will gar our shearers shear?
> Wha will bend up the brags of weir?"

What will our agricultural friends say to this practice of the olden time? or what would they think were their reapers to refuse to work unless to a musical accompaniment? In 1722 Hamilton published a translation from the ancient into the modern Scottish dialect, of Henry the Minstrel's *Metrical Life of Wallace*. This production has not added to his fame. It is generally admitted to be much inferior in vigour and gracefulness of expression to the original. It has, however, rendered this interesting work familiar to many who might otherwise have been scared from its perusal by the difficulties of an almost obsolete tongue.

Towards the termination of his life, Hamilton resided at Letterick, on the south of Dychmont, where he died in 1751, at an advanced age. The readers of Burns will remember that in one of his finest epistles he alludes to Hamilton, in company with Allan Ramsay and Ferguson,[38] as occupying a position on the Parnassian[39] heights to which he could never hope to climb. We give the verse in which the allusion occurs,

> "My senses wad be in a creel
> Should I but dare a hope to speel40
> Wi' Allan or wi' Gilbertfield
> The braes o' fame,
> Or Ferguson, the writer chiel,
> A deathless name."[41]

---

[38] William Hamilton of Gilbertfield (c.1665 – 1751), Allan Ramsay (1686 – 1758), Robert Ferguson (1750-74).
[39] Mount Parnassus in Greek mythology was the home of the Muses.
[40] climb
[41] From 'Lines to William Simson' (1785).

Now the name of Gilbertfield is seldom heard, while that of the unknown ploughman has become a household word wherever the English language is spoken.

The house of Gilbertfield is fast falling into a ruinous state.[42] It was last inhabited by a gamekeeper in the employment of the Duke of Hamilton. This individual, a stalwart Englishman, as some of our readers may remember, was accidentally shot by a young man belonging to this city a few years since. After this melancholy occurrence it was deserted, and is now only used as a kind of storehouse by Mr. Weir, a neighbouring farmer. With the permission of this gentleman we examined the interior of the edifice with considerable interest, but discovered nothing worthy of special remark. A number of the apartments are entire, and might yet be rendered habitable; the winds, however, have free entrance by the shattered windows, and the walls have already begun to manifest symptoms of dilapidation, while the swallow and the starling have taken possession of its deserted chambers. The prospect from the turret windows is extensive and beautiful.

We may remark, however, *en passant*, that besides having been the residence of the above bard, Cambuslang parish has given birth to several individuals who have attained distinction in the world of letters. It was the birth-place of Mr. Loudon,[43] the celebrated horticultural writer, although, so far as we have learned, there is nothing remembered of him on the spot; and of Dr. Claudius Buchanan,[44] the author of *Asiatic Researches* and other works. Relations of the latter, we believe, are still residing in the village. It is also whispered, *sub rosa*,[45] that the clever authoress of *Rose Douglas*,[46] a recent meritorious work of fiction, was born not quite a hundred miles from the manse of Cambuslang, and gleaned a number of the

---

[42] The castle is now a ruin, having partially collapsed in the mid-twentieth century.
[43] John Claudius Loudon (1783 – 1843), author of *An Encyclopaedia of Gardening* and other horticultural works.
[44] (1766 – 1815) chaplain to the East India Company and sponsor of Bible translation.
[45] secretly
[46] Sarah Robertson Whitehead (1817 – 1875) who published *Rose Douglas* in 1851.

characters introduced into that production from real personages who lived, or are still living within no very great distance of that locality.

Setting "a stout heart to a stey brae," we now leave the dreary abode of the old poet, which we commend to the attention of our local artists, and commence the ascent of Dychmont. A short though somewhat wearisome walk brings us to its brow, which is 600 feet above the ocean level. There were formerly traces of ancient buildings at this place, but they are now almost totally obliterated. The common nettle, however, grows abundantly in some spots, and it is well known that this plant seldom grows unless in the vicinity of human habitations, or near places where they have once been. In the depopulated Highland glens, the sites of the ancient clachans are generally marked by a profuse growth of the nettle. It is said that about fifty years ago ruinous remains were very extensive on Dychmont, but that they have been gradually removed for the purpose of building walls and constructing roads. Spirit of Oldbuck,[47] what a desecration! But reverence for the antique does not seem to be a Cambuslang virtue. The Lady Chapel, as we have already remarked, exists but in name; and the ancient castle of Drumsargard, which stood about a mile to the east of the church, has totally vanished, the plough having long ago passed over its site. About sixty years since it remained a stately ruin,[48] but it too was pulled down by ruthless hands for the mere sake of its building materials, and that in a district where excellent sandstone is to be had almost for the lifting!

The prospect from the summit of Dychmont is of the most extensive and varied description, embracing the vale of Clyde from Tintoc to Dumbuck. To the east are seen towering in pride Bothwell Castle's ruined walls, the church of Bothwell, with the extensive woods of Hamilton, and far away on the horizon the Tweeddale and Pentland hills. To the north and north-west the spectator sees Cambuslang, Rutherglen, and Glasgow, with towns, villages, gentlemen's seats, and comfortable farm-steadings innumerable, while

---

[47] The title character in Sir Walter Scott's *The Antiquary* (1816).
[48] According to the 1910 edition of *Rambles*, the stones were actually removed in the early 18th century.

the serrated ramparts of the Highland mountains bound with their wild beauty the far-stretching line of vision. To the south are the woods of Crossbasket and the romantic glen of the Calder, with the dreary moorlands beyond Kilbride. Altogether the circle of scenery visible from this "coigne of vantage" is of the most rich and varied description, and would of itself amply reward a summer day's journey. Dychmont, we may mention, is the subject of a descriptive poem of considerable merit by the late John Struthers,[49] author of the "Poor Man's Sabbath," who resided for some time in this vicinity.

Having now reached the boundary which prudence allows to our ramble (after resting our somewhat wearied shanks for a brief space), we commence our homeward walk. Instead of returning by Cambuslang, however, we cross the hill in a south-west direction, and by a country path make our way to the Greenlees Toll on the Glasgow and Muirkirk road. From this a smart walk of an hour and a-half's duration brings us by Rutherglen to our own good town.

---

[49] 1776 – 1853

No. IV. Blantyre and Bothwell

In a letter to Mrs. Dunlop, the bard of Coila[1] remarks that one of his dearest aims was the acquisition of sufficient means to enable him "to make leisurely pilgrimages through Caledonia, to sit on the fields of her battles, to wander on the romantic banks of her rivers, and to muse by the stately towers or venerable ruins, once the honoured abodes of her heroes." Almost every individual of an imaginative temperament must have experienced a similar desire. The stream which has been ennobled by song, the field where freedom has been won in blood, and the gray ruin where in ages long past the great and the good have dwelt, will always attract the pensive wanderer, and by their associations awaken in his bosom emotions of sympathy and reverence. What Scotchman but has felt a yearning to visit the "banks and braes o' bonnie Doon,"[2] or the green sylvan windings of Tweed, and to croon to himself amidst the scenes of their birth, the songs and ballads which have been linked to their names, and which lend unto them

"A music sweeter than their own?"[3]

What patriot but has longed to muse on the spots where a Wallace and a Bruce have struggled and bled for the honour and independence of their native land, or by the shattered and "howlet-haunted biggins"[4] which have been rendered sacred by their presence, or that of some of their gallant compeers? It is, indeed, a pleasant way of studying the history of one's country, thus to wander up and down, deciphering its principal incidents, as they have been inscribed by the faithful and loving hand of hoar tradition on her own green breast; and to find that though the plough may have passed over the blood-stained soil of the battle-field, and though the defacing influences of centuries and the elements may have banished comfort and security from the once proud

---

[1] Robert Burns (1759 – 1796) to his friend Frances Anne Wallace Dunlop (1730 – 1815).
[2] Poem by Burns, 1791.
[3] From 'A Poet's Epitaph' (1800) by William Wordsworth.
[4] That is, owl-haunted. From 'On the Late Captain Grose's Peregrinations through Scotland' (1789) by Robert Burns.

and impregnable tower, leaving it lonely, picturesque, and desolate, still the memory of "what has been" lingers in living hearts, the cherished treasure of sire and son, shedding a halo of sentiment around each hallowed spot, which bids defiance alike to duration and to change.

Scotland is peculiarly rich in this interesting species of lore; but even in Scotland there are few localities wherein it exists more largely, or is associated with more beautiful objects, than in those through which in our present ramble we crave the company of our readers. In deference to the tropical weather which marks the close of June, we are fain to depart to some extent from our pedestrian rule, and take advantage of the means of transit afforded by the "rail." Taking our start, then, from the Caledonian terminus on the south side of the river,[5] we are soon careering away in capital style from

"Gude Sanct Mungo's toun sae smeeky,"

in a direction almost due east. There is something exceedingly exhilarating to us denizens of the city in a short railway excursion. The eye, relieved from the monotonous lines of street and their tumultuous streams of life, revels in the freshness and beauty of the everchanging scenery which seems in very gladness to go dancing past. One moment we have the winds playing over the wavy wheat; another brings us a group of jolly haymakers, with a gush of fragrance from the new-mown swaths; anon sweeps past a band of hoers, thumping away among the shaw-crowned ridges of the potato field, "that flits ere ye can mark its place,"[6] to be succeeded by a bloomy tract of beans, suggesting "odorous" comparisons. Now we have the mansion of wealth, with its green lawns and old ancestral trees;[7] next a lowly cottage, with its kail-yard, its flower-plot, and its bee-hives – the guid wife, mayhap, nursing her baby at the door, and half-a-dozen curly-headed younkers tumbling on the green. Here we have a bridge rushing dinsomely past, there a village with its picturesque spire, and ere the

---

[5] This terminus was at Bridge Street.
[6] From 'Tam o' Shanter' (1791) by Robert Burns.
[7] A reference to 'The Homes of England' (1827) by Felicia Hemans.

spectator can learn its name from the venerable lady at his side, behold it is among "the things that were," and a landscape with cattle *a la* Cooper[8] invites his inspection, and as rapidly disappears. Talk of a picture gallery! why there is none that for variety and richness can bear comparison, even for a moment, with the living panorama of the rail. We are much amused on the present occasion with the vagaries of a botanical friend, who attempts to exercise his vocation and exhibit his scientific acumen by enumerating the various species of plants which he detects growing along the line. While the train at starting moves slowly, he keeps calling our attention every now and again to what he calls "magnificent specimens" of his floral favourites; but when the increasing speed sends the daisy in rapid pursuit of the dandelion, the dock a-hurrying after the nettle, and the wild rose seems in danger of breaking her neck in an extremity of haste to escape from threatened embraces of the stalwart and jaggy thistle, our friend's head seems all at once to grow light, he appears fain to gaze at the more distant portions of the landscape; and to our infinite relief, we hear no more of his long-winded Latin names until we have arrived at our destination.

The line between Glasgow and Blantyre, a distance of some seven miles, passes through a delicious tract of country. There are two intervening stations, Rutherglen and Cambuslang, at both of which we stop, although we are somewhat surprised to observe that no passengers are either taken up or set down, while the booking-offices have rather a dreary do-little appearance. We should imagine, indeed, from the limited extent of these towns – the condition of their inhabitants, who are principally weavers, miners, or agricultural labourers – and the comparative shortness of their distances from the city, that the returns from either will cut but a shabby figure in the sum total of the company's revenue. There are several fine views of the Cathkin and Dychmont hills from the line, looking southward; while the vale of Clyde, with occasional glimpses of its waters, forms the principal attraction to the north. In about half-an-hour after starting, we are set down at Low Blantyre, which we immediately proceed to

---

[8] Thomas Sidney Cooper (1803 – 1902), landscape painter.

inspect. This neat and cleanly little village is finely situated on a high bank which overlooks the Clyde, here a beautiful stream about eighty yards in width. The houses, which are arranged in squares and parallelograms, are the property, and entirely occupied by the operatives of Messrs. Henry Monteith & Co., whose extensive mills and dyeworks are immediately adjacent. Every attention seems to have been paid by this eminent firm to the moral and physical welfare of the inhabitants. They have erected a chapel in connection with the Established Church, capable of accommodating 400 sitters; and we understand that they annually contribute a handsome sum towards the maintenance of the clergyman. During the week the edifice is used as a schoolhouse, for the education of the village children; the teacher being partly supported at the expense of the Company. All the means and appliances of cleanliness, to boot, have been apparently provided for the population. An abundant supply of water, for culinary and other purposes, is furnished from the works; while an extensive building, with a spacious green attached, affords every facility for the necessary scrubbing and bleaching. Altogether this appears to be quite a model of a manufacturing village; everything in apple-pie order – the tenements comfortable and tidy-looking – and the inhabitants seemingly healthy and cheerful. The oldest of the Blantyre Mills was erected in 1785 by the late Mr. David Dale[9] and his partner Mr. James Monteith.[10] Another was built in 1791. Shortly thereafter, premises for the production of the beautiful Turkey-red dye, for which the firm has long been celebrated, were erected; and gradually, from time to time since that period, the establishment has been extending, until now, we believe, upwards of 210 horse-power is required for the propulsion of the machinery, and about 1,000 individuals are engaged in conducting the various operations.[11]

Following the downward course of the river, we now direct our steps towards the ruins of the ancient Priory of Blantyre,[12] which are

---

[9] 1739 – 1806, industrialist and philanthropist.

[10] b.1759, one of a family of textile businessmen.

[11] The last of these mills was pulled down at the start of the 20th century.

[12] The ruin of a monastery founded in the 13th century. Little of it remains.

situated in a beautiful and secluded spot, about three-quarters of a mile from the village. The footpath leading to the Priory lies along a finely wooded bank, the leafy luxuriance of which forms a delightful shade to protect us from the vertical radiance of the midsummer sun. Under the trees the earth is carpeted with a rich profusion of vegetation. We observe many of our most graceful uncultured grasses, with their drooping plumes and silken panicles, waving by the margin of the Clyde, which, from the impulse of the dam at the Blantyre Works, runs here with considerable velocity. In the deeper recesses of the wood, we find the elegant little melic grass (*melica uniflora*) intermingled with the glossy leaves of the wood-rush and other sylvan plants. We also observe the

"Stately foxglove fair to see,"[13]

(*digitalis purpurea*) nodding its towering crest of crimson bells, the broad-leaved helleborine (*epipactis latifolia*), with its curiously plaited foliage, and those most beautiful of our indigenous geraniums, the wood crane's-bill (*geranium sylvaticum*) and dusky crane's-bill (*geranium phæum*) growing in great abundance; while the pink-flowered woundwort, the purple-tufted vetch, the yellow bed-straw, and a bright profusion of kindred blooms are thickly strewn wherever an opening in the leafy canopy overhead permits an entrance to the solar beams. The time of the singing of birds is nearly past, but occasionally the joyous chant of the wood-warbler, or the merry trill of the wren resounds through the green gloamin', and drowns for a time the hum of countless insects which seem to be enjoying their little hour of life with music and dance in the genial summer air.

After a pleasant ramble through the tangled mazes of the wood, we arrive at the Priory, which is situated on a precipitous rock rising to a considerable height above the Clyde. The building, which is of a fine-grained red sandstone, has apparently been at one period of great extent. It is now, however, a complete wreck. A portion of the walls and gables, with several windows and a fireplace, on the verge of the precipice, with a kind of vaulted chamber now threatening to fall in,

---

[13] From 'Elegy On Captain Matthew Henderson' (1788) by Robert Burns.

are all that has been spared by the hand of Time. There are several trees growing among the ruins, and the walls are partly covered with the mournful ivy,

> "Still freshly springing,
> Where pride and pomp have passed away,
> To mossy tomb and turret grey
> Like friendship clinging."[14]

On the opposite bank are the extensive remains of Bothwell Castle; and the view of this lordly edifice, proud even in decay, as seen from the Priory window, with the murmuring Clyde between, forms altogether one of the most interesting and lovely landscapes imaginable. We well remember that, in a conversation which we had several years since with the late Professor Wilson of Edinburgh,[15] who lived for some time at Hallside in this vicinity, he talked in the most enthusiastic terms of this scene, and stated his conviction that it surpassed anything of a similar character in Scotland. The eloquent Professor further remarked that many a summer evening hour he had spent in wandering about this interesting spot. Little is known of the history of the edifice. To it, in its utter desolation, the lines of the poet are peculiarly applicable,

> "Lonely mansion of the dead,
> Who shall tell thy varied story?
> All thy ancient line have fled,
> Leaving thee in ruin hoary."[16]

It seems from an old document to have been founded in 1296, and to have been a cell of the Abbacy of Jedburgh, the inmates of which are said to have found shelter here occasionally when the incursions of English marauders rendered the border counties insecure. The names

---

[14] From 'The Harebell' by 'a lady'.
[15] Professor John Wilson (1785 – 1854), author and professor of Moral Philosophy at the University of Edinburgh, who wrote for *Blackwood's Magazine* under the pen name Christopher North.
[16] From 'The Ruined Castle' (1818) by 'M'.

of Friar Walter of Blantyre, and Frere William, Prior of Blantyre, are mentioned in ancient historical documents. At the Reformation the establishment was suppressed, and the benefice, which was of limited extent, bestowed in name of James VI on Walter Stewart, a son of Lord Minto, who was first entitled Commendator of the Priory, and afterwards Lord Blantyre. At what period the structure was permitted to fall into decay is unknown, but from the *Description of the Sheriffdom of Lanark*, published by Hamilton of Wishaw[17] about a century and a-half ago, it appears that at that time it was the occasional residence of Lord Blantyre. Such are almost the only incidents of an authentic nature which history furnishes regarding this ancient edifice and its former inhabitants.

Tradition says that a vaulted passage under the Clyde formerly existed between the Priory and the Castle of Bothwell; and Miss Jane Porter, in the Scottish Chiefs, has taken advantage of this alleged subaqueous way to heighten the dramatic effect of her story, the scene of which – as most novel readers are doubtless aware – is partly laid here. On our first visit to the Priory – a goodly number of years since – our guide, a school-boy from the adjacent village, told us that according to a winter evening tale current in the neighbourhood, the popular hero, Wallace, in a season of difficulty once found shelter from his foes among the cowled inmates of this establishment. By some means or other the usurping Southrons learning where their terrible opponent was concealed, a large party of them at the dead hour of night determined to secure him and earn the handsome reward offered for his apprehension. To effect this they surrounded the building, with the exception of that portion overhanging the precipice, which from its altitude they considered perfectly secure. While they were thundering at the portal, however, and demanding the surrender of the Knight of Ellerslie, that doughty chief, nothing daunted, slipped out by one of the windows, leaped at once over the rock, and fording the Clyde, made his escape undiscovered. As a convincing proof of the truthfulness of the legend, we were then taken to see an indentation in the solid rock below, which bore some resemblance to a gigantic

---

[17] William Hamilton (d.1724), Scottish antiquarian. The work was published in 1710.

footmark, and which we were seriously informed had been caused by the foot of Wallace on that eventful evening. A fine spring issues from the ground at this spot, the waters of which flow into the sacred footprint; and we need hardly say that it was with a deep feeling of reverence for "Scotia's ill-requited chief"[18] that, on the occasion alluded to, we knelt down and took a hearty draught from the alleged pedal mark. Our faith, we are sorry to say, is not now quite so strong. On our present visit we scarcely discern the resemblance to a footprint which was formerly so obvious; and although we dip our beard in the gratefully cold and crystalline water, the delicious awe which we experienced then comes not again over our spirit.

"Woe's me, how knowledge makes forlorn!"[19]

and how Time rubs the painted dust off the butterfly-wing of youthful fancy! How wofully defaced is now the creed of our sunny boyhood! The fairies are banished from the leafy solitude; no wandering ghost in the glimpses of the moon haunts the ruined tower of other days. Well indeed might the poet Campbell exclaim, –

"Whence science from creation's face
Enchantment's veil withdraws,
What lovely visions yield their place
To cold material laws!"[20]

Had the royal Dane lived in our matter-of-fact age be would have found that there is nothing now in heaven or earth which is undreamed of in our philosophy; nothing to relieve the mind from a "Dryasdust"[21] and stern reality. Whether we are happier in our dreary wisdom and prying scepticism than our ancestors were in their gorgeous ignorance and unsuspecting credulity, is to our mind somewhat problematical. Several of our poets besides the bard of Hope have expressed regret

---

[18] From 'Jean of Lorn; or, The Castle of Gloom' (c.1807) by James Bannantine.
[19] From 'Holy Flowers' by Mary Howitt (1799 – 1888).
[20] From 'To the Rainbow' (1821) by Thomas Campbell.
[21] A reference to Jonas Dryasdust, a fictional character created by Sir Walter Scott.

for the decay of the old spirit of belief. Wordsworth says in one of his finest sonnets,

"Great God! I'd rather be
A pagan, suckled in a creed outworn,
So might I, standing on this pleasant lea,
Have glimpses that would make me less forlorn;
Have sight of Proteus rising from the sea,
Or hear old Triton blow his wreathed horn."[22]

But to our tale. After lingering for a considerable time at the Priory, and about its picturesque environs, we retrace our steps to Blantyre, where we cross the Clyde by an elegant suspension bridge,[23] and proceed to Bothwell, which is situated on a gentle eminence about half-a-mile to the north-east. By the way we pass a neat little United Presbyterian Church, recently erected by a congregation the members of which reside principally in the adjacent villages. Bothwell, like most other ancient Scottish towns, is somewhat irregular and scattered; but, unlike the majority of them, it is remarkable for a characteristic appearance of cleanliness and comfort. It is composed principally of plain one or two-storeyed edifices, built with a peculiar and somewhat highly-coloured red sandstone, which seems to be abundant in the neighbourhood. Most of the houses have garden-plots attached to them, and the neatness and luxuriance of these attest the general taste and industry of the inhabitants. A love for flowers, we are happy to observe, is becoming more common among our population generally; but it is evident, from the fine condition and profusion of rarer kinds around Bothwell, that this is no new love among her people. In the vicinity a considerable number of elegant villas and cottages have been built in tasteful situations. Many of these, we understand, are, during the summer months, occupied by the families of some of our most respectable citizens, and by invalids who find here the benefits to health which result from a genial atmosphere, and an exquisite series of walks amidst scenery of the loveliest description. Near the west end

---

[22] From 'The World Is Too Much with Us' (1807).
[23] This bridge has been replaced twice, the current version being erected in 1999.

of the village is the parish church, a handsome structure in the Gothic style, which was erected in 1833. At the east end of this building, and attached to it, is the ancient church of Bothwell – a fine specimen of the ecclesiastical architecture of other days. This edifice, which is said to have been founded in 1398, by Archibald, Earl of Douglas, is 70 feet in length and 39 in breadth. The roof, which is arched and of considerable height, is covered with sandstone flags, hewn into a curved form resembling tiles. It has been lighted by a large window in the east end, and a range on either side. Inside we are shown carvings of the armorial bearings of the noble families of Hamilton and Douglas, and a stone which was taken from the base of the old spire, with the words "Magister Thomas Dron," or Tron, inscribed on it in Saxon letters. This is supposed to have been the name of the individual who built the church. We are sorry to observe that this time-worn edifice is at present in a shamefully neglected condition. The glass is out of the windows, permitting a free passage not only to the sparrows, which are flying thickly about the nave, but also to the winds and the rain, which have already wrought sad dilapidation on the mouldering walls. The heavy tiles, too, are beginning to manifest a tendency to obey the law of gravitation by tumbling inward. There has of late been but little care taken of this interesting relic of the past. It is to be hoped, however, for the credit of the neighbouring gentry, that measures may speedily be adopted for its preservation from the utter ruin which now seems impending over it.[24] Leaving the dreary precincts of the old church, we next, with considerable labour, ascend the church tower, which is 120 feet in height, and which commands a prospect of great extent and beauty. At the spectator's feet, looking eastward, is the village with its gardens and orchards, some of which are of great extent; beyond is the green expanse of Bothwell haugh, the palace and town of Hamilton, with the wooded grounds of the Duke; while the fertile vale of Clyde stretches away in the distance, –

"To where vast Tintoc heaves his bulk on high,

---

[24] The church has been restored several times and is still in use.

IV. Blantyre and Bothwell

His shoulders bearing clouds, his head the sky."

In the opposite direction are seen Blantyre and the leafy policies of Bothwell Castle, Dychmont, and the high grounds of Kilbride, with the spires of Glasgow towering amidst smoke, and the picturesque outlines of the Highland mountains bounding the misty horizon. After lingering on this commanding pinnacle, enjoying the splendid bird's-eye view which it affords of the country round, until our head becomes somewhat light, and we begin to experience that peculiar yearning to take the shortest way down, which one is startled to feel when looking over a precipice, we descend from our elevated position to the quiet church-yard below. In glancing over the memorials of departed mortality, with which the rank sward is thickly studded, our attention is particularly directed to a headstone, with the following curious inscription, the perusal of which, we are afraid, would have ruffled the equanimity of a Lindley Murray,[25] even amidst the solemnizing influences of the field of graves : "Erected by Margaret Scott, in memory of her husband Robert Stobo, late smith and farrier, Goukthrapple, who died May, 1834, in the 70th year of his age :

"My sledge and hammer lies declined,
My bellows' pipe have lost its wind;
My forge extinct, my fire's decayed,
And in the dust my vice is laid;
My coal is spent, my iron is gone,
My nails is drove, my work is done,"

Bothwell manse, which is immediately adjacent to the church, is, without exception, the most delightful dwelling place of its class which we have ever witnessed, and that is surely saying a great deal in its favour, as everyone knows that, go where you will, "from Maidenkirk to John o' Groats,"[26] the most pleasant of habitations in country or in town is almost invariably that of the clergyman.[27] It is a neat and not

---

[25] 1745 – 1826, grammarian.
[26] That is, in the whole of Scotland. From 'On the Late Captain Grose's Peregrinations through Scotland' (1789) by Robert Burns.
[27] This manse was replaced in 1865 by another manse that is now a private dwelling.

overly large two-storied edifice, situated in a sweet sunny nook, embowered amongst fruit trees, and surrounded by gay parterres and green hedge-rows. It is just the sort of place that one could fancy a poet should be born in, and here accordingly the light of this world first dawned upon that most eminent of Scotland's poetesses, Joanna Baillie. Her father, the Rev. James Baillie, D.D., was sometime minister of this parish. He had previously officiated in the Kirk of Shotts, and it is said that his gifted daughter narrowly escaped being born in that most bleak of parishes, as the flitting between the one locality and the other had just been effected when the little stranger made her appearance. The following record of her birth and baptism is extracted from the parish register of Bothwell, where we saw the original entry, on a page crowded with similar announcements regarding the debut of the sons and daughters of worthy farmers and weavers in the neighbourhood, the majority of whom will doubtless ere now have gone to their final reckoning, without leaving the faintest

"Footprints on the sands of time."[28]

"Joanna, daughter lawful to the reverend Mr. James Baillie, minister of the Gospell att Bothwell, and his spouse Dorrete Hunter, was born the eleventh day of September, and baptized in the Church of Bothwell upon the twelfth day of the said month by the Rev. Mr. James Miller, minister of the Gospell att Hamilton, 1762." From this it appears that the future poetess, who was born on the day after the flitting, was baptized in the open church when she was only one day old. Although Miss Baillie left her natal place at an early age, she seems even when far advanced in life to have recurred with peculiar pleasure to the happy days which, in the morning of her existence, she spent here. In a poetical address which she presented, when her long day of life was drawing near the gloamin', to her sister Agnes, on the birthday of the latter, she says,

"Dear Agnes, gleamed with joy and dashed with tears,
O'er us have glided almost sixty years

---

[28] From 'A Psalm of Life' (1838) by Henry Wadsworth Longfellow.

Since we on Bothwell's bonnie braes were seen,
By those whose eyes long closed in death have been.
Two tiny imps, who scarcely stooped to gather
The slender harebell 'mong the purple heather,
No taller than the foxglove's spiky stem,
That dew of morning studs with silvery gem.
Then every butterfly that crossed our view,
With joyful shout was greeted as it flew;
And moth, and ladybird, and beetle bright,
In sheeny gold were each a wondrous sight.
Then as we paddled barefoot side by side
Among the sunny shallows of the Clyde,
Minnows or spotted par with twinkling fin,
Swimming in mazy rings the pool within,
A thrill of gladness through our bosoms sent,
Seen in the power of early wonderment."[29]

Nor was the attachment of the poetess to the beautiful place of her birth a mere empty sentiment, as the following circumstance, which we learned from a friend in Bothwell, will abundantly testify. About a month previous to the demise of Miss Baillie, an old lady – the widow of a respectable inhabitant of Hamilton, and a former acquaintance of the Baillie family – was suddenly reduced to a state of abject penury by the burning of her house. Some of those who had known her in "better days" got up a subscription for the purpose of relieving her necessities, and amongst others the aged poetess was written to by a granddaughter of the clergyman by whom she had been baptized. Although in bad health at the time, she immediately sent an answer to the appeal, enclosing an order for £15, and expressing an earnest desire to be informed of any other cases of an urgent nature which might occur among the old town's-folk. This was probably the last letter which the hand that had so ably delineated the passions of humanity ever penned; and thus, in the graceful performance of an act of charity, the curtain of time fell upon all that was mortal of this kind-hearted

---

[29] From 'Lines to Agnes Baillie on her Birthday'(1840).

and unassuming woman of genius. We need hardly add that the memory of this last expression of her love for the "old familiar faces" is fondly cherished in the hearts of many; for, as she herself says

"Words of affection, howsoe'er express'd,
The latest spoken still are deem'd the best."[30]

Adjacent to the church of Bothwell is the parish school a handsome edifice of modern erection, in front of which we are pleased to observe a neatly kept flower-plot.[31] The schoolroom is a spacious apartment, hung round with maps and other "means and appliances" of a tuitional description. The average number of pupils in attendance is said to be somewhere about ninety. Attached to the establishment is the dwelling-house of the teacher, Mr. Hunter, and the place altogether has a look of "bienness" and comfort which to our imagination seems to indicate that the lines of this important functionary have, in Bothwell, fallen in an exceedingly pleasant place.[32] Besides the parish school, we understand there are other two seminaries in the village – one in connection with the Free Church, and the other a private school which is under the superintendence of a lady; so that the shooting of the young idea in Bothwell would seem to be abundantly provided for.

After visiting some friends in the vicinity, and benefiting materially by their kind hospitality, we next wend our way to Bothwell Bridge, the scene of the Covenanters' overthrow on the 22nd of June, 1679. The particulars of this engagement are familiar to every reader of Scottish history. The Covenanters,[33] driven to desperation by the cruelties of Claverhouse[34] and his myrmidons,[35] and encouraged by the victory which they had achieved at Drumclog a short time

---

[30] Also from 'Lines to Agnes Baillie on her Birthday'.
[31] This school survives but has been converted into flats.
[32] A reference to Psalm 16.6.
[33] Members of a movement to resist secular power over the Church of Scotland and oppose governance by bishops.
[34] John Graham of Claverhouse, later Viscount Dundee (1648 – 1689).
[35] The followers of Achilles in Homer's *Iliad*, used figuratively to mean minions or henchmen.

previously,[36] assembled to the number of 4,000, determined to wrest by force of arms, from an unwilling government, the right of worshipping their Maker in the form which conscience dictated to be most in accordance with his Word. For the suppression of this "rising" a large army was immediately collected, the command of which was entrusted to the Duke of Monmouth,[37] assisted by Claverhouse and Dalziel,[38] both officers of great energy and experience. The army of the king advanced to Bothwell on the north side of the river, while the Covenanters were encamped on the southern bank, and held possession of the bridge, at that period a narrow and, in the middle, considerably elevated structure, which was defended by a fortified gateway. Immediately previous to the commencement of hostilities the spirit of insubordination broke out in the camp of the Covenanters. The house was divided against itself, and utter ruin was the necessary consequence. The moderate Presbyterians and those of extreme opinions differed as to the extent of the privileges which, in the event of success attending their efforts, they should demand of the government. In the midst of their wrangling and bickering, the Royalists attempted to force the bridge. After a determined struggle with a party of 300 men, under the gallant Hackston of Rathillet[39] and Hall of Haughhead,[40] to whom the defence of this important post was entrusted, the attacking party was ultimately successful. This object attained, they immediately passed over, with their cannon in front, and formed in order of battle on the south side of the river. Here the conflict was resumed, and for some time sustained with considerable warmth; but at length the Covenanters, dispirited by their repulse on the bridge, disadvantageously posted, and wanting that union so essential to success in arms, were thrown into confusion and totally routed; 400 were killed, principally in the retreat, by the merciless troopers of Claverhouse and Dalziel, and not fewer than 1,200 were taken

---

[36] 1st June 1679
[37] James Scott, 1st Duke of Monmouth (1649 – 1685) He was the illegitimate son of Charles II.
[38] Sir Thomas (Tam) Dalziel of the Binns (1615–1685)
[39] David Hackston (d.1680).
[40] Henry Hall (d. 1680), an elder in the Church of Scotland.

prisoners, many of whom were afterwards executed. The author of the "Clyde"[41] gives a graphic account of this disastrous action in the following lines:

> "Where Bothwell Bridge connects the margin steep,
> And Clyde below runs silent, strong, and deep,
> The hardy peasant, by oppression driven
> To battle, deemed his cause the cause of Heaven;
> Unskilled in arms, with useless courage stood
> While gentle Monmouth grieved to shed his blood;
> But fierce Dundee, inflamed with deadly hate,
> In vengeance for the great Montrose's fate,
> Let loose the sword, and to the hero's shade
> A barbarous hecatomb[42] of victims paid.
> Clyde's shining silver with their blood was stained,
> His paradise with corpses red profaned."

This difference in the dispositions of Monmouth and Dundee, or Claverhouse, as he was then called, is quite in accordance with history and tradition. The former is said to have enjoined on his soldiers mercy to their vanquished countrymen; and a pleasing story regarding him is current in Bothwell. An old house in the village, recently demolished, is said to have been the scene of a council held by the commanders of the royal army, previously to the attack on the bridge. While the council was sitting a little child, unobserved by its mother, had strayed into the house. After a lengthened search had been made by the anxious parent for her lost babe, she at last ventured to peep into the apartment where the military chiefs were assembled, and there, sure enough, she found it seated on the knee of the gentle Monmouth, who was fondly caressing it, and endeavouring to amuse it with the glittering hilt of his sword. The ferocity with which Claverhouse pursued and cut down the unfortunate Covenanters after their overthrow on this occasion, is well known; but we think the poet is wrong in supposing, as he does in the

---

[41] John Wilson (1720-1789) best known for the tragedy 'Earl Douglas'. He wrote the poem 'Clyde' in 1764.
[42] great loss of life

above lines, that it was caused by a feeling of revenge for the fate of the great Montrose.[43] More probably it was the result of his own fiendish passions, stirred into extraordinary activity by shame at the recent defeat which he had sustained at the hands of a few undisciplined peasants.

The aspect of the bridge and the ground in its vicinity is completely altered since that period. The gateway has been removed; and, in 1826, the width of the original structure was increased by 22 feet.[44] The banks of the river, which is here about 71 yards in breadth, are of great beauty, and retain no traces of the fierce and disastrous struggle which they once witnessed. Below the bridge, and above it on the south side, they are finely wooded, and brightened with a profusion of wild flowers, fully justifying the opening line of the old song,

"O Bothwell bank, thou bloomest fair."[45]

Above the bridge, on the north side, is the spacious expanse of Bothwellhaugh, formerly the property of James Hamilton, who shot the Regent Murray at Linlithgow in 1569.[46] Leaving the bridge, and taking an easterly direction, we proceed by a delightful path, through fields of waving grain, to the farm-steading which is situated where the dwelling-place of this dauntless individual once stood. The buildings are of modern erection, and nowise remarkable unless from associations connected with their site. Several exquisite views of the palace and pleasure grounds of Hamilton, however, are obtained from points in this vicinity, which are well worth visiting;[47] and about a

---

[43] James Graham, 1st Marquess of Montrose (1612 – 1650), was hanged drawn and quartered.
[44] The width was increased again in 1871, and a monument to the battle was erected by the bridge in 1903.
[45] By John Pinkerton, an Edinburgh historian, published 1783. Pinkerton originally pretended that this song and others were ancient Scottish songs but later admitted to writing them himself.
[46] James Hamilton was a supporter of Mary Queen of Scots. James Stewart, Earl of Moray was Mary's half-brother and ruled Scotland on behalf of Mary's son James VI (later James I of England) after Mary was forced to abdicate.
[47] Hamilton Palace was demolished in the 1920s. Most of the grounds were incorporated int Strathclyde Country Park.

quarter of a-mile to the east of it there is a picturesque old bridge over the south Calder, which, according to popular opinion, is of Roman construction.[48] It consists of a single arch of twenty feet span, high backed, narrow, and without parapets. The pavement is composed of small round stones apparently taken from the channel of the rivulet, and the interstices are thickly studded with grass and

"Weeds of glorious feature."[49]

This curious structure, now somewhat timeworn and dilapidated, has altogether a strange old world aspect, and taken in connection with the rippling dark brown water, and its appropriate sylvan accessories, would form an excellent subject for the landscape painter.

Returning to Bothwell, we now proceed in a direction westward from the village, to visit the celebrated ruins of Bothwell Castle, and the beautiful pleasure grounds of Lord Douglas.[50] This nobleman, with a liberality which is in the highest degree commendable, permits strangers to have access to his extensive policies on certain days of the week. How favourably does such a generous attention to the wishes of his less favoured countrymen contrast with the exclusive spirit which is unfortunately so generally manifested by our modern lords of the soil, and how grateful should the tourist in search of the picturesque feel for the privilege which is thus considerately and handsomely accorded him! It is satisfactory to learn that his lordship's confidence in the popular taste seems to be fully appreciated, and has been but seldom abused. Many hundreds annually traverso the beautiful enclosures, and enjoy the lovely sights around the ancient castle, yet the amenities of the place are but seldom violated.

A walk of about half-a-mile from the magnificent gateway, which is surmounted by a carving of the Douglas arms, along a pathway neatly fringed with verdure, in some places passing through

---

[48] Still in existence, now in Strathclyde Country Park. The bridge is medieval rather than Roman, but it is sited near some Roman ruins.

[49] From 'Muiopotmos: Or The Fate Of The Butterflie' (1590) by Edmund Spenser.

[50] James Douglas, 4th Baron Douglas (1787 – 1857).

lawns of closely-cropped velvet turf, in others beneath the shade of majestic trees, brings us to the front of the spacious mansion of Lord Douglas.[51] The architecture of this edifice, which is of modern erection, is of the most unpretending description. It consists of a central compartment and two wings, the material of the walls being the fine red sandstone prevalent in the district. The principal apartments are said to be very extensive, and furnished in the most elegant and tasteful manner, and the walls of the various rooms hung with pictures by artists of eminence. At a short distance to the west of the house, on a bold green bank which slopes from the Clyde, are the stately ruins of Bothwell Castle, the most extensive and imposing relic of feudal architecture which our country can boast. Some idea of the former grandeur of this structure may be formed when we mention that its shattered remains cover a space which is in length 234 feet, and in breadth 99 feet. The walls are in some places 15 feet in solid thickness, and in height nearly 60 feet. The principal front looking towards the Clyde consists of a lengthened wall pierced irregularly with loopholes and windows, and flanked at either end by a lofty circular tower. The interior presents the appearance of a large court, at the east end of which are the remains of certain windows, which seem to indicate that here stood the chapel of the establishment. There are also several rooms and vaults in a considerable state of preservation; but although specific names have been given to some of these places, nothing certain regarding them can now be known, and the visitor may therefore give his fancy free scope, and people them again as seemeth best to his own mind. The walls are in some places beautifully clad with ivy and other climbing plants, such as the clematis, the greater convolvulus, and the many-tendrilled hop, while the wall-flower and the nettle nod mournfully from the summits and the crevices of the walls; and the starling, the owl, and the daw have long had their homes in the mouldering towers. To quote again from the "Clyde:"

"The tufted grass lines Bothwell's ancient hall,

---

[51] Bothwell House had been rebuilt several times since the 17th century. The house at this time was a neoclassical mansion on a design by James Playfair. It was demolished in 1926 after being damaged by fire and subsidence

The fox peeps cautious from the creviced wall,
Where once proud Murray, Clydesdale's ancient lord,
A mimic sovereign held the festal board."[52]

With regard to the origin of this noble pile little is now known. In the reign of Alexander II.[53] the barony and castle of Bothwell were held by Walter Olifard, the Justiciary of Lothian, who died in 1242. During the troublous period which followed the death of Alexander III.[54] it fell into the hands of the usurper, Edward I. of England,[55] who resided here for some time in the year 1301. In 1309 Aymer de Vallance[56] was appointed governor, and it was while residing here that this individual negotiated the betrayal of Wallace with the ever-infamous Menteith.[57] At the period when Bruce gained the battle of Bannockburn, Bothwell Castle was held by a Sir Walter Fitzgilbert, as we learn from the following passage in Barbour:

"The Earl of Herford frae the melle,
Departed with a great menay,
And straucht to Bothwell took the way,
That in the Inglismennys fay
Was holden as a place of wer;
Schyr Walter Gilbertson was ther
Capitaine," & c.[58]

After the above decisive victory, of course the Southrons were speedily relieved of their unjust possession, and Bruce conferred the barony and castle on Andrew Murray, Lord Bothwell, his own brother-in-law. It seems to have fallen again into the hands of the English, however, after the death of Bruce, when Scotland was again invaded

---

[52] Sir Walter Murray, 1st Lord of Bothwell (d. 1278), who began the construction of Bothwell Castle. He was co-Regent of Scotland in 1255.
[53] Reigned 1214 – 1249.
[54] Reigned 1249 – 1286.
[55] Reigned 1272 – 1307.
[56] Aymer de Valence, (c. 1275 – 1324) 2nd Earl of Pembroke.
[57] Sir John Menteith of Ruskie (c. 1275 – c. 1329).
[58] From 'The Bruce' (c.1375) by John Barbour.

by Edward III., as several documents, still in existence, written by that monarch, are dated at Bothwell. After passing in succession through the hands of the potent families of Douglas, Crichton, Hepburn, and Stewart, it was finally settled on the ancestors of the present possessor in 1715.

The scenery in the vicinity of the castle is of the finest description, including several views of the reaches of the Clyde, with its wooded banks, above and below, of the most striking description. A fine feature in the landscape is the old Priory of Blantyre, which, as our readers are already aware, is situated on a rock of red sandstone immediately opposite. Wordsworth, the poet, who visited this delightful locality, truly remarks, – "It can scarcely be conceived what a grace the Castle and Priory impart to each other." He further adds, – "The river Clyde flows on, smooth and unruffled, below, seeming to my thoughts more in harmony with the sober and stately images of former times, than if it had roared over a rocky channel forcing its sound upon the ear."[59]

Leaving the precincts of this magnificent and awe-inspiring relic of bygone pomp and power, we now proceed by a shady woodland path to visit the extensive gardens of Lord Douglas, which are situated a short distance to the eastward. Having through the kindness of a friend received an introduction to Mr. Turnbull, head-gardener to the establishment, we are received with the most obliging courtesy by that gentleman. Mr. Turnbull, whose fame in his profession has, we believe, extended even beyond the Tweed, may well be somewhat vain of the flourishing condition of his numerous plants, indigenous and exotic. Fruits and flowers are equally abundant, and superior in quality. Such pines, grapes, and peaches, it has seldom been our fortune previously to witness; while in the floral departments, things "rich and rare"[60] seem to be here collected from every country and clime. We are shown all imaginable vegetable curiosities and

---

[59] These words are in fact by *Dorothy* Wordsworth, not her brother William. They come from *Recollections of a Tour Made in Scotland A.D. 1803*.
[60] Possibly a reference to the work of botanist Joseph Banks (1743 – 1820) who went with Captain James Cook to Brazil, Tahiti and Australia, and later encouraged the collection of new species of plants for Kew Gardens.

rarities, such as pitcher plants, sensitive plants, cacti of every possible shape, and many many others, which, but to name, would puzzle a Linnæus.[61] The collection of roses is very extensive, and our visit fortunately happens at the very nick of time to witness them in their hours of bloom. In one conservatory are no less than two hundred distinct species of heaths, many of which are exquisitely beautiful, and all are in the most healthy and luxuriant condition. Time would fail us, however, were we to attempt to indicate even the leading features of the bloomy wealth – the pansy, the pelargoniums, the calceolarias, the fuchsias, and the cacti, which in greenhouse and on lawn, are strewn profusely yet tastefully about. Suffice it to say, that to any individual of taste, a visit to this place alone would far more than repay a ramble to Bothwell. With many acknowledgements of his kindness, we take leave of our friend Mr. Turnbull, and by a pleasant, though somewhat tortuous route through the woods, return to Bothwell.

Feeling somewhat tired with our devious peregrinations and the sultriness of the day, we rest in the village for an hour or two, after which we pass over the river to Blantyre, and by the "last train" we are in a brief space safely deposited at the terminus, whence some dozen of hours ago we took our start.

---

[61] Carl Linnaeus (1707 – 1778), Swedish botanist who developed the naming system for classifying plants and animals.

No. V. Rutherglen and Cathkin

The horizon to the southward of Glasgow is bounded by a range of gently swelling hills, finely wooded, yet with beautiful green slopes intervening, which are exceedingly refreshing to the eye of the spectator, who, haply in "populous city pent,"[1] yearns to wander forth where summer is strewing with bloom the leafy dells, and making the nestling birds rejoice in their green solitudes. For true it is, that while

> "Many a flower is born to blush unseen,
> And waste its sweetness on the desert air,"[2]

full many a heart, alive to the charms of nature, is, at the many same time, doomed to undue confinement by the hard necessities of artificial life, and left to pine and fret amid the weary cares of the city. The hills alluded to are familiarly known as the "Cathkin Braes," and our present purpose is to request the company of our gentle readers on a ramble through the intervening country and along their summits.

Leaving the City then by Rutherglen-loan, on the south side of the river, this sweet morning in the "leafy month of June,"[3] we proceed cheerily on our route. It is some time, however, before we get completely beyond the region of smoke. If fashionable Glasgow is progressing towards the setting sun, her manufacturing industry is moving at an equally rapid rate in an opposite direction. If crescents, squares, terraces, and villas, of every imaginable order and disorder of architecture, are rising at the west end, mills, printworks, and foundries are almost as profusely springing up by way of counterbalance towards its eastern extremity. In the direction in which we are now proceeding, where a few years since there were nothing to be seen but gardens and fields of waving grain, there is now a large community of factories and workshops, and a perfect forest of tall chimneys, The sight of such a vast extension of our manufacturing capabilities is doubtless highly

---

[1] From book 9 of 'Paradise Lost' (1667) by John Milton.
[2] From 'An Elegy Written in a Country Church Yard' (1751) by Thomas Gray.
[3] From 'The Rime of the Ancient Mariner' (1798) by Samuel Taylor Coleridge.

gratifying to our local pride, yet, while muttering something about the flourishing of Glasgow, we are fain to hasten on our way, as we feel but a limited degree of pleasure in lingering where our lungs are necessarily made to perform the rather disagreeable functions of a smoke-consuming apparatus.[4]

About half-a-mile beyond the outskirts of our manufacturing Babel, the road crosses the Rutherglen Burn, which having its origin in the Cathkin hills, after an exceedingly devious course, falls into the Clyde at Little Govan[5], nearly opposite the well-known bathing place in Glasgow Green. Close to the bridge which here spans the rivulet are the Shawfieldbank printworks. Immediately adjacent is an extensive dam, surrounded with trees and thickly interspersed with aquatic vegetation. This is a favourite haunt of the water hen (*gallinula chloropus*), which may be here observed by the disciple of the good old Gilbert White of Selborne,[6] swimming about among the green sedges and "puddock pipes" (as the *equiseta*[7] are familiarly called), in search of the small fishes and larvæ on which it feeds. At present, while the process of nidification[8] is going on, they are seldom to be observed near the margin of the water; but in the gray autumnal mornings we have often surprised scores of them in a neighbouring field, and been amused to see their helter-skelter movements in returning to the water, when the alarm-note was raised. Previously to the formation of this dam, an ancient tumulus or burial-mound occupied a portion of the space now covered by its waters. This relic of a prehistoric antiquity was removed about the end of the last century.

Passing Shawfield Toll, we walk about a mile between lengthened ranges of those hateful "dikes," now so common around our large towns, and which are always so unwelcome to the pedestrian. Their tediousness, however, is relieved in the present instance by green boughs, which, in spite of exclusive owners, seem determined to find

---

[4] See chapter 1, footnote 15.
[5] Polmadie
[6] Reverend Gilbert White (1720 – 1793), gardener and author of *The Natural History and Antiquities of Selborne*.
[7] horsetail plants
[8] nest building

their way over the stony enclosures, and by the singing of birds which know not of artificial boundaries. We soon arrive at the ancient burgh of Rutherglen. Although now a comparatively small and insignificant member of the burgh family, Rutherglen boasts a greater antiquity than her extensive and opulent neighbour. Her territories, it is alleged, at one period even included the site of the present manufacturing capital of the west; and tradition yet tells that the architects who erected our venerable Cathedral were indebted for bed and board to the Ruglen folk of that day. According to a legend common in our boyhood among the auld wives of Glasgow, but of course banished by that general diffusion of philosophy which has given Jack the Giant-Killer his quietus, and blighted the wondrous bean-stalk, it was said that the Hie Kirk was the work of a race of wee pechs (Picts) who had their domiciles in Rutherglen. These queer bits o' bodies, it was added, constructed a subterranean passage between the two localities – a work which throws the famous Thames Tunnel completely into shade;[9] and as they were stronger than ordinary men, they experienced no difficulty in transporting their building materials through this bowel of the earth without equestrian aid. Had any of the juvenile listeners round the winter evening hearth dared to hint a doubt of the credibility of this story, he was forthwith silenced by the corroborative tale of the Highland piper. This worthy (who, as we have since learned, is made to do similar service for sundry other apocryphal passages of a kindred description) is said to have volunteered, a goodly number of years ago, with his pipes and his dog to explore this famous underground way. According to the story, be entered one day playing a cheery tune, and confident of a successful result, but, as the good old lady who narrated the circumstance to us was wont to say, with bated voice, "he was never seen nor heard tell o' again." The sound of his pipes, however, was heard some hours afterwards in the vicinity of Dalmarnock, and to the ears of those who heard it, seemed to repeat, in a wailing key, something like the ominous words,

"I doot, I doot, I'll ne'er get out."

---

[9] Built by Marc and Isambard Kingdom Brunel and completed in 1843.

79

Rambles Round Glasgow

After this tragical event the mouth of the mysterious tunnel was very properly ordered to be closed up, and so effectually has the command been obeyed, that every after-search for it has proved utterly unavailing.

Rutherglen consists principally of one street, which lies in a direction nearly east and west, and is about half-a-mile in length. This thoroughfare, which is broad and well paved, has a number of wynds or narrow streets branching off to the north and south. Like most old towns, it has been built without any fixed plan, and has consequently somewhat of an irregular and straggling appearance. The houses have but little pretension to architectural elegance. They are mostly plain two-storeyed buildings, with a considerable sprinkling of low thatched cottages, which give it a somewhat old-fashioned and primitive aspect. Near the centre of the town is the parish church, a quadrangular edifice of modern erection. The steeple of a small though very ancient church, on the site of which the present one was built, stands in the vicinity, a venerable memorial of bygone ages, and associated with recollections of several interesting events in Scottish history.[10] According to Blind Harry, the biographer of Wallace, a peace was concluded here between England and Scotland in 1297. In describing the circumstance the minstrel says, in lines the orthography of which will puzzle some of our readers, we dare say, –

> "At Ruglen kirk ye traist yan haiff ye set
> A promise, maid, to meet Wallace; but let
> Ye day offyis approchyt wonderfast,
> Ye gret Chanslar and Aylmer yidder past.

> "Syne Wallace came, and his men weil beseyne,
> With hym fifty all arrayt in greyne,
> Ilk ane of yaim a bow and arrowis bar,
> And lang swerds ye whilk full scharply schar."[11]

---

[10] The 'modern' church from 1794 was replaced in 1902 with a church by the architect J. J. Burnett, but St Mary's Steeple, from about 1500, still stands next to it.
[11] From 'The Wallace' (c.1477) by Blind Harry, also known as Henry the Minstrel.

V. Rutherglen and Cathkin

From the same authority we learn that it was also at this place that the "fause Menteith"[12] engaged for English gold to consign his name to eternal infamy, by the betrayal of the peerless Knight of Ellerslie,[13]

> "A messenger, Schir Aylmer, has gart pass
> On to Schir Ihon, and sone a tryst has set
> At Ruglen Kirk, yir twa togydder met."

The old bard then goes on to describe, in indignant language, the paction entered into, and its fatal results.

Like the famous Alloway Kirk,[14] the sacred pile of Rutherglen seems occasionally to have been the scene of diabolical orgies. At least we have the authority of a decent elderly gudewife for asserting that such was the case. According to her, when Mr. Dickson, who suffered sair during the persecution, was in the ministry at Ruglen, the reverend gentleman was riding up the main street of the burgh one night at the witching hour. While passing along the kirk-yard wall, he fancied, to his surprise, that he heard sounds of merriment issuing from his own church. Being a man of some courage, he at once dismounted from his steed, made his way into the grave-yard, which was then, as now, elevated, with its time-honoured elms, a few feet above the level of the street, and, looking into the sacred edifice, which was lighted up as if for a festival, beheld, to his horror and amazement, several of his own congregation, male and female, engaged in some mysterious ceremony, in company with a gentleman in black, whom he at once knew, from a well-known peculiarity of foot, as the enemy of mankind.[15] Provoked beyond forbearance at the desecration of his church, and the evident backsliding of a portion of his flock, he roared out with the voice of a stentor, "Ye'll no deny this the morn, ye limmers!"[16] and turning on his heel, remounted his horse, and commenced making the best of his way home. Not having the benefit

---

[12] Sir John Menteith of Ruskie (c. 1275 – c. 1329).
[13] That is, Sir William Wallace of Elderslie.
[14] Scene of the witches' dance in Robert Burns' 'Tam o'Shanter'.
[15] In folklore, the devil was supposed to be identifiable by his cloven hooves.
[16] scoundrels

of a running stream,[17] however, as the gudeman o'Shanter had, the worthy minister was soon overtaken; and although the powers of darkness durst not injure a hair of his head, yet by their cantrips they contrived to render both horse and rider as rigid as a couple of petrifactions. Stock-still they were compelled to stand, unable to move hand or foot, nor would the band of warlocks and witches release them from this statuesque state, but on condition that his reverence would give his solemn pledge never to divulge the names of those whom he had discovered in such questionable company. This, although with reluctance, he was ultimately fain to do; and so well did he keep his promise, that who the members of the diabolical soirée really were, has never yet been certainly discovered. The old lady added, however, that "there could be nae doot anent the truth o' the circumstance, for it wasna very likely that Mr. Dickson, honest man, was gaun to mak up a leein' story even against siccan deil's buckies."

The Castle of Rutherglen seems to have been at one time a place of considerable strength and importance. This structure, which was said to have been erected by Reuther, a king whose name is associated with the origin of the town, was indeed ranked among the fortresses of the country. During the troubles which broke out in consequence of the contested claims of Bruce and Baliol,[18] the usurper, Edward of England, took possession of this and other castles of Scotland. Robert the Bruce, when he raised the standard of his country's independence, determined to wrest this important place of strength from the English. He accordingly laid siege to it in the year 1309. On hearing of this, Edward sent his nephew, the young Earl of Gloucester, to relieve the garrison. What the immediate result was is somewhat doubtful. Some historians assert that Bruce overcame the garrison, while others are of opinion that he was forced to retire without accomplishing his purpose. In 1313, however, the Scottish king took possession of Rutherglen Castle, having driven the English

---

[17] In 'Tam o'Shanter', Tam escapes because witches cannot cross running water.
[18] Contest between (among others) Robert Bruce, earl of Carrick (d.1295), grandfather of King Robert the Bruce, and John Balliol (1292 – 1306). Edward I of England established Balliol as king, becoming his overlord.

from the country, and made a descent upon England, carrying fire and sword into several of the northern counties.

This is almost the only instance in which the Castle of Rutherglen figures in history. The edifice, however, continued in existence until the battle of Langside,[19] when it was burned to the ground by the Regent Murray, as an act of vengeance on the house of Hamilton, in whose hands it then was. One of the towers was afterwards repaired and fitted up as a residence by Hamilton of Ellistoun,[20] who was then laird of Shawfield and other property in the vicinity. On the decline of the family it was again suffered to fall into decay, and at length became entirely dilapidated, and was levelled with the ground. We may mention that the ruin of the Hamilton family was generally ascribed, at the time, to an immediate judgment of Heaven, drawn down upon them by their persecuting spirit. At the period when our covenanting forefathers made such a noble stand for liberty of conscience and the independence of the national church, the minister of Rutherglen was a Mr. John Dickson. In consequence of an information lodged by Sir James Hamilton of Ellistoun,[21] this good man was dragged from his church, and put in prison. We shall quote a passage from Wodrow's History,[22] to show the sequel: – "Mr. Dickson was kept in durance[23] till the parliament sat, when his church was vacated and he was brought into much trouble. We shall afterwards find him a prisoner in the Bass[24] for near seven years; and yet he got through his troubles, and returned to his charge at Rutherglen, and for several years after the Revolution served his Master there, till his death in a good old age. While that family who pursued him, is awhile extinct, and their house, as Mr. Dickson foretold, in the hearing of some yet alive, after it had been a habitation for owls, the foundation-

---

[19] The Battle of Langside, 1568, between Mary Queen of Scots and her half-brother James Murray. There is a full account of it on pp112-114.
[20] Possibly Sir Claud Hamilton of Shawfield (d. 1614).
[21] Probably James Hamilton, 1st Duke of Hamilton (1606 – 1649) who served Charles I against the Covenanters.
[22] *The History of the Sufferings of the Church of Scotland from the Restoration to the Revolution* (1721–1722) by Robert Wodrow.
[23] imprisonment
[24] Bass Rock, off the coast of Fife.

stones of it were digged up." Such is the story as given by Mr. Wodrow, minister of Eastwood or Pollokshaws, and who wrote immediately after the event. He further says, "The inhabitants there (that is, at Rutherglen) cannot but observe that the informers, accusers, and witnesses against Mr. Dickson, some of them then magistrates of the town, are brought so low that they are supported by the charity of the parish." We shall not take the judgments of Heaven thus into our hands. We shall not say that the curse of the persecutor fell upon this family, and laid their proud mansion in the dust; but we shall ever revere the memories of such men as Dickson and Wodrow, and while we acknowledge that there is prejudice and intolerance in their recorded language, we shall lay the blame rather at the door of their adversaries than at theirs, because persecution is ever the mother of intolerance and all unkindness.

We may mention, before passing from this subject, that the castle stood near the east end of the Back-row, and nearly opposite to where that thoroughfare is intersected by Castle Street. The garden of Mr. John Bryson now occupies the very spot. There is not now, however, even the faintest vestige of the structure. About eighty years ago the foundation-stones were removed. They were very large, measuring five feet in length by four in breadth. Some of the cornice-stones were to be seen in a wall near the town for some years, but they too have disappeared, and now the ancient Castle of Rutherglen has utterly passed away, leaving not even a wreck behind.

Besides the parish church, Rutherglen has no fewer than four other places of worship, viz., a chapel in connection with the Establishment, a United Presbyterian, a Free, and a Roman Catholic church. The inhabitants would therefore seem to have their spiritual wants pretty well provided for. From this abundance of churches it would appear that their religious character is infinitely superior to that of their ancestors, who were occasionally blamed for conduct, in matters ecclesiastical, anything but accordant with propriety, as will be abundantly evident from the following curious facts extracted from the records of the Presbytery of Glasgow:

V. Rutherglen and Cathkin

On 8th May, 1593, the Presbytery ordered their clerk to write a letter to my Lord Paisley, to repair the choir of Ruglen kirk, and at the same time prohibited the playing of pipes on Sunday from sun-rising to its going down, and forbade all pastimes on that day. This order to be read in all kirks, but "especially in that of Ruglen." On the 20th of May, 1595, we find the same reverend court complaining of the introduction of profane plays into the burgh on Sunday, and also of the drawing of salmon and the paying of accounts on that day. From the same source we learn that on the 20th of March, 1604, Sir Claud Hamilton of Shawfield interrupted the minister of Ruglen during sermon in a most barbarous manner, and that Andrew Pinkerton[25] boasted that he had put away four ministers from Ruglen, and hoped he would put away Mr. Hamilton also. He afterwards drew a whinger[26] and held it to the minister's breast, while David Spens[27] said, "he would stick twa ministers, and would not give a fig for excommunication." Two or three years subsequent to these outrageous proceedings, we find a certain James Riddel[28] cutting grass in the kirk-yard on Sunday, and sitting down to the communion-table in spite of minister and session. Altogether, it would seem that in those days the parish of Rutherglen was not in a condition much superior to that of the notorious Dunkeld, the inhabitants of which, according to popular rhyme,

> "Hanged their minister,
> Drooned their precentor,
> Pu'd doon the steeple,
> And brak' the kirk bell."[29]

Things are, however, in a much superior condition now a-days, the inhabitants being generally an industrious, decent, and kirk-going people, attached to their ministers, and especially attentive to the

---

[25] Bailie of Rutherglen in 1667.
[26] A short sword or long knife.
[27] Bailie of Rutherglen in 1661, 1665,1672–74, 1678.
[28] Bailie of Rutherglen in 1669–70 – dismissed for corruption.
[29] From the traditional song 'O What a Parish (The Parish of Dunkeld)'. If the incident did happen, it may have been in Kinkell, rather than Dunkeld.

education of their children, as is sufficiently evident from the attendance of pupils at the two commodious and handsome seminaries which have been erected in connection with the Established and Free Churches. They seem, moreover, to have been tenacious of old customs. The riding of the marches, once an annual ceremony in every Scottish burgh, continued to be celebrated in Rutherglen until 1832, when it was discontinued. We understand, however, that it has since been at least partially revived. Another ancient custom, the baking of sour cakes on St. Luke's eve,[30] is peculiar to the burgh, and is supposed to have had an origin anterior to Christianity itself. We have ourselves witnessed this curious operation in the Thistle Inn of Rutherglen – within the past two or three years. This mystic baking requires for its proper execution the services of some six or eight elderly ladies. These, with each a small bake-board on her knee, are seated in a semicircle on the floor of the apartment devoted to the purpose, and pass the cakes, which are formed of a kind of fermented dough, in succession from one to the other, until the requisite degree of tenuity is attained, when they are dexterously transferred to an individual called the queen, who, with certain ceremonies, performs the operation of toasting. These cakes, which we have often tasted, are generally given to strangers visiting St. Luke's fair. They are somewhat like a wafer in thickness, of an agreeable acidulous taste, and lend an additional relish to the drams usually in extra demand at such times. The lover of old customs would regret the discontinuance of this curious ceremony, the observance of which forms an interesting link between the present age and an impenetrable antiquity.

Rutherglen has long been famed for its horse and cattle fairs, seven of which are held on the main street of the burgh annually, and generally attract considerable crowds of buyers and sellers from all parts of the country. The Clydesdale breed of horses, which has attained such a well-deserved celebrity for its excellent qualities, was generally exposed in greater numbers and in greater perfection at the Rutherglen fairs than at any other market. The principal fairs are the

---

[30] St Luke's Day is 18th October.

Beltane in May, and St. Luke's in November, when the town is generally crowded with strangers. According to the last census, the number of the population was 6,947, of whom 3,430 were males, and 3,517 females. It would therefore appear that there is a trifling excess of the fair sex in the burgh, but the overplus is not sufficiently great to excite anything like serious alarm, more especially as the well known beauty of the Rutherglen lasses is certain to attract a considerable number of wanters from other localities.[31]

After rambling about the burgh for a considerable time, and visiting "Din's Dykes," where two boorish rustics attempted to intercept the unfortunate Mary on her flight from Langside,[32] we proceed towards Cathkin by the Glasgow and Muirkirk road. About a quarter of a-mile on the way we pass through Stonelaw, the vicinity of which is finely timbered, having been extensively planted about sixty years ago by Major Spens,[33] then proprietor of the estate. The botanist would do well to imitate our example, and linger for a brief space in the umbrageous recesses of these beautiful woods, which contain many of our finest indigenous plants. Among these are the periwinkle (*vinca minor*), with its glossy leaves and blue or white flowers, which is more abundant here than we have seen it elsewhere; the hop (*humulus lupulus*); the spreading bell-flower (*campanula latifolia*); the lesser winter-green (*pyrola minor*); the rare mountain currant (*ribes alpinum*); various species of gerania, and many others, which will abundantly repay a leisurely inspection.

In passing Stonelaw our attention is attracted by a kind of tower, near the road, which, although of comparatively modern erection, is quite as picturesque as an ancient feudal keep, being completely embedded in ivy, which is trailing over and around it in the most beautiful profusion.[34] This ivy is at present the haunt of innumerable starlings and sparrows, which appear to be proceeding

---

[31] Both of MacDonald's wives came from Rutherglen. His second wife, Alison, was a bridesmaid at his wedding to his first wife, Agnes.

[32] Mary Queen of Scots was defeated at the Battle of Langside in 1568. A fuller account of this incident is given on pp112-114.

[33] Major (later General) John Stonelaw, Coal Master of Stonelaw Pits (1740 – 1821).

[34] Probably built in the mid-1830s, the tower was eventually demolished in the 1960s.

merrily under its shade with their various domestic duties. During the few minutes we stand looking at it, we count not less than twenty starlings leaving the tower in search of supplies, and nearly as many returning in different directions with the fruit of their raids through the brairded[35] fields around. As for the sparrows, they appear to live on the most harmonious terms with their starry neighbours, and keep up such an incessant chattering that it is obvious they are quite at home, and, as usual, enjoying themselves with characteristic sangfroid. A more than ordinarily well-tempered and philosophic man the inside tenant of that tower must be, or he would infallibly be driven distracted by the noisy intercourse of his feathered friends outside, not to speak of the depredations which their well-known voracity must lead them to perpetrate on his garden. [Since this was written, the tower has been denuded of its covering, and the birds have consequently been forced to betake themselves to other quarters.]

From Stonelaw to Cathkin the road gradually ascends through a delightful succession of gently swelling knolls and fields in a high state of cultivation, interspersed with clumps of wood and fine belts of planting, the haunts of numerous birds, and at this season of love ringing merrily with their sweetest melodies.

Passing Boultrie Loch,[36] a favourite curling place in winter – but which, as an Irishman might say, is in summer no loch at all, but a verdant meadow, being regularly drained every spring, when its alluvial bottom is sown with some kind of cereal crop – we next come to Cathkin House, the fine seat of Humphrey Ewing M'Lea, Esq.,[37] situated at the eastern extremity of the braes, and commanding an extensive and beautiful prospect.[38] Turning to the right, we now leave the road we have hitherto been pursuing, and proceed along the summit of the Cathkin hills on the way to Carmunnock, which lies at the distance of a mile and a-half or so to the west. For a great portion of

---

[35] sprouting or germinating
[36] This loch, in Burnside, is no longer there.
[37] 1773 – 1860. His family owned slaves and sugar plantations in Jamaica.
[38] Built in 1799. It was converted to a children's home and old folks' home before being restored into a dwelling.

this distance, the view is walled in as it were by dense woods; but ever and anon an opening occurs through which the eye is permitted to roam over an exquisite and far-stretching tract of country. We soon arrive at the highest point of the range, which is said to be elevated about 500 feet above the level of the sea. The atmosphere is delightfully clear, so that the landscape, which is spacious and lovely, is seen to great perfection. At our feet, half-hidden among its old ancestral trees,[39] lies Castlemilk,[40] a stately structure of considerable antiquity, and where, it is said, Mary Queen of Scots slept on the night preceding Langside; in the low grounds beyond are seen the burgh of Rutherglen, and our own good city, nestling, as usual, under her canopy of smoke, with a variety of other towns and villages, including Cathcart, Pollokshaws, Paisley, and Renfrew. The course of the Clyde is here seen at a glance from Carmyle to Dumbarton, the glittering waters like the convolutions of a mighty snake turning up to the light every here and there amongst the beautiful wilderness of woods and fields, over which the winds are making their mimic waves of verdure while we stand gazing on the scene. To the east on the far horizon, are Arthur's Seat and the Pentland Hills in the vicinity of old Edina, "Scotia's darling seat;"[41] to the north, Benlomond, Benledi, and the Cobbler, with their giant neighbours; to the west, Gleniffer, and Fereneze braes, with Goatfell peering far away over their green summits. Altogether, the prospect from this spot is one of great interest and magnificence, and embraces, it is said, within its scope no fewer than sixteen counties. Scattered around our feet are the yellow mountain violet (*viola lutea*), the blaeberry plant (*vaccinium myrtillus*) with its pretty little crimson bells, and the golden tasselled broom, forming an appropriate crest to the hill which, as tradition loves to tell, once bore on its brow Scotia's fairest and most unfortunate Queen.[42]

---

[39] A reference to 'The Homes of England' (1827) by Felicia Hemans.
[40] Built in the 15th century by the Stirling-Stuart family. It was demolished around 1970 but the 17th century stable block still survives as a community hub.
[41] From 'Address to Edinburgh' (1787) by Robert Burns.
[42] Mary Queen of Scots stayed at Castlemilk the night before the Battle of Langside (1568).

To the geologist, the Cathkin range presents but few features of interest, being composed principally of one solid and uniform mass of whin. A short distance below the house of the proprietor, however, a beautiful specimen of basalt is exposed to view. The columns above the surface are about thirty feet in height, pentagonal in form, and being extremely regular in arrangement, form a fine natural colonnade. This curious formation, an engraving of which was published in Ure's *History of Rutherglen*[43] about the end of the last century, was discovered a considerable number of years since by some individuals when quarrying for road metal. The proprietors, with commendable taste, have since preserved it from further dilapidation.[44]

A group of gigantic burial mounds, or tumuli, formerly stood upon the Cathkin hills a short distance to the south of Cathkin House. These were formed of unhewn stones, and were of great extent. One, which was opened for the sake of the stones it contained, was found to measure 260 feet, and to consist in the interior of a long gallery, or chamber, containing a number of curious relics, such as brass vessels, beads of glass, and other articles. Another of these rude mansions of the dead, popularly called Queen Mary's Law, measured 18 feet in height and 120 feet in diameter. For several years it served as a perfect quarry to the farmers in the neighbourhood, and at length a chamber was discovered in its interior containing no fewer than twenty-five urns for the reception of the ashes of the departed. These urns, as was the custom, were placed with their mouths downwards, and under each was a piece of white stone. In the centre of this pile another small chamber was disclosed, in which were found a quantity of human bones, with a ring or armlet of cannel coal,[45] and a comb of the same material. Since that period all these interesting structures have been from time to time removed, until there is not even one now remaining. We have conversed with an individual who superintended the removal of several, the stones being used for the construction of dykes and

---

[43] *A History of Rutherglen and East Kilbride* (1793) by Rev. David Ure.

[44] I have been unable to find any trace of this natural structure. There is, however, a large quantity of basaltic stone chippings in the current suburb of Cathkin.

[45] A shiny, hydrogen-rich coal.

barns. He stated that they invariably found one or more urns within them, and that these were formed of unbaked clay, which crumbled into dust shortly after being exposed to the air. It is certainly to be regretted that some of these most interesting and suggestive relics were not spared for the gratification of the antiquary, and as objects of contemplation to the poetic wanderer. Among such tombs there was indeed abundant scope for the most serious reflection. For many a long and dreary century they had kept their trust in defiance of the wind and the rain; and the tale they told was of an age before the light of Christianity had dawned on our isle – of a dark and distant era, when our sires were a band of painted savages, and when the altar-fires of Baal, from the brow of Dychmont, still threw a lurid lustre over the valley of the Clyde.

The old road from Rutherglen to Kilbride passed over the braes of Cathkin, and in our boyish days a considerable extent of their surface was patent to ramblers from that burgh and from Glasgow. The privilege was often abused, as is too frequently the case where such liberties are granted, by thoughtless or evil-disposed parties. Fences were occasionally broken and depredations committed on the plantations and the crops, until at length, a few years since, the proprietor thought proper to exclude the public from the spot altogether. Considerable indignation was excited in the popular mind by this measure, and there was some talk of making a "Harvie's Dyke"[46] affair of it, and endeavouring, through the instrumentality of law, to enforce right of way on plea of immemorial usage. The excitement however, gradually died away, no practical steps, were taken in the matter, and now the silence and solitude of Cathkin are but seldom disturbed by the foot of the holiday wanderer.[47]

Between the summit of the braes and Carmunnock, about a quarter of a-mile to the southward of the road, and on a wild tract of moorland, are the traces of an ancient British camp.[48] To this spot we

---

[46] See pp23 – 24.

[47] In 1886, 49 acres of braes were donated to the city by the manufacturer James Dick to form Cathkin Braes Country Park.

[48] The 'wild tract of moorland' is now Cathkin Golf Course

now direct our steps, disturbing on our way several snipes, which here breed among the moist marshy hollows. We also occasion infinite consternation among the lapwings or peeseweeps, which keep wheeling round our head, and clamouring vociferously as erst their ancestors may have done to the sad discomfiture of the persecuted Covenanters, who, in their hiding-places among the moors, were frequently alarmed lest the cries of the lapwing should attract to their "whereabouts" the attention of the passing dragoons. The elegant and affectionate bird alluded to, from this habit, prompted by love of its offspring, was, we may remark *en passant*, anything but a favourite with the "worthies," and it was even said to be in league with the enemy of our race[49] for the exposure of the faithful. We soon arrive at the camp, the outlines of which are still, after the lapse of many centuries, distinctly visible.[50] It is circular in form, of considerable extent, and is still surrounded by a wide and somewhat deep ditch. From its elevated position, it commands an extensive prospect of the surrounding country. Whatever other purposes, therefore, such an encampment may have been designed to serve, it seems at least to have been well adapted for watchfulness. The view from this interesting footprint of the past embraces within its range the villages of Busby and Eaglesham, with the hill of Ballygeich in the Mearns, and the bleak moorlands beyond Kilbride. The tufted cannach[51] here waves in the blast its snowy plumes, the curious sun-dew (*drosera rotundifolia*) is also met here, with its glittering beads of dew unmelting "in very presence of the regal sun;"[52] with the marsh violet (*viola palustris*) creeping in beauty along the untrod den heath, and the buckbean (*menyanthes trifoliata*) and marsh cinque-foil (*comarum palustre*) rising above the dark moss-water.

Shortly after leaving the camp we arrive at Carmunnock, a pleasant little village, with some score or so of houses, situated at the

---

[49] That is, the devil.

[50] The camp is now a green in Cathkin Braes golf course.

[51] cotton grass

[52] From the play 'William Tell' (1825) by James Sheridan Knowles. This speech by Tell was included in the anthology *The English Orator* by James Hedderwick, MacDonald's friend and editor.

western extremity of the Cathkin hills. The population of the parish, consisting principally of agriculturists and weavers, numbered at the late census 717, being an increase of only ten individuals within the last decade! It has an old-fashioned barn-like church,[53] which stands about the centre of the village, and an exceedingly commodious and well-built school,[54] from which, as we pass, the juvenile Carmunnockians are pouring forth with that dinsome glee which is only heard at the skailing o' the schule, and which at once calls back to the memory of us "children of a larger growth,"[55] the joys of other years.

In the Statistical Account of Carmunnock, published about 1840, there is a fact stated which must fill with envy the assessment-crushed unfortunates of our city parishes. There has hitherto been no levy for poor-rates, and the worthy minister, with justifiable complacency, expresses his belief that such a thing as a compulsory assessment for the support of the poor is not at all likely ever to be required. What a delightful little city of refuge this must appear to the pauper-ridden denizens of Sanct Mungo; what an oasis in the desert, far away from the persecuting tax-gatherer, who, on some pretence or other, is eternally prying into our books, and making town's talk of our most secret affairs! The minister, likewise, boasts that no individual belonging to the parish was ever convicted of a capital crime. Why, the golden age would seem to be lingering at the south-west end of Cathkin braes, and we should not be surprised, if the knowledge of these good matters once gets wind, that the next census will show an infinite addition to the ratio of increase in the population of this really pleasant and picturesque, as well as almost pauperless and felonless parish.

We have now arrived at the prescribed limit of our excursion, and after resting our somewhat wearied limbs, for a brief space, in a tidy country alehouse, which, for cleanliness and comfort, would have

---

[53] Build 1767, repaired around 1840. The building is still in use as the parish church.
[54] Built in 1840 to replace an earlier school. The building is now used by the Carmunock Recreation Club.
[55] From the play 'All for Love' (1677) by John Dryden.

pleased even the fastidious eye of old Izaak Walton,[56] and paying due homage to the maxim of a genuine Scotch poet, who recommends us on the journey of life "Aye to live by the way,"[57] we commence our homeward walk by Cathcart, a distance of some five miles, which, being principally downhill, is speedily accomplished.

---

[56] (1593 –1683) Son of an alehouse keeper and author of *The Compleat Angler*.
[57] Probably a misquote from 'Sae Will We Yet' by Walter Watson (1780 – 1854):
      "As we journey through life, let us live by the way"

The pedestrian plodding wearily along the highway, after a lengthened and devious walk, when some gay equipage dashes rapidly past, spattering the mud around, or leaving a blinding cloud of dust along its track, is apt to feel a passing twinge of envy, and to fancy that their lot must indeed be a happy one who possess so handsome and luxurious a conveyance. He is ready under such circumstances to exclaim, "How much is their mode of progression as a means of enjoyment superior to mine!" Yet there cannot be a greater mistake. For speedy transmission from point to point on matters of business, or for the salutary airing of an invalid, the various equestrian methods of transport may be all very well; but for healthy exercise of the person, and the thorough enjoyment of nature, there is nothing that can for a moment bear comparison with natural locomotion. The man who travels by carriage must keep by the highway; he cannot plunge into the recesses of the wood in search of the wilding flower; the din of the wheels on which he is borne along drowns the sweet voices of the birds. He cannot follow the windings of the footpath through the whispering corn-field, nor trace that fairest line of beauty, the "trotting burn's meander,"[1] which, according to the bard of Coila, forms the favourite haunt of the Parnassian sisters.[2] Then he is continually liable to interruption from the outstretched hand of the toll-keeper; his horses are always getting rid of their shoes at out-of-the-way places, where farriery is an art unknown, or his driver, taking a cup too much, is sure to run over and squelch some unlucky urchin making mud-pies on the middle of the road, or to come tilt against a mile-stone and spill his unfortunate master, who, if he escapes with nothing worse than a dislocated shoulder or a fractured collar-bone, may thank his stars, and consider himself an exceedingly lucky fellow. Really, amidst all our troubles – and we suppose everybody has his share – we have much reason for gratitude to Fortune, that she has not inflicted on us a

---

[1] From 'Lines to William Simson' (1785) by Robert Burns (the 'bard of Coila').

[2] That is, the muses, who in Greek legend lived on Mount Parnassus.

carriage and its cares; and that without encumbrance, save our gray hazel switch, we

> "Can wander away over hill and glen,
> Far as we may for the gentlemen."

There are several ways which the pedestrian may take at pleasure in his rambles from Glasgow to Cathcart. Our favourite route is by Rutherglen. Connecting this burgh and Carthcart, there is a delightful footpath, about a mile and a half in length, through the intervening fields. It is one of those old kirk-roads which, having been in popular use from time immemorial, will, it is hoped, be long preserved from the encroachments of unscrupulous proprietors, who, in so many instances, have of late enclosed and obliterated these "old brown lines of rural liberty."[3] Leaving the west end of Rutherglen by this road, we proceed towards Cathcart in a south-westerly direction. About a quarter of a mile out of the town we pass the cottage of "Bauldie Baird," a plain one-storeyed edifice, which – with its proprietor, a plain blunt man – has attained considerable local celebrity. Honest Bauldie, who is the subject of a certain wicked song, for many years earned a decent livelihood by the sale of "curds and cream," "fruits in their season," and a wee drap of the mountain dew. His edibles and liqueurs, though of a homely description, were always excellent in quality; and the place became a favourite resort of the lads and lasses of Glasgow, who, after the toils of the week, might have been seen during the summer and autumn months, in laughing groups in the garden, enjoying the good cheer which the place afforded. Bauldie had virtuous neighbours, however, who were determined that there should "be no more cakes and ale."[4] Complaints were made by these parties that the stringency of Sabbath rule was occasionally violated on his premises, and ultimately, on the faith of their representations, the licensing court put their veto on his trade as a publican. This at once extinguished poor Bauldie's popularity. His

---

[3] From 'Sonnet on Footpaths' (?1836)by Samuel Plumb.
[4] From Shakespeare's *Twelfth Night*, II.iii.

curds might be as agreeable to the palate as ever, his "grozats"[5] as large and as well-flavoured, but everybody knows that such dainties are rendered much more easy of digestion when they are accompanied by a caulker of the Glenlivet. This necessary addition to the treat Bauldie having been by law forbidden to dispense, the result as that in a short time he found bis occupation in a great measure gone, his garden an unpeopled wilderness, and himself a standing jest for triumphant teetotallers. (Since this was written, poor Bauldie has become a tenant of the narrow house. [6])[7]

At a short distance beyond the cottage of Bauldie Baird, the road passes over the "Hundred-acre hill," a beautiful eminence, which commands a series of delightful views of the surrounding country. On the one hand are undulating fields, in a high state of cultivation, interspersed with gentlemen's seats, comfortable farm-steadings, and picturesque clumps of trees, with Dychmont and the Cathkin braes in the distance; on the other is a wall of moderate height, which serves as a screen to shield from withering blasts a lengthened strip of verdure at its base, which is brightened with the varied hues of many of our sweetest indigenous plants. Among these we observe the handsome yellow goat's-beard (*tragopogan pratensis*), the sweet little field forget-me-not (*myosotis arvensis),* the silver-weed (*potentilla anserina*), the perforated St. John's-wort (*hypericum perforatam*), intermingled with clusters of speedwell, crosswort, and bird's-foot trefoil, forming altogether as lovely a fringe to the brown footpath as poet's eye could wish to scan. Here, too, we find the first rose of summer,

---

[5] gooseberries

[6] That is, has died.

[7] Bauldie Baird's Inn was Canada Cottage, which has since been demolished. The neighbours who complained were the Russell family who lived in Auburn Cottage, which still survives. James Russell was Glasgow's first steamboat harbour master and the grandson who lived with him, James Burn Russell, was later a public health pioneer.

"Sweet blooming alone,"[8]

amid countless kindred buds, on the eve of bursting into light, with their tribute of perfume for the wandering winds. What sad work the majority of our poets have made with the appointed times of the flowers![9] The rose is exclusively a summer flower, seldom blooming in Scotland before the second week of June. Yet how frequently do we see in rhyme the spring months decorated with the "queen of flowers!" Not to talk of minor bards, we find Burns falling into this error; and Thomson, the minstrel of "the Seasons," one of our best descriptive poets, invokes the spring in the following fashion:

> "Come, gentle Spring, ethereal mildness, come,
> And from the bosom of yon drooping cloud,
> While music wakes around, veil'd in a shower
> Of shadowing roses, on our plains descend."[10]

When the masters of the lyre are thus out of joint with the seasons, we need hardly be surprised that with bards of low degree the "confusion becomes worse confounded,"[11] so that were the mirror held up to nature, it would be utterly impossible, we opine, for the goddess to recognize her own features. Shakespeare, that mental triton among the minnows of poetry, is never found thus tripping. Deeply as he must have studied the world within, he had, at the same time, an attentive and loving eye for the minutest of external existences. He knew the season

> "When daisies pied and violets blue,
> And lady's smocks all silver white,
> And cuckoo buds of yellow hue
> Do paint the meadows with delight;"[12]

---

[8] MacDonald appears to be mixing up 'The First Rose of Summer' (?1831) by Robert Gilfillan with 'The Last Rose of Summer' (1813) by Thomas Moore.
[9] See also pp33 – 35.
[10] From 'Spring' (1728) by James Thomson.
[11] From book 2 of 'Paradise Lost' (1667) by John Milton.
[12] From 'Spring', a song in Shakespeare's *Love's Labour's Lost* (1597).

and he could tell, with an exactness as to time that would have pleased even a Linnæus,[13]

> "Of daffodils that come before the swallow dares,
> And take the wings of March with beauty."[14]

On attaining the southern brow of the hill over which we have been walking, a landscape of the most exquisite description bursts upon the view. At the feet of the spectator, and situated at the bottom of a vast green basin, formed by a girdle of gentle eminences, is the elegant church of Cathcart, standing in its field of graves, and surrounded by stately and time-honoured trees. A little beyond is the village of Old Cathcart, half embowered in dark-green foliage, through which the blue smoke is gracefully ascending, with that peculiar effect which is so pleasing to the eye of the painter, and which so frequently tempts his pencil to imitation. To the right is the battlefield of Langside;[15] to the left Cathcart Castle, half hidden among woods, and the "Court Knowe," from which Mary saw her kingdom and crown dashed at one fell swoop for ever from her grasp. It is indeed a lovely, and from its associations a deeply interesting scene. For, as the author of the "Clyde" beautifully says,

> "Here, when the moon rides dimly through the sky,
> The peasant sees broad dancing standards fly;
> And one bright female form, with sword and crown,
> Still grieves to view her banners beaten down."[16]

The fine woods and pleasure-grounds of Aikenhead in the vicinity, also contribute considerably to the beauty of the landscape as seen from this point. After lingering here for some time, we take our way down hill, towards the church. This edifice, which was erected in

---

[13] Carl Linnaeus (1707 – 1778), Swedish botanist who developed the naming system for classifying plants and animals.

[14] From Autolycus' song in Shakespeare's *The Winter's Tale* (1611).

[15] Site of the Battle of Langside,1568, between Mary Queen of Scots and her half-brother James Murray. The suburb nearby is still known as Battlefield. See pp109 – 110 for a full account.

[16] 1764, by John Wilson best known for the tragedy 'Earl Douglas'.

1831, on the site of an old barnlike structure which we well remember, is an elegant building in the modern Gothic style of architecture.[17] It is surrounded by a fine burial-ground, quiet and secluded, where beneath the flickering shadows of several umbrageous old ash trees "the rude forefathers of the hamlet sleep."[18] The pensive rambler may here spend a profitable hour, as many a time and oft in bygone days we have, in meditation among the tombs. Many of the headstones are well worthy the attention of those who love to study the doleful literature of the dead. Among the more remarkable of these is one that marks the grave wherein are interred the ashes of three individuals, who suffered a violent death for their adherence to the principles of the Solemn League and Covenant,[19] in the days when Claverhouse[20] and his troopers rode rough-shod over the consciences of the Scottish people. Many years ago we remember enacting "Old Mortality"[21] on this stone, by removing with our gully[22] the moss which had crept over it and almost obliterated the inscription. Since then a fresh application of the chisel has rendered it perfectly legible, so that we should have had no difficulty in transcribing it for our readers, although it had been effaced from our memory – which, however, from the strong impression it made on our youthful imagination, it has not. It is as follows:

"This is the stone tomb of Robert Thom, Thomas Cook, and Jolin Urie, martyrs for ouning the covenanted work of Reformation the 11th of May, 1685.

"The bloody murderers of these men
Were Major Balfour and Captain Maitland;
With them others were not frie,
Caused them to search in Polmadie.

---

[17] This church was demolished in 1931 but the bell tower survives.
[18] From 'An Elegy Written in a Country Church Yard' (1751) by Thomas Gray.
[19] A covenant to support Reformed Christianity in Scotland.
[20] John Graham of Claverhouse, later Viscount Dundee (1648 – 1689), who opposed the Covenanters during the 1670s.
[21] 1816 novel by Sir Walter Scott, set during the Covenanter conflict.
[22] large knife

As soon as they had them cut found
They murthered them with shots of guns;
Scarce time did they to them allow
Before their Maker their knees to bow
 Many like in this land have been
Whose blood for wingeance cries to Heaven.
This cruel wickedness yow see
Was done in lon of Polmadie.
This shall a standing witness be
'Twixt Presbytrie and Prelacie."

The circumstances of this tragedy are found briefly detailed in Wodrow's history.[23] The martyrs were men of low degree, poor weavers and labourers. They resided in the village of Little Govan (now removed),[24] and they were dragged from their cottages by the dragoons, and murdered in the immediate vicinity. The scene of their death is directly opposite the Fleshers' Haugh of Glasgow Green. In another part of the ground is a curiously carved old headstone, thickly encrusted with moss and lichens, yet in a tolerable state of preservation. At each side of the base is a well-executed sphinx. Immediately above these are a group representing the Saviour, with a balance and scales in his hand, trampling on Death, from whose grizzly form springs a tree emblematic of Life. At the side of the skeleton is a falling figure of Time, with sand-glass and scythe, while before and behind the Saviour is the winged form of an angel. On the reverse side of the stone is the following brief inscription:

"Here lies the corps of Francis Murdoch, Dean of Guild of Ayr, who died March 17th, 1722. Ætatis[25] 53."

We learn from tradition that Francis Murdoch was drowned in the Cart, while on his way from Glasgow to Ayr. The river was then

---

[23] *The History of the Sufferings of the Church of Scotland from the Restoration to the Revolution* (1721–1722) by Robert Wodrow.
[24] The village of Little Govan in present-day Govanhill was replaced by the ironworks known as Dixon's Blazes.
[25] at the age of

crossed by a ford, and a spate prevailing at the time, the unfortunate gentleman was carried away by the angry current, and thus perished.

Church-yard poetry is seldom worth the perusal – the simple green mound, without a line to tell whose dust is mouldering below, making a more eloquent appeal to the heart than the most elaborately sculptured monument or the most high-sounding epitaph. Yet we must say, that when, having with some difficulty brushed aside the long rank grass, we read the following lines, we felt a thrill as if a voice from the lowly mansion at our feet were whispering the words in our shrinking ear. The inscriptions are on a couple of flat stones lying side by side, and covering the ashes of several generations of a family named Hall, who resided when in life at Cathcart Mill. On the one stone, dated 1689, is inscribed –

> "Time's rapid stream we think does stand,
> 　　While on it we're blown down
> To a vast sea, which knows no land,
> 　　Nor e'er a shore would own;
> In which we shall for ever swim,
> 　　Blest through eternity;
> Or sink below wrath's dreadful stream,
> 　　In deepest misery."

On the other, which bears date of 1782, the following is traced:

> "A foe death is not to the just and good,
> Though he appear to us a porter rude;
> But faithful messenger and friendly hand
> To waft us safely to Immanuel's land;
> There, with pure untold pleasure to behold,
> The joys of heaven and brightness of our Lord,
> To which none entered in these fields of bliss
> But by the gate alone of righteousness,
> Not of our own, indeed, but of another
> The anointed Christ, our friend and elder brother."
> "O Meliboce! Deus nobis hæc otia fecit." – Virgil
> "O Melibocus! a God gives us this tranquillity."

102

VI. Cathcart and Langside

A chaste little gothic structure has recently been erected in one corner of the ground by Mr. Gordon of Aikenhead,[26] one of the principal proprietors in the parish, as a family burying place. This, as well as many of the other "sermons in stone"[27] of an humbler description, will be found worthy of leisurely and thoughtful inspection. [The "Adam Blair" of Lockhart's powerful tale was minister of this parish, and sleeps in the auld kirk-yard. The real name is not given in the tale, but the incidents are in the main strictly true.][28]

Leaving the kirk-yard, and passing a handsome school, which, with the manse, is in the immediate vicinity[29] – the latter, like most other edifices of a similar description, being a very pleasant habitation – we soon find ourselves on the banks of the murmuring Cart. The stream in this vicinity winds its seaward way through banks of great beauty, thickly wooded, and, above the village, of considerable altitude. We observe the sand-piper, the sand-martin, and the elegant gray wagtail playing about the margin of the waters, while among the foliage which overshadows their rippled breast is heard the music of many birds. Not the least sweet is the wail of the yellowhammer, which at once, in association with the surrounding scenery, recalls to our mind the memory of a poet who in other days rambled a happy boy on this very bank. We allude to Grahame,[30] the author of the "Sabbath," who in his youth lived for some time in this vicinity. In the "Birds of Scotland" – a production of his genius which has always been an especial favourite of ours, although it has never attained anything like an extensive popularity – he gives a description of the first bird's nest which he ever discovered. The nest was that of a yellowhammer, one of our loveliest though most common songsters, and the scene was the banks of Cart, a short distance below the manse. The passage, which

---

[26] John Gordon (1815 – 1897). The Gordon estate was acquired by the Glasgow Corporation in 1930 and became King's Park.
[27] From Shakespeare's *As You Like It* II.i
[28] *Adam Blair* (1822), a novel by John Gibson Lockhart, son-in-law of Sir Walter Scott, about a minister in a Scottish village succumbing to sexual temptation. In real life the erring minister was George Adam (1700 – 1759) who was deposed in 1746 for immorality but reinstated in 1748 at the request of the parish.
[29] Both since replaced.
[30] The poet James Grahame (1765 – 1811).

to our mind seems an exceedingly fine bit of word painting, is as follows:

"I love thee, pretty bird! for 'twas thy nest
Which first, unhelped by older eyes, I found.
The very spot I think I now behold!
Forth from my low-roofed home I wandered blythe,
Down to thy side, sweet Cart, where 'cross the stream
A range of stones, below a shallow ford,
Stood in the place of the now spanning arch;
Up from that ford a little bank there was,
With alder copse and willow overgrown,
Now worn away by mining winter floods;
There, at a bramble root, sunk in the grass,
The hidden prize, of withered field-straws formed,
Well lined with many a coil of hair and moss,
And in it laid five red-veined spheres, I found.
The Syracusan's[31] voice did not exclaim
The grand Eureka with more rapturous joy
Than at that moment fluttered round my breast."

The author of the "Pleasures of Hope," who like Grahame was a Glasgow callant,[32] also spent some of his happiest youthful days at Cathcart. During vacations he was a frequent visitor and an occasional resident for weeks together at the manse. Nor, indeed, do we know a spot where the fancy of a poet could have been more fitly nursed. The banks of the river and the surrounding country are rich in varied beauty. The gently swelling hill or the verdant mead – the shadowy wood where the cushat[33] loves to dwell, or the leafy lane where the shilfa[34] builds his nest – the dashing waterfall, or the torrent rippling through wild and bosky banks – in short, all the choicest features of

---

[31] Archimedes (c.287 – 212/211 BC) who supposedly exclaimed 'Eureka!' after discovering the method of calculating volume using water displacement.
[32] The poet Thomas Campbell (1777 – 1844).
[33] wood pigeon
[34] chaffinch

landscape, are congregated in the vicinity; while the silent church-yard, the old castle, and the battle-field of Langside, lend to natural beauty the deeper charm of sentimental association. There can be no doubt that much of the fine imagery with which the poet afterwards adorned the productions of his heart-touching lyre, were gleaned by the wandering school boy from the green banks of Cart. After the lapse of many years, during which he had achieved a name among men, and mingled with the loftiest in the land, Campbell came once more to gaze upon the scenery, which,

"In life's morning march, when his bosom was young,"[35]

he had so rapturously enjoyed. He came to experience the disappointment which all must feel who, dreaming not of time and change, return to the haunts of other days. The old familiar faces had departed, and seen in the gloom of sorrow, the landscape seemed less fair, and the very flowers less brilliant than in days o' langsyne. He penned the following lines as an expression of his feelings, and left the place to return no more:

"Oh, the scenes of my childhood and dear to my heart,
Ye green waving woods on the margin of Cart;
How blest in the morning of life I have strayed
By the stream of the vale and the grass-covered glade!

"Then, then, every rapture was young and sincere,
Ere the sunshine of bliss was bedimmed with a tear,
And a sweeter delight every scene seemed to lend,
That the mansion of peace was the home of a friend.

"Now, the scenes of my childhood and dear to my heart,
All pensive I visit, and sigh to depart;
Their flowers seem to languish, their beauty to cease,
For a stranger inhabits the mansion of peace.

---

[35] From 'The Soldier's Dream' (1804) by Thomas Campbell.

"But hush'd be the sigh that untimely complains,
While friendship and all its endearments remains,
While it blooms like the flower of a winterless clime,
Untainted by change, unabated by time."[36]

However it might seem to the tear-dimmed eye of the poet, leaf and flower are as abundant and as beautiful around Cathcart now as ever they were in the past. We can assure the youthful botanist that he will find the steep banks at and immediately above the bridge, peculiarly rich in the material of his study. Any one who has ever glanced into Hooker's *Flora Scotica*[37] (the habitats given in which, we may remark, are the best of all indices to the beautiful in Scotland that we know), must have observed numerous references to localities in this neighbourhood

The village of Old Cathcart is somewhat irregular and scattered. It consists of some score or so of houses, mostly one-storeyed, and with little patches of garden-ground attached to them. Among these are a handsome farm steading, a smithy or cartwright establishment, a snuff-mill, and in the neighbourhood an extensive paper manufactory.[38] It has two public-houses, one of which, that of Mr. Mitchell, is an exceedingly neat and comfortable little place of rest and refreshment. The landlord is an amateur florist, and his small garden plot, with its flower-beds and bee-hives, is a perfect model of neatness and beauty. It seems, moreover, to be a favourite haunt of ramblers from the city, who, with "all the comforts of the Sautmarket,"[39] find besides the charms of rural beauty and quietude in its leafy bowers.

A short distance above the village, on a steep bank which rises over the Cart, are the ruins of the castle, which we next proceed to visit.

---

[36] From Campbell's 'Lines on Revisiting Cathcart' (?1815).

[37] By Sir William Jackson Hooker, published 1821.

[38] The smithy survives as The Old Smiddy pub. The snuff mill has been converted to houses.

[39] An expression taken from Sir Walter Scott's Rob Roy. What Bailie Jarvie actually says is: "For accommodations, ane canna expect to carry about the Saut Market at his tail, as a snail does his caup."

VI. Cathcart and Langside

This structure, a massy square tower, must at one period have possessed great value as a place of security and strength. The date of its erection and the name of its builder are alike lost in a dark antiquity. In the days of Wallace and Bruce it was in the possession of an Alan de Cathcart,[40] who did good service in the cause of Scottish independence. From this individual the present Earl of Cathcart[41] is lineally descended. About the middle of the sixteenth century, the barony and castle of Cathcart were sold by the then possessor to the Lord of Sempil, from whose family it was transferred to the Blairs of Boghen. In 1801 it was purchased by the late Earl of Cathcart,[42] whose son, the present earl, is now its proprietor. On examining the castle, we find it to be one of those stubborn fragments of the past which seem destined to bid an enduring defiance alike to the war of the elements and of time. By the measurement of our staff, we find its walls to be not less than ten feet in solid thickness. It is now roofless and chamberless, with the exception of a vault, wherein darkness is rendered visible by the light which enters at a narrow loophole. Here, probably, in "the good old times" when the law of the land was the caprice of a lordling, the unhappy serfs who happened to displease their feudal superior were kept secure until it might be found convenient to dispose of them otherwise. This place has a damp charnel-house smell, which speedily sends us into the sunshine again. The crumbling tower is in some parts thickly mantled with ivy, the haunt of the starling and sparrow, while the swift builds its nest and the wall-flower waves its golden flowers in the loop-holes and window-places.[43] From the castle there is a fine view of the vale of the Cart, with the modern mansion of the family in the foreground,[44] and a perfect wilderness of foliage around and beyond. There are, indeed, some exquisite snatches of landscape in this vicinity, and we would recommend the locality altogether to the special attention of our

---

[40] Born before 1300, died after 1336.
[41] Charles Murray Cathcart, 2nd Earl Cathcart (1783–1859).
[42] William Schaw Cathcart, 1st Earl Cathcart (1755–1843).
[43] The remaining tower was pulled down in the 1980s because it was unsafe. The base of the walls can still be seen in Linn Park.
[44] Built around 1740, demolished in the 1920s.

Glasgow artists, who, like others, are too apt to run from home in their pursuit of the beautiful.

About a hundred yards or so east from the castle is the "Court Knowe," where Queen Mary stood at the most critical moment of her life. A thorn-tree which threw its shadow over her, and was long called by her name, grew on the spot until the close of the last century, when it fell into decay through age. An upright slab of stone, with a rude carving of the Scottish crown, and the letters "M.R. 1568," now mark the spot.[45] This interesting memento of the beauteous being who in a past age ascended to its site – a queen with thousands of gallant men at her command – and in one little hour thereafter descended from it a hapless fugitive, has been appropriately shaded by a fine clump of trees. We find the speedwell, the king-cup, and the forget-me-not blooming in beauty on the velvet turf that had been dewed with the tears of royalty, and the emblematic

> "Pansy that looks up
> Like a thought earth-planted."

It is indeed a lovely and a fitting place to muse on that fair, ill-fated woman, whose memory is inseparably linked to so many beauteous scenes, and whose story must ever touch the deepest sympathies of the pensive heart. The evening sun is bathing the landscape in mellow radiance while we linger, and the wild birds are singing their vespers as if misfortune and sorrow had never flung their shadows there; but the winds are murmuring a plaintive melody among the trembling leaves, and showering around us the fine gold of the laburnum, which is now becoming dim, as if nature, entering into our feelings, meant to show the evanescence of earthly glory. The landscape seen from this station is extensive and beautiful, including, as is well known, an excellent prospect of the battle-field of Langside. The blue smoke of Cathcart is seen close at hand curling through the trees; beyond is the

---

[45] The stone was placed there in the early 19th century by General Sir George Cathcart. It has since been replaced by a sandstone memorial block erected by his nephew, Earl Cathcart.

church and the shadowy burying-place; and in the distance the spires of Glasgow, relieved against the towering Kilpatrick bills.

Descending from our elevation, we cross the Cart by the old bridge,[46] a structure which bears a considerable resemblance to the Brig o' Doon, and on the sides of which the botanist will find several beautiful though minute species of ferns. We then take our way to New Cathcart, a neat and tidy-looking little village, which lies about the third of a mile to the west. It is of modern origin, and possesses but few features of interest. From thence, along a pleasant country road, we pass by Millbrae to Langside. This little hamlet, which has been rendered remarkable by the decisive skirmish which occurred in its vicinity between the troops of Queen Mary and those of the Regent Murray, on the 13th of May, 1568, is finely situated nearly on the ridge of a long hill which lies at a little distance to the south-west of Glasgow. The story of the battle, with its antecedents and ultimate consequences, is familiar to every student of Scottish history. Queen Mary on her escape from Lochleven, immediately, with the assistance of her friends, many of whom were possessed of great influence, proceeded to organize an army for the recovery of that power which, while in captivity, she had been compelled formally to renounce. In a short period she found herself at the head of a considerable body of troops. With these she was on her march from Hamilton to Dumbarton, when she found herself intercepted by the vigilant and energetic Regent, who having heard of her advance, pushed out from Glasgow with all the forces he could command, and took up a favourable position at the village of Langside. With greater bravery than prudence Mary's party resolved to risk an engagement; and while she proceeded to the position we have previously described, her troops at once formed themselves into order of battle on the north side of Clincart Hill, a gentle eminence adjoining that on which their opponents were drawn up in battle array. Impatient of delay, the inexperienced infantry of the Queen rushed up the hill to the attack, but from the unfavourable nature of the ground, and the superior numbers[47] and discipline of the

---

[46] Now called Snuff Mill Bridge.

[47] In fact Mary had more troops (c.6,000) than Murray (c.4,500).

Regent's troops, after a brief but sanguinary struggle, they were repulsed, and by a decisive charge of cavalry, which was skilfully directed against their flank at a critical moment, they were involved in inextricable confusion, and ultimately put to complete rout. Nearly three hundred of the Royalists, it is stated, fell on the field of battle, while four hundred were made prisoners. The loss of the Regent was trifling in the extreme. On returning to the city he caused thanks to be publicly offered to the Deity for a victory which, on his side, was almost bloodless; and he rewarded the Corporation of Bakers, who had particularly distinguished themselves by their bravery on the occasion, by bestowing on them the lands of Partick, where their mills are now built. Poor Mary, on seeing the overthrow of her friends, took to flight, and, it is said, scarcely closed an eye until she arrived at Dundrennan Abbey in Galloway, nearly sixty miles from the fatal scene.[48] By what route she arrived there we cannot now tell, but several spots in our vicinity are pointed out by tradition as marking the way she took. Between Cathcart and Rutherglen is a place called "Mal's Mire,"[49] where it is said her horse almost stuck fast, in consequence of the muddy nature of the soil. On the same line, but nearer Rutherglen, is a place called the "Pants," it is said from the panting which her steed made while hurrying past. A little to the east of this, at a place called "Din's Dykes," two fellows who were cutting hay lifted their scythes and threatened to take her captive. Some of her friends coming up, however, compelled the haymakers to clear the way, when she passed on; and we next hear of her in a Cambuslang tradition, crossing the Clyde a little below Carmyle, at a place called the "Thief's Ford."[50] Here we lose sight of her until, weary and worn, at the close of the day, she is found at Dundrennan, where a rhyming friend of ours puts the following words of lamentation into her lips, which, as appropriate to the occasion, and hitherto unpublished, we shall present to our readers:

---

[48] This is more like 100 miles. She may have stopped first at Sanquhar, which is about 50 miles from the battlefield.

[49] Now a managed community woodland.

[50] According to the 1910 edition of *Rambles Round Glasgow*, this is a mistake and Mary did not pass this way.

"Loud roars the wind adown the shaw,
The drumlie clouds are big wi' rain,
Fast hameward flees the frichten'd craw,
The sea-bird, screaming, leaves the main;
Sae I, before misfortune's gale,
A waefu' wanderer now maun flee
An exile sad frae all I love,
Despair alone remains with me.

"Thou sun, red sinking down the west,
Oh, haste thee, close the hateful day
With ruin fraught, and stained with gore
Of noblest hearts – my pride and stay.
Triumphant treason's banner floats
O'er purpled Cartha's devious way,
Where hearts that heaved yestreen wi' hope
Lie cauld and lifeless in the clay.

"O God! how bitter is the cup
Thy chastening hand has filled for me
How crushing is the weird[51] of wrath
That I, a worm of earth, maun dree![52]
My country false, my babe estranged,
My name the butt of calumny;
Even hope – the wretch's friend – takes wing,
Nor dares to mock my agony.

"Vain pomp and grandeur of the world,
How false to me your pleasures seem!
Like drewdrops melting in the sun,
Or bubbles on the mountain stream.
Now, I maun bid farewell to pride,
And I maun stoop – oh, thought of woe!

---

[51] destiny
[52] suffer

This aching, crownless, homeless head,
A suppliant to my direst foe.

"Proud land of hills – my fatherland
Adieu! – a long, a last adieu!
Despair is whispering to my soul
I ne'er again shall gaze on you.
Oh, when your hapless Mary's gone,
May brightest fortune be your fa'![53]
Ye'll haply mourn your wrangs to me,
When I for aye have passed awa'."[54]

But all signs of battle have long been effaced from the fair brow of Langside;[55] and it is fervently to be hoped that never again may the soil of our country be stained with the blood of brother fighting against brother, as on that dark day. The very spirit of peace indeed seems brooding over the scene as we pass along the pleasant hill. The farmer is plodding home in the gathering gloaming from the toils of the day. The soft rustle of the waving grain is making sweet music to the passing winds, which have been wantoning through the bloom of the bean,

"And bear its fragrant sweets alang."[56]

The lark is leaving the sky, and seeking its mate on the grassy lea; while the bat comes flickering past, and the bugle of the "shardborne beetle"[57] is occasionally heard in the thickening air. This walk is indeed delicious. The prospect is extensive and beautiful. In the valley beneath, amid richly cultivated fields, the Cart is seen by glimpses winding its devious way; farther off, and in various directions, the spires of Glasgow, Rutherglen, and Cambuslang attract the eye of the spectator; while Cathcart, with its fine church, its picturesque cottages,

---

[53] foe
[54] 'Lament of Mary Queen of Scots' by Hugh MacDonald himself.
[55] A monument commemorating the battle was erected in 1887.
[56] From 'The Lass O' Ballochmyle' (1786) by Robert Burns.
[57] From Shakespeare's *Macbeth* III.ii.

and its old castle peeping over the trees, nestles sweetly on the green slopes below.

The village or hamlet of Langside consists of some score or so of houses, principally one-storeyed cottages, clustering irregularly amidst patches of garden, and finely screened by fruit and other trees. Like most other Scottish villages, it seems to have been left in a great measure to "hing as it grew," and consequently it possesses a picturesqueness of aspect to which our more regularly constructed modern towns are utter strangers. The majority of the inhabitants are weavers, who manage to make ends meet better than the generality of their city brethren, by the cultivation, during spare hours, of their bits of kail-yard, the produce of which adds materially to the comfort of their families. Several of them are famous for the quality of their gooseberries, the excellence of which during July and August tempts numerous parties from the neighbouring city. We have not learned that anything beyond the general tradition regarding the battle, which is common over the country, has been preserved by the inhabitants of Langside. A neighbouring farmer, we are informed, has several times discovered old horse-shoes, bits of bridles, and other relics, while cultivating the fields where the engagement took place; but beyond these no vestige of "what has been" is now in existence.

> "All, all is quiet now, or only heard
> Like mellowed murmurs of the distant sea."[58]

A walk of short duration from the field of battle brings us safely into the artificial day of the lamp-lighted streets.

[The hill of Langside is in process of being covered by ornamental cottages and villas. Already the Clincart Knowe is crowned by a couple of tenements, and even on the very spot where the contest occurred, a number of houses have been erected. These neat and

---

[58] Possibly a misquote of 'The Eolian Harp' (1795) by Samuel Taylor Coleridge:
"and the world so hush'd!
The stilly murmur of the distant Sea
Tells us of silence."

comfortable looking domiciles certainly do not harmonize with the associations of the spot; while a public work, which has just been planted in the basin of the Cart, still more detracts from the amenity of the picture.]

Communities, like individuals, are supposed to have their peculiar idiosyncrasies; and those who are familiar with the popular rhymes and common sayings of Scotland, must be aware that a considerable portion of these "old saws" are devoted to a description of the characteristics, real or imaginary, of the inhabitants of our various towns and villages. For instance, we say the *people* of Glasgow, the *folk* of Greenock, and the *bodies* of Paisley. The Merse,[1] according to the same authority, is famous for its stalwart men; Dunkeld for its votaries of the wee drap; and Edinburgh for its loopy lawyers; while auld Ayr, as every believer of Burns must admit, is unsurpassed

"For honest men and bonnie lasses."[2]

There is one town, however, which is said, *par excellence*, to be productive of "queer folk." This town, as everybody in the West of Scotland well knows, is Pollokshaws, or "the Shaws," as in common parlance it is generally called. How this saying originated we cannot for the life of us surmise, but it has long been quite proverbial – a very household word, in fact; and just on the same principle that we glowered in search of bonnie lasses on our first visit to Ayr, did we keep a sharp look-out for *outré* specimens of humanity when we first passed through Pollokshaws. Disappointment, we need hardly remark, in both cases attended our inspection. The fair maids of Ayr, with all due deference to Burns, who, by-the-by, was said to be no great authority on the subject of female loveliness, we found to be "just like ither folk;" while the special queerness of the Pollokshaws people did not strike us as being particularly obvious. There are doubtless bonnie lasses in the one town and queer folk in the other, just as there are everywhere else; but we rather suspect there is in neither case more than the due proportion. "Old saws and modern instances,"[3] it would therefore seem, do not in all cases quite accord with each other.

---

[1] In Berwickshire.
[2] From 'Tam o' Shanter' (1791) by Robert Burns.
[3] From Shakespeare's *As You Like It* II.vii.

Crossing the Clyde by the elegant and spacious Broomielaw bridge,[4] and passing along Bridge Street, Eglinton Street, and past the front of the Cavalry Barracks, now deserted by its gay cavaliers, [Since this was written, the establishment has been converted into the Poorhouse of the Govan Parish][5] we soon arrive outside the boundaries of the city. A walk of a mile or so farther – during which we pass on the right, Muirhouses,[6] a row of one-storeyed and thatched edifices, and at a short distance to the left, the hamlet of Butterbiggins – brings us to a little village which rejoices in the somewhat unmusical appellation of Strathbungo. There is nothing particularly attractive or worthy of attention about this tiny little congregation of houses. With the exception of the church, a small and neat but plain specimen of ecclesiastical architecture,[7] the houses are for the most part humble one or two-storeyed buildings, inhabited principally by weavers, miners, and other descriptions of operatives. There are, of course, several public-houses in the village; and those who have an eye to the fine arts, as manifested on sign-boards, will be amused, if not delighted, with a unique head of Burns, which is suspended over the entrance to one of them, with a barefaced quotation in praise of whisky attached to it by way of pendant. There is no mistaking the double-breasted waistcoat of the poet; it at once stamps the man. The management of this portion of the drapery is indeed a master-stroke of the artist, as otherwise it might have been somewhat difficult to recognize in the goggle eyes, flabby cheeks, and ridiculously mim mouth, the features of the burly ploughman. Painters now-a-days, and the failing is not by any means confined to those of the Dick-Tinto[8] school, have got such a habit of

---

[4] This bridge, designed by Thomas Telford, was replaced in 1894 but the decorative features of Telford's bridge were incorporated into the new design.
[5] The poorhouse later moved to a new location in the Linthouse area and eventually became the Southern General Hospital, now replaced by the Queen Elizabeth University Hospital.
[6] Where Muirhouse Street now stands.
[7] This church, built around 1840, was replaced by a larger and fancier church in 1888. The site now holds flats but the façade of the 1888 church has been preserved.
[8] A sign-painter turned portrait-painter in the novel *The Bride of Lammermoor* (1819) by Sir Walter Scott.

idealizing their portraits, that it has really become perfectly impossible to recognize even one's most intimate friends on canvas. The flattery that the honest mirror fails to give may be purchased at any time from the venal palette. Since the advent of Gall and Spurzheim,[9] foreheads under the hands of the limners have gradually been expanding in their proportions, like the head-dresses of the ladies in the reign of good Queen Anne.[10] Tomkins is represented with the "front of Jove;"[11] while the jolly countenance of Snooks, to please his sentimental better-half, is "toned down," as the phrase is, to the "pale cast of thought,"[12] until he resembles more the half-starved Hamlet of a strolling company than his own plump and good-natured self. Whatever faults, however, the sign board portrait above mentioned may have – and it must be admitted, we are afraid, that it is not quite a perfect work of art – no one can at least accuse the artist of the slightest tendency to the "reigning vice"[13] of his profession. Want of will or want of power has given him the solitary merit of being an absolute stranger to flattery. Strange as it may seem, Strathbungo has also its poet. In Blackie's *Book of Scottish Song*[14] there is an effusion, not devoid of merit either, addressed to a certain bonnie Jean who flourished in this uncouth-named locality. Lest there should be any doubt on the matter, however, we shall take the liberty of giving a sample of the production:

"The Glasgow lasses gang fu' braw,
And country girls gang neat and clean,
But nane o' them's a match ava
To my sweet maid, Strathbungo Jean.

"Tho' they be dressed in rich attire,
In silk brocade and mous de-laine,[15]

---

[9] Franz Joseph Gall (1758-1828) and Johann Gaspar Spurzheim (1776-1832) who invented the 'science' of phrenology.
[10] Reigned 1702 – 1714.
[11] From Shakespeare's *Hamlet* III.iv.
[12] From Shakespeare's *Hamlet* III.i.
[13] The title of a satirical essay from 1827 by Chauncy Hare Townshend.
[14] Collected by Alex Whitelaw, published by Blackie and Son in 1843.
[15] Muslin-like cloth made of wool.

Wi' busk and pad and satin stays,
They'll never ding Strathbungo Jean."[16]

After this, who shall say what the lyrical muse may not do for Ecclefechan or Tillicoultry!

Leaving Strathbungo, a pleasant walk of about half-a-mile brings us to another village not less ridiculously provided with a name. This is Crossmyloof, a finely situated little hamlet, composed principally of plain and unpretending houses, ranged on both sides of the highway, and occupied chiefly by families of the operative class. A considerable number of the humble edifices, however, have garden-plots attached to them for the cultivation of kitchen vegetables; and it is well known that both here and at Strathbungo many of the handloom weavers are celebrated growers of tulips, pansies, dahlias, and other floricultural favourites. Florist clubs, also, exist among them, which meet regularly for the examination of choice flowers, and for discussing the best means of rearing them to perfection. We have had the pleasure, at various periods, of conversing with several of these bloom worshippers – for such, in truth, they are – and we must admit that we were fairly astounded at the multifarious charms which they could discover and point out in what seemed to our obtuse visual organs a simple tulip or pansy. We could not help, indeed, comparing ourselves, when in their company, to Wordsworth's "Peter Bell," of whom it was said,

"A primrose by the river's brim
A yellow primrose was to him,
And it was nothing more."[17]

What a different affair was a primrose or a pansy to our Crossmyloof friends! It was indeed "a great deal more" than it seemed to the uninitiated. There are some sharp-sighted people who are said to see farther into a millstone than their neighbours. For the truth of the saying we shall not venture to vouch; but most assuredly, for seeing

---

[16] From 'Strathbungo Jean' (1843) by Adam Knox.
[17] Published 1819.

into the mysteries of a tulip or a dahlia, we shall back a Crossmyloof or Strathbungo weaver against the united amateurs of Scotland.

After all, however, there is something very creditable to such individuals in their enthusiastic love of flowers. We know not, indeed, how a working man could spend his leisure hours more harmlessly or pleasantly, than in the cultivation of a little flower-plot. In towns such a privilege is beyond the reach of the operative; but in suburban situations and rural villages, it is exceedingly gratifying to witness the manifestations of such a taste.

The singular name of "Crossmyloof" is accounted for by a popular myth which is yet current in the surrounding country. It is said that, immediately before the battle of Langside,[18] the forces of Queen Mary were drawn up on the site of the village. A council of war was meanwhile held, at which it was debated whether they should, under circumstances in which they were placed, risk a collision with the troops of the Regent. The Queen, always impetuous, was urgent that an attack should at once be made. From this resolution several of her adherents attempted to dissuade her, representing to her the advantages likely to result from delay. Tired at last of their importunities, and eager to decide her fate, the Queen pulled an ebony crucifix from her breast, and laid it on her snowy palm, saying, at the same time, "As surely as that cross lies on my loof, I will this day fight the Regent." From this circumstance, it is said, the spot received its name. It is rather unfortunate for the credibility of the legend, however, that Queen Mary's troops were routed at a considerable distance to the eastward of this locality, having been effectually intercepted by their opponents at the village of Langside, while they were advancing in this direction. Tradition in this, as in other instances that might be mentioned, has taken sad liberties with geography. The story is a pretty one, nevertheless, and will continue, we dare say, to obtain credence at the winter evening hearth, in spite of the sneers of the prying student of history.

---

[18] 1568 – see pp109 – 110.

A little to the north-east of Crossmyloof, on a green hill, within the enclosures of Neale Thomson, Esq. of Camphill,[19] are the vestiges of an ancient British camp.[20] Passing through the fine grounds of Mr. Thomson, which are kept in the most elegant and tasteful order, we now proceed to inspect this interesting relic of other days. It occupies the entire crown of the eminence, and is upwards of a hundred yards in diameter. The vallum, or wall, although nearly obliterated in some places, is yet in a sufficient state of preservation to show the a extent and form which it originally presented. At one extremity there is an elevated platform, or dais, which is supposed to have been the situation occupied by the tent of the commander, or chief of the party, who, in a long vanished century, held possession of this commanding height. From this spot a delightful and wide-spreading prospect of the surrounding country is obtained. Towards the north and east is the vast strath of Clyde, bounded on the right by the sylvan heights of Cathkin and the verdant slopes of Dychmont, and on the left by the picturesque Campsie and Kilpatrick ranges; while stretching far away in front is a lengthened series of fertile fields and gentle undulations, studded with towns, villages, mansions, and farm-steadings, and bounded in the extreme distance by the misty Pentlands. In other directions the views are almost equally extensive and fair; including, within their scope, Neilston Pad, Ballygeich, and the song-hallowed "braes o' Gleniffer."[21] The interior of the camp is thickly planted with trees, the foliage of which forms a delicious shade in the glowing summer or autumnal noon, when, in the words of Tennyson, all around is seen

"The landscape winking through the heat."[22]

After lingering in the leafy shadows of the lonely camp for a brief space, gazing on its sights of beauty, and dreaming of the warriors

---

[19] Mr Thomson (1807 – 1857), a philanthropist, soon afterwards sold his land to Glasgow Corporation for below the market price so that it could be converted into Queens Park.

[20] The age of this 'camp' has never been established, but the earthworks are still in Queens Park, at the top of Camp Hill.

[21] Immortalised in an 1806 poem of the same name by Robert Tannahill.

[22] From 'In Memoriam' (1850) by Alfred Lord Tennyson.

fierce and rude who, in the olden time, peopled its precincts, we descend from our elevation, and passing the spacious and handsome mansion of Mr. Thomson,[23] make our exit from the grounds.

It is said that there is but a short distance between the sublime and the ridiculous. There is certainly but a step from the sentimental to the commonplace, as we cannot resist muttering to ourselves, when a few minutes after leaving the camp and musing on its bygone glories, we find ourselves in the immense Bakery of Crossmyloof, inspecting with interest the manufacture of quartern loaves. This extensive establishment, perhaps the largest of the kind in the queen's dominions, is the property of Mr. Thomson of Camphill, by whom it was erected in 1847, for the purpose of supplying the city of Glasgow with bread similar in quality to that used in London.[24] Commencing operations on a small scale the increasing demand has gradually necessitated an extension of the premises, until at the present time operations are carried on in four large bakehouses fitted up with every requisite convenience for securing cleanliness and expedition. There are no less than twenty-six ovens generally at work, attended by from forty-five to sixty bakers, as the demand increases or diminishes. A number of other hands also are constantly employed in subsidiary operations, such as preparing the yeast, which is done on the premises, removing and packing the bread, &c., while no fewer than six large vans are constantly engaged carrying the loaves as they are prepared to the insatiate city, and distributing them amongst the various agencies. Some idea may be formed of the extent of this monster baking manufactory when we mention, that it requires not less than five hundred sacks of flour on the average weekly, out of which it turns from 40,000 to 43,000 quartern loaves. Mr. Dalgetty the active and intelligent manager, obligingly conducted us over the establishment, explaining the various processes through which the flour must pass ere its final transformation into the wholesome "staff of life." Cleanliness, order, and neatness, pervade every department; and we must admit that

---

[23] Camphill House, which still stands in Queens park.
[24] And specifically for supplying the workers at his Cotton Spinning Adelphi works in the Gorbals.

we have seldom seen a more curious or cheerful sight than we witnessed in one of these lengthened and spacious bakehouses, where thirty well-powdered operatives are busily engaged thumping, turning, cutting, pelting, weighing and kneading immense masses of plastic dough, which, in their experienced hands, rapidly assumes the requisite form and consistency.[25]

Taking leave of our friend, Mr. Dalgetty, we now leave Crossmyloof, and wend our way towards Pollokshaws, which is situated about a mile to the southward. At this point the road diverges, one branch leading to Kilmarnock, by Mearns; the other to Barrhead and Neilston, by Pollokshaws. The country in the vicinity is beautiful in the extreme, and within the last few years a large number of fine villas have been erected in the neighbourhood. The majority of these have gardens and elegant flower-plots attached to them, and altogether the locality has a highly pleasing and attractive appearance. The walk from Crossmyloof to Pollokshaws is of the most pleasant description. On either hand are wide-spreading and fertile fields, relieved at intervals with patches and belts of planting, farm-houses, and gentlemen's seats. About half the distance it is uphill, but afterwards it gradually declines towards the hollow in which, on the banks of the Cart, here a considerable stream, the town is situated.

Pollokshaws is a tidy and thriving little town, somewhat irregular in appearance, and containing a population of about 5,000 individuals. An air of bustle and life about its streets, furnishes a perfect contrast to the dullness and languor which generally prevail in towns of similar extent in the rural districts. There are a number of extensive establishments for spinning, weaving, and dyeing, within its precincts, which furnish employment for the greater portion of its inhabitants, the residue being principally handloom weavers, miners, and agricultural labourers. Calico-printing was also at one period carried on here a considerable extent; but of late years, we understand, this department of trade has been, in a great measure, if not altogether discontinued. The inhabitants have the usual characteristics of a

---

[25] Crossmyloof bakery continued to operate until 1880.

122

manufacturing population. There is the common preponderance of pale faces and emaciated forms, accompanied with that sharpness of intellect which manifests itself in diversity of religious and political opinion. Every shade of political principle, indeed, finds here its own little knot of adherents; while the fact that there are not fewer than nine separate places of worship, great and small, sufficiently indicates the variety of points from which the great question is contemplated. The precise number of schools which are in the town we have not learned, but we understand that this important department of social improvement has not been by any means neglected; while an extensive public library furnishes the necessary intellectual pabulum[26] for the studious portion of the adult population.

The town was erected into a burgh of barony by a charter from the Crown in 1814,[27] the civic affairs of the community being managed by a provost, bailie, and six councillors, with a town-clerk and fiscal. The magistrates and council are elected by popular suffrage, every householder paying a certain amount of rent possessing the privilege of voting. Many of our readers will be interested, we doubt not, to learn that a natural daughter of the Ayrshire bard[28] has been for many years resident in Pollokshaws. This individual is Mrs. Thomson (Elizabeth Burns), the wife of a decent and intelligent handloom weaver of the town. In features and complexion Mrs. Thomson admittedly bears a more striking resemblance to her father than any of his other children. We have had the pleasure of meeting with two of the poet's sons, on both of whom the paternal stamp was obvious; but we were more forcibly reminded of the family lineaments as represented in the best portraits, on being introduced to Mrs. Thomson, than we were on that occasion. She is now pretty well advanced in years, being rather over sixty; her features are consequently somewhat shrunk from their original proportions, but still the likeness is sufficiently marked to indicate, at a glance, her relationship to the departed bard. The mother

---

[26] nourishment
[27] Actually 1812.
[28] That is, Robert Burns.

123

of Mrs. Thomson was Anne Hyslop, of the Globe Tavern at Dumfries. She was the heroine of the beautiful song,

> "Yestreen I had a pint o'wine
> In place where body saw na,
> Yestreen lay on this breast o' mine
> The raven locks of Anna."[29]

Mrs. Thomson never knew her mother; but she fortunately found a kind and affectionate substitute in Mrs. Burns. After remaining for two or three years at nurse in Edinburgh, she was taken to her father's home in Dumfries, where she was brought up along with his other children. She has some faint recollections of her father, who was wont occasionally to take her on his knee and fondle her affectionately; and she remembers vividly the imposing ceremonials attendant on his death and funeral. After the poet's decease she continued to live with Mrs. Burns, of whom she still speaks under the endearing appellation of mother, until her marriage with Mr. Thomson, who was then as a soldier located with his corps in Dumfries. The wedding was celebrated in the house and under the auspices of the bard's kind-hearted widow, who afterwards, even until the year of her death, continued occasionally to manifest her regard for Mrs. Thomson by sending her small presents, accompanied by affectionate inquiries after her welfare.

Mrs. Thomson is now the mother of a considerable family of grown-up sons and daughters, several of whom bear an obvious resemblance to their celebrated grandfather. Her second son, Robert Burns Thomson, is especially the "counterfeit presentment"[30] of him whose name he bears. He is, indeed, a living *fac-simile* in physical appearance of what Burns must have been when in the prime of manhood. A degree more slender in person, or a shade more fair in complexion, from the nature of his employment, he possibly may be; but this, we feel confident, is the extent of difference. Nor is the resemblance only physical. He has in a considerable measure the same

---

[29] From 'Yestreen I had a pint o'wine' (c.1790).
[30] From Shakespeare's *Hamlet* III.iv.

vigorous intellect, and pithy if not rude humour, combined with a manly sense of independence, and a taste for poetry and music, in both of which arts he is indeed no mean proficient. Altogether, he is admitted by all who have the privilege of his acquaintance to be an excellent specimen of the honest, upright, and industrious working man. We know not that, on the whole, we could bestow upon him a more estimable character. Mr. Thomson is of course proud of his descent, but he has not the most distant desire that his "bonnet should be hung on his grandfather's pin." He would be respected for his own sake, or not at all; and we can assure those who would thrust themselves into his company, for the mere gratification of an empty curiosity that they will stand a pretty considerable chance of finding out what it is to be "taken through the whins."[31]

Although he makes no pretension to the character of a poet, Robert Burns Thomson, as we have already hinted, has on more than one occasion, tried his hand at poetic composition. Some of our readers, we dare say, would like to see a sample of verse from the pen of one who stands in the relation of grandson to our great national poet; and at the risk of being deemed guilty of a breach of confidence, we cannot refrain from contributing to their gratification. The only production of his at present in our possession, although of considerable merit, is by far too lengthy for publication in its entire form in our limited space; but we shall venture, nevertheless, to extract a few detached stanzas from it, begging the author's pardon at the same time for the liberty which we are taking. The composition, we may premise, is an elegy on an old military musician, who is represented, after having passed unhurt through manifold dangers by flood and field, as having been at last killed while attempting "some thrawn bars that wadna spell." Passing over several pithy verses invocatory of sorrow, we find the poet exclaiming,

"Ye wakerife lav'rocks, pride of Spring,
Wha speel the lift on dewy wing,
While in the lift ye pendant hing

---

[31] An unpleasant experience – a reference to 'Tam o' Shanter' (1791).

125

In bliss ecstatic,
Lament till mountain echoes ring
Your plaints pathetic.

"And ye wha haunt the leafy spray,
Or warble in the sunny ray,
Or lull the closing ear of day
In haugh or glen,
Sound each your waest in minor key
For him that's gane."

Not altogether unworthy the "old man," we should say; but we must
take another leap over some seven or eight stanzas, and leaving the
tender, try what our author can exhibit of sterner stuff, –

"Mourn ye, wha lift the daily shillin'
Imperial pay for brither-killin'
For Jock, when but a haufins callan,
Left frien's and hame,
And ower the stormy seas gaed sailin'
To fecht for fame.

"In dark Toulouse he met the Franks,
Where biting bullets thinn'd our ranks,
And worthy chiels of heads and shanks
Were rudely shorn,
There bauldly first he cheered the ranks
Wi' fife and horn.

"He clamb the tow'ring Pyrenees,
Where frosts 'neath smiles of summer freeze,
And through the mirk, on hands and knees,
'Thout star or moon,
The foemen's tents he set ableeze,
To licht him doon.

"See half way up Sebastian's wa's,
Tho' death rax doon wi' drippin claws,
His left arm round the steps he thraws,
    His right the horn,
And, charge them hame! he loudly blaws
    To the hope forlorn.

"Ay, mony a fearfu' siege and storm,
In mony a clime baith cauld and warm,
Tho' death and him's been arm in arm
    The maist o's life.
Yet ne'er till now he durst him harm
    Wi' dirk or knife."

But we must refrain. Suffice it to say, that honest John turns out, after all, to be both hale and well, and that the elegy is fortunately only "a false alarm." We shall leave it to our readers to decide whether the scion is altogether worthy of the noble stem from which it sprung. We have our own opinion; but where friendship holds the balance it may well be doubted whether strict justice is administered.

The church of Pollokshaws, or Eastwood, as the parish is sometimes called, is situated on a rising ground at the south eastern extremity of the town. It is a plain quadrangular edifice of somewhat limited extent, and calls for no particular attention from the passing stranger.[32] The church-yard is situated about a mile to the southward, near the site of a more ancient church, which was demolished on the erection of the present structure. Towards this spot we now proceed, passing on our way the fine old mansion of Auldhouse,[33] at present the residence of Walter Crum, Esq., of Thornliebank.[34] It is beautifully situated on the margin of Auldhouse burn, a little streamlet that joins the Cart at a short distance to the northward. The building, which is of

---

[32] This church, built in 1781, was replaced in 1863 with a neo-gothic structure commissioned by Sir John Maxwell, 8th Baronet.

[33] Built c.1631, the building survives and has been converted to flats.

[34] 1796 – 1867, chemist specialising in dying fabric. His Birkenshaw Estate later became Rouken Glen Park.

considerable extent, is, we understand, the property of Sir John Maxwell of Pollok, in the possession of whose family it has been for many years.[35] It has certain architectural features worthy the attention of the antiquary; while the handsome old trees by which it is surrounded, and especially a couple of magnificent and tall specimens of the Spanish chestnut in the garden, will be found peculiarly attractive to those who delight in the study of sylvan beauty. A brief but pleasant walk brings us to the "Auld kirk-yard," in the vicinity of which is a cosie and comfortable looking manse.[36] We find the field of graves, which is protected from human intrusion by a high wall and a well-locked gate, tenanted by a flock of sheep, which seem particularly to enjoy the long rank herbage. They manifest considerable wildness, moreover, and scamper about over green mound and flat stone, as if they were anything but accustomed to receive visitors. The church-yard of Eastwood is of moderate extent, and is shaded at certain parts of its circumference by trees. Its only noticeable features are the burial place of the ancient family of the Maxwells of Pollok, and an elegant monumental structure recently erected to the memory of Wodrow the historian. The former is a square compartment enclosed by high walls of the plainest appearance. The place has a melancholy and rather neglected aspect. The sexton has piled a lot of old planks and mouldering coffins against one of the walls, and on peeping through the doorway we observe the interior to be crowded with loathsome and overgrown weeds. Accustomed as we are to the trim and tidy manner in which the burial-places in our city cemeteries are generally kept, we must admit that we feel rather surprised at the want of attention which is here evinced, and we should really have expected that the last resting-place of an old and honourable family would have been more carefully preserved from the ravages of time and the elements.

The Wodrow monument, which stands almost in the centre of the burial-ground, is a structure of considerable elegance and taste,

---

[35] Sir John Maxwell, 8th Baronet (1791 – 1865). The Maxwell family acquired this land in the 15th century. Most of the Maxwell estate was gifted to Glasgow Corporation in 1966 to become Pollok Park.
[36] Since demolished.

having been executed by our townsman, Mr. John Mossman,[37] a gentleman whose chisel has done much for the adornment of our local cemeteries, and whose contributions, from time to time, to our Fine Art exhibitions have been characterized by merit of no ordinary description. On one side of the massive quadrangular pediment, which is surmounted by a finely carved superstructure, terminating in a sepulchral urn, is the following inscription:

"Erected to the memory of the REV. ROBERT WODROW, minister of Eastwood; the faithful historian of the sufferings of the Church of Scotland from the year 1660 to 1668. He died 21st March, 1754, in the 55th year of his age, and 31st of his ministry.

"He being dead yet speaketh."[38]

The monument has been at one period surrounded by an excellent wire fence, but the woolly occupants of the enclosure having taken a fancy to rub themselves against it, the wires have been bent and displaced, so that there is little to hinder the animals now from scratching themselves against Mr. Mossman's chaste and beautiful carvings.[39]

Robert Wodrow was born at Glasgow in the year 1679; his father, the Rev. James Wodrow, having been at that period professor of divinity in the University.[40] In 1691 he was entered a student in the University of his native city; and, after a short period, in consequence of the extraordinary aptitude which he displayed for historical and bibliographical researches, he was appointed to the office of librarian to that learned institution. While in this situation, which he held for four years, he studied with the greatest earnestness the ecclesiastical and literary history of his native land. At the termination of his academical career, he resided for some time with his kinsman, Sir John Maxwell of Pollok,[41] then one of the Lords of Session. While living at Pollok, a vacancy occurred at Eastwood by the death of Mr. Matthew Crawford, author of a *History of the Church of Scotland* (which is yet,

---

[37] 1817–1890

[38] Hebrews 11:4

[39] The monument still survives in Eastwood Old Cemetery.

[40] James Woodrow did not become a professor until 1692.

[41] 1648–1732

we believe, unpublished), and Mr. Wodrow was appointed, by the patronage of Sir John Maxwell, to the ministry of the parish. Although at that period one of the smallest parishes in the West of Scotland, Mr. Wodrow seems to have been contented with his situation, and continued to perform the duties of his calling in it till his death, which, as has been already noticed, occurred in the thirty-first year of his ministry. Besides taking a prominent part in the public business of the Church, Mr. Wodrow composed a *History of the Sufferings of the Church of Scotland from the Restoration to the Revolution*, which was published in two folio volumes, and several other works of a religious and literary nature, all of which are deservedly held in high esteem. He seems also to have devoted a considerable portion of his leisure time to the study of antiquities and natural history. George Crawfurd,[42] a contemporary and friend of Wodrow's, in his *History of Renfrewshire*, mentions a collection of fossil shells which he had made, and characterizes him as "a gentleman well seen in the natural history of the country." Altogether, the old minister of Eastwood seems to have been a truly estimable and worthy individual, an ornament to the Church to which he belonged, and a valuable as well as voluminous contributor to the literature of his country. In Fox's *History of the early part of the Reign of James the Second*,[43] that eminent statesman has passed a eulogium upon his fidelity and impartiality as a historian; while the esteem in which his memory is held by the literary antiquaries of Scotland may be inferred from the fact, that a Society under his name has been established in Edinburgh for the publication of old works of an ecclesiastical nature.

A little to the south of the Eastwood burying-ground, in a fine hollow, watered by the Auldhouse burn, is the village of Thornliebank, with the extensive manufacturing establishment of the Messrs. Crum, in which the greater portion of the inhabitants are employed. The manufacture of cotton is carried on here on an enlarged scale, the works embracing every process from the spinning of the raw material to the finishing of the most beautiful dyed and printed fabrics. Walter

---

[42] 1681 – 1748
[43] By the Liberal politician Charles James Fox, published posthumously in 1808.

Crum, Esq.,[44] one of the leading partners of this wealthy and enterprising firm, is well known as one of the most eminent practical chemists of the present day.

Retracing our steps to Pollokshaws, we now proceed to visit the seat of Sir John Maxwell, Bart., of Pollok, which is situated in a delightful position, on the north bank of the Cart, a little to the south-west of the town.[45] The house is a spacious edifice, four storeys in height, and of the plainest architectural appearance; comfort and commodiousness, rather than ornamental grandeur, having been obviously attended to in its construction. It was erected in 1753 by the great-grandfather of the present possessor,[46] who died a few weeks after its completion. The castle previously occupied by the family, which stood a little to the eastward, was shortly afterwards entirely demolished, with the exception of a small portion, apparently the remains of a massive tower, which was pointed out to us, embedded in the garden-wall.[47] The offices of the present mansion now occupy the site of its more warlike predecessor. On an eminence in the vicinity, which commands a magnificent prospect of the country for many miles around, a still older castle formerly stood.[48] Not a vestige of this ancient structure now remains to mark its whereabouts. Desolation as complete has fallen upon it as that predicted for his own mansion by Thomas the Rhymer,[49] when he said, in bitterness of spirit,

"The hare shall kittle on my hearth-stane."

While we stand musing on the spot, the redbreast is piping his dreary autumnal song on a spreading beech which has been planted on the site of the vanished towers, and we see the glossy plumage of the pheasant glancing in the sunbeam, as, disturbed by our presence, it glides away

---

[44] 1796 – 1867

[45] This is Pollok House, which still stands in Pollok Park and is open to the public.

[46] Sir John Maxwell, 2nd Baronet (1686 – 1752).

[47] This was the second castle on the site, built c.1368 by Sir John Maxwell, 4th Knight of Pollok.

[48] Probably built by Sir John Maxwell of Nether Pollok, 1st knight of Pollok, between 1270 and 1306.

[49] Sir Thomas de Ercildoun, Laird of Learmont (d. 1298).

into the shade of the tangled underwood. Crawfurd, who wrote in 1710, mentions in his minute and curious *History of Renfrewshire*, that in his day the remains of the drawbridge and fosse were still visible.

The gardens and pleasure grounds of Pollok are on a princely scale of magnificence. The Cart, which is spanned by an elegant bridge in the vicinity of the house, winds beautifully through the park, which is finely sprinkled with clumps of wood and picturesque sylvan individualities (to make use of a Johnsonian phrase) every here and there standing "alone in their glory," and exhibiting to the practised eye the distinguishing peculiarities of their various species. We have seldom, indeed, witnessed finer woodland studies than are to be found in the spacious park of Pollok. Old Evelyn[50] would have travelled a long summer day, and reckoned himself amply repaid for his labour, by the sight of a single group of wych-elms which grace the bank of the river a little to the east of the mansion. These fine trees were described in Mr. Strutt's *Sylva Britannica*,[51] published in 1826, a splendid but expensive work, the Scottish division of which was dedicated to Sir John, then Mr. Maxwell, younger, of Pollok. The principal member of the group was measured a number of years since for Mr. Loudon's work on trees,[52] and was found to be ninety feet in height, and four feet in diameter at a yard and a half from the ground. Nor is it only in modern times that the grounds of Pollok have been shadowed by sylvan giants. Several years ago an immense trunk of oak was discovered in the bed of the Cart at this place. With great difficulty it was excavated from the gravelly bank, when it was found to be not less than twenty feet in circumference. This immense mass of primeval timber has since been scooped out, and formed into a summer-house, in which character we saw it in the garden, and had the pleasure of resting ourselves for a brief space in its capacious interior.[53]

---

[50] John Evelyn (1620 – 1706), diarist and author of *Sylva, or A Discourse of Forest-Trees*.

[51] Joseph George Strutt. *Sylva Britannica* was first published in 1822.

[52] *An Encyclopaedia of Trees and Shrubs* (1842) by John Claudius Loudon.

[53] Built in 1850, this summer house no longer survives.

The ancient and honourable family of the Maxwells of Pollok, to whom the greater portion of the parish of Eastwood or Pollokshaws belongs, is descended from the Maxwells of Carlaverock, and has been located here since the end of the thirteenth century. An ancient document, of date 1273, is still in existence, which bears the signature of "John Maxwell, Lord of Nether Pollok," the ancestor of the present Sir John.[54] The representatives of the family have at various periods taken a prominent position in the history of the country. In the reign of Queen Mary Sir John Maxwell, who had been knighted by that fair but ill-fated monarch,[55] adhered faithfully to her cause through all her misfortunes. On the escape of Mary from Lochleven and her flight to Hamilton, she sent a communication to Sir John, ordering him to come to her aid with his friends and servants. This royal missive is still carefully preserved at Pollok. It is as follows:

"To our Traist Friend,
"Ye Laird of Nether Pollok,
"Traist friend, we greet you weill. We dowt not bot ye know that God of his gudnes has put us at libertie; quhome we thank maist heartlie. – Quhairfore desires you wt all possible diligence faill not to be heir at us in Hamylton wt all your folks friends and serwands bodin in feir of weir as ye will do us acceptable service and pleasure Because we know yor constance. We need not at this put to mak langer Lyr but will byd you fairweill.
"Off Hamylton, ye V. of Maij 1568. (Signed) MAIRIE R."

The summons was obeyed, and Sir John and his friends were engaged on the losing side at the decisive skirmish of Langside. A number of other papers of considerable antiquity are preserved in the family archives, among which are a letter from James VI. to the Laird of Pollok, requesting provision for the Prince's baptism – a curious trait of the times; and the original of the Solemn League and Covenant, with the signatures of the King and Council, dated 1587.[56]

---

[54] Sir John Maxwell of Nether Pollok (1243 – 1306), 1st knight of Pollok.
[55] Sir John Maxwell of Cowglen (1524 – 1577).
[56] A covenant to support Reformed Christianity in Scotland.

After a lengthened and extremely pleasant stroll through the policies and gardens of Pollok, we return to Pollokshaws, whence, we proceed to visit the ruins of Haggs Castle, which are situated about a mile to the west of the town. This ancient and time-worn edifice, with its belt of trees, forms a fine feature in the landscape for a considerable distance around. In its "better days" it has combined architectural elegance with a degree of strength necessary to the security of its inmates in those "good old times" when the strong hand was to an inconvenient extent the law of the land. The walls are in some places upwards of five feet in thickness, while the durability of the material of which they are composed is obvious from the excellent state of preservation in which the carvings on their exterior surface still exist. Several vaults or chambers (we are puzzled to say which) are still quite entire; in one of which, at the eastern gable, is an immense fire-place, redolent of hospitable associations, and which must have been capable of roasting at once a whole ox, supported by a couple of wethers,[57] or a perfect host of minor culinary subjects. The place has now a dark, dismal, and chilly appearance, as if many many years must have elapsed since the cheerful blaze illuminated its capacious jaws, or the jagged flames roared in its bat-haunted chimney. An elegant window and several finely carved ornaments still adorn the principal front of the edifice. Over the main doorway, on a triangular stone, there is an antique inscription, now almost illegible, from which it appears that the castle was erected in 1585 by Sir John Maxwell[58] and his spouse Margaret Conyngham. The legend is as follows:

"1585
NI DOMIN
ÆDES STRVXE
RIT FRUSTRA STRVIS.
SIR JOHN MAXWELL OF POLLOK KNIGHT
AND D. MARGARET CONYNGHAM HIS WIFE
BIGGET THIS HOUSE."

---

[57] That is, rams.
[58] Sir John Maxwell, 12th Laird of Pollok (d. 1593).

The Latin portion of this inscription, from its arbitrary construction and curious abbreviations, has been a fruitful source of controversy to the Jonathan Oldbucks[59] of the neighbourhood. Many and various have been the readings which have been suggested and contested with a warmth peculiar to antiquarian discussion. The most abstruse meanings have been discovered and proclaimed with flourish of trumpet, but only to be denounced and exploded by the lore of succeeding savants. Not being prepared with a theory of our own, we shall, with due deference to more learned authorities, give the most recent, and what seems to our non-professional intellect the most plausible translation, which is, that it is only a fanciful rendering of the passage from Psalms – "Unless the Lord build the house, they labour in vain who build it."[60]

Concerning the history of this interesting edifice extremely little is known. It seems to have been used as a jointure house[61] by the family of Pollok, and, indeed, was probably built for that purpose. During the time of the persecution in Scotland it appears that the Knight of Pollok, who belonged to the Covenanting party, occasionally concealed within its walls the outlawed ministers who had been driven from their homes by fear of Claverhouse[62] and his bloodthirsty myrmidons.[63] Information was on one occasion lodged with the Episcopal Archbishop of the district that conventicles and prayer meetings were held at the castle of Haggs under the auspices of its proprietors; and Wodrow mentions that in 1676 Mr. Jamieson,[64] the ejected minister of Govan, "gave the Sacrament in the house of the Haggs, within two miles of Glasgow, along with another clergyman." The family of Pollok suffered severely for the attachment which they thus exhibited to the cause of the Covenant. By a decree of the Privy

---

[59] Jonathan Oldbuck is the title character in *The Antiquary* (1816) by Sir Walter Scott.
[60] Psalm 127.1
[61] A provision for a widow on the death of her husband.
[62] John Graham of Claverhouse, later Viscount Dundee (1648 – 1689), who opposed the Covenanters during the 1670s.
[63] The followers of Achilles in Homer's *Iliad*, used figuratively to mean minions or henchmen.
[64] Alexander Jamieson

Council, dated December 2, 1684, a fine of £8,000 sterling was inflicted on Sir John Maxwell for the alleged crime of receiving into his house and holding converse with the nonconformist ministers. On refusing to pay this enormous sum – for such in those days it really was – the worthy knight was condemned to imprisonment for sixteen months. The worthy baronet alluded to does not seem to have lived long after this period, as we find that a Sir George Maxwell was the Lord of Pollok in 1688.[65] This individual is known in local tradition as the bewitched baronet. On one occasion Sir George was seized with a severe illness, and as the doctors could do nothing for him his malady was ascribed to witchcraft. Suspicion led to certainty. A young vagrant woman having heard of the dread surmise, undertook to discover the offenders. This she at once set about, and to the astonishment of all, she accused several of the most respectable tenants on the Pollok estate. These parties she had private reasons for hating; and by cunningly secreting images of clay stuck full of pins about their houses, and afterwards pretending to find them, she lent an air of probability to her foul accusations, which in those days were sufficient to consign her victims to the tar-barrel. A special commission was ordered by government to investigate the matter, consisting of several Justiciary lords and the leading gentlemen of Renfrewshire. The result was, that the charges were found clearly proven, and no fewer than seven persons were actually sentenced to be strangled and burned – a sentence which, however monstrous it may now appear, was rigidly carried into effect. Full details of this melancholy event may be found in a work entitled *The Renfrewshire Witches*;[66] and still, as a clever modern ballad on the subject, by Mr. Peter M'Arthur,[67] states

> "The story is told by legends old,
> And by withered dame and sire,
> When they sit secure from the winter's cold

---

[65] MacDonald appears to be mixing up his Maxwells, as it was Sir George Maxwell (1622-1677) who was fined for his Covenanting activities, and the same George who was the witch hunter.

[66] *A History of the Witches of Renfrewshire* (1809) by John Millar.

[67] 1805 – 1881, poet and painter.

All around the evening fire:
How the faggots blazed on the Gallowgreen,
Where they hung the witches high;
And their smouldering forms were grimly seen
Till darken'd the lowering sky."

We are happy to observe that the Sir John Maxwell of our own day, with praiseworthy taste, has adopted measures for the proper preservation of this fine old building. A dung hill, which a few years since stood in its vicinity, has been removed, and certain portions of the walls, which were threatened with speedy prostration, have been strengthened and supported; while the entire building has been enclosed and placed under the charge of an individual who is always ready to admit parties wishing to inspect it, but whose presence necessarily acts as a check on the wanton or evil disposed.[68]

From Haggs, in a north-west direction, there is a fine country road, leading, by a farm-house, on a gentle but commanding eminence, to the Glasgow and Paisley Canal. By this route we return to the city, where we arrive somewhere about that dubious hour, "between the gloamin' and the mirk,"[69] which calls the star into the sky, the bat into the air, and (bathos apart) the most useful of the trio, the lamplighter into the street.

---

[68] Haggs Castle was fully restored and is now a private residence.
[69] From 'When the Kye Come Hame' (1823) by James Hogg.

The people of Scotland unquestionably owe a deep debt of gratitude to their Covenanting forefathers; to those brave men who, in defiance of a persecuting government, nobly, and ultimately with entire success, asserted their right to worship the God of their fathers according to the dictates of their individual consciences. Narrow-mindedness, bigotry, and superstition – the errors of the age in which they lived – to a certain extent, it may be admitted, existed among them; but it is unquestionable that it was to their stubborn and long-continued resistance to the aggressions of a dissolute and overbearing court that we are, in a great measure, indebted for the civil and religious liberty which, happily, we are now privileged to enjoy. It has latterly become fashionable in certain literary circles to underrate the character and services of these hardy and perhaps somewhat rude pioneers of spiritual freedom. Scott, in his *Old Mortality*,[1] and *Tales of a Grandfather*,[2] has rendered them but a scanty measure of justice; while in the *Lays of the Cavaliers*,[3] a recent poetical publication of merit, the heartless mercenary, Claverhouse,[4] and his merciless minions are exhibited as models of excellence; whereas rebel and traitor are the best names which the writer has to bestow on his Covenanting countrymen. Blind loyalty to a crowned rake finds, it would seem, more favour with such parties than steadfast and honest adherence to principle. It is satisfactory to know, however, that, despite these attempts to throw a halo of false sentiment around their persecutors, the memory of the Covenanters is still fresh and unfaded in the hearts of the Scottish people. Old Mortality is at rest with his fathers. The clink of the venerable man's renovating hammer is no longer heard on the lonely moor, or in the green church-yard where the martyrs, after "life's fitful fever, sleep secure;"[5] but the homely inscriptions on their

---

[1] 1816 novel by Sir Walter Scott.
[2] 1828 – 1830
[3] 1849 by William Edmondstoune Aytoun.
[4] John Graham of Claverhouse, later Viscount Dundee (1648 – 1689), who opposed the Covenanters during the 1670s.
[5] From Shakespeare's *Macbeth* III.ii.

memorial stones are still religiously preserved from the effacing influences of time, and the tale of their sufferings, their struggles, and their triumphs, is still heard at the cottage-hearth. As the poet has well said, though

"The martyr's hill's forsaken
In simmer's dusk sae calm,
And there's nae gathering now, lassie,
To sing the e'ening psalm;
Yet the martyr's grave will rise, lassie,
Aboon the warrior's cairn,
Though the martyr sound may sleep, lassie,
Aneath the waving fern."[6]

Among the haunts of the Covenanters there are few which are more interesting, or which are more frequently visited, than the lonely farm-house of Lochgoin, situated in the moorlands of Fenwick, some fourteen or fifteen miles to the south-west of Glasgow.[7] In a pilgrimage

"O'er moors and mosses mony, O,"[8]

to this humble and sequestered domicile, which we have long desired to visit, we now entreat, in imagination, at least, the company of our gentle readers. At an early hour on a fine morning of August we bid adieu to the city, and proceed, by way of Cathcart, towards Eaglesham. The newly arisen sun is shining brightly over the Cathkin Braes, while

"Ilka blade o' grass wi' its ain drap o' dew"[9]

---

[6] From 'The Covenanter's Lament' (1836) by Robert Allan.
[7] The farmhouse, which was rebuilt in 1858, is now within Whitelee Windfarm.
[8] MacDonald may be confusing Burn's 'The Bonie Moor Hen' (1788) –"O'er moors and o'er mosses and mony a glen" – with the song 'Glasgow Peggy' (c.1819) – 'They rode through moors & mosses mony'.
[9] From 'Ilka Blade o' Grass Keps its ain Drap o' Dew' (c.1832) by James Ballantine.

is radiant with tints that might well "pale the ineffectual fires"[10] of the overly-vaunted Koh-i-noor;[11] and the webs of the field-spider, spread on the green hedgerows, and beaded with the tears of the bygone night, would take the shine, we have no doubt, out of Queen Isabella's much talked of, and richly begemmed pair of bracelets.[12] The luxuriant wheat, a perfect wall of bread, with the first faint russet tinge of autumn, is waving on the fertile fields, and contrasting sweetly with the fresher verdure of the oat and the silken awns of the bearded bere.[13] The potato ridges are blooming as if such a thing as the destructive aphis had never existed; while the bean, not yet denuded of its flowers, lends a honeyed fragrance to the passing winds. Every now and again a country girl with her sour-milk cart passes onward to the thirsty city; or "gangrel bodies,"[14] such as wandering dealers in delf,[15] packmen, and votaries of the gaberlunzie profession,[16] may be observed commencing their daily rounds among the scattered farms and villages. It is really astonishing to witness the numbers of these poor creatures who daily issue from our wynds and vennels to pick up a precarious living beyond the police boundaries, partly by charity and partly by the disposal of some humble description of merchandise. One-half the world in reality does not know, and perhaps does not much care, by what a variety of shifts the other half manages to gain its meagre subsistence.

At a distance of some five or six miles from Glasgow we pass the villages of Clarkston and Busby; the former a small cluster of houses situated at the junction of four roads, one of which was formerly the way from our city to Kilmarnock. The formation of the

---

[10] From Shakespeare's *Hamlet* I.v.

[11] A huge diamond that was surrendered to Queen Victoria in 1849 after Britain annexed the Punjab.

[12] Possibly referring to Isabella I of Spain's jewels, which were said to have been pledged to fund Columbus' voyage to the new world, or possibly MacDonald is thinking of Marie Antoinette's pair of diamond bracelets which were inherited by the Duchess of Parma in 1851.

[13] barley

[14] vagrants

[15] peat or sods

[16] That is, tramps or beggars.

new line by Pollokshaws and Newton of Mearns has, however, long diverted the traffic from this route. There is nothing of particular note in or about the village to interest or attract the rambler. Busby lies a short distance to the east, on the banks of the Cart, which are here of the most picturesque description. It is of considerable extent, the population being upwards of one thousand in number, and principally engaged in manufacturing operations. At the north end of the village, in a deep ravine, is an extensive cotton-spinning establishment, belonging to Messrs. Crum & Co.; while about half-a-mile farther up the stream are the printworks of Messrs. Inglis & Wakefield. The houses in the village are generally of a superior description, and the place altogether has a comfortable and tidy appearance. There is a handsome dissenting meeting-house in the vicinity, and we understand that there are also several seminaries for the education of the rising generation. Busby, singularly enough, seems to form the junction-point of three parishes, part of it being situated in Mearns, part in East Kilbride, and a portion in Carmunnock, the church of which, being the most convenient, is generally attended by that section of the inhabitants who adhere to the national Establishment.[17] The country around Busby is of the most beautiful description, being composed of gentle pastoral undulations and fertile slopes, while the steep winding banks of the Cart, with their rich garniture of woods, present many scenes which might well please the eye of the poet or the painter.

Leaving Busby and proceeding to the southward, at the distance of about a mile, according to our reckoning, we arrive at Waterfoot, where, the Earn, a fine stream which comes meandering westward from the Mearns Moor, joins the Cart. A more lovely spot than that in which the union of the Cart and the Earn is thus consummated it would be difficult indeed to imagine. With Moore we might well say,

"There is not in this wide world a valley so sweet,
As the vale in whose bosom the bright waters meet;"[18]

---

[17] That is, the Church of Scotland.
[18] From 'The Meeting of the Waters' (1808) by Thomas Moore.

but brightness is not, by any means, a characteristic of either stream. They are both wanderers of the moors, with a rich brown tinge in their bosoms that suggests ideas of liquid amber, or a pretty strong infusion of tea. Immediately after the "meeting of the waters," they tumble lovingly together down a rocky steep that churns them into a foamy whiteness, which rivals in fairness the breasts of the ducks and geese that are swimming gracefully about in the dancing eddies. There are broken grounds and trees, and cottages and bridges, and an old mill, with picturesque wheel, strewn about in that beautiful confusion which the artist so dearly loves, and which he so often transfers to his canvas. It is just the very sort of place, in short, where a langsyne poet would have expected to meet a water-kelpie, and where a modern naturalist, with greater probability of success, we dare say, would linger lovingly in the hope of discovering the lonely water-ouzel.

The Earn, (what a sweet name!) as some of our readers will perhaps remember, was the stream of the celebrated Christopher North's[19] boyhood. On its banks he first donned his world-famous sporting-jacket. While living in the Mearns manse, as he did for several happy years, he could almost hear its murmuring voice in his bed-chamber, inviting him to its margin; "full many a time and oft," we need not doubt, he listened to the call of the charmer, and leaving books and bookish cares behind, stole forth, a truant Izaak Walton,[20] to angle for the rich red-speckled trout in its brown waters. The lonely angler catches more than fish. He may not fill his creel, but he can hardly avoid filling his soul with sweet memories. A burn-side is indeed "a joy for ever."[21]

> "The muse nae poet ever fand her,
> Till by himsel' he learned to wander
> Adown some trottin' burn's meander,

---

[19] (1785 – 1854) Penname of the lawyer and critic Professor John Wilson who wrote for *Blackwood's Magazine*.
[20] (1593 –1683) Author of *The Compleat Angler*.
[21] From 'Endymion' (1818) by John Keats.

And no think lang.”[22]

Nay, we feel persuaded that even the most prosaic of mortals, if put on a proper regimen of burn-side wandering, might, by the benign influence of the "cold water cure," be transformed, if not into a veritable poet – for it seems he is born, not made – at least into a something infinitely superior to the mere worldling:

But we must for the present bid adieu to the Earn and proceed on our way to Eaglesham. We shall again meet the stream, however, and find it nursing another genius, whose name also our country will "not willingly let die."[23] From Waterfoot to Eaglesham – a distance of some three miles – the country becomes by gentle degrees more elevated. The road, which is straight almost as an arrow's flight, consequently presents what, in the language of the rail, is denominated "a pretty steep gradient." A marked change in the productive capabilities of the soil is also observable here as the rambler passes along. From a richly agricultural, it gradually assumes a decidedly pastoral character. The yellowing wheat disappears altogether, and we find instead a predominance of somewhat cold-looking pasture lands, relieved, at considerable intervals, with patches of oats, barley, and potatoes – the former much greener and thinner than in the warm lowlands which we are leaving behind. A straight road is seldom much to our liking; but, although somewhat stiff, the walk from Waterfoot to Eaglesham is really one of a very pleasant description. The way is fringed on either side by some of our sweetest wild flowers, while the surface of the country is of a fine undulating nature, with every here and there a picturesque farm-steading surrounded with its straggling belt of trees. It is somewhat provoking, however, to the sentimental traveller, while he is thus hedged into a right onward path, to see the Cart, a little to the left of him, at "its own sweet will,"[24] turning and winding with ever-varying curve amidst its banks of freshest green. What a contrast it presents in its playful gambollings here a to its staid

---

[22] From 'Lines to William Simson' (1785) by Robert Burns.
[23] From 'The Reason of Church Government urged against Prelaty' (1642) by John Milton.
[24] From 'Composed upon Westminster Bridge' (1802) by William Wordsworth.

and sober self – "alike, but oh! how different"[25] – in the lower part of its course! It is really worth the while of our "Seestu"[26] friends to make a pilgrimage to this district for the express purpose of witnessing the boyhood of their native stream. Not crabbed age and youth are more essentially opposite in their characters. The dull, sluggish, and withal filthy waters, which wash the shipping at the classic Sneddon, are here sportive, joyous, and pure, while every link and turn presents a new portraiture of sylvan or flowery loveliness. There is a deep moral in the contrast, which we have no doubt our sagacious readers will expiscate for themselves. Truth is said to have her habitation in a well; but the pensive observer will occasionally find her bathing in the rippled flow of the lonesome river.

The present village of Eaglesham is of comparatively modern origin – an ancient hamlet of the same name having been demolished in 1769 by Alexander, tenth Earl of Eglinton, to make way for it, he having some time previously drawn up a plan for its erection. It is consequently regular in its appearance, and consists principally of two lengthened rows of houses running from east to west, which are situated opposite each other on the sides of a kind of shallow valley or glen, in the face of a gentle declivity. At the upper end the rows of houses are 100, and at the lower 250 yards apart. Each house has a plot of garden-ground in its rear; while the space in front, down the middle of which a rapid streamlet gushes, is partly wooded and partly of a smooth sward, interspersed with trees, which forms the bleaching green and playground of the village. Between the rows at the lower end are situated a meal-mill, the Eglinton Arms Inn, and the parish school. Midway up, in a considerable hollow, lies the extensive establishment of the Eaglesham Spinning Company. Half-hidden from the eye, and with everything about them clean and orderly, these important works, contrary to what might have been expected, do not in the least detract from the rural aspect of the locality. The machinery is driven by an immense water-wheel of iron, about 45 feet in diameter, and of 50 horse-power. For the propulsion of this, 740 cubic feet of

---

[25] From 'The Mountain Echo' (1806) by William Wordsworth.
[26] That is, Paisley.

water per minute are required; yet so ingeniously is the fluid conducted to and from the wheel that it is neither heard nor seen within the walls of the factory.[27]

At the south-east corner of the village is the parish church, a small octangular building of the most unpretending appearance. This structure was erected in 1790, on the site of a still more diminutive edifice of considerable antiquity, by Archibald, the eleventh Earl of Eglinton.[28] It is surrounded by an extensive burying-ground, in which, with our usual penchant for "sermons in stones,"[29] we linger for some time, to the sad discomfiture of a pretty numerous flock of sheep which are nibbling the verdure from the grassy mounds of the dead. There are differences of taste, no doubt, among men, but, for our part, we should really not like to have our mutton brought to us from the church yard. We know one place where the field of graves is reserved for the minister's cow, and we have more than once in our peregrinations come across a clerical pony meditating among the tombs; but, in truth, we think this custom of turning the fertilizing properties of decaying mortality into profit would be considerably "more honoured in the breach than the observance."[30] Let the Eaglesham sexton endeavour to find perquisites without violating the amenities of the grave; as for the professional offenders we have alluded to, we shall not presume to interfere with their proceedings. As Burns has said, and as doubtless he knew to his cost,

"Corbies and clergy are a shot richt kittle[31]."[32]

There are a considerable number of old memorial stones in the Eaglesham burying-ground, but none which call for special remark, with the exception of a monument erected to the memory of two individuals who were put to death for their adherence to the Solemn

---

[27] The mill burnt down in 1876.
[28] This church survives and still serves as the parish church.
[29] From Shakespeare's *As You Like It* II.i.
[30] From Shakespeare's *Hamlet* I.iv.
[31] risky
[32] From 'The Brigs of Ayr' (1786) by Robert Burns.

League and Covenant,[33] in the reign of the Second Charles.[34] The structure is of comparatively recent erection, but the inscription is evidently old, and has probably been transcribed from a more ancient head stone. It is as follows:

"Psalm cxii. 6.– 'The righteous shall be in everlasting remembrance.'

"Here lie Gabriel Thomson and Robert Lockhart, who were killed for owning the covenanted testimony, by a party of Highlanders and dragoons, under the command of Ardincaple,[35] 1st May, 1685.

"These men did search through moor and moss,
To find out all that had no pass;
These faithful witnesses were found,
And murdered upon the ground.
Their bodies in this grave do lie;
Their blood for vengeance yet doth cry;
This may a standing witness be
For Presbytery 'gainst Prelacy."

Besides the parish church there are several other places of worship in Eaglesham. The inhabitants are principally weavers and factory workers; and as usual amongst a manufacturing population, considerable diversity of opinion prevails. Free Church, United Presbyterian, and Morisonian[36] meeting-houses are pointed out to us, each having its own little knot of adherents; while there is a sprinkling of Roman Catholics, and also of those who, as our informant remarks, "care for none of these things."

Altogether, the village, both in respect to situation and arrangement, is one of the most attractive that we have yet witnessed. It is indeed a pleasant habitation. The children, who in noisy groups are playing about as we pass, have a freshness and rosiness of complexion which the parents of the city might well look upon with

---

[33] A covenant to support Reformed Christianity in Scotland.

[34] Reigned 1660 – 1685.

[35] Archibald MacAulay, laird of Ardincaple from 1681 to 1705.

[36] The Evangelical Union, a universalist sect founded in 1843 by James Morison.

envy; while the very weavers have a colour in their cheeks which tells of salutary airs, and a not overly close attendance on the loom. This is accounted for by the circumstance that most of them have a patch of ground in the vicinity of the village, which they cultivate at spare hours, and which not only adds considerably to their domestic comfort, but administers to their bodily health by the out-door exercise which it induces. It is this combination of the manufacturing with the agricultural employments which, in general, renders the country weaver a more comfortable as well as a more robust and healthy individual than the webster of the town.

The barony of Eaglesham, which includes nearly the entire parish, was for many generations the property of the Montgomeries, who latterly became Earls of Eglinton. It came into their hands originally through a Robert de Montgomery, in the twelfth century. For two hundred years it continued the chief seat of this noble family, which has ever been honourably distinguished in the annals of our country. In the fourteenth century the baronies of Eglinton and Ardrossan were obtained by the marriage of John de Montgomery with Elizabeth, daughter and heiress of Sir Hugh Eglinton, by a sister of Robert II., King of Scotland. This gentleman vanquished and took captive Harry Percy (the "Hotspur" of Shakespeare)[37] at Otterbourne, and afterwards received a handsome sum by way of ransom for that gallant though unfortunate knight. Near Eaglesham the vestiges of an ancient castle are still pointed out, which is said to have been erected with the English gold obtained on that occasion.[38] Some of our readers, we daresay, will remember the old ballad wherein the exploits of this doughty warrior are celebrated:

> "The Gordons good in English blood
> They steeped their hose and shoon;
> The Lyndsays flew like fire about,
> Till all the fray was done.

---

[37] He features in the series of plays about the rise of the House of Lancaster: *Richard II*, *Henry IV* parts 1 and 2.

[38] Polnoon Castle, which fell in to ruin probably sometime in the 18th century.

"Tre Percy and Montgomerie met,
Of other they were richt fain,
They swakked swords until they swat,
And their red blude ran between.

"'Yield thee, yield thee, Percy,' he said,
'Or I swear I'll lay thee low!
'To whom shall I yield,' said Earl Percy,
"Since I see that it maun be so?'

"As soon as he knew it was Montgomerie,
He stuck his sword-point in the ground;
But the Montgomerie was a courteous knight,
And quickly took him by the hand.

"This deed was done at Otterbourne
About the breaking of the day;
Earl Douglas was buried at the bracken bush,
And the Percy led captive away."[39]

Sir Hugh Montgomery, the son of this hero, has also obtained a ballad immortality. Those who are familiar with "Chevy Chase," (and who is not?) will at once remember that this gallant knight was slain on that fatal field by an arrow from the bow of a stout English yeoman, –

"The gray goose-wing that was thereon
In his heart-blood was wet."[40]

In our own day the Eaglesham estate has departed from the Montgomery family. It is now in possession of Allan Gilmour, Esq.,[41] a merchant prince of our own good city, one of a class which, by the

---

[39] From the traditional ballad 'The Battle of Otterburn'. The battle took place in 1388.
[40] From the traditional ballad 'The Ballad of Chevy Chase', which probably dates from the 15th century.
[41] International timber merchant and shipowner (1775 – 1849). At the time MacDonald was writing, the estate had in fact passed into the sole ownership of his brother, James Gilmour (1782 – 1858).

peaceful conquests of industry and commerce, are, in modern times, gradually stepping into the shoes of the ancient lords of the soil.

After a little rest and needful refreshment at Eaglesham, we proceed towards Lochgoin, which is situated in a bleak moor, some four or five miles to the south-west. For about one-third of this distance there is an excellent country road, but after that the rambler must plunge into the bowels of the moorland, and trust very much to chance, or his own skill in regard to the cardinal points, as to whether he shall ever reach his destination. In some places there are faint traces of a footpath, but these are continually disappearing, or leading you astray – sometimes into a brown moss-water burn, at others into a fine green spot that, siren-like, smiles in your face while luring you to wet feet. There are several extensive lochs or reservoirs in the moor. After passing in succession three of these, which are named respectively Picketlaw Loch, Mid Loch, and Dunwan Loch – the latter of which, a broad sheet of water, supplies the Eaglesham mills – we fairly lose our reckoning. It is in vain that we endeavour to recover ourselves by observation of the sun, which is shining brilliantly in the zenith, so we resign the reins to fortune, and determine to enjoy the wild beauty of the scenery. We are surrounded by bleak hills and wide morasses, stretching far as the eye can reach. In the words of a poet who spent his boyhood here,[42] we are encircled

> "By hills and streams,
> And melancholy deserts, where the sun
> Saw, as he passed, a shepherd only, here
> And there, watching his little flock."[43]

The wild cry of the curlew or the plover alone breaks the dreary silence, unless when the startled snipe springs from the rushy brink of a mossy pool, with a whirr and a shrill alarum-note, as the unwonted presence of man scares it from its solitary haunt. Yet Flora has her favours for the botanist even here. The snowy tufts of the canach[44]

---

[42] Robert Pollok (1798 – 1827), born at North Muirhouse.
[43] From 'The Course of Time', 1827.
[44] cotton-grass

wave gracefully in the breeze; the grass of Parnassus (*Parnassia pulustris*), with its beautiful corolla; and the bog asphodel (*narthecium ossifragum*), with their golden bloom, make the desert to rejoice. Here also are the sun-dew (*ilrosera rotundifolia*), with its beads of pearl; the cinque-foil (*commarum palustre*), with its deep purple petals; and numerous other cultureless inhabitants of the untrodden wilds, –

> "Born to blush unseen,
> And waste their sweetness on the desert air."[45]

While we are paying our devoirs[46] to the goddess of scent and bloom, a stranger luckily heaves in sight, whom we at once hasten to meet. We have, he informs us, wandered considerably from the right track, which he points out; and at the same time describes certain landmarks, by observing which we shall be less likely to lose our course in future. He also gives us directions where we shall find a celebrated spring, the water of which he praises for all imaginable good qualities, and which he advises us by all means to visit. Taking leave of our obliging informant with a liberal outpouring of gratitude, we again proceed on our way, which, as formerly, lies

> "O'er mosses, slaps, moors, hags, and stiles."[47]

We do not again lose ourselves, however, and soon arrive at the "Woofield well," to which we were so kindly directed. It is a tiny springlet, which bubbles out of a green bank, fringed with white-flowered water-cress, beneath a rocky declivity, near the east end of Lochgoin. Time out of mind, as we are informed, it has been a favourite rendezvous of the sportsmen on the Eaglesham moors. Nor do we wonder at the circumstance, for more limpid water or more intensely cold we certainly never tasted. It has apparently been designed by Nature as the scene of a pic-nic. Behind is the towering trap-rock;[48] before is the dark placid waters of Lochgoin, unfretted by

---

[45] From 'An Elegy Written in a Country Church Yard' (1751) by Thomas Gray.
[46] duties
[47] From 'Tam o' Shanter' (1791) by Robert Burns.
[48] Any dark igneous rock such as basalt.

the shadow of bush or tree, with the dreary expanse of the moor and a perfect wilderness of hills in the distance. Pulling out our vasculum,[49] which ere starting we took the precaution to charge with a liberal allowance of provender, we set to work with an appetite which only a wanderer in such wilds can thoroughly appreciate; while a teetotaller would be delighted to witness our frequent and deep potations of Nature's own delicious brewing. It is questionable, however, whether he would sympathize altogether with our audible aspiration for a thimbleful of the forbidden dew at the termination of our repast. Be that as it may, it is something to our regret that the necessities of the locality enforce the iron rule of "touch not, taste not, handle not." [50]A kenning[51] of the creature would have formed such a treat in judicious combination with the almost gelid water!

We have scarce concluded our meal, *al fresco*, when we observe two lads from a neighbouring farm-house unmooring a boat on the loch below. One of them frankly accosts us, and offers us a passage, if we choose, to the west end of the water, a distance of perhaps two-thirds of a mile, where the farm of Lochgoin is situated. Closing with the offer, a very short period sees us gliding over the glassy surface of the lake to our destination.

The farm of Lochgoin is somewhat like an oasis in the dreary waste. Around the house are a few patches of oats and potatoes, with a small garden for kitchen vegetables and the hardier kinds of flowers. Fruit trees there are none, for the best of all reasons – they could not exist in such an exposed and barren situation. There are a few of our hardiest trees, however; but even these have a dwarfed and miserable appearance. For miles around stretches the wild moor land, barren and desolate as it came from the hand of Nature, and the only practical use of which is as pasture for sheep and cattle. Some idea of the soil of this bleak Shetlandish locality may be formed from the fact that we find the farmers, as we pass, making hay on fields where the moisture, oozing from the ground, is from two to three inches in depth. The farm-

---

[49] A metal container usually used for collecting botanical samples.
[50] Colossians 2.21
[51] tiny amount

steading of Lochgoin is a low range of houses, partly of recent erection and partly of considerable antiquity. The larger and most comfortable looking portion is devoted to the accommodation of cattle. The present occupant of Lochgoin is Mr. Thomas Howie,[52] the descendant of a long line of ancestors, who have for many generations dwelt on the same spot, and who have been throughout honourably distinguished for their attachment to the cause of religious liberty. The founder of the family is said to have been one of the persecuted Waldenses,[53] who in 1178 fled from his native land, and found a safe though solitary place of rest and peace at Lochgoin. The date of his arrival, with others indicating the various periods at which alterations and additions to the original tenement have been made, are carved on the lintel of the principal doorway. During the dark days of religious persecution,

"When the minister's home was the mountain and wood,"[54]

in the reign of Charles II., who was, in sad truth, no "merry Monarch" to Scotland, and that of his bigoted and priest-ridden brother James II., whom England flung from her like an unclean thing, Lochgoin formed a frequent asylum to those who had sacrificed their all for conscience' sake. Cameron, Peden,[55] and others, often found shelter under its hospitable though humble roof. For this the house was plundered not less than from ten to twelve times; while its inmates were as often driven to seek safety in the moors by the revengeful dragoons, who, by the way, it is some consolation to know, must have had considerable difficulty in finding their way on horseback to the place. The names of James Howie,[56] the possessor of the farm, and that of his son, were also placed on the fugitives' roll, and exposed on the church doors; while it appears from a proclamation, dated May 5, 1679, that they were both denounced as rebels and dangerous persons. Nevertheless,

---

[52] 1776 – 1863
[53] Members of a twelfth-century French Christian movement that emphasised poverty and simplicity.
[54] From 'The Cameronian Dream' (1821) by James Hyslop.
[55] The Covenanters Richard Cameron (c.1648 – 1680) and Alexander 'Prophet' Peden (1626 – 1686).
[56] d. 1691. His son was John Howie (1665 – 1755).

they continued firm to their principles, and although exposed to great hardships and perils both survived until after the Revolution. John Howie, father of the present possessor, was the author of the *Scots Worthies*,[57] a work which contains biographical sketches of the leading personages who struggled and died for the covenanted work of Reformation in those times, and which has obtained an almost unrivalled popularity in the rural districts of Scotland.

At the time of our visit Mr. Howie is in the fields busy with his haymaking, but we are received in the most kindly manner by the goodwife, who at once proceeds to show us certain relics of the Covenanters, which have been religiously preserved in the family. These are the Bible and sword of Captain John Paton,[58] one of the worthies who fought for his principles at Pentland and Bothwell Bridge, and who was afterwards executed at Edinburgh for his share in these transactions. The captain also served with the Covenanters against Montrose;[59] and certain marvellous stories are told of his exploits with the sword in question, after his party had been routed at Kilsyth. In the memoir of him which is published in the *Scots Worthies*, the following extraordinary statement appears regarding his prowess on this unfortunate occasion:

"Having made the best of his way through the enemy, he fell in with Colonels Hacket and Strachan.[60] All three then rode off together, but they had not gone far till they were encountered by about fifteen of the enemy, all of whom they killed except two. When they had gone a little farther, they were attacked by about thirteen more, and of these they killed ten, so that only three of them made their escape. But upon the approach of about eleven Highlanders more, one of the Colonels said in a familiar dialect, 'Johnny, if thou dost not something now, we are all dead men.' To him the Captain answered,

---

[57] John Howie (1735 – 1793), biographer. *Scots Worthies*, published 1775, was officially titled *Biographia Scoticana*.
[58] d. 1684
[59] James Graham, 1st Marquess of Montrose (1612 – 1650).
[60] Robert Halkett (b.1617) and Archibald Strachan (d.1652).

'Fear not, for we will do what we can before we yield, or flee before them.' They killed nine of them and put the rest to flight."

The Captain's other feats, many of which are sufficiently wondrous, will be found recorded in the book alluded to. The sword is now rusty and time-worn, but even at its best it must have been a light blade, and all unlikely to do such deadly work. It is said at one time to have had a series of nicks on its edge, corresponding to the number of years during which the persecution lasted. These emblematic notches are not now visible. The Bible is dated 1652, and has the following inscription on the inside of one of the boards:

"Captain John Paton's Bible, which he gave to his wife from off the scaffold, when he was executed for the cause of Christ at Edinburgh, on the 8th of May, 1684. James Howie received it from the Captain's son's daughter's husband, and gave it to John Howie, his nephew."

Besides these interesting relics, we are shown the banner which waved above the heads of the Covenanters at the battle of Drumclog,[61] when the bloody Claverhouse was sent to the right about by a handful of undisciplined peasants. It is of white linen, and has the figures of a Bible and crown, supported by the thistle, rudely traced on it with a reddish pigment, and the motto,

"Phinick[62] for country and covenanted work of Reformation."

An old drum also, which beat the alarm on that memorable morning when the troopers hove in sight as the Covenanters were engaged in prayer on the lonely moor, is also placed in our hands, and we need scarcely say excites our deepest interest. An antiquary would be delighted with a collection of ancient silver coins which is in the possession of the family; and we cannot help picturing to ourselves the

---

[61] 1st June 1679
[62] That is, Fenwick.

ecstasy which a Monkbarns[63] might have felt had he been shown into the spence of Lochgoin, as we are, and permitted to examine the extensive assortment of old books which it contains. These were principally purchased, as we understand, by the author of the *Scots Worthies*, and many of them must have been of inestimable service to him for purposes of reference in the composition of that work. We pull out a number of them at random, and find them to be generally of a religious or historical character, and nearly all of venerable date. One old Bible interests us considerably; it is of date 1599, and was "Printed by the deputies of Christopher Smart, printer to Queen Elizabeth." It is still in a good state of preservation, and contains a number of curious engravings, amongst which we observe a map wherein the geographical position of the garden of Eden is lucidly delineated. Altogether, we are highly gratified by our visit to this out-of-the-way nook; and we do not wonder that many hundreds annually, as we are informed is the case, should be attracted to its precincts. The wild beauty of the locality, the associations of an interesting nature which are entwined around it, and the venerable relics of the past which it contains, must ever render it a sacred spot in the eyes of those who sympathize with the trials and struggles of those brave men, from the darkness of whose sufferings has arisen for us the day-star of a brighter era.[64] As we take leave of the obliging matron, and set out on our homeward way, we cannot help repeating the following lines from a genuine Scottish poet, which seem to us peculiarly applicable to the place:

> "And from that lonely rugged spot
>   Ascended rich and rare
> The incense of the contrite heart,
>   The sacrifice of prayer;
> And angels from the heights of heaven
>   Did look complacent down

---

[63] Jonathan Oldbuck of Monkbarns, title character in Sir Walter Scott's *The Antiquary* (1816).

[64] The rebuilt farmhouse now houses a Covenanters Museum, and there is amonument to John Howie nearby.

On honoured heads that soon should wear
The martyr's glorious crown."[65]

Before leaving Lochgoin, we may mention that the prospect from the vicinity of the house, looking towards the south and west, is of the most spacious and beautiful description, including within its range Loudon hill, near which the battle of Drumclog was fought, and an extensive portion of the Ayrshire coast, with Ailsa Craig and the picturesque mountains of Arran in the distance. The atmosphere is delightfully clear, and we consequently behold the land of Burns spread, as in a map, at our feet; while, on the blue sea beyond, the white sails are gleaming here and there like snowy specks of cloud on the summer sky. The motion of these fair children of the deep is of course imperceptible in the extreme distance, and to our gaze they seem

"As idle even as painted ships
Upon a painted ocean."[66]

It is always monotonous and wearisome to retrace one's steps on an excursion, and we determine, instead of returning by Eaglesham, to take a circuitous course, and to make our way home by Mearns. With this intention we strike across the moor in a northerly direction, towards the hill of Ballygeich. The way is rough enough in all conscience, and forcibly brings to our mind the exclamation of the Highlander on seeing the roads which General Wade had constructed through the wilds of his native country,

"Had you seen these roads before they were made,
You would hold up your hands and bless General Wade!"

The road from Lochgoin to Ballygeich is not yet made, and we would recommend any one who has a desire thoroughly to appreciate the benefits of modern road-making to try the walk from the one place to the other. The distance may be somewhere about two miles, and by

---

[65] 'The Mountain Sanctuary' (1834) by David Veddar.
[66] From 'Rime of the Ancient Mariner' (1798) by Samuel Taylor Coleridge.

dint of leaping, wading, and scrambling, we manage to get over them in rather more than an hour.

The hill of Ballygeich is, with the exception of Mistilaw and the hill of Staik, the highest eminence in the county of Renfrew, being about 1,000 feet above the level of the sea. It is principally composed of the trap-rock[67] prevalent in the district; but several specimens of barytes have been found in its vicinity, and a species of stone which bears extreme heat without renting, and has consequently been found well adapted for the construction of furnaces and ovens. It is also reported to contain silver and lead ores; but it must be admitted that nothing of the sort comes under our observation. The prospect from its summit, however, fully repays us for any disappointment which we may experience on this score. It indeed commands an extensive and beautiful series of landscapes, embracing many counties within its scope. On one hand are the moors of Fenwick, with the fertile woods and fields of Ayrshire, the giant rock of Ailsa, and the towering Goatfell in the distance; on the other, the grand basin and vale of Clyde, with Glasgow, Paisley, and countless other towns and hamlets in its capacious bosom, while a perfect wilderness of Bens rise proudly on the dim horizon. This was a favourite haunt of the author of *The Course of Time*,[68] who was born and spent his early years in the vicinity. Here the youthful poet came full oft to feast his expanding soul with the elements of beauty and sublimity; and those who are familiar with his great poem will doubtless recollect that several of its most striking passages are evidently descriptive of the scenery which was here impressed upon bis memory. We may mention, however, that in our admiration of the landscape here, we unfortunately dropt our vasculum, which, for the benefit of the non-initiated, we may explain to be a sort of japanned tin-canister, used by botanists for the convenient conveyance of their specimens. It has been our companion on many a flower-gathering excursion; and although of no great value

---

[67] Any dark igneous rock such as basalt.

[68] Robert Pollok (1798 – 1827). His very popular *The Course of Time* was published in 1827.

in a pecuniary sense, we have a sort of affection for it, which makes us regret its loss considerably.

Leaving Ballygeich and proceeding in a north-west direction by Moorhouse, we soon, after crossing the Earn by a rustic bridge, arrive at the Glasgow and Kilmarnock road, about nine miles from the city. Being somewhat fagged with our devious wanderings, and evening drawing rapidly on, we make an effort and push smartly homeward. Including a few minutes' rest at Newton-of-Mearns, we get over the distance in about two and a-half hours. Latterly, we must admit, the mile-stones, to our fancy, appear somewhat "lang o'coming," but this is scarcely to be wondered at, when it is considered that our peregrinations must have extended, by a moderate computation, considerably over thirty miles.

> "'That's the Forth,' said the Bailie, with an air of reverence
> which I have observed the Scotch usually pay to their distinguished
> rivers. The Clyde, the Tweed, the Forth, and the Spey are usually
> named by those who dwell on their banks with a sort of respect and
> pride." *Rob Roy*.

Not only are the above remarks of the author of *Waverly*[1] true with
regard to the larger rivers of Scotland, but they also hold good with
respect to the most diminutive of her streamlets and burns. The Scotch
have a perfect passion, indeed, for the "living waters" with which their
beautiful country is everywhere so delightfully intersected. Every one
of them, from the greatest even unto the least, is duly named, or
christened if you will, and the music of their names – for they are
nearly all concords of sweetest sound – flows into the very hearts of
those who dwell among their green banks and braes, and not
unfrequently comes welling forth again in never-dying melody. Glance
at the glowing pages of Scotia's matchless book of song, and you will
at once learn the depth and fervour of that affection which the natives
of the cannie North bear to the running waters of their "ain countrie."
Beyond the Tweed the traveller often asks in vain at the dull
chawbacon[2] the designation of brook or stream. The wee'est toddlin'
bairn in Scotland, with the faintest development even of "the gift of
the gab," can at once name its own natal burn; and not only that, but
would volunteer on the instant to show the stranger the favourite pools
where the little minnow and the "beardie"[3] have their haunts, and the
shallows where the weans of the clachan best love to paidle among the
tiny wavelets. The bard of Coila,[4] who has invested many waters with

---

[1] Sir Walter Scott (1771 – 1832)
[2] unsophisticated rural dweller
[3] stickleback
[4] Robert Burns (1759 – 1796)

a music sweeter than their own, never touched a deeper chord than when, in his love-fraught lay of Langsyne, he makes the long-parted friends recall the wadings of life's young day. How many bosoms have melted in tearful sympathy over the two simple lines,

> "We twa hae paidi't in the burn,
> Frae morning sun till dine."

We have seen gray-headed men, "loof locked in loof," crooning them in trembling tones together; while the saut, saut pearls of memory were trickling down each furrowed cheek; and we have seen young men and maidens fair encircling in alternate links the festive board, and chanting them in loving and heartfelt harmony. In the lowly cottage and in the lofty hall they find a sympathetic echo; at home, amongst our own gray hills, or ayont the faem[5] in the land of the stranger, wherever two or three of Scotia's callants are gathered together, there is heard, midst mingling tears and smiles, the song of songs that brings them back the happy days of youth, and the remembrance of their ain burn-side.

First, and most beautiful of rivers to our heart and eye, is our own dear Clyde.

> "Let others love the tangled Forth,
> Or mountain-shadowed Spey,
> The Don, the Dee, wake others' glee,
> Fair Tweed or queenly Tay.

> "From all their charms, with open arms,
> We turn in love and pride
> To thy green ways and flow'ry bráes,
> Our own, our native Clyde."[6]

Yet is our love anything but exclusive. We love thee also, O sylvan Tweed! although to us thou art but a name. Yarrow, albeit

---

[5] beyond the sea
[6] From 'To the Clyde' by Hugh MacDonald himself.

unvisited, is dear unto our heart, for sake of those who have sorrowed and sung by her side. The Doon, the Lugar, and the Cart have, since our earliest days, been in name familiar as household words to our ear and our soul in the lyrics of Scotland's, sweetest singers, and we have since gazed upon their material charms with ever-increasing admiration and delight. As well attempt to

"Count the leaves of all the trees,
Count the waves of all the seas,"[7]

as to reckon the number of our beloved waters. Yet we have undoubtedly favourites among the wimpling murmurers. Clyde is, of course, the foremost and the best; then there is the tiny Earn, the beautiful brown-tinted Earn, that winsome wanderer by, lonely paths whom we are now about to unveil. Thou too, reader, must be numbered among her admirers, or we shall henceforth have serious doubts of thy taste.

Our first introduction, we may premise, to the Earn was through the inspired writings of Christopher North,[8] some score of years ago. How lovingly the "old man eloquent" babbled of its charms! It was the stream of his boyhood; and the golden light of langsyne flickered round his pen as in memory he delineated its beauties. He was once again the yellow-haired stripling, roving at will among the wild moors – a lonely but happy familiar of bird, and beast, and flower, with insatiate spirit feeding on the beautiful. He had again donned for the first time the sporting jacket, and was treading the plashy brink of the brother loch, or threading the mazes of the amber Earn, waging deadly war with the red-speckled trout. The description was, in truth, steeped in richest poesy, and made such an impression on our youthful imagination, that we determined to make a pilgrimage to the locality for the express purpose of gazing upon the loveliness of what seemed to our mind's eye a species of fairy land. Years passed away, however, and the Earn was still to us a waking dream. *The Course of Time*, which

---

[7] Probably from Rose Lambart Price's very loose translation of Catullus VII.
[8] (1785 – 1854) Penname of the lawyer and critic Professor John Wilson who wrote for *Blackwood's Magazine*.

afterwards fell into our hands, recalled it more vividly to our memory. The author of that noble poem[9] was born in the immediate vicinity of this moorland stream, and spent the happiest portion of his too brief existence "here below" amongst its lonely banks and braes. Again we purposed a ramble amid the scenery which genius had hallowed by the light of its presence; but again time was permitted to slip away, and although we obtained on several occasions a passing glimpse of the Earn, our resolve to spend a long summer day

"Adown its sweet meander"[10]

remained unaccomplished. A friend, who is familiar with every turn and winding of the stream, however, has at length persuaded us to include the vale of the Earn in our series of Rambles, and we have consequently now to request the company of our readers on this our long-proposed and long deferred excursion.

It is a lovely August morning. Phœbus, to use the words of honest Allan Ramsay, has begun

"To speel the Olympian brae
Wi' a cart-lade o' bleezin' day;"[11]

while the yellow fields below reflect untarnished the radiance of his slanting beams. Leaving the city and its smoky atmosphere, how deliciously fresh and cool is the breath of the young autumn as we meet it among the dewy hedge rows! A slight touch of frost lingers in the air, and the beads of evening are still unmelted on the lace-work of the field-spider, which clings to bush and tree. How loudly sounds the horn of chanticleer[12] among the scattered farm steads! how liquid soft the pipings of the robin among the rustling foliage of the birch! Blessings upon thy bright black eye and thy swelling breast of red, sweet songster of the autumn day! The blackbird's golden bill is silent now in the

---

[9] Robert Pollok (1798 – 1827). His very popular *The Course of Time* was published in 1827.
[10] From 'Lines to William Simson' (1785) by Robert Burns.
[11] From *The Gentle Shepherd* (1725)
[12] cockerel

162

woodland glade; the voice of the throstle is mute in the leafy choir, while the lark is heard no more in the far blue vault of heaven, showering his merry music-drops o'er mead and moor; but thou hast still a lay of love for the waning year, "most musical, most melancholy." When the fields are bare, and the barn-yards are crowded; when the plough is at rest, and the stream has ceased to flow; when the glory has departed from the forest, and the storm sweeps pitiless over the flowerless lea, thou art still heard in the fitful pauses of the blast, like hope in the breast of affliction, singing thy notes of solace and of "promised joy."[13] But whence come those jocund voices – those loud-ringing bursts of laughter? From the gladsome harvest field, from amid the fast-falling grain. See, here are the reapers, a merry, motley crew of many-coloured garb, with the waving gold before them, and thick-strewn stooks in lengthening rows behind. Old age and youth side by side are striving here together. That ancient matron with the flannel mutch[14] would scorn to lag behind the blooming buff-capped kimmer[15] on the next rig; yon gray-haired carle, observe, is in advance of the swankie chiel' who calls him neighbour. "There is life in the old dog yet." Cupid, with a reaping-hook instead of his customary bow, is also there. How slyly that swain with the blue plush vest is shearing his way into the affections of the sonsie queen beyond him! The fellow is actually doing half her work, although sorely tantalized for his gallantry by that wicked wag of an Irishman, whose rude jest brings the burning blush to the cheek of the conscious maiden, and sets the field in a roar. But we must end our contemplation of the picturesque group, and move upon our way. We too have a harvest to gather. Passing bonny Cathcart, with its blue smoke curling over the trees, its fine old castle, and its fine new kirk; Clarkston, with its roadside cottages; and Busby, with its hives of industry; we soon arrive at Waterfoot, the lovely meeting-place of Earn and Cart, and the last sweet scene in the former streamlet's devious but withal brief pilgrimage. By the by, while waiting for our friend, who trysted to

---

[13] From 'To a Mouse' (1785) by Robert Burns.
[14] cloth head covering
[15] girl

foregather with us here, we may mention that we have "a craw to pick" with Christopher the Great in regard to this same water of Cart. In his most beautiful article "Our Parish," when talking of the stream which is even now murmuring a welcome to its amber tributary at our feet, he says, "The Cart! – ay, the river Cart – not that on which pretty Paisley stands, but the Black Cart, beloved by us chiefly for sake of Cathcart Castle, which, when a collegian at Glasgow, we visited every play-Friday, and deepened the ivy on its walls with our first sombre dreams."[16] Now, old man (though Heaven bless thee for thy remembrance of the castle of our boyish love), we have here caught thee tripping. This is in truth none other than the veritable White Cart which, far below, and after many a beauteous sweep and playful winding, washes the walls of Paisley's time-honoured town, thy own loved place of birth. That thistle-top, which with our trusty switch we send whizzing into the yeasty foam, will, mill-dam interruptions excepted, most assuredly, ere tomorrow's dawn, dance over the "Hammils"[17] and past the fragrant Sneddon to meet the Black Cart at Inchinnan Bridge.

[Alas! since this article was penned, the "old man eloquent" has gone to that bourne towards which all travellers are tending, and from whence no straggler e'er returns. Peace to his ashes!]

After lingering for a brief space at Waterfoot, gazing on the mingling waters as they gush in music over the shelving rocks, and watching the wagtails flitting in graceful curves from stone to stone, we are greeted with the blythe good morrow and kindly smile of our friend Mr. Pollok,[18] brother of the bard, who has left his haymaking for a day to introduce us with all the honours to his native stream. "Cobbie's isle" first claims our attention. This is an insular patch of land, situated in a fork of the Earn, which flows into the Cart by two channels – one a mill-lade, the other the natural bed of the water. On this tiny isle there is a one-storeyed cottage, which for many years was inhabited by an eccentric old man, a cooper to profession, who had a

---

[16] From *Recreations of Christopher North* (1868).
[17] a waterfall in Paisley
[18] David Pollok, who wrote *Life of Robert Pollok* (1843) about his brother.

pet gander called "Cobbie," which he loved exceedingly. The snow-white bird, indeed, was the pride of the venerable cooper's heart. He loved to see it gliding over the smooth mill-dam with its companion shadow, or breasting the dancing foam-flakes below the rocky linn. Often, in the summer afternoons, would he stand for hours at the end of his cot, gazing upon the evolutions of his feathered favourite, or feeding it from his hand as it floated near the gravelled margin. But "all that's bright must fade," and poor Cobbie went at length the way of all living. The man of hoops and staves was disconsolate, and mourned his bereavement many days. To perpetuate the name of the lost one, however, he conferred its name upon the island of his habitation. The neighbours around, to please the old man, adopted the designation; and now, though years have elapsed since he also passed away, the name of Cobbie still clings to the spot.

Along the flowery margin of the Earn, in a south-westerly direction, we now wend our devious way. With daylight brilliance in the picture, instead of the moon's pale beams, the playful streamlet here realizes, in the minutest feature, Burns's inimitable description,

> "Whiles ower a linn the burnie plays,
>   As through the glen it wimples,
> Whiles round a rocky scaur it strays,
>   Whiles in a well it dimples;
> Whiles glitterin' in the noontide rays,
>   Wi' bickering dancing dazzle,
> Whiles cookin' underneath the braes
>   Below the spreading hazel."[19]

Now it is leaping in whiteness over some channel stone; now it sweeps sullenly 'neath some overhanging cliff, lichened and gray, or velveted with the greenest of moss; and anon it reflects in its glassy bosom some solitary birch or drooping group of saughs.[20] How richly tangled with vegetation is its brink at every sunny turn! The wild rose-bush with its fast reddening hips, the bramble with its tempting bunches of ebon-

---

[19] From 'Halloween' (1786) by Robert Burns.
[20] willows

dye, and the hazel with its clear brown clusters, in bosky luxuriance, are projecting over the steep banks, and form a screen of beauty to the jinking, gurgling, foam-fretted wanderer below. Didst ever see such stately thistles as compose yon hoary-headed group, now flinging their fairy parachutes to the passing breeze? We trow not; – and see, here is Scotland's ain blue-bell, not "lurking lowly unseen,"[21] but trailing with a graceful pride over the brow of yonder precipice in miniature, and side by side with the crimson belts of heather, and the bright golden tufts of the bird-foot trefoil, while the green plume of the bracken hangs sweetly over them, and curtains their loveliness from "the garish eye of day."[22] This is Windmill[23] farm-steading to the left, and you may observe that, compared with the crops we have seen in our own warm vale, the "stuff hereabouts is still unco green." It promises well, however, and we doubt not that yonder now empty barn-yard will see another sight and tell a far other tale some half dozen weeks hence. The district around us is rather of a pastoral than an agricultural character. The spiky wheat is seldom seen here; but it is from these green hills that Glasgow receives her spates of sour dook,[24] her humplucks of rich yellow butter, and her kebbucks innumerable of palatable cheese.

After pursuing for an hour or so "the linked sweetness long drawn out"[25] of the sportive Earn, which in truth does not seem to know its own mind for two consecutive minutes, but keeps turning and winding, now hither, now yont, zig zagging fantastically from right to left, and occasionally even manifesting a decided inclination to retrace its steps, we arrive opposite the farm of Floors, at a picturesque bend where formerly stood the mill of Ross. There is here a fine linn, some ten feet in height, which in bygone days gave motion to the wheel, but which is now singing its eerie tune to the echoes of an unbroken solitude. Of the mill not one stone remains upon another. A few stately

---

[21] From 'Their Groves O'Sweet Myrtle' (1795) by Robert Burns.
[22] From *Alfred* (1815) by Henry James Pye.
[23] Actually Wind-Hill.
[24] buttermilk
[25] From 'L'Allegro' (1645) by John Milton

ash trees, through which the blue smoke from the miller's hearth may have curled long ago, wave drearily over the spot – sole vestiges of what has been. In his boyhood, our friend remembers coming with a "melder"[26] to the miller of Ross, who had a bien and a braw house then:

"Hens on the midden, ducks in the burn were seen,"[27]

while a gaucy[28] gudewife, with a bairn in her arms, graced the door-cheek, and watched with motherly pride a number of wee toddlin' things, with flaxen hair and rosy cheeks, who were tumbling before her on the green. But all is dull and lifeless now. The cheerful din of the happer is heard no more; the loud laugh of the jolly miller, the prattle of playful children, and the crowing of the household cock, all, all are now silent. Nature has resumed her peaceful sway. The rank nettle waves on the site of cheery but-and-ben, and the solitary hare may kittle undisturbed on the cold hearth-stone.

We are now in the immediate vicinity of the ancient castle of Mearns, and for a brief space must turn aside from the Earn to visit the time-honoured edifice. A few minutes' uphill walk brings us to Auldtoun Farm, where we are welcomed with a delicious bowl of cold milk, and are introduced by our friend to the farmer's niece, Katie Pollok, a bonnie bit sonsie Scotch lassie, dressed becomingly in shortgown and coat. Katie we soon discover to be fond of flowers, and enthusiastically in love with the auld tower. After showing us her pansies, which she denominates "step-mothers and daughters," a goodly show, we proceed to the castle-hill, accompanied by a sagacious collie,

"Whase gaucy tail, wi' upward curl,
Hings ower his hurdies wi' a swirl."[29]

---

[26] a portion of corn for grinding
[27] From *The Gentle Shepherd* (1725) by Allan Ramsay.
[28] Healthy-looking
[29] From 'The Twa Dogs' (1786) by Robert Burns.

The Castle of Mearns is situated on the summit of a commanding knoll, the steep and somewhat rugged sides of which are densely covered with wood. The structure consists of a strong quadrangular tower, the walls of which are from seven to eight feet in thickness, and are pierced at irregular intervals by windows and loopholes. In former times this sturdy keep, which is still in an excellent state of preservation, was surrounded by a thick wall, which has now disappeared, with the exception of a few vestiges of the foundation.[30] There are also traces of an ancient drawbridge. But little is known of the origin or history of Mearns Castle. According to tradition it was erected at an early period by a chief of Mearns, named Johnston, whose residence previously was on a less elevated position in the neighbourhood. Being disturbed one morning while at breakfast by a party of his enemies, Johnston, who seems to have been too partial to a quiet meal for that rude age, resolved to build a place of strength wherein he could enjoy himself without fear of his foes. The present edifice was the result; but it is said that its erection cost the chief so many slices of his barony that, when it was finished, he had scarcely wherewithal to purchase a breakfast. In the pithy words of Katie Pollok, "for sake o' his guts he had e'en biggit himsel' oot at the door." The first authentic circumstance regarding the Mearns Castle which occurs in history, was its transfer by marriage, with an heiress who bore the surname of Macgeachin, to the Maxwells of Carlaverock, in the reign of Alexander the Second.[31] After remaining for several centuries in the family of Maxwell, it was ultimately sold by the Earl of Nithsdale about the year 1648 to Sir George Maxwell of Nether Pollok, from whom it shortly afterwards passed into the possession of Sir Archibald Stewart of Blackhall, whose descendant, Sir Michael Shaw Stewart,[32] is the present proprietor.

The interior of the edifice, which is still in good preservation, has in recent times been the scene of more than one festive assemblage. The members of the Mearns troop of Yeomanry cavalry, previous to

---

[30] The tower survives but now forms part of Maxwell Mearns Castle church.
[31] Reigned 1214 – 1249.
[32] 1826 – 1903. He was the seventh baronet and a Conservative MP.

their disembodiment, held several of their annual balls within the precincts of the ancient hall, when the rank and beauty of the district graced it with their presence. For a number of years past, however, it has been entirely deserted, the doors and windows having been securely blocked up, while the minister of the parish has been entrusted with the keys. Under these circumstances we might have found some difficulty in effecting an entrance, but for an event which, to the serious injury of the castle, had occurred a short time previous to our visit. The fortalice,[33] during a late thunder-storm, was actually struck with a shaft from heaven, which effectually demolished the barricades in the windows, and thus cleared a passage which affords free ingress. A flag-staff on the summit had apparently attracted the electric fluid, which, in its passage to the earth, caused a large rent in the wall from top to bottom, and, with the force of the concussion, drove the window-boards out with such force that some of the splinters were afterwards found at a distance of many yards. We now make our way into the hall without leave of the minister, for which his reverence, we dare say, will readily excuse us. It is a spacious apartment, of somewhat modern aspect, having been replastered and otherwise altered, apparently to render it more suitable for ball-room purposes. Descending by a narrow staircase, we next enter a dark vaulted chamber underneath, the gloom of which is only rendered visible by the scanty radiance admitted by a narrow loop-hole in the thick wall. This was probably the prison or dungeon of the establishment in "the brave days of old" when mercy to a vanquished foe was a virtue somewhat sparingly exercised. Our fair friend, Katie, seems rather unwilling to enter this dreary den, and on our asking the reason of her reluctance, says – "I dinna ken, but folk say it's no a canny place. I've never seen onything ill in't mysel; but some tinkler bodies that took up their lodgings in the ha' abune got sic a fricht wi' something doon here that they were fain to take French leave, and never durst venture back again. So I think we'll be jist as weel to slip awa' up the stairs." Taking Katie's advice, we now ascend to the battlements of the tower, from which we obtain a splendid prospect of the surrounding country. To the south are the

---

[33] outwork of the fortification

dreary moors of Eaglesham, swelling gradually upwards to Ballygeich, and fretted with numerous flocks and herds. Westward, amidst a very sea of verdant knolls, clumps of wood, and yellow fields are Mearns Kirk and the Newton, with Dod Hill and Neilston Pad in the distance. To the north and east is the great valley of the Clyde, studded with towns, villages, and mansions, while the Renfrewshire, Kilpatrick, and Campsie hills rise proudly beyond, and the blue mountains of the Gael are faintly visible on the misty horizon. Beautiful, indeed, is the wavy bosom of the Mearns, as it lies outspread before us in the warm sunshine of the autumn noon. Merry groups are busy in the fields, and the blue smoke curling over cottage and hall gives pleasant indication of happy hearths. Yonder, observe, is the fine old baronial house of Nether Pollok; there again is Broomhouse, with its green lawn and shadowy trees; while here is the manse of Mearns,[34] half hidden among foliage – the home of Christopher North's boyhood. Could you fancy a more appropriate place for the nurture of a youthful poet? Over these sunny braes ran the yellow-haired boy, gathering insensibly the rich stores of natural imagery with which he has since delighted the world. Where we are now sitting he has sat; and often, in his dreams of day or night, would the features of the landscape on which we are now gazing in rapture flit across the inward eye of that eloquent old man,

> "For there's no place half so sweet on earth,
> As the home of life's young day."[35]

"From morning sun till dine"[36] we could linger in truth on this venerable tower, companion of the wall-flower which nods at our feet to the passing gale, and monarch of the wide realm of beauty which we survey; but the day is wearing on apace, and we have still many

---

[34] This manse had been built on the site of the one in which 'Christopher North' spent his childhood.

[35] Possibly a misquote of 'Jeanie Morrison' (18) by William Motherwell:
"I 've wandered east, I 've wandered west,
> Through mony a weary way;
> But never, never can forget
> The luve o' life's young day!"

[36] From 'Auld Lang Syne' (1788) by Robert Burns.

links of the Earn to unravel ere our darg[37] is done. So, fair Kate, we must descend to Collie, who is waiting patiently for us behind the stile. What a delicious spring we have here under the trees – clear as the glittering crystal, and cool as December's ice! Doubtless thou hast arranged thy snood in this unwrinkled mirror ere now, Kate, as the flowers even now are doing. That drooping foxglove seems to admire its own fair image exceedingly, and stoops as if it fain would kiss the purpled water. It is a pleasing floral illustration indeed of the old song,

> "Keek into the draw-well, Janet, Janet,
> There thou'lt see thy bonnie sel',
> My jo, Janet."[38]

Bidding Katie a kind farewell, we now return to the margin of the Earn. For some distance above Ross mill, the course of the stream is somewhat tame. It still keeps turning and winding playfully; but the banks are less bold, and the channel is less frequently interrupted by those shelving rocks which prevail farther down. Now and then we meet with a murmuring rapid, however, where the angler might linger with a fair hope of tempting the speckled trout to rise to the treacherous fly. The sand-lark loves these gravelly shallows, and as we move along it keeps fluttering before us with its querulous cry of "kee-lee-leep," from which it has received its common Scottish name. Vegetation is gradually becoming less dense as we advance into the breast of the moor. The iris and the meadow-sweet still accompany us, however, with the "leddie's thistle"[39] and a rich variety of tall grasses, which wave gracefully to and fro with every breath of zephyr. Occasionally a field of oats steals down almost to the edge of the water, "a' fading green and yellow," and every now and then the potato ridges intercept our path with their crowns of mingled shaw and bloom. Few and far between we meet a tuft of saugh, a stunted hazel, or a scraggy mountain ash devoid of berries. Yet there is a pleasing appearance of coming plenty on the neighbouring braes and round the cosie-looking

---

[37] day's work
[38] Traditional song dating to the seventeenth century.
[39] milk thistle

farmsteads. The golden feet of autumn indeed are visibly advancing o'er the rustling grain; and are not her blushes beginning to be obvious on the cheek of the apple? Well, indeed might our friend, the author of "Wee Willie Winkie," exclaim – were he now by our side, as we could almost wish for his own sake he were –

> "O hairst-time's like a lippen cup
>   That's gien wi' furthy glee;
> The fields are rich wi' yellow corn
>   Red apples bow the tree;
> The genty air, sae leddy like,
>   Has on a scented gown;
> And wi' an airy string she leads
>   The thistle-seed balloon."[40]

Passing "Humbie Brig," and the fine farm of Titwood, we soon arrive at the bleachwork of Hazelden, where we cross to the south or Eaglesham side of the Earn. A few minutes' walk farther, during which we pass Hazelden Head, Hazelden Mains, and various other places with Hazelden prefixes, brings us to the lands of North Moorhouse, the birth-place of Robert Pollok,[41] the gifted author of *The Course of Time*. The banks of the stream are here of the most beautiful description. On either side they rise, in softest verdure, to a considerable height in natural terraces, some of which are scooped out into smooth green dells, with a regularity of outline which seems to be rather the production of art than of nature. This indentation, carpeted with horsetail, which is known by the name of "Chaumer Braes," looks as if it had been designed for a Covenanting place of worship. How beautifully adapted it is to be the local habitation of such a group as the pencil of Harvey can so well delineate![42] Or might it not rather be a meeting-place for the moonlight fairies, a fit spot for Oberon and Titania to hold their mimic court? The thick-coming fancies of a Noel

---

[40] From 'Hairst' [harvest] (c.1842) by William Miller.
[41] 1798 – 1827
[42] Sir George Harvey (1806 – 1876), Scottish artist best known for religious scenes, who was the brother of the Baillie Alexander Harvey mentioned on p7.

Paton[43] could not, I ween, be introduced on a more appropriately decorated stage. Here the youthful poet spent his early days. When a wee, wee boy, our companion, his elder brother, has often taken him to these green and lonely braes for company when watching his father's kine. Together they have paidled in the stream which murmurs even now as sweetly as in other days at our feet; together they have gathered the wild flowers, which then, even as now, adorned each sunny nook; and who can doubt that the scenery of this very spot mingled in the heaven of his imagination, afterwards so beautifully depicted in the great poem which has become even as a household word in the religious homes of his country! Like Robert Nicoll, another true poet of the hillside, he might well have said,

> "I thought the little burnie ran,
>> And sang the while to me;
> To glad me, towers came on the earth,
>> And leaves upon the tree;
> And heather on the moorlands grew,
>> And tarns in glens did lie.
> Of beauteous things like these I dream'd,
>> When I was herdin' kye."[44]

But let us turn aside to yonder knoll, to visit the poet's favourite gowk (*Anglice*, cuckoo) stone. This was a ponderous mass of granite, whereon it was observed the cuckoo, on its annual migrations to the vale, loved to sit and pipe its cheery but monotonous song. Here it was first seen in the early summer by the neighbouring peasantry, and here, when the "pea puts on its bloom,"[45] it chanted its well strain. Alas! alas! it is rent and shivered now. We were not destined to witness it in its entirety. Two short weeks since a bolt from on high alighted upon the gowk stone, and shattered it fearfully. Several massive fragments still mark the spot, but a considerable portion has been scattered, like

---

[43] Joseph Noel Paton (1821 – 1901), artist and poet who was particularly interested in folklore.
[44] 'Youth's Dreams' (1835)
[45] From 'To the Cuckoo' (1770) by John Logan.

chaff to the winds, by the resistless stroke of the lightning. 'Tis a "sorry sight" to our companion, who loved the stone for its association with memories of sweet langsyne; and we sympathizingly assist him to gather the debris into its place, that the gowk in future springs may still continue to haunt the spot.

Resuming our walk by the Earn we encounter two votaries of the "gentle art," earnestly lashing the rippled bosom of the stream. "Well, what luck have ye had to-day, lads?" was our inquiry, after the usual compliments had passed. "Oh, jist middlin'," was the reply of the foremost disciple of old Izaak;[46] "the water's ower clear an' the licht ower strong the day for the burn-trout." "We've had a rise or twa, though," interposed the other, "and I daursay, if we had twa-three worms, we micht dae no that ill yet." Patience and hope are indeed necessary mental qualifications for successful angling. The weather, somehow or other, is almost always adverse to the sport – at least if we are entitled to form an opinion from the answers, evasive or apologetical, which we have invariably received from the numerous piscators encountered in our walks. A well-filled creel is a thing we have seldom or never seen. Yet hear the burn-side Munchausens[47] over their toddy, and miraculous indeed are the draughts which they have one and all brought home! Well, well, it is doubtless a harmless hobby; but how we have enjoyed the quiet meaning smile which has played over a conscious matron's features the while her lord and master was triumphantly recounting the number and weight of his finny captures!

Immediately after taking leave of the anglers, which we do with the expression of a hope that their sport may prove better farther down, we pass a little ford where the Moorhouse people are in the habit of crossing the stream when making a "short cut" to the village of Mearns. Many a time and oft the future poet has "buckled his breeks" and forded the Earn at this spot, when on his way to school at the Kirktoun. Here, also, it was that, in company with a cousin of his own,

<hr>

[46] Izaak Walton (1593 – 1683), author of *The Compleat Angler*.
[47] Baron Munchausen, fictional character known for his tall tales. From Rudolph Erich Raspe's *Baron Munchausen's Narrative of his Marvellous Travels and Campaigns in Russia* (1785).

he concocted a notable scheme for out witting honest "uncle Andrew," the particulars of which, as they exhibit the quiet humour of the youth, we may as well narrate. Andrew Pollok, a brother of the poet's father, and then, as now, tenant of North Moorhouse, had been troubled, it appears, for some time with a pain in his back, and, complaining of it, was advised by some of the neighbours to take the doctor's breath on the subject. Outdoor wark, as it so happened, was geyan thrang at the time, and it was not convenient for the gudeman to go over to Mearns in person. As young Robin Pollok and his cousin went daily to school at the village, however, it was settled that they should call on the medico, and get something from him to rub the place affected with the painful symptoms. Accordingly, having received their instructions and a small phial to bring the desired lotion, the two boys set out for school. Lingering at the ford, however, a notion struck the young poet (who, by the by, had then no love for doctors or their stuffs), that were they to fill the phial with the amber-coloured water of the Earn, it would not only save them the trouble of going out of their usual course, but would perhaps be as effectual a cure to uncle Andrew's back as anything in the shop of the village Esculapius.[48] On submitting the project to his equally mischievous cousin, he of course declared it excellent, and at once agreed that it should be put in practice. On returning from school, accordingly, the phial was filled, and carefully corked, after which it was placed in the hands of the expectant patient. "An' what did the doctor say, callants, when he gied ye this?" quoth the unsuspecting uncle. "Oh, he jist said ye were to keep your back close to the fire, and get the balsam weel rubbit in till't," was the unhesitating reply. The prescription was immediately applied; and whether from the effects of imagination, or, as is more probable, from those of the heat and friction combined, uncle Andrew at once declared that he felt considerably relieved. The mischievous urchins, who had been gravely watching the operation, no sooner heard this, however, than with a glance at each other they both burst into an uncontrollable fit of laughter, and made with all speed for the door. Suspicion being aroused by these circumstances, an examination of the contents of the phial was

---

[48] Greco-Roman god of healing

instituted, when the trick was discovered. "Wait till I catch the young scoondrels," says uncle Andrew, who started up in wrath; "Lod, I'll thraw their necks for daurin' to mak' game o' me." They were of course wise enough to keep out of his reach while the anger continued, and, as his back was really the better of the operation it had undergone, his temper was soon mollified, and the "twa Rabs" were again admitted to the old man's good graces.

Proceeding onward, we shortly afterwards arrive at the embouchure of the Langlee burn, a tributary of the Earn. At Logan's Well, a short distance farther west, the stream whose course we have been pursuing divides into Blackloch burn and Floak burn, its two principal sources, and loses its distinctive name. We are now at the head of the vale, and in the very heart of the Mearns Moor. Around us, on every side, a dreary expanse of brown heathy hills and dark morasses stretches away to the horizon. Here and there a few comparatively fertile spots enliven the waste; each with a cluster of ash trees, and a little wreath of blue smoke marking the sites of the thin strewn pastoral farms. Yet there is a peculiar beauty in the wild landscape, all bleak and dreary as it is. Ascending the heights of North Langlee, a quiet secluded farm, the peeseweep[49] flutters round our head with its plaintive cry, and the snipe starts from our path on its tortuous flight; while at our feet we have the meeting of the various waters which form the lovely Earn. The Black Loch, the Floak, the Lochcraig, the Wintry Wells, and the Langlee Burns, within the compass of a few acres, are seen turning and twining, each in its own little vale, as they severally hasten to the congregated stream in which they are so soon to lose their individual existence. "Frae a'the airts the wind can blaw"[50] they seem to gush to this lovely tryst; and, as we gaze upon their rippled links, all glittering in the light of the bright autumn sun, there is a pleasing harmony in the music of their many waters. The age of kelpies is past, we fear; but were it not so, we should almost expect to find one of these water-demons lurking among the plashy

---

[49] lapwing

[50] That is, from all the points of the compass. From 'Of A' The Airts The Wind Can Blaw' (1788) by Robert Burns.

nooks below our present position. If Dr. Jamieson's description of the water-kelpie is true, however, we can very well dispense with his presence. Just fancy such a monster as the following lines depict coming up that green dell:

"He rushes bare, and seggs for hair
　　Whaur ramper-eels entwined;
Of filthy gar his eebroos war,
　　Wi' esks and horsegeils lined.

"And for his een wi' dowie sheen,
　　Twa huge horse-mussels glared;
From his wide mou a torrent flew,
　　And soop't his reedy beard.

"Twa slauky stanes were his spule banes,
　　His brisket braid a whin;
Ilk rib sa bare a skelvie skair,
　　Ilk arm a monstrous fin.

"He frae the wame a fish became,
　　Wi' shells a' covered ower :
And for his tail the grisly whale
　　Could never match its power."[51]

A gruesome tyke, indeed, the kelpie must have been. At Benan Linn, where we now turn, however, we meet nothing so dreadful. A delicious little picture it is, with its foamy fall of ten feet or so, its deep dark pool below, and its fine bosky banks. Our friend says it is just a Fall of Foyers[52] in miniature – a statement which we can neither controvert nor affirm, as we have never seen that most romantic of Highland cascades. But see! there is the water-ousel, disturbed by our presence, flitting away down the stream. A lonely and a lovely little bird it is, haunting such scenes as this, and seldom seen but by

---

[51] 'The Water Kelpie' (1803) by John Jamieson.
[52] On Loch Ness.

"untrodden ways."[53] Oh that we had the pencil of a Harvey, that we might delineate this picturesque nook, and bear a reflex of its quiet loveliness to our city home! This may not be, however, and wherefore should we repine? It is already engraven ineffaceably on our memory, and amidst the haunts of men and the withering cares of life, it will be to us a solace and a joy; for true it is that

"A thing of beauty is a joy for ever."[54]

Turning eastward, and passing the North and South Langlees, a brief walk brings us to South Moorhouse, the residence during youth and the greater portion of the brief period of manhood allotted to him on earth, of Robert Pollok. It is an ordinary farm-steading, no way distinguishable in appearance from the other establishments of a similar nature scattered over the moor. The buildings are plain, one-storeyed edifices, and consist of the usual "but-and-ben" for the accommodation of the farmer's family, with barns, byres, milkhouses, &c. To the west of the house is a garden, screened on three sides by a belt of trees, all planted, we understand, by the poet's father, with the exception of three tall ashes, which, with an elm unfortunately blown down some years since, have stood there from time immemorial. To these the poet in his great work makes affectionate allusion, in the following lines:

> "Four trees I pass not by,
> Which o'er our house their evening shadow threw;
> Three ash, and one of elm. Tall trees they were,
> And old, and had been old a century
> Before my day. None living could say aught
> About their youth; but they were goodly trees;
> And oft I wonder'd, as I sat and thought
> Beneath their summer shade, or in the night
> Of winter heard the spirits of the wind
> Growling among their boughs—how they had grown

---

[53] From 'She Dwelt Among the Untrodden Ways' (1800) by William Wordsworth.
[54] From 'Endymion' (1818) by John Keats.

No. IX. The Earn, Mearns Castle, and Moorhouse

So high in such a rough tempestuous place;
And when a hapless branch, torn by the blast,
Fell down, I mourn'd as if a friend had fallen."[55]

It was at South Moorhouse that *The Course of Time* was written; and on expressing a desire to see the room in which the poet sat when engaged in the work of composition, we are considerably shocked on being shown into a place now occupied as a stable. This in former times was the "spence;"[56] but on a strange tenant coming to the farm, some seven or eight years ago, he took up his residence in another part of the establishment, and turned his horses into what had previously been the haunt of the Muses. This is really too bad and most certainly evinces a sad deficiency of taste somewhere. Surely such a spot, hallowed as it is by the most interesting associations, might well have been devoted to nobler uses. Every season the fame of Pollok attracts numerous visitors to Moorhouse; and there is something absolutely humiliating in the idea that the very scene which is perhaps most intimately associated with his memory should be thus degraded. We nevertheless linger for a considerable time within the precincts of the apartment, picturing to ourselves the pale student over the midnight oil, giving "a local habitation and a name"[57] to the bright forms which his teeming imagination so abundantly bodied forth. In this corner stood the little table on which he wrote, and which had to be altered to suit his sore breast, for even then death was wrestling with him. Often during progress of the work he required to pause from sheer fatigue or bodily weakness, when with a sigh he would gaze out of this little window on the silent hills, or take a short walk to a neighbouring height, to inhale the free winds as they came fresh and cool from the bosom of his beloved Earn. Alas! his was a melancholy fate. In the hour of hope, when fortune was just beginning to smile upon his prospects, he was stricken down. In the same year he was ordained to the ministry, published his great poem, and died.[58] The completion of

---

[55] From *The Course of Time* (1827) by Robert Pollok.
[56] parlour
[57] From Shakespeare's *Midsummer Night's Dream* V.i.
[58] 1827

his work was indeed the signal of his departure. We may mention that some kind hand has planted an ivy at the door of the poet's study, and that it is creeping with its green leaves over the lowly wall. We pull a sprig from it as a memorial of our visit, on taking leave of the spot.

From the braes in the vicinity of South Moorhouse an extensive and beautiful prospect of the country for many miles around is obtained. One commanding height, called the Head of the Moyle, brings at a glance the whole course of the Earn, from Waterfoot to Logan's Well, before the spectator's eye, with North Moorhouse, the poet's birthplace, and South Moorhouse, the residence of his early years. Here it was proposed to erect a monument to his memory, and certainly a more appropriate site could not have been selected for the purpose. We trust, for the honour of Scotland, that the scheme may be yet accomplished.[59] After lingering here for some time, we visit North Moorhouse, the scene of the poet's birth. It is situated on an eminence which slopes beautifully downwards to the margin of the Earn. It is a low thatched edifice, resembling considerably the "auld clay biggin'" on the banks of Doon, where Burns made his *entrée* into the light of this nether world.[60] The farm consists of about 100 acres, and was rented by the poet's father from the Earl of Eglinton. Robert Pollok was born here in 1798. On our arrival at the door we are warmly received by a couple of sagacious collies, who are evidently not much accustomed to the visitations of strangers, and are consequently exceedingly desirous of making an acquaintance with our nether extremities. We keep them at bay, however, with the aid of our trusty hazel, until a young female makes her appearance from the interior, when we are speedily relieved from their boisterous attentions, and at once invited to "come ben." The picture that presents itself to our gaze on entering would delight a Landseer.[61] The apartment is a perfect model of the cosie auld warld Scottish farmer's ha'. A large fire-place projects from the wall, over which is suspended an immense cauldron

---

[59] A monument to Robert Pollok was eventually erected at the junction of Ayr Road and Old Mearns Road in 1900, and still stands there.
[60] North Moorhouse was rebuilt with two storeys and a slate roof.
[61] Edwin Landseer (1802 – 1873), painter known for his paintings of animals.

simmering on a blazing peat-fire. Around the sides and against the rafters are hung fowling-pieces, fishing-rods, and a variety of agricultural implements; while tables and chairs of venerable fashion are scattered in picturesque confusion athwart the floor. Our friends the collies – their passion having rapidly subsided – are already disposing themselves in attitudes of gracefulness and ease in their accustomed nooks beside the ingle, while a sedate cat is composedly washing her face in the winnock bole.[62] On explaining our errand, we are civilly requested by the girl to step into the spence, where we are shown the "very bedstead" in which the poet was born. The chamber has been but little altered since the event which gave to Scotland another child of song. We need scarcely say that we inspect the place with feelings of no ordinary description. Pollok's *Tales of the Covenanters*[63] were among our earliest Sabbath school prizes, and their perusal was to us a source of deep and tearful interest. *The Course of Time* in after years, despite its gloomier features, we read with anything but a limited degree of admiration; while the sad fate of the bard, struck down in the very noon of hope, and long ere the noon of life, lends a tragic hue to his memory which but the more endears it to our heart. Yet somehow we cannot associate the bard with the humble apartment of his nativity. It is too "cabined, cribbed, confined;"[64] and our fancy keeps wandering away to the realms beyond the *Course of Time* which he has so powerfully and vividly described, and in which alone his imagination had "ample scope and verge enough"[65] for its due exercise. Pollok died of consumption at Millbrook, Southampton, in the twenty-ninth year of his age.[66] He was buried at the locality where he died, and the place which knew him once shall know him no more for ever, although for his sake it will long be visited and venerated by the pensive rambler.

---

[62] window ledge

[63] 'Helen of the Glen', 'The Persecuted Family' and 'Ralph Gemmell', published anonymously in the 1820s then released as a collection after Pollok's death.

[64] From Shakespeare's *Macbeth* III.iv.

[65] From 'The Bard' (1757) by Thomas Gray.

[66] A granite memorial obelisk to Robert Pollok stands in the grounds of Holy Trinity church, Millbrook.

Leaving Moorhouse we cross the Earn, and proceed to Hazeldenhead, the residence of our obliging friend, Mr. Pollok, where we are indeed most hospitably received by his good lady, and where, after our devious pilgrimage, we certainly do ample justice to the good things set before us. The sun is setting in the ruddy west before we tear ourselves away, but a lippin' "doch-an-dhoris"[67] from the hand of our kindly hostess sends us lightly on our homeward path; and passing by the fine hamlet of Mearns Kirk to Clarkston and Cathcart, we arrive within the smoky precincts of the city just as the stars are beginning to twinkle over the darkening world below.

---

[67] a trusty parting drink

"Now westlin' winds and slaughtering guns
Bring Autumn's pleasant weather,
The muircock springs on whirring wings
Amang the blooming heather;
Now waving grain wide o'er the plain
Delights the weary farmer,
And the moon shines bright, as I rove at night
To muse upon my charmer." – Burns.[1]

How rapid are the steps of the year, and how marked with change! Every footfall is on a new flower, every succeeding glance is greeted with a fresh mutation of scene. Gray Winter unfolds his mantle of gloom, and forth cometh with sunshine and song the gentle young Spring. April and May, her lovely handmaidens, with leaves and flowers adorn the earth, and pass away; while June, the golden-sceptred, stalks athwart the gowany meads and the waving brairds, to be followed in turn by the eldest born of Summer, rosy July, with his burning radiance bleaching the new-mown hay, and bringing the rich russet hue of ripeness to the whispering grain. Next cometh August, a mature and stately matron, bidding us "lift up our eyes and behold how the fields are already white unto the harvest."[2] September, full-handed and crowned with mellowing fruits, treads close upon her heels, to give place in turn unto the wild October, with his "coat of many colours,"[3] which "chill November's surly blast"[4] rends pitilessly from his shoulders, leaving pale nature once more drapeless and cold in the stern embrace of the Frost King. Another circle is completed, another span of our allotted pilgrimage is meted out unto us; and, looking

[1] 'Song Composed in Autumn' (1783).
[2] John 4.35
[3] From the story of Joseph, Genesis 37.3.
[4] From 'Man Was Made to Mourn' (1784) by Robert Burns.

mournfully back on the days we have wasted or misspent, we ask in weary bitterness of heart, "Is another of our years really dead?"

There are few localities in the vicinity of our city which will more abundantly repay a visit from the rambler than the vale of the Levern and the adjacent country. If our readers have any doubts of the fact, let them favour us with their company this beautiful autumnal day, and we are mistaken if, at its close, they are not effectually removed. Let us be supposed then as starting on our way to the terminus of the Glasgow and Barrhead Railway. The train is in waiting, the engine in harness, giving an impatient snort now and then, as if eager for the journey, while the guards and other officials are running to and fro as if they had an overwhelming amount of business on hand, and were afraid they would never be able to accomplish it before the ringing of the decisive "third bell." It is all make-believe, however; passengers come slowly in, and one can see at a glance that the fellows *could* easily, and we doubt not *would* willingly, manage double the traffic that passes along this quiet yet beautiful and well-managed little line. The "last man," who comes in puffing and blowing at a furious rate, having at length taken his seat and commenced wiping his reeking and high-coloured visage, there is a slamming of doors, a cry of "all right," a shrill whistle, and we are rushing away as if on the wings of the wind, among the dewy fields. We speedily pass Strathbungo, Camphill, Crossmyloof, and the wood-crowned heights of Langside. Haggs Castle, dreary even in the level radiance of morning, goes flitting past, frowning amidst its encircling trees on the surrounding landscape.

Passing Pollokshaws and the wide-spreading policies of Sir John,[5] the country opens finely to our view, presenting a gently undulating surface, covered with luxuriant crops, and studded with gentlemen's seats and comfortable farm steadings, with here and there a tall chimney peering up amidst the verdant fields, and indicating that the riches of the country are not confined to its surface. Leaving Kinnishead,[6] where the train rests a few moments, and looking

---

[5] Sir John Maxwell, 8th Baronet (1791 – 1865). See chapter VII.
[6] Kennishead

westward, we obtain a view of "Crookston Castle's ruined wa',"[7] towering in the distance, and calling to remembrance the story of Scotia's fair ill-fated queen, the beautiful Mary of many sorrows.[8] Ere we have time to heave a sigh, however, over the sad associations of the scene, the unsympathizing and most unsentimental engine whirls us past the red hills of the Hurlet, amid sights and scents unholy, past Nitshill, with its quarries, coal-pits, and belching volumes of smoke, and about half-an-hour after starting, deposits us safely at Grahamstone, a clean and tidy-looking suburb of Barrhead, nestling finely at the base of the Fereneze Braes, and overlooking a picturesque sweep of the murmuring Levern.

The village of Barrhead is entirely of modern origin, having sprung into existence subsequently to, and in a great measure in consequence of, the establishment of manufactures on the Levern. Within the memory of persons still living there was scarcely a single house on the site of this now extensive and thriving community. The first printfield was erected at Fereneze in 1773; the first bleachfield about the same time; and the first cotton mill (which was also the second in Scotland) at Dovecothall in 1780. Since that period the public works have gradually increased in number, until now the Levern and several tributary streamlets are beaded, as it were, with industrial establishments. No other water in Scotland of anything like equal dimensions, we verily believe, contributes nearly so much to the manufacturing prosperity of the country, as does the Levern in its short course of some six or seven miles. A sadly tortured streamlet it is, in truth. What with dams, and lades, mill-wheels and colouring matters of every hue, with which its bosom is fretted and stained at every turn, it has really a pitiable common-sewer aspect by the time it gets sneaking into the Cart beyond Crookston. Its pollution, however, is associated with the prosperity of the Barrhead people. Their print fields, factories, and bleachfields, are dependent on its originally

---

[7] From 'Crookston Castle's Lanely Wa's' (1808) by Robert Tannahill.
[8] See p211 ff.

pellucid waters, and without them their "decline and fall"[9] would speedily be consummated. Long, therefore, may it continue a willing and useful drudge! Lackadaisical poets may whine over the decay of sentiment, and puling painters maunder about the destruction of the beautiful; but to our mind the most interesting of streams is that on the banks of which exists an industrious, a comfortable, and an intelligent population.

Barrhead is composed of a congeries[10] of villages on the south side of the Levern, to which they are all less or more contiguous, and bearing respectively the names of Barrhead, Newton, Ralston, Dovecothall, &c. These divisions are only locally known, however, and indeed, properly speaking, they now form but one united community, and are generally known under the collective name of Barrhead, a designation derived from a certain farm which formed the site of the earliest built houses in the locality. The village consists principally of one street, running from east to west, and about half-a mile in length, with a number of irregular and straggling offshoots. The houses are for the most part plain two storeyed edifices, without the slightest pretensions to architectural elegance. They have generally a snug, comfortable look, however, and in the rear of the majority we were pleased to observe a well-stocked kailyard, with abundance of curly headed greens, and a proportionate quantity of leeks and onions. Many of the shops would not discredit Glasgow or Paisley. There are no fewer than four places of worship in the village – namely, one connected with the Establishment, a Free, and a United Presbyterian, while a Roman Catholic chapel crowns a rising ground in the outskirts. It would seem, therefore, that the spiritual wants of the inhabitants are by no means inadequately provided for. In the matter of seminaries for the instruction of the rising generation, also, the supply, as we understand, is anything but defective. One of these, the Bourock School,[11] a spacious and well-aired apartment, abundantly furnished

---

[9] Reference to *History of the Decline and Fall of the Roman Empire* (1776) by Edward Gibbon.
[10] jumble
[11] Demolished sometime before 1910.

with the means and appliances of juvenile tuition, we visit, and are specially gratified by the aptitude and proficiency manifested by the various classes under the judicious management of our friend, Mr. John Murray, teacher of the establishment. Nor is the machinery for the intellectual improvement of the adult population defective. We observe several shops for the sale of books and periodicals, and we learn that for many years a Mechanics' Institution has maintained a comparatively vigorous and healthy existence in the village. Under the efficient management of a committee composed principally, if not entirely, of intelligent artisans, the institution, by its interesting annual courses of lectures on science and literature, which are generally well attended, must undoubtedly be instrumental in the diffusion of many useful and refining influences among the operatives of this important district. The library of the Levern Mechanics' Institution, a catalogue of which we had lately the pleasure of inspecting, is really one of a highly valuable character. It contains altogether about fifteen hundred volumes in the various departments of literature, science, and art, among which are many of the works of our best modern authors. Among the recent additions we may mention Dr. Wilson's *Prehistoric Annals*,[12] Macaulay's *Essays*,[13] Hanna's *Life of Chalmers*,[14] and Cockburn's *Biography of Jeffrey*.[15] Of a truth we live in a marvellous age. Think of such productions, even as they issue from the press, circulating in the houses of our working men, ye sceptics of human progress! and acknowledge the fallacy of your misgivings. "The world still moves," say we with Galileo of old (though in a different sense), let the misanthrope and the doubter murmur as they may "I have taken note of it," says the royal Dane; "the age is grown so picked, that the toe of the peasant comes so near the heel of the courtier, that he galls his kibe."[16] What would Hamlet have said had he lived in our day!

Of course there are other aspects in which we might look at Barrhead. There are no lack of public-houses of high and low degree

---

[12] *Prehistoric Annals of Scotland* (1851) by Daniel Wilson.
[13] *Critical and Historical Essays* (1850) by Thomas Babington Macaulay.
[14] *Memoirs of the Life and Writings of Thomas Chalmers* (1851) by William Hanna.
[15] *Life of Lord Jeffrey* (1852) by Henry Cockburn.
[16] From Shakespeare's *Hamlet* V.i.

in the village, most of which look as if they did a pretty fair stroke of business. Anything but an encouraging symptom we must admit this to be. Still, the Barrheadians – what a name! – do not seem in this respect to be "ony waur than their neebors." On a Saturday night, of course, there is occasionally a spree; but the strong infusion of pugnacious Irish blood among the population, will easily account for this fact; while the absence of a proper police force leaves riotously inclined parties in a great measure to the freedom of their own will. The navvies, indeed, who are the principal offenders in this respect, and who revel in the Donnybrook[17] license accorded to them, are not unfrequently heard to apostrophize the village affectionately, as "Sweet little Barrhead! where there's never a jail nor police-office."[18] The quiet and orderly inhabitants, however, who fortunately form an overwhelming majority, are doubtless tempted occasionally to wish that they had either a "jail or a police-office" among them, for the purpose of keeping these mischief-loving vagabonds in due subordination. It is said that midnight rows have become much less frequent since the establishment of a Roman Catholic priest in the locality a few years since. If this is really the case, it is but fair that his reverence should receive due credit as a peacemaker. Would that the priestly influences were never directed to the furtherance of less beneficial purposes!

In the vicinity of Barrhead there are a number of handsome mansions, generally surrounded with umbrageous timber, pleasure grounds, and gardens. Among these we may mention Trees, the residence of James M'Culloch, Esq., situated on a gentle declivity of the braes;[19] Fereneze House, the seat of John Graham, Esq. of Fereneze and Craigallion; and Arthurlee House, the seat of William Lowndes, Esq.[20] A little to the eastward of the village, on the north bank of the Levern also, there are the remains of an ancient keep, called "Stewart's

---

[17] free-for-all brawl
[18] A very grand police station was built later in the 19th century. It still stands, although the local police force has now moved to a more modern building.
[19] Now Fereneze Golf Clubhouse.
[20] Now a community centre.

Rais," or more frequently by the inhabitants, "the auld Tower." This relic of antiquity is now in a sadly dilapidated condition, and seems fast hastening to utter destruction. It is quadrangular in form, and the massive walls, which are now shattered and crumbling, have been evidently at one period of great strength. A strong arched roof, which formerly spanned a chamber in the interior, was demolished at no very distant date, along with certain portions of the exterior walls, for the purpose of erecting an edifice in the vicinity. Extremely little is to be learned either from history or tradition concerning this structure. According to Crawfurd,[21] the quaint old historian of Renfrewshire, it formerly belonged to a family named Halrig, a branch of the house of Darnley; and he mentions that he had seen an antique charter, of date 1484, whereby the lands of Halrig and Rais were granted to Alexander Stuart, upon the resignation of his father, Hector Stuart, by John, Lord Darnley and Earl of Lennox. At what period it passed from its former lords we cannot now ascertain; but in recent times it has more than once changed proprietors. None of these parties, however, seem to have taken any special care of the "auld Tower." As the sole relic of bygone days which the village can boast, we should certainly have imagined that parties connected with the locality would feel an interest in its preservation from impending destruction. This does not, we regret to say, appear to be the case, and in all probability, ere many years have elapsed, this ancient home of the haughty Stuarts will be numbered among the things that were.[22]

Leaving Barrhead. in a south-easterly direction, we now proceed towards a curious basaltic hill, called "the Craig of Carnock," situated about a mile and a-half from the village. Our course lies through a pleasant country path, amidst green hedgerows, belts and clumps of planting, and fertile fields, the cereal coverings of which, "a' fading green and yellow"[23] in the rich radiance of an autumnal day, are rustling sweetly in the westlin' breeze. The waysides also are

---

[21] George Crawfurd (1681 – 1748).

[22] The tower finally disappeared in the 1930s, with its remaining stones being used as road-building material.

[23] From 'Song composed in August' (1783) by Robert Burns.

fringed with indigenous bloom – the purple-tufted vetch, the golden bed-straw, and the fragrant meadow-queen – while at intervals the wild raspbushes, adorned with their crimson berries, offer a tempting refreshment to the passing bird, and doubtless attract from time to time the attention of little bare-footed ramblers from the neighbouring. village. The time of roses is past, but the hips and the haws will soon put on their "red, red coats;" the coral beads are even now in clusters on the drooping mountain ash, while the bramble trails over every ditch with its delicious load of fast-purpling fruit. Well does the light-hearted school-boy love the rough stemmed bramble, with its jetty bunches creeping over the waste; and often, in sunny days of yore, have our fingers and lips known the stain of its juicy blobs, when in juvenile raids from the town,

> "The bramble berries were our food,
> The water was our wine,
> And the linnet to the self-same bush
> Came after us to dine.
> And grow it in the woods sae green,
> Or grow it on the brae,
> We like to meet the bramble-bush
> Where'er our footsteps gae."[24]

As we gradually ascend, see how picturesquely varied the surface of the surrounding country becomes. Now we have a gray lichened crag cropping out with its crown of heather and tangled foliage; now we have a little runlet jinking among the seggans, and singing a sweet undersong as it steals down its tiny glen; and anon we have a far-stretching landscape, with yellow slopes, "like golden shields flung down from the sun,"[25] in the foreground, and high towering hills beyond. But now, brown Carnock, like a couchant lion,

---

[24] 'The Bramble' (1841) by Robert Nicoll.
[25] A misquote of 'September 1819' by William Wordsworth. The original reads
"The sylvan slopes with corn-clad fields
Are hung, as if with golden shields,
Bright trophies of the sun!"

appears to our left, and we must turn aside to place our foot upon his head. As we proceed, what dreary, weather-beaten mansion, so desolate looking among its "old ancestral trees,"[26] have we here, rising as if to intercept our farther progress? This is Glanderston House,[27] formerly a seat of the Mures of Caldwell, and still, although for many years deserted by its lords, not unworthy, as you will perceive, of a leisurely inspection. So here, by the grass-grown gate, let us for a few minutes give ourselves pause, while we endeavour to summarize its story.

"In this parish of Neilston," says old Crawfurd, writing in 1710, "is Glanderston, the residence of William Mure, upon a small rivulet, adorned with regular orchards and large meadows, beautified with a great deal of regular and beautiful planting. The house was of an old model, which the present generation thought fit to demolish, and in place of the old one hath raised a pretty house of a new model, with several well-finished apartments." The lands of Glanderston, as we learn from the same authority, were conferred, in 1507, by Matthew, first Earl of Lennox, upon his brother, John Stewart, from the family of whom they passed, by marriage, into the possession of John Mure of Caldwell, who disposed of them to his brother-german,[28] William Mure, in 1554. The house and lands of Glanderston, subsequently to Crawfurd's time, passed into the possession of a gentleman named Wilson,[29] an eccentric personage, of whom tradition still preserves certain rather discreditable memorials. An instance may be narrated. It is said that Mr. Wilson, who was a professed Episcopalian, on first coming to reside on his estate, called his domestic servants together one evening for the purpose of reading prayers according to the formula of the English Church. It is well known that the Scotch peasantry have a peculiarly strong repugnance to prayers which are not of an extemporaneous nature. Accordingly the unusual service was scarcely commenced by the master of the household (who, by the by,

---

[26] From 'The Homes of England' (1827) by Felicia Hemans.
[27] The remains of the house had entirely disappeared before 1910.
[28] That is, full brother.
[29] Probably Alexander Wilson, mid-eighteenth century.

was supposed, uncharitably enough, to be rather the waur o' the wee drap at the time), than certain whisperings and suppressed titterings were heard among the audience. Mr. Wilson, whose temper was anything but apostolic, paused, and with an eye of fire looked around, when of course every face was at once screwed into an expression of the most rigid gravity and demureness. Suppressing his passion at the unseemly interruption, he again proceeded, without audible remark, with his devotions. Before he had uttered half a dozen sentences, however, the smothered laughter broke out more loudly than before. This was too much for the excitable laird. Up he got "like a prophet in drink," as Burns has it, flung the prayer-book to the wall, and casting a withering scowl on the now terrified domestics, burst out into a torrent of profanity, denounced those present as a pack of graceless -- - and declared they might all go to the --- for him, as he would never pray for a single soul of them again. "This unchristian resolution," said our informant, a venerable old dame, "the thochtless cat-witted body stuck till like a bur, and ye may guess that nae gude cam o't. He took sair to the dram, fell into straits, sell't his property to Mr. Speirs o' Ellerslie, whose family ha'e been ever sin syne in the lairdship o't; and it's said," continued our somewhat garrulous authority, "that he afterwards dee't in the Gorbals o' Glasgow, no without folk suspeckin', however, Gude forgi'e us! that he had laid hauns on himsel'."

A century and a-half have not passed without making alterations for the worse on what Crawfurd calls the "pretty house of a new model," and its adjuncts. The edifice is still entire, and with a somewhat auld warld aspect maintains an air of picturesque dignity, with its craw-stepped gables and windows, surmounted with peaked entablatures. Over several of the windows alluded to the date 1697 appears, with the initials T.W. and W.M. elegantly carved in the dark stone. The orchards are no more; but a considerable portion of the fine old trees, including a stately avenue of beech, still adorn the vicinity. Where the rivulet formerly meandered an extensive dam is now formed – not at all, in our opinion, to the disadvantage of the landscape, however much it may have tended to the obliteration of its ancient characteristics.

We may mention, before leaving Glanderston, that the house has got rather a dubious name among the country people around. For some years it was totally uninhabited, at which time it was, in appearance, dreary and desolate in the extreme. Latterly it has been partially occupied by various parties; but it has been rumoured that "strange noises" have been from time to time heard by the residents within its gloomy walls. One nervous lady who resided for some months in the edifice was in the habit of waiting outside in the afternoons, afraid to venture within until accompanied by her husband, in whose presence his ghostship did not, it seems, choose to indulge in any of his noisy pranks. A gamekeeper now resides on the premises, a sworn foe to "vermin and trespassers" of all descriptions. We are not aware whether spirits of mischief belong to either of these classes; but we are inclined to suspect they do, from the fact that not one of them has dared to show his face inside, by night or by day, since the burly individual alluded to has taken up his quarters there.

To the east of Glanderston, and in its immediate neighbourhood is "the Craig of Carnock"[30] – a detached hillock of basaltic formation – presenting a sort of *fac-simile* in miniature of "Arthur's Seat."[31] From certain points of view it has a precisely similar resemblance to a lion crouching preparatory to the fatal spring. Up this romantic eminence we now wend our toilsome way, and in a few minutes reach its commanding summit. Here there is a species of chair or throne, formed by nature in the solid rock, and popularly called the "Queen's Seat," from a tradition that the beauteous Mary on one occasion rested on the spot. Being somewhat "forfoughten"[32] with our speel, we make no stand on the score of ceremony whatever, but plump ourselves right down into the royal resting-place. A regal prospect indeed now greets our gaze. At our feet is an old-fashioned farm-steading, where cattle are finely grouped around the door, and where

---

[30] Now usually known as Duncarnock.
[31] Extinct volcano in Edinburgh.
[32] worn out

"Hens in the midden, ducks in dubs are seen."[33]

Stretching away to the eastward is the undulating expanse of the Mearns, with the parish church and the old tower rising amidst a very sea of wavy knolls. Turning to the north we have the reservoirs of the Gorbals Gravitation Company[34] mapped before us, with Upper Pollok peeping from its girdle of leaves, and far over the smoke of our own good town, the fells of Campsie looking blue in the distance. Barrhead, Neilston, and the vale of Levern, with the sunny Fereneze range, meet our eyes in succession, as we vacate our throne and gradually turn from the westward toward the south. Nor is the summit of the Craig unworthy an attentive inspection. At one place the columns of basalt, projecting from the soil, and strewn in ponderous fragments around, bear a striking resemblance to a Druidical circle. One vast and somewhat regularly formed mass might well seem a rude altar designed for direst sacrifice. The impression that pagan rites may have been celebrated here is somewhat strengthened by the remains of a green embankment, which is evidently of artificial origin, and which may be easily traced for some distance around the spot. Let some of our archæologists visit the Craig by all means, and investigate the matter.

Making our descent by the southern end of the Craig, where, on the steep declivity, there is a perfect stream, as it were, of rocky fragments, confusedly hurled from the impending brow by the decomposing elements, and passing round the margin of the loch-like dam, we now direct our steps through the fields towards Neilston Pad, which, like a vast pillion (whence its name), rises to the horizon before us. Passing Burnside Farm, where the members of the establishment – young and old, collie and all – are busy with their hay-harvest, and where we are regaled with a bowl of cold milk by the gaucy[35] gudewife; and by Muirhead, where we are greeted by the house-dog's honest but rather annoying bark, and along a delicious flower-fringed

---

[33] From *The Gentle Shepherd* (1725) by Allan Ramsay.
[34] A water company set up in 1846 to supply the southside of Glasgow.
[35] healthy-looking

field-path, familiar to our tread in other days, we arrive at the farm-house of Snipes, nestling near the foot of the lofty Pad. At the base of the Pad there is an immense mass of trap,[36] many tons in weight, half-embedded in the soil, and evidently precipitated at some former period from the rugged cliffs above. There is also a similar ponderous fragment beneath the western brow of Carnock. In accordance with that strong tendency to myth-manufacture which exists in the minds of the Scottish peasantry, we have of course a legend regarding the masses of rock alluded to. It is briefly as follows: In those days when there were giants in the land (a period of which chronology unfortunately takes no cognizance), two of these Titanic gentlemen resolved to have a trial of strength. The test agreed upon was "throwing the stone," an exercise at which, being Caledonian giants, they were probably both proficients. Accordingly, one took his stand on Carnock, and raising a huge rock, hurled it with such force that it alighted at the very foot of the Pad, which may be about a mile and a-half distant. This, it must be conceded, was a pretty fair throw, and sufficient to take the shine out of any ordinary opponent. Nothing daunted, however, the other gigantic competitor walked leisurely to the summit of the Pad, and tearing a vast piece from the cliff, poised it for a moment on his upraised arm, and pitched it with such force that it fairly cleared the Craig of Carnock, and fell on the farther side, where it still remains as a weighty testimony of his superior prowess, and a striking proof of the degeneracy into which the people of modern times have fallen.

Leaving the Giant's Stone, we now ascend the Pad by a circuitous path which slopes gradually upwards to the summit, which is about 800 feet above the level of the sea. In form the Pad is a spacious table-land, somewhat quadrangular in shape, with steep precipitous sides, which are partly covered with a dense bosky wood, and partly with a close velvety sward, fretted with projecting crags, and intersected by sheep-walks. From its elevation and its isolated position, the Pad commands a series of delightful prospects. Looking southward we have the bleak expanse of the Mearns Moor, with here

---

[36] Dark igneous rocks such as basalt.

and there a solitary farm-house; while the long loch, treeless and bare, lies glittering among the dreary hills. This lonely moorland loch is the birthplace of the Levern, which is seen meandering in its downward course towards the scene of its labours in the vale below. To the south west, through a fine opening in the hills, the spectator has a wide tract of Ayrshire spread before him, with the Arran mountains and the rock of Ailsa in the distance. The white sails of passing vessels and the dark hulls of stately steamers, with their smoky trails, floating far over the blue waters, are distinctly visible; while to the north and east are seen the villages of Neilston and Barrhead, the town of Paisley, and our own cloud-capp'd city, with the wide basin of the Clyde, bounded by the far mountains of the Highlands. Every change of position, indeed, brings a new picture into view, while each succeeding one seems to surpass its predecessors in variety, grandeur, and loveliness. But pen or pencil would fail to convey even the faintest conception of the landscape-features visible from the Pad, so we must even leave the imagination of the reader to complete the outlines of the sketch we have so imperfectly indicated. But the summit of the Pad has charms of its own, independently of the picturesque. As we linger on the spot we see the timid hare hirplin' past, and the partridges in whirring coveys circling round. The wheat-ear, that beauteous haunter of lonely places, flits before us as we move; and see, among the crimson bells of the heather, now in its prime, the nest of a mosscheeper,[37] with five wee gaping gorlins clad in puddock hair.[38] What a cosie beild is theirs, with its screen of rich red blossoms! The parent bird, with a chirp of maternal anxiety, keeps hovering near, as we hang in pensive admiration over her helpless little ones. Poor thing! thou hast no cause to fear that we will harry thy lowly home. We have seen the day, indeed, when our hand knew not ruth towards the wild bird's treasure, but that was long ago in our thoughtless boyhood. We have since learned mercy in our own bereavement, and we would address thee,

---

[37] meadow pipit
[38] juvenile plumage

lovely little flutterer of the waste, in the words of one who dearly loved such harmless creatures as thou art, –

"I'm truly sorry man's dominion
Has broken nature's social union,
And justifies the ill opinion
    That mak's thee startle
At me, thy poor earth-born companion,
    And fellow-mortal"[39]

So, fare-thee-well, wee birdie! and may neither cruel hawk nor bare-footed urchin invade thy little chamber of bloom. Now we approach a nook

"Where the blaeberries grow
'Mang the bonnie bloomin' heather,"[40]

and we are at once upon our knees. How delicious are the rich ripe blueish-purple berries of this lowly bit bussie, and here we have them in gowpens! Of a truth this is the choicest of our indigenous wild fruits, so pleasant is it both to eye and palate. Many and many a sunny hour have we spent streekit upon the heather, prying among the myrtle like leaves for the purple beads; but never have we found them more abundant than here. Should the linnet come to the self-same bush we are afraid he would dine but sparely. There is still plenty for bird and body, however; so, with deep-dyed lips, we tear ourselves away from the table which we have so opportunely found furnished for our refreshment in the wilderness. The acid juice of the sourock[41] removes the stains incarnadine from lips and fingers; and, nothing kenspeckle, we descend on Neilston.

The village of Neilston is finely situated on the brow of a gentle eminence, overlooking a considerable expanse of country. It is a compact, neat, and withal somewhat old-fashioned little township, with few features calling for special remark. While Barrhead has been

---

[39] From 'To a Mouse' (1785) by Robert Burns.
[40] From 'The Braes o' Balquidder' (1824) by Robert Tannahill.
[41] sorrell

going a-head, Neilston has remained comparatively stationary. The houses are for the most part plain two-storeyed edifices, some of which have evidently stood the tear and wear of many years. There is a considerable number of shops of various descriptions, some of which are large and showy, but the majority have an old world and decidedly village aspect. The church, a handsome edifice with an elegant spire, was erected in 1763, on the site of a more ancient ecclesiastical structure, one of the Gothic windows of which, however, has been preserved, and now forms the principal adornment of its less pretending successor. Since the period of its erection the church has undergone various alterations and repairs, and judging from outward inspection seems to be now in excellent condition.[42] The church-yard is a spacious area, and contains numerous headstones and monumental structures, none of which, however, strike us as being in any way remarkable. On the occasion of a dispute in 1826 between the heritors of the parish and the poorer class of the parishioners on the subject of church accommodation, Dr. Fleming,[43] the late minister, preached for eight successive years, summer and winter, in this church-yard. During this time an expensive and annoying litigation was carried on between the parties, which ultimately terminated, as is generally known, in the virtual success of the minister and the poor of his congregation. The heritors, meanwhile, for the most part attended public worship in a neighbouring dissenting meeting-house, which Dr. Fleming, who was a keen wit, had satirically called "the Jawhole," as being a sort of receptacle for the refuse of his congregation. One Sunday, during the Doctor's open-air services, a goose was thrown over the wall of the church-yard, by one of the discontented heritors, as was not unnaturally supposed. The poor animal on alighting in the crowd set up a loud cry, which at once distracted the attention of the auditory from the discourse of the minister. The Doctor on observing the occurrence paused for a moment, and drawing his fingers over his beard, drily observed, "Poor thing, what a pity it is they did not send

---

[42] This building survives and is still the parish church.
[43] Rev. Alexander Fleming (1769 – 1844) who wrote the Neilston parish chapter of the *New Statistical Account of Scotland* in 1840.

ye down the road to gabble with kindred cattle in the Jawhole; but I daresay," he continued, "it is perhaps as well that when they have not the grace to show their own faces here, they should at least send a suitable proxy."

The origin of the name of Neilston is a favourite subject of speculation, and has been accounted for in various ways by local etymologists. Certain parties derive it from an imaginary general of the Danish monarch Haco, named Neil, who, flying from the fatal field of Largs,[44] was overtaken here and put to death. Over his grave a tumulus, according to the custom of the age, was erected, and called Neilston, from which, according to this theory, the locality ultimately received its name. Others find its origin in a stone erected over a supposed Highland chief, named Neil, who was killed (for the purpose, we suspect) at the battle of Harlaw,[45] in the reign of Malcolm III. Unfortunately for these specious derivations, an ancient document, the "Chartulary of Paisley Abbey," mentions that in 1160, many years before the Danish invasion or the insurrection which was terminated at Harlaw, Robert de Croc of Crocstown, assigns the patronage of "Neilstoun" to the monks of St. Mirren's, on condition that masses should be regularly said for the benefit of his soul. This leaves us still out at sea in our etymological speculations on this momentous question, where we must probably be content to remain, unless we adopt the shamefully simple solution that Neilston may have received its name from some individual rejoicing in the Celtic cognomen of Neil, who may have resided here at some period, and left his name as a legacy to the locality.

Proceeding down hill, in a south-west direction, to the Paisley and Irvine road, and passing Crofthead Mill, and the handsome residence of its proprietor, a few minutes' walk brings us to the ruins of Cowdon Ha', situated on the summit of a steep bank, beneath which, by the side of the high way, the Cowdon Burn rushes murmuring on to its junction with the Levern in the immediate vicinity. "In this parish of Neilston," says old Crawfurd, "lie the lands of Cowdon, which gave

---

[44] Between Norway and Scotland, 2nd October 1263.
[45] Over the Earldom of Ross, 24th July 1411.

the first title of Lord to Sir William Cochran, afterwards Earl of Dundonald. An ancient family of the Spreuls did possess the forementioned lands for many years." From the Spreuls it passed into the possession of the Cochrans, from whom it was ultimately transferred to the Mures of Caldwell, who still retain it. With regard to the origin or history of the mansion, which has now mouldered away to a few crumbling vestiges, we now know almost nothing.[46] The spot is still "beautiful exceedingly," however, with its rows of time-honoured trees, which stand drearily round the decaying walls, like mourners at a death bed. Alas! for the pride of earth – for those who call themselves the lords of the soil, and who strut and fret their little hour of vain glory upon the stage,[47] but who, even like the common herd, must pass away and be heard of no more! Well has the royal bard of Israel said – "Men heap up wealth, yet do not know to whom it will pertain."[48] "A cadet noble family of Darnley," says the late Rev. Dr. Fleming, in describing his parish, "held Arthurlee; Glanderston was possessed by the ancient and highly respectable family of the Mures of Caldwell; Neilstonside was held by a descendant of Sir William Wallace's family of Elderslie; the barony of Side belonged to a cadet of the honourable house of Skelmorlie; Cowdonhall was long possessed by the distinguished family of the Spreuls, and by Sir William Cochran of Dundonald. Not one of all these has now a house in the parish, nor an acre of land in it, saving Lord Glasgow and Colonel Mure. All has changed hands. What a striking lesson! *Sic transit gloria mundi.*"[49]

> "But some must laugh, and some must weep,
> Thus runs the world away." [50]

The Irvine road, along which our course now lies, sweeps through a broad valley, bounded on one side by the Fereneze range,

---

[46] The ruins are still visible in Cowden Glen, near Lochlibo Road.
[47] A quote from Shakespeare's *Macbeth* V.v.
[48] That is, King David. The quotation is from Psalm 39.6.
[49] Thus passes away the glory of the world.
[50] From Shakespeare's *Hamlet* III.ii.

which here turns somewhat abruptly to the south-west, and on the other by a series of detached hills which stretch away towards the Mearns Moor. The scenery is finely varied, and, as we proceed, the heights on either hand gradually approximate, and the landscape assumes a more quiet and secluded aspect. At Shilford toll, which we soon reach, we turn aside, and ascend by a green lane the braes to the right. On attaining a considerable elevation, and moving a short way towards the west, our gaze is arrested in sweet surprise by the prospect of a lovely little lake sleeping in the verdant bosom of the valley we have just left. This is Lochlibo, certainly one of the most picturesque lakes in miniature that our country can boast. It is only sixteen acres in superficial extent, but gazing on its varied beauties, the spectator never dreams of finding fault with its diminutive size. In form it is nearly oval, and being protected on either side by lofty and well-wooded hills, its waters are generally smooth as a mirror, and reflect with delightful effect the dense umbrageous green of the encircling trees. The beauties of Lochlibo seem almost to have turned the head of good William Semple, who, in his work on Renfrewshire,[51] indulges in a description of the locality which can only be paralleled by the celebrated "Groves of Blarney."[52] Listen to his strangely inverted depiction, gentle reader: "The small lake or basin at the east end, which is formed by the gentle current, is surrounded by a number of young planting, and shrubs of various kinds, which separate it from the other parts of nature, and shade in this retreat a kind of silence by solitary paths, which are now and will be long frequented by sentimental visitors, and a safe asylum for the tuneful bird." Other and abler pens than Semple's, however, have attempted to do justice to Lochlibo. The late Dr. Fleming was enthusiastic in its praise, and asserted that it was superior to Rydal, in Cumberland, while Miss Aird[53] has thrown the halo of poesy over its material charms. Lochlibo abounds in perch and pike, while its surface is enlivened with the graceful heron and the wild duck, which, like "the swan on still St. Mary's Lake," as described in the poetry of

---

[51] Semple wrote a 'Continuation of Crawfurd's History of Renfrewshire' (1782).
[52] By Richard Alfred Millikin (1800) – worth looking up for its amusement value.
[53] Marion Paul Aird (1815 – 1888). This poem is found in her *Heart Histories* (1853).

Wordsworth, "floats double duck and shadow."[54] Lugton Water, we may also mention, has its origin here. This lovely stream, in its meandering course, adorns the pleasure grounds of Eglinton, and after passing "the Castle o' Montgomerie,"[55] falls into the Garnock near Kilwinning.

In the immediate vicinity of our present position is Corkindale Law, to which we now proceed, and in a brief space find ourselves located on its verdant summit, which, although not more than 900 feet above the level of the sea, commands a circle of scenery surpassing in extent and beauty anything that we have ever previously witnessed. We have had our foot on the brow of Benlomond, on the rugged crest of Goatfell,[56] and on many other Alpine peaks "baith hereaboots and far awa,"[57] but the prospects of Corkindale Law seem to our mind vastly superior to those which can be obtained from any of these high places of the land. Yet so gentle is the ascent, and so smooth appears the surface when the top is once attained, that the spectator can scarcely suppose he is even standing on a hill. To attempt anything like a full description of a landscape range so extensive and varied, is out of the question. We can only indicate a few of its more prominent features. We may mention, then, in the first place, that on an ordinary clear day, such as this on which we have fortunately fallen, half the counties of Scotland, with portions of England, and, it is said, of Ireland also (though for this we will not vouch), are within the range of vision. Looking to the north we have the Kilpatrick hills, the rock of Dumbarton, the vale of Leven, with a glimpse of Lochlomond and several of its islands; while Benlomond, Benledi, the Cobbler, and countless other cloudcapt peaks are seen, heaving their heads to the sky on the misty horizon. Turning to the east we have the fertile valley and basin of the Clyde, from Tintoc (which is seen from crown to base) down to Kilpatrick. The three wards of Clydesdale, indeed, with their innumerable towns, villages, and mansions, are spread as it were at

---

[54] From 'Yarrow Unvisited' (1803).
[55] Eglinton Castle
[56] On Arran.
[57] From the traditional song 'The Ewie wi' the Crookit Horn'.

your feet; while the Campsie, western Lomonds of Fife, Bathgate, and Pentland hills are visible beyond. Direct your face now to the south, and immediately before you are the Lead, Cumnock, and Sanquhar hills, with the heights of Kirkcudbrightshire; while Saddleback and Skiddaw, in Cumberland, loom dimly in the distance. The most beautiful prospect of all remains, however, and by turning to the south-west it bursts upon you in all its grandeur and variety. At your feet are seen the woods and glades of Eglinton, with a wide expanse of Ayrshire, sloping gradually downward to the sea, on the irregular margin of which are visible the towns of Irvine, Troon, and Ayr, with the brown hills of Carrick, and far away the opening of Lochryan and a portion of Galloway. Amid the waters, on which numerous snowy sails are moving to and fro, the huge rock of Ailsa stands proudly up, while the Arran hills and the headland of Kintyre are stretched out on the horizon. In certain states of the atmosphere, it is said, the mountains of Morn and Newry, in Ireland, are visible far over the blue waves; but as they do not choose to come within our ken, we shall not venture to include them in our outline. And an outline merely it is, in truth and of necessity; for who could paint the infinite blendings of light and shadow, the ever-varying colours, and the life of which the wondrous picture is composed? Let those who would comprehend its magnificence, themselves visit the favoured spot where now we linger amid the beauty of earth, and sea, and sky.

Long, indeed, might one linger here without exhausting the varied features of loveliness which on every point of the compass are profusely scattered. The scenes amid which we have hitherto been deviously rambling are here brought before us at a single glance. On the living map we can at once trace the courses to and fro of our numerous excursions, while we recall the many hours of gladness which we have spent among them. But the sun is wearing towards the far west, and our shadow indicates the way we must now be going. Descending from our elevation, we return by a field-path which sweeps round the southern shoulder of the Fereneze range to the vale of the Levern. Nearly opposite Neilston, which is now seen in the enchantment of distance towering on the north-east side of the stream, we arrive at the opening of Killoch Glen, a beautifully wooded and romantic defile in the braes along which we have been proceeding. Down this glen the Killoch Burn rushes, to its junction with the Levern, over a succession of precipitous rocks, forming in its progress three picturesque cascades, which resemble in a striking degree – although they are, of course, on a much smaller scale – the celebrated Falls of Clyde. There is a footpath along one side of the ravine, from which the several falls are seen to great advantage through partial openings in the trees, the umbrageous foliage of which forms a delightful natural setting for the various pictures. In the lower and upper falls, the water, with considerable din, is precipitated in one foaming mass over their respective declivities, which, reckoning by the eye, may be from ten to fifteen feet in height. The mid fall, which is much higher than either of the others, is broken by projecting rocks, on which the brown waters are churned into whiteness only to be again dashed into the dark hollow below. In the channel of the stream the wagtails are fitting about while we thread the shadowy mazes of the glen; and the trill of the redbreast, sole songster of the autumn day, blends sweetly with the voices of the rushing waters. Two little urchins are at the same time douking, like juvenile kelpies, in one of the linns, the snowy whiteness of their bodies contrasting finely with the rich amber fluid in which they are half immersed, while their shrill exclamations of delight, as they "splash" each other in very wantonness of spirit, ring joyously in the green gloaming of the wood. Nor has Flora been unkind to this fairy glen. Feathery breckans fringe every rock, while the steep sloping banks are profusely tangled with intermingled verdure and bloom. It was here, on a sweet spring day of langsyne, that we first made the acquaintance of the wild hyacinth or craw-flower, the odorous woodruff, and the silver starwort – a winsome trio; and wherever now in our walks we meet these floral favourites, a vision of Killoch flashes athwart our memory, with the "old familiar faces" of our companions on the occasion. The Muses have also flapped their radiant pinions over this hallowed scene.

No. X. Barrhead and Neilston

Tannahill[58] sings of "Glen-Killoch's sunny brae," and Scadlock,[59] a humble poet of the locality, has devoted several effusions to its praise. The productions of this nameless son of song, who was a friend and correspondent of Tannahill, are generally possessed of but little merit, yet he is occasionally happy in his descriptive sketches of nature, while a vein of genuine tenderness is manifested in several of his lyrics. We shall bid farewell to Killoch by repeating two of his simple stanzas in reference to the scene, but which are not, as our readers will observe, by any means applicable to its present aspect, –

"Cauld the norland wind doth blaw,
Deep the fields are clad wi' snaw;
While wither'd is the birkenshaw,
        And Nature's wae and dreary.

"Hark! the storms around us swell,
Raving doon Glen-Killoch dell,
Where aft wi' thee, my bonnie Bell,
        I've wander'd blythe and cheery."[60]

Leaving the glen at its upper extremity, we now proceed along the summit of the Fereneze Braes, in a northerly direction, and speedily arrive at an old thorn, well known in the neighbourhood as the "Kissing-tree." The stem and branches of this sturdy old bush or tree are thickly studded with nails, which have been driven in, from time to time, by youthful lovers who are in the habit of visiting the spot. From the toughness of the wood, it is no easy matter to send a nail "home" into it; and the swain who manages to accomplish the feat, in presence of his sweetheart, is held fully entitled to "ae fond kiss"[61] on the spot. Success in the operation, we may however mention, is considered an augury of constancy. Hence the appropriateness of the reward.[62]

---

[58] Robert Tannahill, poet (1774 – 1810). His poem about Glen Killoch is 'Gloomy Winter's Noo Awa''.
[59] James Scadlock (1775 – 1818), copper-plate engraver and poet.
[60] Published posthumously in 1818.
[61] Reference to Robert Burns' poem of this name (1792).
[62] The kissing tree, full of nails, fell down sometime around 1860.

From the "Kissing-tree" a fine prospect of the vale of Levern, almost from its origin in the long loch until it loses itself in the Cart, is obtained, with Neilston Pad, Craig of Carnock, and a wide extent of country beyond. The villages of Neilston and Barrhead, also, are here seen to great advantage; the latter seemingly almost at the feet of the spectator.

> "But wat ye wha's in yon toun
> The e'enin' sun shines sweet upon?
> There's kind friends in yon toun,
> Your humble servant waiting on."[63]

So, regretting that we have neither a nail nor a lass, we bid adieu to the nail-coated thorn, and make our way down hill to Barrhead, where we shall bid our wearied readers a courteous good night, as we have "a craw to pluck in mine host's" with a genial "squad" of the natives. So, *au revoir*!

---

[63] From 'O Wat Ye Wha's in Yon Toun' (1795) by Robert Burns.

GLASGOW and PAISLEY, although situated some seven miles or so apart, are, by the facilities of steam transit, now placed, so far as regards time, in almost immediate juxtaposition to each other. A quarter of an hour now suffices to transport the traveller, on business bent, from the Broomielaw to the Sneddon – from the smoky domains of our beloved Sanct Mungo to those of his venerable brother in the "odour of sanctity," Mirrinus. So far as speedy communication is concerned, the railway has left us almost nothing to wish. The country which lies between the great industrial centres of the Clyde and the Cart, however, is of the most beautiful and fertile description, and contains, moreover, several objects of historical and sentimental interest, the due inspection of which requires a more leisurely mode of progression than that of the iron way. Our readers will therefore be pleased to accompany us in our present ramble, as on former occasions, *a la pied.* We may hint, however, for their encouragement, that there is a probability of our being driven to the rail by fatigue on our return, as we propose lading them round a pretty considerable circuit, and into digressions innumerable.

Our favourite route to Paisley is, of course, the longest one, which is that by the margin of the Canal.[1] Taking our start from Port-Eglinton, a short walk brings us to Shields Bridge, at which point, on the south side of the water, the picturesque little village of Pollokshields has recently sprung into existence, with a degree of rapidity which fairly rivals the go-a-head Yankee system of town development. This miniature community is composed of elegant cottages and villas, each edifice having its own belt of garden ground walled in, and tastefully planted in front with flowers and shrubs, and in the rear with kitchen vegetables. The greatest variety of architectural taste, moreover, seems to prevail in this rising suburban settlement.

---

[1] The Glasgow, Paisley and Ardrossan Canal, begun in 1807. It was purchased by the Glasgow & South Western Railway Company and largely converted into the Paisley Canal railway line in the 1880s. Shields Bridge over the former canal no longer exists.

Some two score or so of tenements are already erected, or are in process of erection, and scarcely two of them are similar in design or construction. Each individual proprietor seems to have had his own ideal in "stone and lime," and every man's house is as unlike his neighbour's as possible. Should the same determined diversity of style continue to prevail, Loudon's *Encyclopædia of Cottage Architecture*[2] must soon become a dead letter, so far as Glasgow is concerned, as a walk through Pollokshields will be as instructive to the student as a perusal of that ponderous though valuable volume, with its endless disquisitions on projecting porches, ornamental chimney-stalks, peaked gables, rustic arcades, and mullioned windows. It must be admitted, however, that so far as it has gone, this variety has, on the whole, an exceedingly pleasing and picturesque effect, and that we know few places in the vicinity of our city where we would more readily wish for a snug cottage home, if "the lamp of Alladin" were for a brief period ours.

The banks of the canal between Glasgow and Paisley, artificial though they be, are as rich in natural beauty as the winding margin of many a river. In various places they are finely wooded, while throughout their entire length they are fringed with a profusion of our sweetest wild flowers. Every here and there, also, glimpses of the surrounding country are obtained – in some cases extending for many miles around, and embracing scenes of great fertility and loveliness. As we pass along, the reapers in picturesque groups are busy in the bright yellow fields. Occasionally, also, the voices of juvenile strollers from the purlieus of the city are heard on the tangled and bosky banks, where they come in search of the hips and haws and the blackboyds, which, however, have scarcely yet attained the necessary degree of ripeness. At intervals, "few and far between,"[3] one of the Company's boats passes lazily to its destination; while every now and again a solitary angler gazes despairingly at his float, and mutters "Nothing doing" to our passing inquiries concerning his piscatorial success. About four miles from the city, the Cart approaches within a few feet

---

[2] 1833
[3] From *The Pleasures of Hope* (1799) by Thomas Campbell.

of the canal. At this point of the stream we find the yellow water-lily (*nuphar lutea*) growing abundantly, with its broad cordate leaves and bright golden flowers covering the surface of the water. A number of other fine plants also are thickly strewn along the alluvial margin. Among these are the handsome wood crane's-bill (*geranium sylvaticum*), several stately species of thistle, flinging their snowy locks to the passing breeze, and the rough burr-reed with its green sword-like leaves guarding the shallows of the streamlet, and forming an impervious shade for the water-hen. A dense wood on the opposite side of the Cart at this place, forming part of the extensive estates of Sir John Maxwell of Pollok,[4] seems to be well stocked with game and other wild birds, and we have often heard with delight their peculiar cries and notes while lingering at the spot during the spring and summer gloamings. Here, too, we have observed for several successive seasons a pair of those sweet, though in this part of the country somewhat rare songsters, the black-cap warblers (*curruca atricapilla*), which seem to have bred in the vicinity, although with all our skill (and in our school-days it was famous) we have failed to discover the well screened nest.

About half-a-mile farther on we pass the spot where, on a green bank of the Cart, stood for several centuries the picturesque castle of Cardonald. This venerable relic of other times has, however, been demolished within these few years, and a neat modern farm-steading has been erected on its site.[5] This was at an early period a seat of the Stewart family, who held extensive possessions for a lengthened series of years in Renfrewshire. In the reign of James the Sixth,[6] Walter Stewart, Prior of Blantyre, was lord of Cardonald. From him it passed into the hands of Lord Blantyre, his heir, in whose family it has continued ever since. Crawfurd,[7] in his *History of Renfrewshire*, mentions that in his day the lands of Cardonald were well planted and "beautiful with pleasant gardens." The remains of these are still in

---

[4] See p128, note 35.
[5] Build in 1848. The buildings survive but the steading has been converted into three houses.
[6] Reigned 1567 – 1625.
[7] George Crawfurd (1681 – 1748).

existence. On the fine green lawn which lies between the modern edifice and the canal, and which is thickly strewn with cow slips in the early summer, are a number of stately old forest trees, while the garden still contains several fruit-trees of great age and considerable size. In front of the present house is a stone taken from the walls of its more venerable predecessor, on which is carved the figure of a casque or helmet, with the motto "Toujours avant" (always forward), and the initials J. S., date 1565. At a short distance to the north, on a bend of the Cart, are the extensive meal mills of Cardonald, with a group of cottages and kail-yards, occupied apparently by the operatives engaged in the establishment. A more delightful locality altogether it were difficult to imagine. Wood, water, and variety of surface, are here to be seen in beautiful combination; and we can only regret that it has been divested to a considerable extent of the charm of historic association, by the removal of the "howlet haunted biggin"[8] which for so many generations graced the scene with its presence.

Immediately after passing Cardonald the ruins of Crookston Castle are seen on a rising ground to the west, towering proudly over the intervening woods. Crossing the canal at this point, and passing along a somewhat circuitous route, we find our way, after a walk of about a mile, to this interesting and highly romantic spot, which, from its connection with the name and memory of the unfortunate Mary, must ever be dear to the sentimental rambler. In the time of Crawfurd this venerable building, which is situated on a bold bank of the Levern (which joins the Cart at a short distance to the north), consisted of "a large keep and two lofty towers with battlemented wings." Since that period a considerably greater portion of its walls have owned the crumbling influences of time and the elements. Only one shattered tower has kept its original altitude, and even it has been in a great degree indebted for its preservation to the considerate attention of Sir John Maxwell,[9] on whose property it stands, and who has caused its rent sides to be secured and bound together by strong iron bars. The

---

[8] That is, owl-haunted. From 'On the Late Captain Grose's Peregrinations through Scotland' (1789) by Robert Burns.
[9] Sir John Maxwell, 8th Baronet (1791 – 1865).

same gentleman has also, within the past few years,[10] procured the removal of the debris which in the course of centuries had accumulated around the base of the edifice, and by that means has brought to light a number of antique doors, windows, and staircases, with several other curious architectural features, which had been long hid from the gaze of the antiquary. A couple of vaulted chambers – one of which is in total darkness, and the other only lighted by a narrow loop-hole – are all that now remain in anything like a state of entirety. One is almost afraid to surmise to what vile uses such dreary dungeons may have been put in the rude days of old, when a lordling's caprice was cause sufficient for imprisonment or even death to the helpless and haply unoffending serf. On climbing with some difficulty the narrow and decayed staircase, and gazing on the thick darkness which reigns in one of these cheerless cells, we can almost fancy that we hear the sigh of some hopeless captive floating through the gloomy and stifling air; and we must admit that we are fain to return to the blessed light of day, while a feeling of pride and gratitude springs up in our heart, to think that in our land not even the vilest criminal can now be condemned to such a loathsome and unwholesome den. The rampart and moat of the castle, which are of considerable extent, and convey a vivid idea of the magnitude and grandeur of the edifice in its days of pride and power, may still be distinctly traced. The barony and castle of Crookston seem to have derived their name from Robert de Croc, a gentleman of Norman extraction,[11] who held extensive possessions here in the twelfth century. In the following century the heiress of this individual was married into the illustrious family of Stuart, who thereby became lords of the extensive baronies of Crookston, Darnley, Inchinnan, Neilston, and Tarbolton. Every student of Scottish history is aware that Henry Darnley,[12] the heir of this ancient and noble house, having won the affections of his Queen, the beautiful but unfortunate Mary, was married to her in the year 1565. Tradition asserts that it was at Crookston, one of the seats of the handsome though foolish young lord,

---

[10] This was in 1847 in commemoration of Queen Victoria's visit to Scotland.
[11] Actually Robert Croc. It is not known whether he was Anglo-Saxon or Norman.
[12] Henry Stewart, Lord Darnley (1546 – 1567).

that the brief courtship of the ill-fated lovers took place; and an old and beautiful yew-tree, which stood in the garden a little to the east of the castle, was said to have been a favourite haunt of the royal lovers in the hours of gentle dalliance which preceded their ill-assorted and ultimately tragical union. The remains of this fine old tree were removed in 1817 by Sir John Maxwell,[13] it having been sadly destroyed previously by the depredations of ruthless relic-hunters. A portion of the timber, we may mention, has been appropriately formed into a model of Crookston Castle. This interesting object is preserved at Pollok House, where the visitor is also shown three large sections of the yew, which seems to have been a tree of considerable age and size. The number of snuff-boxes, drinking-cups, and ornaments of various kinds, said to be formed out of Queen Mary's tree, is almost incredible. Every curiosity-collector, from the Land's End to John o' Groat's, can boast one or more fragments of it; although it must be admitted that, like the wood of the "true Cross" which was so extensively diffused during the Middle Ages, the genuineness of the article is, to say the least of it, in many instances extremely problematical.

Sir Walter Scott has made a sad blunder in his novel of *The Abbot*,[14] by representing Mary as witnessing at Crookston the battle of Langside.[15] It is well known that the unfortunate Queen stood on an eminence near Cathcart during that decisive engagement, which occurred at least four miles to the east of Crookston. The intervening ground, also, is of such a nature as to render Langside invisible from this locality. On being informed of the error which he had thus made, Sir Walter at once admitted the fact, in a note to the revised edition of the *Waverley Novels*, but he refused to alter the text, as he considered that by so doing the dramatic interest of the romance would be considerably diminished. Another error regarding the stream which flows past the castle has been perpetuated by many who have written concerning Crookston. This fine rivulet is the Levern, and not the White Cart, as has been generally believed. The fact that the junction

---

[13] Sir John Maxwell, 7th baronet (1785 – 1844). The tree was cut down in May 1816.
[14] Published 1820.
[15] In 1568. See pp109 – 110 for an account of the battle.

of these two streams occurs in a beautiful spot about half-a-mile to the northward of the ruins has probably led to this confusion of their names.

The memory of Scotia's unfortunate Queen – a memory steeped in tears – has been associated with many a lovely scene, but with none more so than Crookston. Pennant,[16] who visited the spot in 1772, truly says, – "The situation is delicious, commanding a view of a well-cultivated tract, divided into a multitude of fertile little hills;" and Scott has made Queen Mary remark,[17] that the castle commands a prospect as wide almost as that which is seen from the peaked summit of Schehallion. Alike rich in material beauty and sentimental interest, it is no wonder that Crookston is annually visited by thousands of pilgrims, or that it has ever been a favourite haunt of the poetic brotherhood. The author of "The Clyde," to whom we have been previously indebted for several apt quotations, thus describes the spot:

"Here raised upon a verdant mount sublime,
To heaven complaining of the wrongs of time,
And ruthless force of sacrilegious hands,
Crookston, their ancient seat, in ruin stands;
Nor Clyde's whole course an ampler prospect yields
Of spacious plains and well-improven fields,
Which here the gently rising hills surround,
And there the cloud-supporting mountains bound." [18]

Tannahill alludes to the ruins in one of his sweet lyrics, –

"Through Crookston Castle's lonely wa's
The wintry wind howls wild and dreary."[19]

And our own Motherwell, who many a time and oft lingered in pensive mood by the time-honoured pile, has celebrated its charms in one of

[16] Thomas Pennant (1726 – 1798), Welsh writer and traveller.
[17] In *The Abbot.*
[18] From 'The Clyde' (1764) by John Wilson.
[19] 'Gloomy Winter's Noo Awa'' (1807) by Robert Tannahill.

his most elegant compositions, of which the following are the concluding lines:

> "'Tis past – she rests – the scaffold hath been swept,
> The headsman's guilty axe to rust consigned
> But Crookston, while thine aged towers remain,
> And thy green umbrage woos the evening wind
> By noblest natures shall her woes be wept,
> Who shone the glory of thy festal day;
> Whilst aught is left of these thy ruins gray,
> They will arouse remembrance of the stain
> Queen Mary's doom hath left on history's page –
> Remembrance laden with reproach and pain,
> To those who make like me this pilgrimage!"[20]

Many an anonymous bard also has endeavoured to express in verse the feelings which the shattered and dreary tower, with its wall-flowers scenting the dewy air, and its clamorous train of daws startling the echoes with their hoarse cries, has excited in his breast. One of these nameless voices of the heart we must give, –

> "Thou proud memorial of a former age,
> Time-ruined Crookston; not in all our land, –
> Romantic with a noble heritage
> Of feudal halls in ruin sternly grand, –
> More beautiful doth tower or castle stand
> Than thou! as oft the lingering traveller tells,
> And none more varied sympathies command;
> Though where the warrior dwelt the raven dwells:
> With tenderness thy tale the rudest bosom swells.
>
> "Along the soul that pleasing sadness steals
> Which trembles from a wild harp's dying fall,
> When fancy's recreative eye reveals
> To him lone musing by that mouldering wall,

---

[20] From 'Cruxtoun Castle' (?1832) by William Motherwell.

What warriors thronged, what joy rung through thy hall,
When royal Mary – yet unstained by crime,
And with love's golden sceptre ruling all
Made thee her bridal home. There seems to shine
Still o'er thee splendour shed at that high gorgeous time:
How dark a moral shades and chills the heart
When gazing on thy dreary deep decay!"[21]

A favourite haunt withal of Flora is Crookston, and the botanist will find in its shady moat a number of our most beautiful, and several of our most rare indigenous plants. Among these are the cuckowpint (*aram maculatum*), with its curiously formed flowers in spring, and its spikes of bright scarlet berries in the autumn months; the tuberous moschatell (*adoxa moschatellina*), and a rich variety of others. The trailing bramble, the brier with its soft-folding blossom, the sloe, the hazel, the rowan-tree, and the haw, are strewn in the most picturesque profusion around the spot – a very girdle of arborescent beauty to the hoary tower. It would almost seem as if Nature loved especially to adorn the scene which had been hallowed by the presence, in a long past age, of the fairest and the most unfortunate that ever bore the sceptre and crown of regal dignity. How often must the fond fancy of the exiled Queen have flown from the gloom of her dreary prison-walls to this fair spot, which every season decks with a beauty of its own! Burns has put words of lamentation into the mouth of Mary; and it would almost seem that the scenery of Crookston was in his mind's eye when he penned the following verse, so true is it to the character of its spring landscape:

"Now blooms the lily by the bank,
The primrose down the brae,
The hawthorn 's budding in the glen,
And milk white is the slae,
The meanest hind in fair Scotland
May rove their sweets amang,

---

[21] From 'Lines to Crookston Castle (1817) by 'SP' but later attributed to Alexander Carlile, thread manufacturer and poet.

But I, the Queen of a' Scotland,
Maun lie in prison strang."[22]

Crookston is lovely at all times and seasons; but we feel, while musing by its hoary towers, that the period most appropriate to wander by the "lonely mansion of the dead"[23] is indeed that in which we have made our rambling pilgrimage to the locality. The primrose and the violet of spring have long been numbered among the things that were; the last rose of summer has fallen from the leafy brier; the lark is silent in the meadow, and the merle[24] in his noontide bower. The gathering harvest in the whitened fields, the woodlands falling into the sear and yellow leaf,[25] the harebell hanging its head as if in woe, and even the liquid pipings of the red-breast telling of approaching decay to everything of bloom, are all suggestive of pensive feeling, and appropriately harmonize with that "luxury of woe" in which one loves to indulge beneath the shattered wall, around which, as with the ivy, melancholy memories are entwined.

Before leaving Crookston, we may mention that after the tragical death of Darnley the estates and honours of Lennox were bestowed upon Charles Stuart, second son of the Earl of Lennox. This individual, however, dying without issue, they were resigned to the crown by Robert Stuart, Bishop of Caithness, the next in lineal succession. After this the lands and castle of Crookston passed through a variety of hands, until they were finally purchased from the Montrose family, in 1757, by Sir John Maxwell,[26] the ancestor of the present proprietor, who, as we have previously remarked, has exhibited his respect for the memory of her whose brief residence here has for ever hallowed the locality, by the judicious measures he has adopted for the preservation of the mouldering edifice. But for the attention which he has thus manifested, the stately remains of Crookston Castle must soon

---

[22] From 'Lament of Mary, Queen of Scots, on the Approach of Spring' (1791) by Robert Burns.
[23] From 'The Ruined Castle' (1818) by 'M'.
[24] blackbird
[25] A reference to Shakespeare's *Macbeth* V.iii.
[26] Sir John Maxwell, 3rd Baronet (1752 – 1758).

have been levelled with the dust, and the place which has known its pomp and grandeur for many a long century should have known them "no more for ever." The antiquary, and he who loves to drop the tear of sympathy over the dark fate of the unfortunate Mary, will have reason for many years to feel grateful to him who has thus preserved from impending destruction such an interesting memorial of "what has been." We may also mention that there is a fine portrait of the beauteous Queen of Scots preserved at Pollok House, as also authentic portraits of her not less ill-fated grandson, Charles the First, and the Infanta of Spain, who, it will be remembered, was at one period destined to be his bride.

Retracing our steps to the canal, we pursue our devious way by its margin toward Paisley, which is still some three miles to the northward. On either hand, as we pass, a succession of fertile fields in all the brightness of autumnal gold, and many of them already shorn or in process of being speedily so, present a series of those rural pictures which the famous American reaping machine threatens soon to banish from our land. In an age of change, while steam is jostling us in every direction, the hairst-rig remained unaltered all its primitive simplicity, a picturesque relic of other times, even as it was when the fair gleaner Ruth

"Stood in tears amid the alien corn."[27]

How our poets and our painters, those dreamy worshippers of the beautiful, have revelled in the cheerful groups of autumn, weaving in immortal verse or tracing on the living canvas those combinations of the graceful in form and the pleasing in colour, which, once seen, become unto the heart "a joy for ever!"[28] Listen to one who first saw the light in the city of our own habitation, the author of "The Sabbath," and who looked with an attentive and a loving eye on all the "shows and forms" of ever-varying nature, –

"At sultry hour of noon the reaper band

---

[27] From 'Ode to a Nightingale' (1819) by John Keats.
[28] From 'Endymion' (1818) by John Keats.

Rest from their toil, and in the lusty stook
Their sickles hang. Around their simple fare,
Upon the stubble spread, blythsome they form
A circling group, while humbly waits behind,
The wistful dog, and with expressive look
And pawing foot, implores his little share."[29]

A delicious picture in words, which some of our artistic friends might well translate into the language of the glowing canvas. Or what say they to the following from the same pen, "alike, but oh how sweetly different!"

"The short repast, seasoned with simple mirth,
And not without the song, gives place to sleep;
With sheaf beneath his head, the rustic youth
Enjoys sweet slumbers, while the maid he loves
Steals to his side, and screens him from the sun."[30]

About a mile to the north-west of Crookston, and on the south side of the White Cart, are the spacious mansion and grounds of Hawkhead, one of the seats of the Earl of Glasgow.[31] This fine old house, which is screened in every direction by extensive and beautiful woods, is somewhat irregular in its appearance. According to Crawfurd, "it is built in the form of a court, and consists of a large old tower, to which there were lower buildings added in the reign of Charles the First[32] by James Lord Ross and Dame Margaret Scott, his lady, and adorned with large orchards, fine gardens, and pretty terraces, with regular and stately avenues fronting the said castle, and almost surrounded with woods and enclosures, which add much to the beauty of this seat." This was, we understand, the first instance in Renfrewshire in which the formal and stiff style of Dutch gardening was introduced. The house, too, was among the earliest in which

---

[29] From 'September' in 'The Rural Calendar' (1807) by James Grahame.
[30] This passage comes immediately after the preceding one in 'The Rural Calendar'.
[31] This building became part of Hawkhead Asylum (later Leverndale Hospital) in 1914 and was finally demolished in 1953.
[32] Reigned 1625 – 1649.

modern comfort was combined with the strength of former times. In 1782 the Countess-Dowager of Glasgow made considerable improvements on this favourite estate, and formed a new garden, four acres in extent, and more in accordance with the taste of our day than its stately but quaint and old-fashioned predecessor. We have seldom seen finer masses of foliage than the bosky banks of the Cart present at this place; while in spring and early summer

> "The spot is wild, the banks are steep,
> With eglantine and hawthorn blossomed o'er,
> Lychnis and daffodils, and crow-flowers blue."[33]

The Duke of York – the persecuting Duke whose name still stinks in the nostrils of the Presbyterian peasantry of Scotland[34] – when in the plenitude of his power in 1681, "dined at the Halcat with my Lord Ross," as we learn from an ancient chronicler,[35] who records the event as one of a memorable nature.

The Hawkhead woods seem to furnish a favourite haunt for the rook. As we pass we are amused to see an immense flock of these sagacious birds flying about a neighbouring field, intermingled with vast numbers of starlings – a kindred species which of late years has increased to an almost incredible extent in the districts around Glasgow and Paisley. In our bird-nesting days a starling was indeed a *rara avis*. We had a tradition in our school that a few starlings from time immemorial had haunted the creviced walls of Bothwell Castle and the shattered towers of Crookston; but for miles around the country, as every disciple of Gilbert White[36] in this neighbourhood well knew, such a thing as a bird of this species was seldom seen. Another proof of their scarcity, if such were wanted, was the handsome prices which they could always command in that most curious of marts, the bird-market. Some seven or eight years ago, however, they began to increase in numbers around Paisley, where they were treated

---

[33] From 'Hawthornden, a Sketch' (1823) by David Moir.
[34] Later King James VII and II, who was deposed in 1688 in the Glorious Revolution.
[35] Robert Law, who wrote *Memorialls, Or, The Memorable Things that Fell Out Within this Island of Brittain from 1638 to 1684.*
[36] Reverend Gilbert White (1720 – 1793), gardener and author.

with the utmost kindness and consideration; breeding-boxes for their special accommodation being suspended on every second tree and chimney-top. Under these fostering influences the starlings "multiplied and replenished," until at present they are almost as common in that town as the house-sparrow. More recently they have begun to congregate in and around our city; and so plentiful have they already become, that a fine young specimen can be purchased in the season, by the juvenile ornithologist, at the price of an old song; while those who, like ourselves, are in the habit of perambulating the country, must have been startled by the vast flocks, often consisting of many thousands, which assemble in the autumn and winter months in the neighbouring fields.

About half-a-mile from Paisley the canal is carried over the Cart by a handsome aqueduct bridge.[37] This structure, from which a fine view of the town is obtained, is 210 feet in length, 27 in breadth, and 30 in height. The span of the arch is not less than 84 feet. At a short distance to the west of this, and quite adjacent to the canal, are the remains of the ancient castellated mansion of Blackhall, in bygone times a seat of the Ardgowan family. Crawfurd mentions that in his day the grounds of Blackhall "were adorned with beautiful planting." The glory, however, has now departed from the locality.[38] The gardens and shrubbery are no more, while the edifice itself has a blackened and exceedingly dreary aspect. A few minutes' walk from this hoary relic of the past brings us into the bustling centre of Paisley, where, in the meantime, we shall leave the reader to make the acquaintance of the "bodies" as he best may.

---

[37] When the canal closed, this aqueduct was converted into a railway bridge, which is still in use.

[38] Blackhall Manor has since been renovated and is now a private house.

The town of Paisley is of considerable extent and importance, being the fifth in respect to magnitude in Scotland. In population it formerly ranked next to Glasgow and Edinburgh, but latterly it has been outstripped in the march of progression by Aberdeen and Dundee; the number of its inhabitants at the late census being 47,952, while those of the two latter towns were respectively 71,973 and 78,931.[1] Paisley is finely situated on both sides of the White Cart, about seven miles to the south-west of Glasgow, and three miles above the junction of that stream with the Clyde. It covers, altogether, a surface of nearly two and a-half miles square. The main line of street, extending from the suburb of Williamsburgh in the east to Millerston in the west, is about two miles long; while several of the other main thoroughfares, such as Causeyside and George Street, are likewise of considerable length. The original portion of the town is chiefly built on a fine terrace-like eminence, which runs in a direction westward of the Cart, and commands an extensive prospect of the surrounding country. By means of recent additions, however, it is now spread far and wide on both sides of this elevation. The new town, which lies on the opposite side of the river, was commenced by James, eighth Earl of Abercorn, so recently as 1779. Previously to that period the suburb of Seedhill, with Walneuk, Smithhills, and a few other contiguous streets, were the only portions of the burgh which existed on the east side of the Cart.

Although Paisley, under the name of Vanduara, was at an early period the site of an extensive Roman encampment – vestiges of which are still visible in some places; yet it seems, like its more extensive and wealthy neighbour, to have had an ecclesiastical origin. In the twelfth century, when Walter Stewart[2] founded a monastery here, it appears there was not even a village in the neighbourhood; but that one gradually arose afterwards, for the accommodation of the retainers of the monks, and the numerous pilgrims attracted to the locality by the fame of its patron saint. Slowly increasing in extent, it was created a

---

[1] The current figures are: Paisley – 77K; Aberdeen – 229K; Dundee – 149K.
[2] Walter FitzAlan (c.1106 – 1177), Steward (Stewart) of Scotland, hence the name.

burgh of barony in 1488, although so lately even as 1695 the population only amounted to 2,200. Crawfurd, writing a few years subsequent to the latter date,[3] says, that in his time the town consisted of one principal street, about half-a-mile in length, running westward from the river, and having some lanes and wynds branching off in various directions. About the same period, Hamilton of Wishaw,[4] whose curious and interesting work we have more than once had occasion to quote, thus briefly describes the town: – "Paisley is a very pleasant and well-built little town, plentifully provided with all sorts of grain, fruits, coals, peats, fishes, and what else is proper for the comfortable use of man, or can be expected in any other place of the kingdom." It was only after the Union[5] that the manufacturing energies of the town began to be thoroughly developed, and the germs were laid of that prosperity which it has since attained. The manufactures of Paisley at first consisted principally of linen and muslin fabrics, in the production of which it ultimately gained considerable celebrity. This branch of textile manufacture was afterwards in a great measure superseded by the production of flax and cotton thread, in the preparation of which it acquired a high degree of excellence, and for which it still retains a wide-spread reputation. Silk and linen gauze, of great elegance and beauty, also formed for many years staple articles of produce in this enterprising community; but one of the more recent and important additions to the departments of skilled industry in which her population has been engaged, is that of shawl weaving, in which, for variety and beauty of pattern and richness of colour, she is almost unrivalled. The weaving of tartans, and other textures of a similar nature denominated tweeds, has also, of late years, been successfully introduced; and, at the present time, there are many hundreds of artisans engaged in and around Paisley in the printing of shawls and plaids, principally composed of fine woollen fabrics, and remarkable for the elegance of their designs, the brilliancy of their tints, and, above

---

[3] George Crawfurd, author of a *History of Renfrewshire*, writing in 1710.

[4] William Hamilton (d.1724), Scottish antiquarian who wrote *Descriptions of the Sheriffdoms of Lanark and Renfrew*.

[5] Union of Scotland with England and Wales, 1707.

all, for their remarkable cheapness.[6] This latter feature, indeed, has caused the elegant though less substantial printed shawl in a great measure to supersede that of the loom, which, from the complexity of the machinery necessary to its production, and the greater amount of labour which it requires, is necessarily much more expensive. Altogether, in manufacturing skill and taste, as well as in commercial enterprise, Paisley has continued to occupy a prominent position among the industrial centres of our country, and, in certain departments, has even manifested a superiority which is in the highest degree creditable to the productive capabilities of her population.

Nor has the pre-eminence of Paisley been entirely confined to the successful production of textile fabrics. The people of Paisley are generally admitted to possess a highly respectable intellectual status, and it is well known that the town has given birth to several individuals who have attained distinction in various departments of literature and art, whose names their country

"Will not willingly let die."[7]

Among these are Alexander Wilson,[8] author of "Watty and Meg," and other poems of great merit, and also of a valuable work on the ornithology of America, famous alike for the vigorous eloquence of its descriptions, and the striking fidelity of its pictorial illustrations; Robert Tannahill[9], with the single exception of Burns, the sweetest lyrical poet of Scotland; Professor Wilson,[10] one of the most eloquent of our prose writers, and a poet of no mean powers; and Henning,[11] the restorer of ancient Grecian art. Besides these, the undoubted heirs of fame, Paisley has produced a perfect host of minor bards, principally

---

[6] The Indian-inspired motifs used on the shawls became known as paisley pattern after the town.

[7] From 'The Reason of Church Government urged against Prelaty' (1642) by John Milton.

[8] 1766 – 1813

[9] 1774 – 1810

[10] Professor John Wilson (1785 – 1854), who often wrote under the pen name Christopher North.

[11] John Henning (1771 – 1851), sculptor who made a copy of the Parthenon frieze, with the destroyed parts recreated from sketches.

intelligent operatives, who have lightened the intervals of labour with literary study, and many of whose productions are highly creditable to their authors.

In general architectural appearance the town of Paisley presents few features calling for particular attention from the tourist. Its streets are for the most part narrow and tortuous, while even its most handsome edifices suffer in effect from the contiguity of less imposing structures. Of late years a material improvement has been effected in the spacious area which is bounded on one side by the County Buildings. This extensive pile, which is in the form of an ancient feudal castle, and to which large additions have recently been made, is situated on the west bank of the Cart, in the immediate vicinity of the Glasgow and Paisley Joint Railway Station, which has been built in a harmonizing style of architecture. It was erected between 1818 and 1821, at an expense of about £28,000, and contains a court house and offices for the transaction of various departments of public business, together with a chapel, jail, and house of correction.[12] Immediately adjacent is the Government School of Design – a building which forms a standing proof of the necessity which existed at the period of its erection for such an institution. It is, indeed, one of the most ineffective specimens of design which, in a public edifice, we have yet witnessed. If architectural taste were a sin, the designer of this might well boast of clean hands.[13] There are, however several fine buildings in the vicinity, among which we may mention those forming the row facing the railway, a banking house[14] near the ancient "hole in the wa'," [15] and the reading room establishment at the Cross, the hall of which is adorned by Fillans's splendid bust of Professor Wilson.[16]

The most interesting public building in Paisley, and, of course, one of the first to which we direct our attention, is the venerable and

---

[12] This building was demolished in the 1960s and replaced by the Piazza shopping centre.
[13] Designed by a Mr Lamb. This institution became the Paisley Art Institute, which is now based in Oakshaw Street East. Its original building does not survive.
[14] Now a pub called The Bankhouse.
[15] A 9-foot wide passageway which was widened in 1845 into Gilmour Street.
[16] By James Fillans (1808 – 1852). This bust is now in the Paisley Museum.

time-honoured Abbey Church,[17] which was originally founded and munificently endowed, in 1160, by Walter, the High Steward of Scotland, the original progenitor of the royal Stuarts. The descendants of this nobleman afterwards, at various periods, bestowed liberal donations, both in money and lands, upon the establishment, until it ultimately became one of the most wealthy and influential in the kingdom. "Gray Paisley's haughty lord"[18] held undisputed sway over a wide extent of territory; while its ecclesiastics, of high and low degree, were accommodated in a style of splendour unsurpassed even in the celebrated monasteries of Dunfermline and St. Andrews, although these were specially patronized by royalty. Like their confreres of Melrose,

"They wanted neither beef nor ale,"[19]

nor a bountiful supply of all those creature comforts which the produce or limited commerce of the country could afford. In the time of Edward I. of England,[20] according to Fordun,[21] the Abbey was pillaged and burned to the ground by the invading Southrons, because the abbot, with a genuine spirit of patriotism, refused to acknowledge the authority of the usurper. After the independence of the nation, however, had been firmly established on the memorable field of Bannockburn, the Abbey was rebuilt on a superior scale of magnificence, the church being not less than 265 feet in length, while both the nave and the transepts were furnished with lateral aisles. It was in the cathedral form, that of a cross, and was surmounted by a lofty steeple. The greater part of what now exists is supposed to have been erected in the fifteenth century, under the superintendence of

[17] Paisley Abbey survives and still functions as a church.
[18] From 'Cadyow Castle'(1801) by Sir Walter Scott.
[19] From the old satirical song:
"Oh the monks of Melrose made fat kail
On Fridays when they fasted.
They wanted neither beer nor ale,
So long's their neighbours' lasted."
[20] Reigned 1272 – 1307
[21] Johh of Fordun, fourteenth century chronicler.

Abbot Thomas Tarves, who died in 1459, and Abbot George Shaw, who bore sway over the brotherhood from 1472 to March, 1498. One of the architects seems, from an ancient inscription on the transept door of Melrose, to have been a John Murdo, who further seems to have been concerned in the erection of several other ecclesiastical edifices of importance. The inscription was originally as follows, although it is now much defaced:

> "John Murdo sum tym callyt was I,
> And born in Parys certainly,
> And had in keping all mason werk
> Of Santandrays, ye hye kirk
> Of Glasgu, Melrose, and Paslay,
> Of Nyddsdall, and of Galway;
> I pray to God and Mary bath,
> And sweet St. John, kep this haly kirk fra skaith."

 At this period the monastery was surrounded by gardens and orchards of great extent, which, with a park for fallow deer, were protected from lay intrusion by a high wall upwards of a mile in circumference, erected by the aforementioned Abbot Shaw, as appears from an inscription on a stone which once formed part of it, and which is now built into the side of a house in the vicinity.[22] The words are as follows, with the exception of the fifth line, which has been totally effaced:

> "Thei callit ye Abbot Georg of Schawe
> About yis Abbay gart mak this wawe,
> A thousand four hundreth zheyr
> Auchty and fyve, the date but veir;
> Pray for his salvatioun
> That made this noble foundacioun."

How excellent in old Abbot Shaw to secure his vineyard and his deer-park, from which he would doubtless derive many a dainty venison pasty, and then to solicit the prayers of the faithful for this act of selfish

---

[22] The stone was later removed to Paisley Museum.

prudence! To our "heretic" understanding, it would certainly appear that the bigging of the "wawe" would receive "its own exceeding great reward" in the protection which it afforded to the creature comforts of the monastic brotherhood. It is to be hoped, therefore, that the jolly old monk had other claims on the devotional sympathies of his neighbours, as otherwise we are afraid there would be but few beads counted on his behalf.

The Abbey of Paisley continued to flourish until the Reformation, when the establishment was overthrown, and a considerable portion of its architectural splendour destroyed. The nest was then to a great extent pulled down, and the rooks who had lived for centuries on the fat of the land were driven ignominiously from their ancient haunts. The last of the abbots was hanged at Stirling, in 1571, for his adherence to the cause of Queen Mary. The revenues and rich endowments of the Abbey were at the same time secularized, and erected into a temporal lordship, which was bestowed, for what equivalent we have not learned, upon Lord Claud Hamilton,[23] who was created Baron of Paisley, a title which, with a considerable portion of the monastic territory, is still preserved by the Abercorn family.

There are few finer specimens of Gothic architecture in Scotland than the ancient Abbey Church of Paisley. Although shorn of its original fair proportions, and denuded of many of its most delicate ornamental features, it still retains a sufficiency of both to impress the spectator with a vivid idea of its pristine beauty and magnificence. The western front presents an elevation of a singularly dignified and regular character. It is composed of a great central and two side compartments, separated and flanked by buttresses, the carvings of both door and windows being in an excellent state of preservation. The interior of the edifice, with its "long-drawn aisles and fretted vaults,"[24] its massive pillars and its richly decorated windows, while it delights the eye, has a peculiarly solemnizing influence on the mind. While

---

[23] 1546 – 1621
[24] From 'An Elegy Written in a Country Church Yard' (1751) by Thomas Gray.

standing in the nave we cannot help repeating to ourselves Milton's beautiful lines in "Il Penseroso,"[25] –

> "Oh let my due feet never fail
> To walk the studious cloysters pale,
> And love the high embowed roof,
> With antique pillars massy proof,
> And storied windows richly dight,
> Casting a dim religious light:
> There let the pealing organ blow
> To the full-voiced quire below,
> In service high and anthems clear,
> As may with sweetness, through mine ear
> Dissolve me into ecstasies,
> And bring all heaven before my eyes."

Of course we are not likely soon to hear the "kist of whistles"[26] at work the Abbey Church of Paisley, but of we frequently heard an excellent vocal band chanting the notes of praise within its walls, and the thrilling effect we shall not easily forget. On the present occasion all is silent, however, and we feel that there is an eloquence in the very stillness of the place which is more suggestive of sentimental emotion, and which touches a deeper chord in our bosom than the sweetest strains of the singer, or the most stirring appeals of the preacher. Was the reader ever alone in an old church? It is good for man to be occasionally alone; and in such a place as Paisley Abbey, with its gloomy aisles and solemn echoes, the pensive rambler will find as moving "sermons in stone"[27] as ever Shakespeare's banished Duke found in the green solitudes of Arden.

To the south of the nave is Saint Mirren's Aisle, a small chapel twenty-four feet square, which, in the palmy days of the Abbey, was specially dedicated to its patron saint. This is commonly called the "Sounding Aisle," from a remarkable echo which it possesses, and

---

[25] 1632
[26] That is, the pipe organ.
[27] From Shakespeare's *As You Like It* II.i

which is caused by certain peculiarities in its construction. The noise produced when the person who attends us slams the door forcibly in closing it, is really startling. We must admit, however, that the effect falls far short of that described by Pennant,[28] when he visited the spot in the early part of last century. Either the echo has got lazy in our day, or the good old man, as not at all improbable, may have exercised more than the usual traveller's license in his narrative of its reverberative feats.[29] Nearly in the centre of the aisle is an altar-tomb, on which is the recumbent figure of a woman, with the hands folded as in prayer. The design and workmanship of this structure are of an elaborate and delicate description; and, according to tradition, it is said to have been erected to the memory of Marjory Bruce,[30] daughter of the hero of Bannockburn, who rejoiced, while in life, in the somewhat unpoetical name of "Queen Blearie." Antiquarian research, however, can discover nothing to confirm the popular story, so that the monument, like many others, may be said to have survived the memory which a fond affection commissioned it to perpetuate. The "footprints" which we would fain leave behind us "on the sands of time"[31] are ever, alas! being washed away by oblivion's advancing tide. A lesson of humility may well be gleaned for the children of pride from the costly memento in St. Mirren's Aisle, which has now "no tale to tell."[32] Go to my lady's chamber, and tell her, though beauty, wealth, and a name among the great ones of earth, are hers, that "to this favour she must come at last."[33]

A short distance to the south-east of the Abbey is the suburb of Seedhill, where, on the 6th of July, 1776,[34] Alexander Wilson, the poet and ornithologist, was born. To this locality. we now wend our way. The house, as we are informed, was demolished a few years since, and

---

[28] Thomas Pennant (1726 – 1798), Welsh writer and traveller who visited Paisley during his second tour in 1772.
[29] The echo was almost entirely destroyed in 1902 when the transept was restored.
[30] 1296 – 1316
[31] From From 'A Psalm of Life' (1838) by Henry Wadsworth Longfellow.
[32] From 'The Knife Grinder' (1797) by George Canning.
[33] From Shakespeare's *Hamlet* V.i.
[34] Actually 1766.

another has since been erected in its stead, which is at once pointed out to us, on inquiry, by a gash old weaver. The edifice is a plain two-storeyed one, and has a small tablet of marble prominently inserted on its front, with the following inscription:

"This Tablet was erected, in 1841, by David Anderson, Perth, to mark the birthplace of Alexander Wilson, Paisley poet and American ornithologist."

In the immediate vicinity of the house the Cart is precipitated over a rugged range of rocks, the projecting portions of which are well known to the juvenility of Paisley as "the Hammills." This was a favourite haunt of the poet in his early years, as indeed it still is with the boys of the neighbourhood, who, in the bathing season, according to our weaver friend, may be seen "ploutering about in the foamy water, or clustering around the craigs like as many eemocks.[35]" Our friend, who, to our surprise, remembers Wilson, says, "he was a tall, thin, swanky fallow; and that he never took kindly to the loom." Of the latter fact we were well aware from the poet's own writings. In "Groans from the Loom," a composition which he indited when about to desert the shuttle for the pack, he bitterly sings, –

"Good gods! shall a mortal with legs
So low uncomplaining be brought,
Go, hung, like a scarecrow, in rags,
And live o'er a seat-tree on nought?"

It is well for the world that Wilson was not content to

"Creep through life a plain day-plodding weaver."[36]

Had he taken kindly to the loom the feathered tribes of the vast American forests had yet in all probability remained comparative strangers to us. The galling spur of poverty was required to send him forth on his noble mission. The lap of ease is not often the cradle of

---

[35] ants
[36] From 'The Resolve' (1807) by Robert Tannahill.

genius. Had the loom been more remunerative, or had the pack never been lost, the name of Wilson had not now been a familiar word on both sides of the Atlantic.

The poetry of Wilson is characterized by merit of no ordinary description, and evinces considerable fertility of fancy, keenness of satire, with a tendency to coarseness, and a masculine vigour of intellect. With the exception of the inimitable "Watty and Meg," and the "Loss of the Pack," however, his poetical productions have never attained anything like an extensive popularity.

After lingering in conversation with our new acquaintance for a considerable time, we retrace our steps to the Cross, and proceed along the High Street, in a westerly direction, to visit the birthplace of Tannahill. By the way we pass the house in which the author of the *Lights and Shadows of Scottish Life*, the sweet singer of the *Isle of Palms*, and the "old man eloquent" of Blackwood's inimitable Magazine, first saw the light.[37] His father, as is generally known, was a respectable Paisley merchant; and the house in which his gifted son was born is situated on the south side of the thoroughfare along which we are passing. It is situated a short distance from a more pretending edifice which stands a a little off the line of High Street, between the points where the latter is joined by the New Street and by Storie Street. The more noticeable structure to which we allude, and which is railed in and screened by shrubbery, was afterwards occupied by Wilson's father, and it was in it that the young poet's earliest years were spent.[38] An old and esteemed friend of ours still remembers seeing the yellow-haired boy spinning his "peerie"[39] on the pavement in front of the house, among the neebor callants. Like other boys, too, he was a rambler in the country around, a seeker of bird's nests, and a gatherer of blaeberries and blackboyds. This we learned from his own lips several years ago, during an interview which we had with him, when we were somewhat surprised to perceive how vividly he remembered

[37] Professor John Wilson (1785 – 1854), who often wrote under the pen name Christopher North.
[38] The building has since been demolished.
[39] spinning top

the various scenes in the neighbourhood of his native town, more especially as he had been removed from the locality at a comparatively early age, and except during occasional visits, "few and far between,"[40] was absent from it almost ever after.

About a quarter of a mile to the westward of John Wilson's birthplace is Castle Street, in which Robert Tannahill made his entrée into existence. The edifice is a lowly one-storeyed biggin', and having undergone considerable alteration, is now occupied by a cowfeeder. The poet's father was a decent and intelligent handloom weaver; and at the period of Robert's birth one end of the building formed the residence of the family, while the other was occupied as a loom-shop. While the poet was still an infant, his father, who seems to have been an industrious and thrifty individual, erected a cottage, with part of his savings, in an adjoining street.[41] To this, when he was little more than twelve months old, the future bard, with the rest of the family, was removed; and here, with the exception of a brief stay in England, he continued to reside until the period of his death. The life of Tannahill presents but few salient features. Having learned reading, writing, and the elements of arithmetic – the poor man's scanty curriculum in those days – he was apprenticed to the handloom weaving at an early age. In his calling, which was at that period a more remunerative one than it is in our day, he was assiduous and attentive, and consequently he soon became an expert workman. His spare hours were principally devoted to reading and study, or to the converse of a few congenial friends; while on Saturday afternoons he was in the habit, either alone or with a chosen companion, of strolling amid the romantic scenery in the neighbourhood of his native town. His favourite haunts on these occasions, during which he enriched his memory with those images of natural beauty with which his verse is so richly adorned, were the braes of Gleniffer, Stanley green shaw, with its castle "old and gray," and the woods of Craigielee, or Ferguslie, all of which he has celebrated in never-dying song. It is this entwining of local scenery, indeed, into the

---

[40] From *The Pleasures of Hope* (1799) by Thomas Campbell.
[41] This cottage on Queen Street was rebuilt after fire damage and is still used by the Paisley Burns Club, which Tannahill helped to found in 1805.

structure of his compositions, that has rendered Tannahill *par excellence* the poet of Paisley. Of numerous poets the town can boast, but no other has stamped his name so generally and so ineffaceable as he has done on the prominent features of the surrounding country. The nook is still pointed out where the poet's loom was situated, and where for so many years he wrought. This also was the place where the greater portion of his poetry was composed, as it is well known that the visitations of his muse most frequently occurred while his hands were busily plying the shuttle. Genius was never with him made an excuse for idleness. His was an honest and industrious poverty, for which he needed not to hang his head. His earnings were at all times amply sufficient for his simple wants, and he could truly and proudly say–

> "Tho' humble my lot, not ignoble's my state,
> Let me still be contented though poor,
> What Destiny brings be resigned to my fate,
> Though Misfortune should knock at my door."[42]

Unfortunately, the contentment which he has here expressed was not at all times experienced. Like most other children of genius, he was throughout life liable to fits of gloomy despondency. His poetry and his letters afford abundant proof of his constitutional proneness to mental depression. Considered as a "shadow of the coming event,"[43] how affecting is the following passage, which occurs in an epistle to his friend Scadlock,[44] so early as 1804:

> "But ere a few short summers gae,
> Your friend will meet his kindred clay;
> For fell disease tugs at my breast,
> To hurry me away."

Ultimately, in 1810, his health, which had never been of a very robust description, sank under the pressure of his dark imaginings. His body

---

[42] From 'Tho' Humble My Lot' (1807).
[43] From 'Lochiel's Warning' (1803) by Thomas Campbell.
[44] James Scadlock (1775 – 1818), copper-plate engraver and poet.

became emaciated, his eyes hollow, and his expressive countenance pallid and careworn. At the same time the wanderings of his mind were rendered obvious, by the incoherent nature of certain poetical effusions which he attempted, and by his jealousy of those whom in his "right mind" he best loved.

> "Black despair,
> The shadow of a starless night, was thrown
> Over the earth, in which he moved alone."[45]

His melancholy fate is too well known to require our recapitulation of its sad particulars.[46] He now rests amid his kindred in the West Relief Church-yard of Paisley. The spot is unmarked by even the simplest memorial.[47] Without guidance, a stranger, however willing to do reverence to the dust of the departed poet, would be unable to find its whereabout. The sod has sunk to the common level, and the grass is as thickly matted as if it had never been disturbed by the implements of the sexton. The memory of Tannahill, however, is still green in the hearts of his townsmen. Many of the older inhabitants, among whom is the poet's younger brother, Mr. Matthew Tannahill,[48] a highly respectable and intelligent individual, now well advanced in years, still affectionately remember his person, and many of the incidents of his life. The poet's watch, purchased by the first money which he saved from his earnings as a journeyman weaver, is in the possession of his brother; one individual religiously preserves a portion of his loom, while several fondly cherish scraps of his handwriting; and his songs, much as they are appreciated over the length and breadth of the land, are doubly endeared to the people of Paisley, from their association with scenes which to them have the charm of familiarity.

With regard to the position which the name of Tannahill is destined to occupy among the bards of his country, a few words must suffice. As a song-writer, in which character his superiority alone

---

[45] From the dedication of 'The Revolt of Islam' (1818) by Percy Bysshe Shelley.
[46] Robert Tannahill drowned himself in a culverted river in 1810.
[47] A grave monument for Tannahill was erected in 1866.
[48] c.1777 – 1857

consists, he can only be compared with Burns, the great master of the lyre. To him alone is he inferior. Strength and vigour are the prevailing characteristics of the Ayrshire peasant – simplicity and tenderness of the Paisley artisan. The former wrung his imagery in a great measure from his own large and burning heart; the latter gathered his principally from the woods and fields. The one touches our feelings; the other pleases our fancy. In the love songs of Burns, the woman is always in bold relief; in those of Tannahill, she is half-hidden among flowers. In "My Nannie O" and "Mary Morrison" we never lose sight of the heroines; in "Jessie the Flower o' Dumblane" and "Gloomy Winter's noo awa'" the bonny lasses are but as lay figures, which the fancy of the poet busks with bud and bloom. The lover revels in Burns; the sentimentalist finds his delight in Tannahill. Variety and power are on the side of the former; sweetness and delicacy on that of the latter. In different walks both are true to the living nature; and the constitution of Scottish hearts must undergo a radical change ere the lays of either can cease to be heard with pleasure in cottage and in hall,

"From Maidenkirk to John o' Groat's."[49]

One of the most recent and most striking architectural additions to Paisley is the Neilson Testimonial, an extensive and stately edifice, which crowns the western and highest extremity of the ridge on which the more ancient portion of the town is situated.[50] The site of this handsome structure, designed by Charles Wilson, Esq., of this city, was formerly a bowling-green, and was remarkable for the extent and beauty of the landscape which it commanded. The establishment has been erected in accordance with the will of the late Mr. John Neilson, a grocer of the town, who bequeathed at his death, which happened a few years since, the sum of £20,000, for the purpose of educating, and, if necessary, clothing and feeding poor children belonging to the community. A moiety of this munificent bequest, as we were informed,

---

[49] That is, in the whole of Scotland. From 'On the Late Captain Grose's Peregrinations through Scotland' (1789) by Robert Burns.
[50] Opened in 1852. The John Neilsen Institution building survives, but has now been converted into flats.

has been expended on the building, which, however much it may contribute to the adornment of the town, is reckoned a "leetle too grand" for the occasion by many of the long-headed natives, for the especial benefit of whose children it was designed. We have no desire, however, to "scaud our tongue wi' ither folk's kail," and other towns besides Paisley have fallen into the error of sacrificing the useful to the ornamental, and erecting a palace where a poor-house would have been more to the purpose.

Leaving this magnificent "Testimonial," and proceeding a little farther to the westward, we arrive at the Cemetery of Paisley – a spacious and most lovely "city of the dead," extending altogether to about forty imperial acres, on both sides of a beautiful green hill. It is intersected by several miles of gravelled walks, neatly trimmed and adorned with a profusion of shrubs and flowering plants. A considerable number of hardy trees also lend additional beauty to the locality, while a variety of tasteful monuments and headstones mark the last resting-places of the departed. In one corner of the grounds we observe an obelisk, erected to the memory of two individuals who suffered for their adherence to the principles of the Solemn League and Covenant,[51] in the days of the Second Charles.[52] On the front of the pedestal is the following inscription:

"Here lie the Corpses of James Algie and John Park, who suffered at the Cross of Paisley for refusing the Oath of Abjuration,[53] Feb. 3, 1685.

"Stay, passenger, as thou goest by,
And take a look where these do lie,
Who, for the love they bore to truth,
Were deprived of their life and youth.
Though laws made then caused many die,
Judges and sizers were not free;
He that to them did these delate
The greater count he hath to make;

---

[51] A covenant to support Reformed Christianity in Scotland.
[52] 1660 – 1685
[53] An oath renouncing the Solemn League and Covenant and promising not to take up arms against the king.

Yet no excuse to them can be,
At ten condemned, at two to die.
So cruel did their rage become,
To stop their speech caused beat the drum;
This may a standing witness be
'Twixt Presbytrie and Prelacy."

The remains of these martyrs, as we learn from another inscription, were originally deposited in the Gallowgreen; but on the occasion of that spot being built upon in 1779, they were removed by the authorities and reinterred here. The present monument was erected by contributions from various denominations of Christians in 1835. On the west side of the obelisk is the following beautiful and appropriate quotation from Cowper:

"Their blood was shed
In confirmation of the noblest claim
Our claim to feed upon immortal truth,
To walk with God, to be divinely free,
To soar and to anticipate the skies;
Yet few remember them – they lived unknown,
Till persecution dragged them into fame,
And chased them up to heaven."[54]

We now proceed to the summit of the eminence, along which there is a splendid avenue, fringed with shrubbery and handsome rows of trees. Near this we are shown the grave of William Finlay,[55] a poet of considerable merit and no limited local fame; but whose "last low bed of earth "is unmarked even by the simplest headstone. Here also lies our old friend, James King,[56] a poet of no mean power, and who was for many years the esteemed companion, and afterwards the correspondent of Tannahill. His narrow bed, however, we fail to discover, although we assisted at his obsequies, probably from the same lack of a funereal index. This neglect, however, is scarcely to be

---

[54] From book 5 of 'The Task' (1785) by William Cowper.
[55] 1792 – 1847
[56] 1776 – 1849

wondered at, when we consider that Wilson and Tannahill are in this respect still unhonoured in the town of their birth. We understand that sites have been selected at the east and west extremities of the avenue we have alluded to, and that money has even been collected for the purpose of erecting monuments respectively to the memory of the authors of "Watty and Meg" and of "Jessie the Flower of Dumblane."[57] There is no immediate indication, however, we regret to say, of these laudable schemes being carried into effect. Paisley, which is so apt to boast of her genius, and with good reason too, must still lie under the reproach of ingratitude to the memories of those who have so widely enlarged her fame and so richly invested her scenery with the charms of sentimental association. Let us hope that this defect in her noble Cemetery may speedily be remedied.

> "Not as a record he lacketh a stone!
> Pay a light debt to the singer we've known;
> Proof that our love for his name hath not flown
> With the frame perishing,
> That we are cherishing
> Feelings akin to the lost poet's own."[58]

[A renewed effort is at present (May.1856) being made to raise a sufficient sum for the erection of a monument to Wilson; and it is confidently anticipated that the work will be commenced during the current year.][59]

No place certainly could be selected more appropriate for the erection of a monument to Tannahill, than the brow of the Paisley *Pere la Chase*.[60] It commands a series of the most lovely, varied, and

---

[57] A bronze statue of Tannahill was erected near Paisley Abbey in 1883. A statue of Wilson by John Mossman was erected near Paisley Abbey in 1874. There is also a modern headstone of Wilson in the cemetery and a bronze monument from 1995 near the Hammills rapids.

[58] From 'Lines Written after a Visit to the Grave of my Friend William Motherwell' (1847) by William Kennedy.

[59] MacDonald is probably referring to an earlier monument that has since been replaced.

[60] That is, the cemetery. A reference to the famous Père Lachaise cemetery in Paris.

comprehensive landscapes that we have ever witnessed. Scotland, rich as she is in material beauty, can boast few such. Some idea of their interest may be formed, when we state, that included within their range is almost the entire "land of Tannahill" – that is to say, the principal scenes alluded to in his songs. Looking northward, we have almost at our feet the spot where once waved the "bonnie wood of Craigielee," not occupied by the gas-work (as Philip Ramsay[61] asserts), which is considerably to the east of it, but now denuded of its leafy covering, and given over to the plough.

> "Far ben its dark green planting's shade,
> Nae cushat[62] croodles amorously,
> Nae mavis down its bughted[63] glade
> Gars echo ring frae tree to tree."

The "Spunkie howe," the "Whinny knowe," still covered with whins, Kebbuckston farm, where the famous wedding was held, and Ferguslie wood,[64] are all in the immediate vicinity; while beyond are the wide-spreading and fertile haughs of Clyde, with the burgh of Renfrew, and our own smoky city, with Tennant's giant towering over it;[65] and in the distance, to the left, are the Kilpatrick range and the misty mountain tops, where

> "Sweet amidst her native hills,
> Obscurely bloomed the Jeanie,"[66]

whose unsophisticated charms won the admiration of the susceptible poet. Turning "to the right about," as the drill-sergeant has it, and looking from this picture unto that, the scene is equally fair, although not quite so spacious. To the right are the Newton woods, just as they

---

[61] Philip Anstruther Ramsay (1798 – 1844), writer for the *Paisley Magazine*, and another friend of William Motherwell.
[62] wood pigeon
[63] twisting
[64] All references to Tannahill's poems.
[65] 'Tennant's stalk', the chimney of the St Rollox Chemical Works in Sighthill. The chimney was demolished in 1922.
[66] From Tannahill's 'The Lass o' Arranteenie'.

were when the bard marked the laverock fanning the "snaw-white cluds,"[67] on the departure of gloomy winter, some half century ago. Then immediately in front are the Gleniffer Braes, with the dark firs still crowning the stey rocky hill, and the "dusky glen," where in the gloaming "the planting taps" are still "tinged wi' gowd,"[68] as in the days o' langsyne. A little nearer are the "auld castle turrets"[69] of Stanley, but an intervening knowe half hides them from our gaze. To the left is Craigie Linn, a delicious little subject for some of our landscape limners – and virgin, so far as we are aware – with Glen-Killoch's sunny brae beyond. In short, the entire features of the fine song of "Gloomy Winter's noo awa," are spread as in a picture before the spectator. We would advise our youthful readers, however, to think twice before they address their sweethearts in the words of the poet, –

> "Come, my lassie, let us stray,
> O'er Glen-Killoch's sunny brae,
> Blythely spend the gowden day
> 'Mong joys that never wearie, O."[70]

In Tannahill's day the braes were free to all; now they are strictly tabooed, and it would be rather an awkward *contretemps* to have one's hinnied whisperings interrupted by the growl of a surly gamekeeper, or to have an action of damages appended to the "joys that never wearie."[71] We have now glanced at two sides of the picture which is seen from this "coigne of vantage," but there is still another over which we must cast an eye. Looking to the westward, a beautiful tract of country is seen, terminating in a fine range of gently undulating hills. In the foreground is the village of Elderslie, the birthplace of the great Caledonian patriot, at whose name

---

[67] From 'Gloomy Winter's Noo Awa''.
[68] From 'The Dusky Glen'.
[69] From 'The Braes of Glennifer'.
[70] From 'Gloomy Winter's Noo Awa''.
[71] Following the 1695 Act for the Division of Commonties, most of Scotland's common land was divided among adjacent landowners during the 18th and 19th centuries, becoming private property.

No. XII. Paisley and its Environs

"What Scottish blood
But boils up in a spring-tide flood"[72]

of love for the land whose independence he so nobly struggled to secure! Beyond are seen the villages of Johnstone and Kilbarchan – the latter of which has long been celebrated as the birthplace of the famous piper, Habby Simson,[73] an effigy of whom, with his drones over the wrong shoulder, still graces the parish steeple.[74] Every one acquainted with Scottish song will doubtless remember the favourable mention made of Habby by no less a personage than Maggie Lauder,

"Weel ha'e you play'd your part, quo' Meg,
Your cheeks are like the crimson:
There's nane in Scotland plays sae weel
Since we lost Habby Simson."

Altogether, as we daresay, our readers will admit, even after the imperfect enumeration we have given, there are few points of vision in Scotland from whence at a glance so many objects of sentimental interest may be seen as from the brow of the Paisley Cemetery, while, even to the merest student of material beauty, it would amply repay a summer day's walk.

A number of the walks round Paisley are of the most delightful description. Within the compass of an hour's stroll in almost any direction, her denizens can command nearly every variety of scenery – including fertile fields, green flowery knolls, heath-covered braes, romantic glens, shadowy woods, clear gushing streamlets murmuring on their way, and silent rivers moving solemnly and slow on their funeral marches to the insatiate sea, – in short, almost all the shows and forms of natural beauty which the eye of the poet or the painter could desire. Nor are the inhabitants devoid of urban sources of enjoyment, intellectual or recreative. The Paisley "bodies" are eminently social, or we might even say clannish. Social and literary

---

[72] That is, William Wallace. From 'Lines to William Simpson of Ochiltree' (1785) by Robert Burns.
[73] c.1550-1620
[74] This wooden statue was replaced with a bronze copy of it in 1932.

241

coteries are more common among them than in any other community with which we are acquainted. We were lately, through the kindness of a friend, invited to an annual potato and herring dinner at Renfrew, in connection with a club which was instituted upwards of half a century ago. The following account of the origin of the club, and probably from the pen of a member, appeared in the *Edinburgh Chronicle* of August 31, 1844:

"It so happened, that on a Saturday in autumn, forty-six years ago, six or eight weavers took their weekly walk down the banks of the Cart and up the side of the Clyde. By the time they reached the ancient burgh of Renfrew they felt inclined for some rest and refreshment. They entered an humble public house to have their wants supplied, but the landlady had nothing in the shape of food to offer them except a meal of potatoes and herrings, which stood ready cooked beside the fire. The homeliness of the fare was rather a recommendation than otherwise, and so well did the company relish the refreshment and the unsophisticated simplicity with which it was served, that they there and then formed themselves into a club, elected a preses[75] and convener, and resolved to return annually, at the same period of the year, and dine on herring and potatoes. Since that time to this the club has been kept up, and the members have attended with great regularity – some of the original members, who still survive, never having been once absent from the dinner. All the original members of the club were weavers, and for a number of years all who attended it continued in the same rank. But, by and by, some of them got up to be merchants and manufacturers; and twenty years ago the herring and potato dinner was attended by thirty-six individuals, and not a tradesman amongst them, the meeting being composed of manufacturers, merchants, bankers, lawyers, &c. The same frugal bill of fare is still adhered to, for the sake of the pleasing associations therewith connected, and to keep in remembrance the 'days of langsyne,' when the members were glad to have plenty of such humble viands as good herring and potatoes. The cost of the feast is sixpence!

---

[75] chairman

The bond of union among the members is not sensual indulgence, but sociality; and simple natural tastes are cherished by the exclusion of all expensive luxuries from the board.

"After the dinner the glass and toast, the speech and song, go round; and it is expected that every person present will give something in the shape of a toast, speech, or song, to keep up the hilarity of the meeting. It is needless to say, though the 'mirth and fun' is seldom either fast or furious, 'the feast of reason and the flow of soul' make the time fleet past with speedy wing, and render the herring and potato dinner day one of the brightest in the year to every member of the club."

To borrow the words of the immortal Gilpin, when next they discuss their feast of tubers and "Glasgow magistrates," "may we be there to see,"[76] or perhaps we should rather say to pree,[77] for the mere sight of the wholesome and savoury viands would prove but a Barmecide treat.[78]

The studiously inclined among the working classes of Paisley are well supplied with the means and appliances of intellectual culture. The Mechanics' and Artisans' Institutions afford, for an extremely moderate subscription, abundance of newspapers, periodicals, and books, with accommodation for harmless amusements, such as billiards and draughts. [Since this was written the Mechanics' Institution has ceased to exist.][79] Such privileges, if properly appreciated and taken advantage of, as it is to be hoped they are, must ultimately have a highly beneficial influence on the character of the population. Somewhat tired with our devious wanderings – for however willing the spirit may be, the flesh is apt under lengthened exertion to become weak – we are fain, as twilight is thickening into night, in company with a friend or two to seek the shelter of a friendly "howff" for rest and a modicum of needful refreshment. "A wee drap

---

[76] From 'The Diverting History of John Gilpin' (1782) by William Cowper.
[77] to sample
[78] A reference to a banquet given by Prince Barmecide in the *Arabian Nights* where all the food was imaginary.
[79] It was formed in 1847 and wound up in 1855.

frae the Saucel"[80] has a decidedly magical influence on both heart and tongue, and certainly sets time askipping with astonishing velocity. It seems as if we had scarcely sat down when the ear-piercing whistle of the "last train" warns us to depart. There is a shaking of hands, a slamming of carriage doors, a brief rush through the darkness, and we are once more pushing our way through the bustling streets of our "ain toun."

---

[80] The Saucel was Paisley's distillery.

No. XIII. Gleniffer and Elderslie

There is a charm of sweetest potency in the lay of the poet when it is wedded to the beautiful in external nature. Both song and scene are doubly enriched by the union. The melodious gush of human feeling passing over the fair bosom of the landscape, like the south wind upon a bank of violets, to borrow an image from the great treasury of imagery, seems, as it were, like "giving and receiving odour."[1] The genius of Burns to many a stream has lent "a music sweeter than its own."[2] It is not the material loveliness of the Doon, the Lugar, and the Ayr, though lovely wanderers by wood and wild are they one and all, that leads the pilgrim's willing feet so frequently to their banks. It is not the beauties which Flora discloses among the green links of the Tweed, the Yarrow, and the Ettrick which bring so many loving eyes to gaze on their rippled bosoms. To those who admire the shows and forms of the great mother in all their native grace, these murmuring beauties of our native land would in any case be dear. But when to their other attractions is added the living light of song; when they are associated with the heart utterances of beings with kindred passions to our own, who have loved, and hoped, and feared – who have joyed and sorrowed, smiled and wept by their gushing channels – then, indeed, do they become unto our souls even as hallowed things, and the spirit yearns to behold them, even as it would to gaze upon an absent friend, and longs to hear their liquid voices as it does for that of one whom we have loved with a perfect love. Few are thy running waters, mine own song-breathing land, which cannot boast their own peculiar strains; and few, indeed, are thy song-haunted streams with which these eyes have not, at one time or other, been gladdened. Beyond the Tweed, however, there are many Yarrows yet unvisited. Shakspeare's Avon is to us a dream; the fairy Duddon and the sylvan Wye, murmur for us in Wordsworth's verse alone; while the Ouse of gentle Cowper we can only see "in the mind's eye, Horatio,"[3] as it floweth in placid sweetness

---

[1] From Shakespeare's *Twelfth Night* I.i.
[2] From 'A Poet's Epitaph' (1800) by William Wordsworth
[3] From Shakespeare's *Hamlet* I.ii.

through the landscape of "The Task."[4] Would it were ours, this sweet September day, to thread the mazes of some one or other of these song-enchanted streams! to tread in the footsteps of departed genius, and to look upon the scenes which, in days gone by, the poet loved and sung! The wish is vain. Even in these days of speedy transit it may not be; so we shall even make a virtue of necessity, and spend our golden interval of autumnal leisure, in a pilgrimage to scenery not less fair, though happily more familiar – the land of our own sweet singer, Robert Tannahill.[5]

The year is falling into the "sere and yellow leaf,"[6] and the reapers are busy among the white fields of harvest. There is still a faint lingering indication of nocturnal frost in the morning air, but the sun, with its golden slants of radiance, from a sky of mingled blue and white, gives promise of a glorious day, as we shape our course towards the terminus of the "South-Western,"[7] on our route to the ancient town of Paisley. Our train is in waiting with a snorting engine at its head, and, punctual to the minute, we find ourselves in rapid motion along the iron way. There is something exceedingly exhilarating in a brief rush by rail a into the country. As with the wings of a bird, we are at once borne from the city's bustling maze into the freshness and beauty of the scattered farms and villages. The sense of sight, which has been "cabined, cribbed, confined"[8] within the weary waste of walls, is again permitted "ample scope and verge enough,"[9] and wanders with a feeling of relief and gladness over the fair face of nature, while in the very depths of our heart we find an echo to the poet's exclamation –

"God made the country, but man made the town."[10]

Brief space for reflection is now afforded to the traveller between the Broomielaw and the Sneddon. There are fine snatches of landscape,

---

[4] William Cowper was the author of 'The Task' (1785).
[5] 1774 – 1810, Paisley poet.
[6] From Shakespeare's *Macbeth* V.iii.
[7] The Glasgow and South Western Railway.
[8] From Shakespeare's *Macbeth* III.iv.
[9] From 'The Bard' (1757) by Thomas Grey.
[10] From book 1 of 'The Task' (1785) by William Cowper.

however, by the way. Dashing past the neat little suburb of Pollokshields – the picturesque villas of which have sprung up as if by enchantment – we have the fine spire of Govan rising over its girdle of ancient elms to the right; and in the distance beyond, the brown Kilpatrick Hills seem as if they were hastening to meet us. Now we have a cosie farm-stead rushing past – then a stately mansion, half-hidden in foliage – and anon we catch a passing glimpse of Crookston's shattered tower rising against the horizon to the left. At length, emerging from the tunnel of Arkleston, the smoke of Paisley is seen curling lazily to the sky, and the train, passing Greenlaw, with its verdant lawns and leafy clumps of trees, soon comes to a pause, and discharges a considerable portion of its living freight.

We have a warm side to Paisley and its "bodies." Some of our happiest days were spent in that locality, and we have never experienced more genuine kindness than amongst its inhabitants. Nowhere else have we such "troops of friends,"[11] and nowhere else do we meet so many smiling faces and frankly extended hands, or so many homes where we are certain of a warm and hearty welcome. Blessings be upon thee and thy denizens, old town! and may the prosperity which now shines upon thee be of long continuance! May thy trade flourish and thy comforts increase! and may the gift of song, in which so many of thy sons have excelled, still find its most faithful votaries in thee! But, talking of poetry, we are reminded that a young poet of most ample promise – one whose name has already travelled far on the wings of fame – was to meet us here;[12] and see, there he is, in front of that stately baronial pile, the County Prison, awaiting our arrival, and, staff in hand, prepared for the pilgrimage we have chalked out for ourselves. As we pass along another friend of kindred spirit is picked up, and, congratulating ourselves on the best day of the season, we thread our way to the "west end," and, after a brief interval, make our exit from the town by way of Maxwellton, in the direction of Gleniffer Braes. This fine range of hills is situated about two miles to the southward of Paisley – the intervening country consisting

---

[11] From Shakespeare's *Macbeth* V.iii.
[12] Alexander Smith, 1829 – 1867, poet and writer.

principally of gently swelling undulations, part of which are covered with trees, but the greater portion being cultivated or under pasture. We are now upon classic ground, amid scenes which have been immortalized in never-dying song. Along the path which we are now treading Robert Tannahill, the weaver poet of Paisley, has often strayed, to glean the sweet natural imagery with which his lyrics are so delightfully interwoven. The place of his birth and his boyhood, the scene of his toils and his pleasures, and, alas! that of his melancholy death, are all in the immediate neighbourhood. Some half-century ago the poet might have been seen stealing out, on this very road, in the summer gloamings, when the midges were dancing aboon the burn, to spend a few hours alone with nature, after the labours of the day were over. These green knolls have often rung with the echoes of his flute; and perhaps these very trees which are now rustling in the autumnal breeze have murmured in harmony with his voice, as he chanted in solitude the new-born song as came welling from his heart. The surface of the country, however, has undergone material alteration since those days. Where the yellow blossoms of the whin or the golden tassels of the broom then waved unmolested in the passing wind, the ploughshare has since passed, and what was formerly a barren wilderness is now a place of cultivated fertility. Were the poet coming to life again, he would scarcely recognize, indeed, the haunts of his early love.

Passing Meiklieriggs Moor, where the monster political meetings of Paisley have been long held, and leaving the Corsebar Farm behind, we soon arrive at the large reservoir of the Paisley Water Company,[13] also a new feature in the landscape since the departure of the poet. At the south west corner of this large sheet of water, and generally entirely surrounded by it, stands the ancient and withal picturesque Castle of Stanley.[14] This venerable pile is alluded to on several occasions in the writings of Tannahill. Every one will remember that most beautiful passage in one of his songs, –

---

[13] Built in 1838 and now known as Stanely Reservoir.
[14] The water level has since been raised and the castle is partially submerged.

No. XIII. Gleniffer and Elderslie

"Keen blaws the wind o'er the braes of Gleniffer,
The auld castle turrets are covered wi' snaw;
How changed frae the time when I met wi' my lover
Amang the broom bushes by Stanley green shaw!"[15]

Writing in 1804 to his friend and brother poet, Scadlock,[16] who was then located in Perth, he also refers to the old tower in the lines,

"If e'er in musing mood you stray
Alang the classic banks of Tay,
Think on our walks by Stanley tower
And steep Gleniffer brae."

This seems, indeed, to have been a favourite haunt of Tannahill. Stanley green shaw, however, is now no more. Its site is swallowed up in the capacious bosom of the reservoir, and where the birks once waved in the luxuriance of summer, the mavis no longer "sings fu' cheerie, O."[17]

Fortunately, at the time of our visit, the water in the "muckle dam" is exceedingly low, in consequence of which the old castle is standing high and dry, so that we are enabled to inspect it minutely. This edifice, which is of unknown date, consists of a quadrangular keep about forty feet in height, with a rectangular tower of equal elevation, originally designed to afford protection to the principal entrance. Round the top there is a cornice, the corbels of which project considerably, and seem at one period to have been surmounted by a series of small turrets. These, with the entire roof, have now disappeared, however, leaving the structure, which is rent and shattered in various places, in an exceedingly ruinous condition. The window embrasures are small and narrow, and the wall is pierced at intervals by loopholes, which have doubtless contributed to the defence of the inmates in the lawless days of old. Every crevice and seam of the weather-beaten castle is overrun with vegetation – lichens, and mosses, and minute ferns – while the long grass waves above the

---

[15] From 'The Braes of Gleniffer' (1807).
[16] James Scadlock (1775 – 1818).
[17] From 'Gloomy Winter's Noo Awa'' (1807) by Robert Tannahill.

walls, imparting to them an aspect of the dreariest desolation. By a huge gap in one of its immensely thick sides we make our entrée to the interior of the solitary edifice. The desolation within is even more striking and affecting than that which meets the eye outside. The sight of roofless and weed-peopled halls, the vestiges of chimneys still black with the fires which a hundred years ago grew dim, of staircases worn by the feet of long, long departed humanity, of vaults which bring the miserable captives of long ago before the inward eye, all strike upon a solemn chord of sympathy within us, and excite to serious meditation upon the transitoriness of all earthly things. Fancy in such a scene has full scope, and immediately begins to summon up the dead. The silent chambers are once more teeming with living forms – knights, and lords, and ladies fair. Here the master of the keep once more prepares him for the fight – from that window the weeping mistress again looks forth upon her warrior's departure, or smiles his welcome home. Pictures of birth, marriage, and death – the land marks of all human life, the events of all earthly homes start up before us, and we joy or sorrow as they come and go, as if the creatures of imagination were still our fellow pilgrims between the cradle and the grave. But see! upon the green floor there, in the shaft of sunlight that comes through yonder loop-hole, a bright-winged butterfly, his glowing tints of red, and black, and brown, resplendent in the light! How rich the contrast of his radiant hues with the verdant lichens, upon which he is couched, and the old gray walls around! 'Tis a speck of living glory on the very heart of ruin. In wrapt admiration we gaze in silence on the gorgeous insect, as he lingers for a moment on the floor of that most ancient hall, and then goes flickering lightly on his way. 'Tis a trifling incident; yet, in such a place and in such a mood as we are, trifles have power to touch the heart. "He preacheth too," as Jean Paul has said. Ay, this

> "Tiny patrician, on whose bannery wings
> Are bright emblazonings,"[18]

---

[18] From 'On a Butterfly in a Church' (1844) by James Headerwick. The poem quotes the words of Jean Paul Richter, German Romantic author: "Hinder him not; he preacheth too."

is but a type of human grandeur – of human life; a thing of beauty for a moment seen, and then for ever lost. Children of a day, we sport from flower to flower, while the sun is in the sky, and death meets us in the dews of gloaming. Full many a butterfly of humankind have these sturdy old walls encircled, who has now gone the way of all living, and long after the trio of friends who are now musing on this beauteous insect of a day have passed the dark "bourne whence no traveller returns,"[19] they will still lift a weather beaten front to the peltings of the pitiless storm. The things our own hands have made are far more lasting than we.

Ascending a narrow stair in the castle, we find ourselves on a commanding platform, which, through a huge gap in the wall, presents a magnificent view of the country to the northward: but, as we shall have the pleasure of witnessing the same landscape on a more extended scale from the brow of the adjoining braes, we shall not linger here to attempt its description. So, making our exit by the channel which time has gnawed in the wall, apparently to permit us a passage, we take farewell of the hoary edifice. About thirty yards or so to the south-west of the castle, however, we again give ourselves pause to examine the shaft and pedestal of a curious old stone cross, which, from time immemorial, stood where the reservoir is now excavated, and which has long been a puzzle to local antiquaries. We find, to our regret, this interesting relic removed from the rude socket in which it stood, and lying ingloriously prostrate on the ground, where it has evidently lain for a considerable time past. This, in popular parlance, is called the "Danish Stone;" and tradition ascribes its origin to some of those roving Norse warriors who were in the habit of favouring our Caledonian sires of a far distant era with occasional visits of a hostile nature. It was supposed that one of their leaders had been slain and was buried at this spot, and that the stone was erected to perpetuate his memory. There can be little doubt, however, that it is in reality a fragment of one of those ancient monumental crosses which were at one time so plenteously erected by our Popish forefathers. Remains of such erections are, indeed, still to be found in various parts of the

---

[19] From Shakespeare's *Hamlet* III.i.

country. Examining the prostrate stone, we find it to be between four and five feet in length, with faint vestiges, barely visible indeed, of sculptured animals upon one of its sides, and traces of wreathed work, better defined, carved upon its edges. What species of animated forms were designed to be represented on this fragment of the past, it would require more acute eyes than ours now-a-days to discover; but we learn from Semple,[20] the county historian, who saw it in 1782, that on what was then the west side, and which is now the upper one, "there were two lions near the base, and two boars a little above." The old stone, however, has forgotten the tale which it was intended to tell; it is now almost a blank, and if permitted to remain much longer on the cold earth, exposed to the action of wind and weather, it will soon be indistinguishable from an ordinary piece of mason-work.[21] To such a favour, indeed, must the proudest monuments of man come at last.[22]

Gradually ascending, we have now the beautiful range of the Gleniffer Braes immediately before us. That dark ravine in our front, surmounted with gloomy firs on either side, is the glen from which the braes derive their name. It is a deep rocky gully, bounded by steep overhanging walls, and with a brawling torrent rushing foamily down its rugged channel. Observe, the fine beech at one side of the entrance is already tinged with gold, as if October had untimely dashed it with his mellowing wing. Fain would we guide thee, gentle reader, up that most picturesque ravine, for well we know its every linn and pool; but my lord's game might chance to be disturbed, or haply we might fall in with some one of his lordship's surly keepers, than whom we had rather encounter a raging bear.[23] So we must even content ourselves with the highway, which, as you observe, slopes beautifully up hill to the westward. Before proceeding, however, we may mention that the

---

[20] William Semple wrote a 'Continuation of Crawfurd's History of Renfrewshire' (1782).

[21] The stone was removed to a store by the Water Company (now Scottish Water) for safekeeping. Its present whereabouts are unknown.

[22] A reference to Shakespeare's *Hamlet* V.i.

[23] This land had previously been open to all, but (following the 1695 Act for the Division of Commonties) most of Scotland's common land passed into private hands during the 18th and 19th centuries.

scene before us is supposed by some to be the "dusky glen" alluded to in Tannahill's fine song beginning

"We'll meet beside the dusky glen, on yon burnside,
Where the bushes form a cosie den, on yon burnside."[24]

The spot certainly agrees in all its features with the scenery referred to in the song; the "birken bower," the "broomy knowes," the "sweetly murmuring stream," &c., are all here as the poet has described them. As if, moreover, to corroborate the statement that this is the veritable "dusky glen," we may record an incident which we have learned on the best authority. One sweet summer evening, about the beginning of the present century, the poet and his brother (Mr. Matthew Tannahill, who still survives, a hale and venerable old man) were taking their usual walk together after the toils of the day, on the braes in this vicinity. By the time they reached the place where we are now standing, that is to say, immediately below Gleniffer proper, the sun was slowly sinking beneath the horizon. The whole vale of the Clyde was filled, as it were, with the level radiance of the departing orb, and the gray hills were glowing in a warm ruddy hue. What principally attracted the poet's attention, however, was the effect which the flood of light had produced upon certain trees in the neighbourhood, which were gilded as with a glittering halo by the effulgent beams. On observing the phenomenon he immediately cried out in ecstacy to his brother, "Look here, Matthew! did you ever see anything so exquisitely beautiful! why, the very leaves glimmer as gin they were tinged wi' gowd." Shortly after this the song appeared, and the poet's brother at once remembered the circumstance which had given birth to the finest verse in the production, –

"Now the plantin' taps are tinged wi' gowd, on yon burnside,
And gloamin' draws her foggy shroud, on yon burnside;
Far frae the noisy scene,
I'll through the fields alane;
There we'll meet, my ain dear Jean! down by yon burnside."

---

[24] From 'Yon Burn Side' (1807).

There is an opinion generally entertained in Paisley and its vicinity, however, that the locale of the song is a certain "dusky glen" on the Alt-Patrick burn, about a couple of miles north-west from our present position. It would be difficult indeed to prove definitely which of the places the poet had in his mind when the effusion was written. We are in favour of the Gleniffer theory from the circumstances above stated, but when the poet's surviving friends refrain from speaking authoritatively on the subject we must be moderate in the advocacy of our views. Either glen is sufficiently beautiful to justify the taste of the author.

The song of "Gloomy winter's noo awa'" is perhaps the most popular, as it certainly is the most exquisite of Tannahill's songs. There is a melodious sweetness in this strain, combined with a tenderness of sentiment and a truthfulness of natural imagery, which have rarely been equalled, and which, unless by a few of the best lyrical effusions of Burns, have never been surpassed. The scene of this delightful lay now lies before us, beautiful even as it was when the poet saw it in the light of his own genius. To the eastward lies Glen-Killoch, towards which, in the song, he invites his "young," his "artless dearie" to stray; to the west are the "Newton woods," over which the laverock fanned the "snaw-white cluds" on the "gowden day" alluded to, while "Gleniffer's dewy dell" opens its verdant bosom before us. We have heard it prosaically objected to this song, that the Newton woods are too far west for the ear to distinguish the laverock's lilt, while Gleniffer is at hand; and that Glen-Killoch is a shade too far east for a couple of lovers to visit within the compass of an easy walk; but assuredly those who made the objection were neither poets nor lovers, or they would have known better the extent of license which both poet and lover require for their enjoyments. To the lover no ramble is too long when his charmer is by his side, and the ear of the poet is gleg beyond the comprehension of ordinary mortals.

What is the "craw-flower" alluded to in this song? is a question to which various answers have been returned. The little celandine of Wordsworth has been pointed out to us as the "craw-flower" of Tannahill, and also the crowfoot or buttercup of our meadows. It is neither of these, however. The craw-flower of the poet is the wild hyacinth of our woods, the *hyacinthus non-scriptus* of the botanist, which, with its tuft of blue-bells, sweetens the breath of May and June. The local name of this beautiful flower is the "crawtae," and by this name also it is mentioned in the writings of Milton, who, it will be remembered, in *Lycidas*, invokes the vales to strew their blooms on the tomb of his lost friend: –

"Bring the rathe primrose that forsaken dies,
The *tufted crowtoe* and pale jessamine,
The white pink, and the pansy freaked with jet,
The glowing violet,
The musk-rose and the well-attired woodbine,
With cowslips wan, that hang the pensive head,
And every flower that sad embroidery wears."[25]

The celandine is not a bell but a star; neither is it blue in colour; and we learn from another song[26] that Tannahill's "craw-flower" *was* blue; but in addition to this, we know that "feathery breckans" fringed the rocks at the season alluded to in the song, and every botanist knows that by the time the fronds of the fern are unfolded the bloom of the celandine is over, while that of the hyacinth is at its prime. The craw-flower of "Gloomy winter's noo awa," therefore, is in reality the sweet-scented blue-bell of the early summer; than which our indigenous Flora can boast but few lovelier flowers. It is just the image which a poet would select for sweetness and modesty in the lassie of his heart.

Our way is now up hill, and as we advance the prospect gradually widens and becomes more interesting. The character of the vegetation also becomes altered. Flowers which are unknown on the rich flats below here bloom profusely in all their native loveliness. The bracken, the heather, and the myrtle-leaved blaeberry lend a kind of Alpine feature to the swelling knolls; while fringing the margin of the path we have the delicate wild pansy, the fairy blue-bell, and the

---

[25] By John Milton (1638).
[26] From both 'Ye Echoes that Ring' and 'Langsyne'.

graceful bed-straws white and yellow. Passing a comfortable looking farm-house, with a few fine umbrageous plane trees by its side, one of which has an immense hollow in its trunk, we at length, in a bend of the road, arrive at a little natural fountain trickling from a green bank by the wayside. The gush is small, but unfailing in the highest noons of summer, and the water is deliciously cool and clear. Full many a crystalline draught are we indebted to that tiny well. Oft in our rambles over these braes, alone or in company with valued friends, have we come for rest and refreshment to this secluded but commanding spot. Many are the blythe groups we have seen circled around it, while each individual in turn dipped his beard in its stainless bosom. Fair faces, too, have we seen mirrored in its waters, while rosy lips have met – substance and shadow – on its cool, dimpled surface. Were we a rich man we should gift thee a handsome basin, thou well-loved little fountain; but silver and gold have we none; so thou must even content thyself with a humble poet's honest meed of praise:[27]

THE BONNIE WEE WELL

The bonnie wee well on the breist o' the brae,
That skinkles sae cauld in the sweet smile o' day,
And croons a laigh sang a' to pleasure itsel'
As it jinks 'neath the breckan and genty blue-bell.

The bonnie wee well on the breist o' the brae
Seems an image to me o' a bairnie at play;
For it springs frae the yird wi' a flicker o' glee,
And it kisses the flowers, while its ripple they preen.

The bonnie wee well on the breist o' the brae
Wins blessings on blessings fu' monie ilk day;

---

[27] A fountain designed by John Mossman was erected at this spot, known as 'MacDonald's Rest', with funds raised by the Glasgow Ramblers' Club. It was moved to Glasgow Green in 1881. The Paisley Old Weavers' Society raised funds for a replacement, erected at MacDonald's Rest in 1883. It still stands there, but the water of the Bonnie Wee Well no longer flows through it.

No. XIII. Gleniffer and Elderslie

For the wayworn and wearie aft rest by its side,
And man, wife, and wean a' are richly supplied.

The bonnie wee well on the breist o' the brae,
Where the hare steals to drink in the gloamin' sae gray,
Where the wild moorlan' birds dip their nebs and tak' wing,
And the lark weets his whistle ere mounting to sing.

Thou bonnie wee well on the breist o' the brae,
My memory aft haunts thee by nicht and by day;
For the friends I ha'e loved in the years that are gane
Ha'e knelt by thy brim, and thy gush ha'e parta'en.

Thou bonnie wee well on the breist o' the brae,
While I stoop to thy bosom, my thirst to allay,
I will drink to the loved ones who come back nae mair,
And my tears will but hallow thy bosom sae fair.

Thou bonnie wee well on the breist o' the brae,
My blessing rests with thee, wherever I stray;
In joy and in sorrow, in sunshine and gloom,
I will dream of thy beauty, thy freshness and bloom.

In the depths of the city, midst turmoil and noise,
I'll oft hear with rapture thy lone trickling voice,
While fancy takes wing to thy rich fringe of green,
And quaffs thy cool waters in noon's gowden sheen.[28]

Let us now glance at the picture which is spread before us, and we verily believe that a fairer one exists not in bonny Scotland. At our feet is the old Castle of Stanley, with its sheet of water glittering in the sun; beyond is the magnificent basin of the Clyde, stretching away to the Campsie and Kilpatrick Hills, with all its garniture of woods and

---

[28] MacDonald extemporised the first two lines of this poem during the ramble described. Alexander Smith threatened to steal the line. MacDonald replied, "If it's worth stealing, it's worth keeping," and finished the poem when he returned home.

fields, mansions and farms, villages and towns, set down as in a map. In the middle distance are Paisley and Renfrew, to the right our own good city with its canopy of smoke, to the left Elderslie, Johnstone, and Kilbarchan. Snatches of the Clyde and its tributary Cart are to be discovered here and there; while long trails of steam mark the various courses of the rail. To the far right we have the Cathkin Braes, to the left Strath-Gryffe, with the hills above Port-Glasgow, and the Mistilaw. On the horizon to the north a grand sweep of the western Highlands meets the view, with Benlomond and a score of other gigantic peaks raising their dun crests against the sky. Such are the landmarks of this glorious amphitheatre; but what pencil or what pen shall do justice to its beautiful details? Of a truth, not ours. The scene, indeed, baffles description. It is on too mighty a scale for words, and it contains within its scope material for countless landscape delineations.

Shortly after leaving the well we reach the summit of the ridge, when our course from a westward direction turns almost due south. We have now reached a kind of table land, consisting principally of moorland pasture, with here and there large patches of cold arable soil, and occasional tracts of peat-bog. The fertile valley which we have been contemplating becomes gradually screened from our gaze by the brow of the hill, and a comparatively sterile tract lies before us. We are now wending our way to a lonely hostelry situated among these dreary moors, and well known to ramblers from Paisley by the appropriate title of the "Peeseweep Inn."[29] A few minutes' walk brings us to the spot. The house is a lowly one-storeyed edifice, with a peat-stack at one end, a rowan-tree in front, and a kail-yard behind. Above the door there was formerly a spirited representation of the bird from which the inn takes its name.[30] The Dick-Tinto[31] who executed the picture so well in other respects, however, had, by some oversight or other,

---

[29] The Peeseweep Inn lost its licence in 1889 and fell into disuse in the 1930s. It is now completely gone.
[30] The lapwing.
[31] A sign-painter turned portrait-painter in the novel *The Bride of Lammermoor* (1819) by Sir Walter Scott.

neglected to furnish the poor bird with a crest. This omission was naturally the cause of considerable jocularity among the gangrel bodies who frequented the house; and whether offended at this circumstance or not we cannot take upon ourselves to say, but the peeseweep has taken wing from its former position, and the inn is at present without a sign. On making our *entrée* we are kindly received by mine hostess of the Peeseweep, and are at once shown ben to the spence. An abundant supply of excellent bread, butter, and cheese, with a jug of milk which never knew the pump, soon grace the board. Our lengthened walk has given appetite an edge of exquisite keenness, and the destruction which immediately ensues is really awful to contemplate. A flowing caulker concludes the repast; and, let the grumblers in the Times, who have recently been crying out against the rapacious charges of our modern Bonifaces,[32] hear and wonder – our united bill is somewhat under a couple of shillings!

Leaving our inn – the landlord of which is certainly in his charges a sad laggard behind the spirit of the age – we now turn in a westerly direction, and pursue our way by a pleasant country path for about a-quarter of a mile, until we arrive at a bridge, which crosses a fine frolicsome burn that leaves a moorland loch a little to the southward, and pursues a devious downward course to the Black Cart, which it joins somewhere in the vicinity of Linwood. This is the Alt-Patrick burn, and down its winding way it is our intention, even at the risk of encountering the gamekeeper, to continue our pilgrimage. Gamekeepers, after all, are but men, and a "soft answer turneth away wrath."[33] We have seldom, indeed, come in contact with specimens of this unpopular genus in our numerous trespasses by wood and wild; and, in the few instances where we have, a civil word or two – and "civility costs nothing" – have generally brought us off with flying colours. So, without a thought of evil consequences, we follow the guidance of the streamlet, and sure a more playful or more beautiful little water never tempted poet's foot to stray adown its sweet meander,

---

[32] Landlords – from the name of the landlord in *The Beaux' Stratagem* (1707) by George Farquhar.
[33] Proverbs 15.1

and no think lang.[34] The inimitable verse of Burns is, in truth, justified in every feature,

> "Whiles ower a linn the burnie plays,
> As through the glen it wimples;
> Whiles 'neath a rocky scaur it strays,
> Whiles in a well it dimples:
> Whiles glitteringto the nightly rays
> Wi' flickering dancing dazzle;
> Whiles cooking underneath the braes
> Beneath the spreading hazel."[35]

Now it seems to sleep in some sweet pool, as if loath to leave a spot so fair; anon it is rippling merrily onward, foaming round some projecting rock that seems to bar its passage, making sweet music to the enamelled stones; and again it leaps playfully over some tiny linn, and gushes rapidly on its way, with foam-bells winking on its dark brown breast. Leisurely we follow its many links and turns, stooping at frequent intervals to regale ourselves on the wild fruits with which its tangled margin abounds. The blackboyd is here in many a jetty bunch, while, strange conjunction, the blae berry, the hindberry, and the strawberry are all to be gathered at once in the same nook. Such a meeting of berries we have never seen before. It would almost seem as if July, August, and September had agreed among their sweet selves to enrich at once with their peculiar fruits this favoured burn. How we enjoy the treat! The omniverous appetite of our schoolboy-days seems to have revisited our inner man once more, while our heart beats lightly in our breast as in the days o' langsyne, when

> "We plundered the hazel, the bramble, and sloe."[36]

As we advance the banks become more steep and bosky, presenting at every turn glimpses of beauty which would fill the painter's heart with joy. Anon, hazels and rowans of richest red are added to our sylvan bill

---

[34] A reference to 'Lines to William Simson' (1785) by Robert Burns.
[35] From 'Halloween' (1786) by Robert Burns.
[36] For the origin of this song, see pp31 – 32.

of fare. At one spot of peculiar loveliness we turn to scan our poetical friend's countenance, expecting to find him in rapt admiration, gazing on its charms. No such thing; the sensuous scoundrel absorbed in the mysteries of a rasp-bush, which he is despoiling of its crimson gems with an avidity approaching to the sublime; while his companion is gazing with a fox-and-grape[37] sort of expression at an un-come-at-able cluster of blushing rowans! Steeper and more steep are the banks becoming, and at length we hear the roar of a waterfall, hidden in foliage, and half-drowning the sweet song of the redbreast with its din. Who would have thought the sportive streamlet could have mustered such a volume of voice? Passing through the gloaming of the wood, we obtain a glimpse of the cataract, which may be about thirty feet in height. The water is dashed down in one white sheet, which has a most pleasing effect as it is seen through its green vale of overhanging boughs. It is a thing to be seen, however, rather than painted, as the intervening foliage somewhat destroys its pictorial capabilities. Immediately below the fall the stream winds pleasantly away through a vast green basin, which has apparently been scooped out by the floods of countless ages. The waters in this uninterrupted channel soon resume their gentle character, and while we rest by its margin a picturesque group of cattle are lazily wading in the foam-fretted shallows. This, we suspect, is the scene of Tannahill's little pastoral drama, "The Soldier's Return," which, as a whole, is admitted to be the least successful of the weaver poet's productions. Indeed, in several recent editions of his poems, it is omitted altogether, with the exception of the fine songs with which it was so profusely interspersed. Some of these are among his most successful efforts; and in one of them he makes his heroine allude to natural beauties similar to those of this locality, when she is about to leave Glenfeoch, and her "mammy and her daddie, O," to go in search of her "braw Hieland laddie, O." The wild fruits, amid which we have been revelling, are specially dwelt upon, as witness:

---

[37] From Aesop's fable, 'The Fox and the Grapes'.

"The blaeberry banks now are lonesome and dreary, O;
Muddy are the streams that gushed down sae clearly, O;
Silent are the rocks that echoed sae gladly, O,
The wild melting strains o' my dear Hieland Laddie, O.
He pu'd me the crawberry, ripe frae the boggy fen;
He pu'd me the strawberry, red frae the fossy glen;
He pu'd me the row'n, frae the wild steep sae giddy, O;
Sae loving and sae kind was my dear Hieland Laddie, O."

Who can doubt that the sweet singer of Paisley has often, in his country rambles, come down the glen as we have now done! or that like us, he has partaken freely of the banquet which Nature spreadeth for our acceptance in the wilderness! We now bid adieu to this charming little glen, where we have spent a couple of hours right pleasantly; and we doubt not that the laird will heartily forgive our harmless, though unauthorized intrusion into his most beautiful domains. We shall certainly accord unto him an equal privilege when he deigns to visit the broad, very broad lands which rejoice in our lairdship. Like those of the famous "Tom Tiddler,"[38] however, we are afraid they will be somewhat difficult of discovery.

And now for Elderslie. The distance may be somewhere about a mile and a half, and as our shadows are waxing ominously long, we must not loiter by the way. Indeed, as there is little of a noticeable nature on the route, we may as well, with the reader's leave, just skip over the intervening space, and deposit ourselves at once in that classic locality. Elderslie, or "Ellerslie," as it is occasionally spelled, is a small straggling village, principally consisting of two ranges of commonplace-looking houses, erected on either side of the highway leading westward from Paisley, and at a distance of fully two miles from that town. The population, who are for the most part of the operative class, numbers about one thousand two hundred, or thereby. It is as the birthplace of Scotland's great warrior-chief, Sir William

---

[38] A children's game in which a child defends a small heap of stones from other children.

No. XIII. Gleniffer and Elderslie

Wallace, however, that Elderslie is chiefly remarkable. As Burns has poetically said, –

> "At Wallace' name what Scottish blood
> But boils up in a springtide flood!
> Oft have our fearless fathers strode
> By Wallace' side,
> Still pressing onward red-wat-shod,
> Or glorious died."[39]

The spot on which he was born, the scenes of his numerous battles with the enemies of his country's independence, his various hiding-places in seasons of adversity – indeed, every place and object associated with the name of Wallace, is hallowed in the memory of every true-hearted Scotsman, This brave but ill-requited chief[40] was the eldest son of Sir Malcolm Wallace of Elderslie, by a daughter of Sir Ronald Crawford, Sheriff of Ayr. Near the west end of the village a house is pointed out as the identical edifice, in which the hero first saw the light. Approaching the spot, and making inquiry, this structure is pointed out to our admiring eyes by an individual of somewhat crusty appearance, who is apparently about to enter the auld biggin'. At a glance, we perceive, from its architectural character and comparatively modern aspect, that the edifice is of much more recent origin than the date assigned to it. On expressing our doubts on this point to the individual alluded to, he retorts, "Ay, but ye're lookin' at the wrang place a' thegither; it's no the big house ava, but this wee place here whare Wallace was born. Come in by – never mind the dog – lie doun, sir! (addressing the dog aforesaid, a most fierce and villainous-looking mastiff that was straining with dreadful violence on its chain to reach the intruders) – come in by, and gang in at that door, that's Wallace's kitchen." So saying, he turns on his heel, and disappears, *sans ceremonie*, in the doorway. Entering the kitchen, we find it to be a dark

---

[39] From 'Lines to William Simson' (1785) by Robert Burns.
[40] A reference to 'Jean of Lorn; or, The Castle of Gloom' (c.1807) by James Bannantine.

low-roofed chamber of small dimensions, but with a fire-place sufficiently capacious to have cooked a supper, not only for Wallace, but at the same time for a large section of his army. This part of the structure is decidedly ancient; but we should imagine it must have been erected long subsequent to the days of our hero. There can be little doubt, however, that it was on this very site that the home of Sir Malcolm Wallace once stood. Unvarying tradition affirms the circumstance; and, as if to corroborate this, in some measure, about thirty years ago a stone, bearing the following inscription in Roman characters, was dug from the foundation of the garden wall: "W. W. W. Christ is only my Redeemer." The initials in this are supposed to refer to two proprietors of Elderslie, who bore the name and surname of William Wallace. This curious relic is now, we understand, in the possession of Alexander Speirs, Esq. of Elderslie.[41] In the garden there is a venerable old yew-tree, which is popularly known as "Wallace's Yew," not, we imagine, from any supposed connection with the hero, but simply from the situation in which it stands.[42] Repassing our canine friend, who again takes the full length of his tether, and upon whom we feel every inclination to bestow a little wholesome chastisement, we now proceed a short distance farther east, for the purpose of paying our respects to the famous "Wallace oak." This sylvan giant is now the merest wreck of what it was even a few years ago. Time and the storms of centuries have done their share of the work, but, worse than all, the relic-hunters, have been unceasingly nibbling at the once stately tree. Little more than the blackened torso, indeed, of the old oak remains, with a few straggling shoots alone showing symptoms of vitality. According to tradition, Wallace and some of his followers, on one occasion, when hotly pursued by the vindictive Southrons, found shelter and safety among the leafy branches of this tree. We shall not inquire too curiously into the probability of the story, lest in this

---

[41] Archibald Alexander Speirs (1840 – 1868). It was later removed to Houston House.

[42] The tree was damaged by fire in 1978 and by storms in 2005. It is dying of Ganoderma fungus infection, but cuttings have been taken from it to eventually replace it.

sceptical age we get laughed at for our pains; but the fact that the ancient and sadly scathed oak has been for centuries associated with our favourite national hero's name should render it an object of interest to every patriotic Scottish breast. In the year 1825 the trunk of the Wallace oak measured 21 feet in circumference at the base, and 13 feet 2 inches at the height of 5 feet from the ground. It was then 67 feet in altitude, and the branches extended 45 feet east, 36 west, 30 south, and 25 north, covering altogether a space of 19 English poles. Since then it has been sadly shorn of its fair proportions, and probably in the course of a few years it will be numbered among the things that were. [This prediction has been more speedily verified than we anticipated. In the dreadful storm of February, 1856 – a storm which will long be remembered for its destructive effects – the grim old sylvan, with thousands of its less remarkable peers, was levelled with the dust. Hundreds of relic-hunters, on hearing of the event, hastened to the spot, and, with saws and whittles, commenced a vigorous dissection of the prostrate giant. Mr. Speirs of Elderslie, however, hastened to the rescue, and had the shattered trunk conveyed to his residence at Renfrew.][43] Taking off our hats in reverence to the decaying giant, we bid it farewell, and turn our faces toward home. The light is beginning to thicken, and the "lengthening train of craws"[44] are hieing them away to their roosting-places in the distant woods. Half-an-hour's smart walk brings us to Paisley, where we receive a kindly welcome in the domicile of our friend and companion.

---

[43] The remains of the oak have since been lost.
[44] From 'The Cotter's Saturday Night' (1786) by Robert Burns.

One of the most interesting, if not of the most picturesque walks in the vicinity of our city is that down the margin of the river to the "Water Neb," where the mingled streams of the Black and White Carts, blended with the Gryffe, pour their watery tribute into the bosom of the Clyde. From the facilities of transit afforded by the river steamers, which are continually passing and repassing between the Broomielaw and the various watering-places on the coast, almost every denizen of our city must be perfectly familiar with the landscape features of the country in this direction. Every turn and bend, every house and tree along the channel is an old acquaintance, whose aspect is quite as well known as those of the Laigh Kirk steeple,[1] the statue of King William,[2] or the ancient Westport well.[3] The beautiful, however, can never become commonplace; familiarity with nature never begets contempt, the Dominie's dictum notwithstanding. Often as we have traversed on foot, or afloat, the seaward windings of our native stream, we have still found something to excite our admiration afresh, some hitherto overlooked charm to endear its verdant banks still more to our affections.

> "Scenes must be beautiful which, daily viewed,
> Please daily, and whose novelty survives
> Long knowledge and the scrutiny of years, –
> Praise justly due to those that I describe."[4]

So sang Cowper in laudation of his favourite Ouse, and so, with greater truth, may we sing of our stately and ever beautiful Clyde.

Glasgow may well be proud of her river, and of the valuable improvements which, by the energy and perseverance of her sons, have been effected on it as a commercial channel. Originally obstructed by

---

[1] Now the steeple of the Tron Theatre, Trongate.
[2] Equestrian statue of William of Orange, now in Cathedral Square.
[3] A double-spouted well at the junction of Trongate and Virginia Street. It was Glasgow's most used well before the city had a piped water supply. The well was filled in sometime before 1880.
[4] From book 1 of 'The Task' (1785) by William Cowper.

fords and shallows, it was insufficient for the transport of the humblest "gabbart."[5] It has gradually been cleared and deepened, however, until in our day it is freely traversed to and fro by barks of stateliest build and the most gigantic proportions. Not quite a century has elapsed since Mr. Smeaton reported to the authorities that the depth of the river at Govan Pointhouse was only one foot three inches at low water; nay, there are men still alive who remember fording it when they were boys, with their "breeks scarce buckled aboon the knee;" and now such "leviathans afloat"[6] as the "Glasgow" and the "Simla"[7] steam unimpeded down its course, when going forth to brave the billows of the stormy ocean. Old M'Ure, the quaint historian of the city, writing about the beginning of the last century, complacently sings,

> "More pure than amber is the river Clyde,
> Whose gentle streams do by thy borders glide;
> And here a thousand sail receive commands
> To traffic for thee into foreign lands."[8]

Considering the depth of the river at the period, we have our suspicions that the good old man must have exercised the poetic license to its full extent in his enumeration of the shipping, and that he must have had Dumbarton and Greenock in his eye when he talked of "foreign lands." This is all the more likely, as we find that a few years earlier, Patrick Bryce, tacksman of the Gorbals coal-heugh, complained that he could not get his coals loaded at the Broomielaw, from the scarcity of water, and that he had to crave license from Sir George Maxwell to have them transported through the lands of Pollok to a place of embarkation near Meikle Govan.[9] How the enterprising coalmaster and the sage historian would stare, if they could rise from the land of shadows, and

---

[5] barge
[6] From 'The Battle of the Baltic' (1801) by Thomas Campbell.
[7] International steamships. The Simla was launched in 1854 and later converted into a sailing ship. The City of Glasgow was launched in 1850, transferred to Liverpool, and lost at sea in 1854.
[8] From *The History of Glasgow* (1736) by John McUre.
[9] Govan was formerly divided into Meikle Govan (now Govan) and Little Govan (now the Gorbals, Polmadie and Govanhill).

be for a time permitted to gaze on the busy, bustling scene which our harbour now presents; or if they could witness the lengthened vista of towering masts which is to be seen from the Glasgow Bridge, stretching away into the distance, and enlivened by never-ceasing arrivals and departures! Clyde floweth not now past the "borders" of the town. Far and wide, since the days of M'Ure, has the city spread its ever-extending labyrinths, and the stream which then was its border has now become as one of its central streets. The giant steam, too, has since arisen, increasing indefinitely the productive powers of man, and in defiance of wind and tide annihilating time and distance by its wondrous powers of transit. Marvellous indeed would the changes which have occurred appear in the eyes of the old historian, and proudly would he acknowledge that his native town, since he left the scene, has amply justified its motto of happy augury, "Let Glasgow flourish!"

Taking our way down the southern bank of the Clyde along the crowded quays, and passing spots where, in our own recollection, green fields, hedgerows, and trees once occupied the space where stately vessels are now moored, we soon arrive at the picturesque, and despite its vicinity to the city, still rural-looking village of Govan. The walk in this direction has long been a favourite one with the denizens of Sanct Mungo, who, on Saturday afternoons, or on Sundays after the skailin' of the kirks,[10] love to stroll by the waterside to "snuff the caller air," as Ramsay has it,[11] and to gaze upon the landscape, well pleased to see that green is still the livery nature loves to wear. The gradual extension of the harbour has, however, divested the banks in a great measure of their natural charms. Many of our readers, we dare say, will remember the bitter lines which the bard of Hope penned, when, after an absence of many years, he revisited the haunts of his boyhood in the vicinity of Glasgow. On these very banks he had wandered many a happy day, and often, when far away, we need not doubt, his fancy would bring back to his gaze the joys of langsyne and the scenes with which in his mind they were associated. He sought the Clyde, but the

---

[10] dispersal from church
[11] Actually from 'The Holy Fair' (1785) by Robert Burns, not Allan Ramsay.

hand of improvement had wrought what to his eye was a woful change, and he sang in the fullness of his sorrow the following

"LINES ON REVISITING A SCOTTISH RIVER

"And call they this improvement? – to have changed,
My native Clyde, thy once romantic shore,
Where Nature's face is banished and estranged,
And Heaven reflected in thy wave no more;
Whose banks that sweetened Mayday's breath before
Lie sear and leafless now in summer's beam,
With sooty exhalations covered o'er;
And for the daisied green-sward, down thy stream
Unsightly brick-lanes smoke and clanking engines gleam,

"Speak not to me of swarms the scene sustains,
One heart free tasting Nature's breath and bloom
Is worth a thousand slaves to Mammon's gains.
But whither goes that wealth, and gladdening whom?
See, left but life enough and breathing room
The hunger and the hope of life to feel,
Yon pale mechanic bending o'er his loom,
And childhood's self as at Ixion's wheel,[12]
From morn till midnight tasked to earn its little meal.

"Is this improvement? where the human breed
Degenerates as they swarm and overflow,
Till toil grows cheaper than the trodden weed,
And man competes with man like foe with foe,
Till death that thins them scarce seems public woe?
Improvement! Smiles it in the poor man's eyes,
Or blooms it on the cheek of labour? No!
To gorge a few with trade's precarious prize,
We banish rural life and breathe unwholesome skies

---

[12] In Greek mythology, king of the Lapiths who was tied to a spinning wheel of fire for eternity for trying to seduce Hera.

"Nor call that evil slight; God has not given
This passion to the heart of man in vain,
For earth's green face, the untainted air of heaven,
And all the bliss of Nature's rustic reign;
For not alone our frame imbibes a stain
From fetid skies; the spirit's healthy pride
Fades in their gloom; and therefore I complain
That thou no more through pastoral scenes shouldst glide,
My Wallace's own stream and once romantic Clyde."[13]

The sweet singer of Hope seems to have been altogether in a despairing mood when his muse gave utterance to this most doleful effusion. Poets, however, have seldom been remarkable for devotion to the study of political economy. They are generally conservative of the beautiful, even to the sacrifice of the useful. Wordsworth raised his voice against the intrusion of the rail into the green solitudes of Cumberland, and Campbell could see nothing to admire in the commercial elevation of the Clyde, although the prosperity of his country was thereby infinitely enhanced. The splendid discoveries of a Watt,[14] or the ingenious application of these discoveries to the propulsion of vessels by a Bell,[15] were nothing in his eyes to the preservation of a flowery bank. We have no sympathy with the maudlin sentiment which is ever selfishly crying, "Woodman, spare that tree," when the said tree is a public inconvenience; or, "Injure not the lovely banks of that stream," when the so-called injury would be productive of benefit to a whole community. Such was not the purpose which pervaded the genius of Burns. He mourned the impending fate of the "wee modest crimson-tipped flower," but he turned not the ploughshare aside to spare its bloom. Addressing it, he says, –

"For I maun crush aneath the stour

---

[13] By Thomas Campbell (1826), best known for 'The Pleasures of Hope'.
[14] James Watt (1736 – 1819), inventor who greatly improved the steam engine.
[15] Henry Bell (1767 – 1830), engineer who pioneered the steamship and co-built the PS Comet.

> Thy slender stem;
> To spare thee now's ayont my power,
> Thou bonnie gem."[16]

While regretting the destruction of the beautiful, he well knew that the right onward furrow of utility was not to be interrupted by a sickly sentimentality. Wordsworths and Campbells may foolishly protest in measured phrase against the march of improvement, and gild their maunderings with the richness of an exuberant fancy, but the ploughshare of progress can neither be stayed nor turned aside from its course, although here and there a flower may be "crushed beneath the furrow's weight."

The village of Govan, like most other old townships, is a long straggling congregation of houses, having been permitted apparently to "hing as it grew," each individual proprietor "biggin'" where it best pleased himself, and without the most distant regard for the opinion or convenience of his neighbour. It is, in fact, the most curious and eccentric little townie that we know, and always wears, to our fancy, a kind of half-fou aspect. At two places, the Pointhouse and the Ferry, it comes rambling down towards the river; but, as if startled at its own temerity, it staggers rapidly away back, zigzagging into nondescript lanes and wynds, the irregularity of which would break the heart of any individual whose bump of order had an extraordinary degree of development. It has a predominance of thatched houses, too, as if in its sturdy independence it was determined to retain its straw bonnet in defiance of the innovating slate. Altogether Govan has a genuine old world look, which is perfectly unique in these days of improvement and change, and which forms a not unpleasing contrast to the stiff though stately angularity of our own somewhat overgrown town.

In the vicinity of Govan there are a considerable number of elegant villas, embowered in cosie garden-plots, screened amidst hedgerows and trees, and generally occupied by well-to-do citizens of the Western Metropolis, who can afford to combine the pleasures and profits of the city with the charms of rural retirement. These are in

---

[16] From 'To a Mountain Daisy' (1786) by Robert Burns.

many instances so situated as to command a view of the river, with its steamers and sailing vessels ever passing and repassing on their watery way; while the country around, with its fertile haughs, gentle undulations, belts and clumps of trees, all chequered with the verdant fences of the thorn, presents many a sweet snatch of landscape of the fairest English type. The village itself, as seen from the margin of the Clyde, with its handsome church and elegant spire – a *fac-simile* of that at Stratford-on-Avon, the birth and burial-place of the great dramatist – has an exceedingly fine effect, and has often tempted into action the imitative skill of the artist. The church is a chaste Gothic structure, and the church yard is one of the most beautiful that we know.[17] It is surrounded by a girdle of tall and rugged elms, which throw their chequered shadows over the green mounds below, lending an air of quiet and seclusion to the spot, which harmonizes appropriately with those sombre reflections which the field of graves is so well calculated to excite. We linger for a brief space among the silent mansions of the dead, poring over the records of mortality on the tomb stones which are scattered around, but nothing calling for special remark rewards our search. There is a dreary monotony in the tales of the auld kirk-yard. They were born and they died is ever the sad legend – repeated with endless iteration, and to be repeated till time shall be no more; a few short years of difference the only variation. The redbreast perched on the roof of the church piping the dirge of the departing year, and the yellow leaves dancing in the air to his melancholy strain, are also but sad repetitions of sounds and symbols which season after season have thrilled the heart of man with the same unwelcome moral, that "the end of all these things is death."[18]

Adjacent to the church of Govan is the manse, a plain but comfortable looking habitation, surrounded by a garden, and commanding a fine view of the Clyde where it is joined by the

---

[17] This church, which was only built in 1826, was replaced with the current structure in 1883. The kirkyard has had some old stones removed for their preservation but is otherwise still there.

[18] From *Practical Discourses on All the Parts and Offices of the Liturgy* (1716) by Matthew Hole, probably taken from Romans 6.21.

Kelvin.[19] The predecessor of the present worthy incumbent, Dr. Leishman, was the celebrated Mr. Thom, [20] whose caustic wit and keen spirit of satire have ever since his day furnished our local *Joe Millers*[21] with an inexhaustible supply of anecdotal lore. The pungent genius of this preeminently witty minister is also obvious in a collection of sermons, tracts, and letters, which was published in Glasgow about the commencement of the present century, but which is now only to be found in the libraries of the curious. We may also mention that an individual who resides in Govan preserves religiously the wig of the reverend wit.

The antiquary or the relic-hunter will find but little to attract his attention in Govan. Formerly there was an ancient green tumulus called "the Doomster's Knowe," near the bank, a short distance east of the ferry; but within the past few years, to the chagrin of the local Oldbucks,[22] this interesting memorial of the pre-historic past has been levelled to permit the extension of a neighbouring dyework! *Sic transit gloria mundi.*[23] An individual in the village, who combines the professions of publican and poet, and who has deservedly attained considerable celebrity under his Parnassian *nom de guerre*[24] of "Buc," has several objects of antiquarian and sentimental interest in his possession, which will repay the inspection of the curious. Among these are the chair on which Burns habitually sat by his "ain fire-end"[25] at Dumfries, and (incongruous association!) the Bible of Wishart, the Scottish martyr.[26] With regard to the genuineness of the chair we have no doubt, but as to the authenticity of the legend which "Buc" has attached to the antique Bible – and a curious old blackletter copy it is – we have our own misgivings. Poets, "with reverence be it spoken," are not the most trustworthy authorities in regard to matters of fact.

---

[19] The manse was demolished in the late 19th century.
[20] Rev. William Thom (1709 – 1790).
[21] A reference to the book *Joe Miller's Jests* (1739) by Elijah Jenkins.
[22] Jonathan Oldbuck is the title character in Sir Walter Scott's *The Antiquary* (1816).
[23] Thus passes away the glory of the world.
[24] That is, his pen name. Mount Parnassus in Greek mythology was the home of the Muses
[25] From 'Our Ain Fire-End' (1842) by William Miller.
[26] George Wishart (1513 – 1546), martyred at St Andrews.

"Buc" himself, by the by, a thing that does not always happen, is the most interesting piece of furniture in his own house, as every one must admit who has had the pleasure of hearing him recite some of his beautiful and heart-touching effusions. [Alas! since this was written, poor "Buc" has been called hence. His widow retains the relics we have mentioned.][27]

We may mention, before leaving Govan, that besides a weaving and a silk-spinning factory, it can boast of an extensive dyework; and that from building-yards erected by the enterprising firms of Tod & M'Gregor on the north,[28] R. Napier & Sons, J. & G. Thomson, and Smith & Rodger on the south side of the river, it has recently produced some of the most handsome specimens of marine architecture that have ever graced the bosom of the Clyde.

The walk from Govan to Renfrew, a distance of some four miles along the margin of the river, is in the highest degree pleasing, but it presents few features calling for particular remark. On both sides the country is somewhat flat, partaking, in this respect, as well as in its general fertility, more of the softer character of English landscape than of that which is peculiar to our own mountain land. An abundance of trees and hedgerows still further heightens the illusion, so that, as we pass along, without tasking our imagination overmuch, we could almost fancy ourselves rambling through some genial scene in "merry England," were it not for the Kilpatrick Hills towering in the distance, and reminding us by their familiar features that we are still located on the kindly breast of our "auld respected mither."[29] Wordsworth talks somewhere of a river wandering "at its own sweet will,"[30] and a lovely sight it is to see a streamlet turning and winding like a playful child in very lightsomeness of heart. No such vagaries, however, are permitted, in this part of its course, to the Clyde. It is here "cabined, cribbed, confined,"[31] and compelled to own the mastery of man, and like a steed

---

[27] "Buc" was Alexander Buchanan, landlord of the Waverley Inn in Water Row.
[28] This was the yard that build the SS Simla and SS City of Glasgow, mentioned above. It was sold to Handyside and Henderson in 1872.
[29] From 'The Author's Earnest Cry And Prayer' (1786) by Robert Burns.
[30] From 'Composed Upon Westminster Bridge' (1802).
[31] From Shakespeare's *Macbeth* III.vi.

in harness, carry his burdens, and do his drudgery. Passing in succession the houses of Broomhill, Fairfield, Linthouse, and Shieldhall,[32] each girt with its own gardens and groups of trees, tinged with the variegated hues of autumn, we arrive opposite Scotstoun, the fine mansion of Miss Oswald,[33] which is beautifully situated on the right bank of the river. Scotstoun and Renfield (now Blythswood)[34] have been elevated to poetic honours by the author of "The Clyde," who thus celebrates their charms in his fine descriptive poem:

"Where Scotstoun shines afar with snowy light,
And beauteous Renfield captivates the sight,
His ample mirror Clyde to both displays,
Where each her image with delight surveys;
So at one glass two rival beauties stand
Their charms admiring, one on either hand:
Now self-approved, each looks with lofty scorn
Now sinks each bosom, with black envy torn;
Now triumph flashes from each lovely eye,
Now pride, desponding, heaves the unwilling sigh."[35]

"A plague o' both your houses,"[36] honest John, say we, for a couple of "capernoited[37] biggins." The jealousy of the rival houses, however, was, after all, only a fond fancy of the poet, as our readers will readily believe, when we assure them that the one tenement is situated a good mile farther down the river than the other. It is not often that our author

---

[32] Linthouse (known as Mansionhouse) was demolished in 1921 but the portico was preserved and is now in Elder Park. Shield Hall has also been demolished and some of the estate makes up the grounds of the Queen Elizabeth University Hospital. The land on which the other houses stood was largely swallowed up by the shipyards.
[33] Elizabeth Oswald (1767-1864). The Scotstoun estate extended from the river up to Great Western Road. Some of the estate was later turned into Victoria Park. Scotstoun House stood near what is now Ardsloy Place. It was demolished in the 1890s during the construction of the Lanarkshire & Dumbartonshire Railway.
[34] Blythswood House stood on what is now Renfrew Golf Course. It was demolished in 1935.
[35] From 'The Clyde' (1764) by John Wilson.
[36] From Shakespeare's *Romeo and Juliet* III.i.
[37] peevish

stretches the professional license so far as in this instance. His descriptions are generally correct, and his reflections appropriate and judicious. We have frequently, in the course of our rambles, had occasion to quote from "The Clyde," – a poem which, we humbly think, is far from being so well known as its merits deserve. Dr. Leyden characterized it as "the first Scottish loco-descriptive poem of any merit," and remarked that the author's "descriptions of rural scenes and occupations are always true to nature, and often diversified by striking and picturesque touches."[38] The poet traces the Clyde from its origin down its entire course, glancing at every scene which is remarkable for natural beauty or historical association, until its waters are lost in the wide Atlantic. To the people of Clydesdale his delineations of scenery should prove especially interesting; and we are only surprised that it has never attained a more extensive popularity. Before taking leave of Wilson, we may mention that it was while occupied as a teacher in Rutherglen that "The Clyde" was partially composed and prepared for the press. He was afterwards invited to become superintendent of the Grammar-school of Greenock. This situation his necessities compelled him to accept, although one of the conditions of his engagement was that he should for ever renounce "the profane and unprofitable art of poem-making."[39] To this bitter condition he seems ever after to have rigidly adhered, although, as might have been expected, not without murmuring. Many years afterwards he thus expressed himself in a letter to his son: – "I once thought to have lived by the breath of fame; but how miserably have I been disappointed, when, instead of having my performances applauded in crowded theatres, and being caressed by the great, – for what will not a poetaster in the delirium of possession dream! – I was condemned to bawl myself to hoarseness among wayward brats, to cultivate sand, and wash Ethiopians for all the dreary days of an

---

[38] From *Scenes of Infancy: Descriptions of Teviotdale* (1803) by Dr John Leyden, poet and linguist.

[39] According to the 1910 edition of *Rambles*, this condition of employment was only a joke by the novelist John Galt, which John Leydon, Wilson's biographer, took seriously.

obscure life, the contempt of shopkeepers and brutish skippers." He died at Greenock on the 2d of June, 1789.

A short distance to the west of Scotstoun, and on the opposite side of the river is Elderslie House, the seat of Alex. Spiers, Esq.,[40] finely embowered in trees, and with a spacious and beautiful park in its front. This handsome edifice was erected in 1777-78 by the great-grandfather of the present possessor, who named it after the birthplace of the great Scottish patriot, of which he was also proprietor. The house has since been extended and improved, while the numerous and graceful sylvan groups with which the lawn toward the Clyde is thickly studded, render its appearance peculiarly pleasing and attractive.[41] About thirty years ago an ancient stone was dug from the foundation of "Wallace's house" at Elderslie, which is still, we understand, carefully preserved at this stately residence.

Passing the spot, and crossing a filthy and stagnant-looking water, half canal and half stream, which here joins the Clyde, and which rejoices in the unmusical but appropriate name of "Pudyeoch," we find ourselves in the burgh of Renfrew, the capital of the shire, and although far from the greatest, certainly the most ancient of its towns. Renfrew was formerly designated "Arenthrou;" and, remembering an old rhyme which we learned in our boyhood –

"Arenthrou! Arenthrou!
There's yill[42] and whisky there for you,
And a cut o caller[43] sawmon,"

we at once look about for a place where we may have the wants of our inner man properly satisfied. The "caller sawmon" are not so plenty now-a-days as they were when our rhyme first saw the light, but the "yill and whisky" are quite as abundant and good as in days of yore, while there is no lack of the more substantial creature comforts. The town of Renfrew proper is situated about half-a-mile from the margin

---

[40] Archibald Alexander Speirs (1840 – 1868).
[41] Elderslie House was built on the ruins of a former castle on Kings Inch. It was demolished in the 1920s and Braehead shopping centre now stands on the spot.
[42] ale
[43] fresh

of the Clyde. It is of no great extent, and consists principally of one main street with a number of lanes or wynds branching off irregularly from it. Architecturally speaking, Renfrew has but few claims to attention, the houses for the most part being of the humblest and most unpretending description. Many of them are old-fashioned thatched edifices, of a highly venerable and occasionally even picturesque appearance. The whole town, including a number of suburban villas and cottages, has an air of neatness and quietude which has an exceedingly pleasing effect. At the cross there is a townhouse and jail, attached to which is a somewhat diminutive spire, with a clock. The dwarfishness of this spire, or steeple, is rather a sore subject with the inhabitants, and has been the occasion of much banter and even bickering between them and their Paisley neighbours. A threat of carrying away the "steeple" will raise the bile of a Renfrew man at once. Formerly the mischievous Seestu'[44] lads were in the habit of coming down, and while placing their shoulders to the wall of the structure, crying out, "I say, Jock, gie's a hand with this lift," to any Pudyeochian who might chance to pass. The result generally was an appeal to fisticuffs, when the jesters had frequently to pay for their joke with a sound drubbing. Of course, we pass the "steeple" without a hint as to its stability.[45]

The illustrious house of Stuart, from which such a lengthened series of our kings and queens have sprung, had at an early period their principal residence in the vicinity of Renfrew. No vestige of the edifice now remains, but its whereabout is indicated by certain names which still cling to the locality. The site where once the proud embattled keep reared its stately towers is called "Castlehill" to this day, while the "Orchard," the "King's Meadow," and the "Dog-row" are the names of places in the immediate neighbourhood, and probably derived from their connection with the ancient home of the Stuarts. "Baron of Renfrew" is still one of the numerous titles to which the eldest son of the reigning monarch of our country is by birth entitled; and we

---

[44] A nickname for Paisley.

[45] The town hall was replaced in 1872. The new building has a much more impressive steeple.

understand that considerable disappointment was experienced in the burgh, on the occasion of the Queen's visit to the Clyde, that the heir-apparent did not land, when passing, to inspect his Barony, and the spot where once stood the home of his fathers. [46]

The educational wants of the juvenile population of Renfrew seem to be well supplied. Besides several private schools, there is a large seminary at the western extremity of the town, designated the "Blythswood Testimonial." It is of elegant architectural proportions, and was erected by subscription in 1842, in honour of the late Archibald Campbell, Esq., of Blythswood.[47] This institution, which is highly ornamental to the locality, has been endowed by the Town Council, and is conducted, we understand, in an efficient and superior manner. It were well that more of our testimonial builders imitated this excellent example, and united the useful with the ornamental in their monumental structures. The memory of Mr. Campbell will be none the less effectually perpetuated that it has been associated with an edifice in which utility and beauty are combined.[48]

Leaving Renfrew we now take our way to Inchinnan, which lies about a mile to the westward. About midway we pass the spot where the unfortunate Earl of Argyle was wounded and taken prisoner, after the failure of his imprudent expedition in the year 1685.[49] After the dispersion of his troops in Dumbartonshire the Earl crossed the Clyde, and, disguised as a countryman, was endeavouring to make his escape towards Renfrew. He had just forded the Cart, which is in the immediate vicinity, when he was recognized and attacked by two militiamen. These he managed to keep at bay with the aid of his pistols, but, assistance coming up, he was ultimately wounded and disarmed. We are shown a large stone on which tradition asserts the ill-fated noble man leaned himself after his capture, and which is said to have been stained by the blood which flowed from his wounds. This interesting relic is within the policies of Blythswood, and is situated a

[46] The future King Edward VII visited the Clyde in 1847 and 1849.
[47] 1763 – 1838
[48] Blythswood Testimonial School was demolished in the late twentieth century.
[49] This was Argyll's Rising, when Archibald Campbell, 9th Earl of Argyll, attempted to overthrow James II & VII.

few yards off the road. It is a large sandstone, about two tons in weight, and had probably at a still earlier period formed the pedestal of a crucifix, or monumental pillar, as it is hewn into a form which would adapt it for such a purpose. It is elevated considerably, however, at one end, and is now thickly crusted over with mosses and lichens. There are certain veins of a ruddy nature in the stone, which, in wet weather, give a tinge of red to portions of its surface. These ruddy spots are, or we should rather say were, supposed by the superstitious to be the effect of the sanguinary stains which it had received on the occasion alluded to.[50] Archibald, Earl of Argyle, as the readers of Scottish history are aware, was beheaded, by the "Maiden,"[51] at Edinburgh, on the 30th of June, 1685, rather less than a fortnight after his capture.

A few minutes' farther walk brings us to Inchinnan Bridge, which is situated immediately above the junction of the Gryffe and the White Cart, over both of which it is erected.[52] The prospect from this point is very beautiful, including "the meeting of the waters," which, after a brief union, are absorbed in the bosom of the Clyde at the "Water-neb," about half-a-mile to the south. For several hundred yards before the Cart and Gryffe intermingle, they are only separated from each other by a narrow stripe of land, thickly covered with willows, which, at the period of our visit, are turning up in the breeze the silver lining of their leaves with a most delicious effect. The fine plantations of Blythswood also lend an air of sylvan grandeur to the spot, and materially heighten the loveliness of the picture. Old Pennant,[53] who had a keen eye for the picturesque, said in reference to the scenery in this vicinity, that it was "the most elegant and softest of any in North Britain."

About two hundred yards from the bridge, on the margin of the Gryffe, is the church of Inchinnan, a small edifice in the Gothic style, with a massive square tower and supported laterally by buttresses. This

---

[50] This stone can still be seen in the gardens of the Normandy Hotel, Renfrew.

[51] An early guillotine.

[52] Actually a pair of similar bridges. The westernmost one still carries traffic over the Black Cart (of which the Gryffe is a tributary). The course of the White Cart was changed and the easternmost bridge is now landlocked.

[53] Thomas Pennant (1726 – 1798), Welsh writer and traveller.

structure was erected in 1828 on the site of an old building which had previously been removed. It is surrounded by a church-yard of limited dimensions, but which is girded with trees and shrubs, and which forms altogether one of the most quiet and secluded resting-places of the dead that can be well imagined.[54] Gray would have been delighted with it.[55] A little vestry at the end of the church is quite embedded in ivy of the most rich and glossy green, which is also beginning to straggle up one of the side walls:

> "Creeping where no life is seen,
> A rare old plant is the ivy green."[56]

A horse chestnut tree, as we linger, is showering down its broad yellow leaves with low rustling whisper of dreariest import; while a gloomy yew – nature's perennial mourner – stands unmoved and solemnly by, garnished with its deep red berries, like drops of blood intermingled with its funereal foliage.

> "Cheerless, unsocial plant! that loves to dwell
> Midst sculls and coffins, epitaphs and worms;
> Where light-heeled ghosts and visionary shades,
> Beneath the wan cold moon (as fame reports),
> Embodied, thick, perform their mystic rounds:
> No other merriment, dull tree, is thine."[57]

In a long-vanished age the church of Inchinnan, with all its revenues, belonged to the Knights Templars. On the suppression of the order, in 1312, their property was conferred on the Knights of St. John, who held it until their dispersion at the Reformation. Strange to say, a number of the Templars' tombstones are still to be seen in the churchyard. Centuries have passed away – the houses in which they

---

[54] This church was replaced in 1904 and the new church was demolished in 1965 to allow expansion of Glasgow airport, but the kirkyard is preserved.
[55] A reference to 'An Elegy Written in a Country Church Yard' (1751) by Thomas Gray.
[56] From 'The Ivy Green' (1836) by Charles Dickens.
[57] From 'The Grave' (1743) by Robert Blair.

dwelt have "left not even a rack behind"[58] – the place which knew them once shall know them no more for ever – and yet here still, in despite of time and change, are the memorial-stones of the Knights, with the symbols of their calling uneffaced. The swords of the cross are still there, but the names of the bearers have utterly perished. There are four narrow-ridged stones, each having the form of a warrior's brand[59] in relief sculptured upon one side of it. There are also a number of flat stones somewhat in size and form like a coffin, each with a cross upon it, but varying in the style of execution. The majority of these interesting fragments of the past are still in a tolerable state of preservation. They are lying exposed in the church-yard, however, and consequently are liable to be trampled on and injured. They are surely entitled to a little more care.

The manse, a plain but neat building, is situated in the immediate vicinity of the church.[60] The Rev. Laurence Lockhart, minister of the parish,[61] is a native of our own city; his father, Dr. Lockhart, having been minister of the College Church for many years. [62] His brother, Mr. J. G. Lockhart, editor of the *Quarterly Review*, and author of a variety of miscellaneous productions, both in prose and verse, has attained a highly respectable name in the literature of his country.[63] [J. G. Lockhart is now among the men that were. He was born in 1793, and died in 1854. A monument either has been, or is about to be raised at Dryburgh Abbey to his memory, by a party of surviving friends, among whom are some of the most eminent living names in the literature of England.][64]

Before we leave Inchinnan the shades of evening have begun to lower, and

---

[58] From Shakespeare's *The Tempest* IV.i.
[59] sword
[60] The manse was demolished in 1965 along with the church.
[61] 1795 – 1876
[62] Rev Dr John Lockhart (1761 – 1842). He was minister of Blackfriar's Church on High Street, which was the church of the University of Glasgow.
[63] John Gibson Lockhart, son-in-law of Sir Walter Scott.
[64] There is now a memorial stone over Lockhart's grave in Dryburgh Abbey, where it lies right next to Sir Walter Scott's.

No. XIV. Govan, Renfrew, and Inchinnan

"The gloomy night is gathering fast."[65]

We therefore hasten back to Renfrew, taking the route down the margin of Cart to the Clyde, and from thence across the fine lawn of Blythswood. On arriving at Renfrew we find a steamer roaring at the wharf, and proceeding on board, are speedily wafted to the Broomielaw.

---

[65] From 'Farewell to the Banks of Ayr' (1786) by Robert Burns.

The finely wooded vale of the Kelvin, next to that of our own river, has long formed one of the most favourite haunts conveniently accessible to our citizens, many of whom, both old and young, we have no doubt, must find its name a talisman capable of exciting their sweetest langsyne memories. Our purpose on the present occasion is to notice, in our usual cursory manner, a few of the more remarkable objects and scenes which meet our gaze during a walk of a few miles, principally in the track of the Kelvin, immediately above its *embouchure* into the Clyde. Taking our start from the Pointhouse,[1] on a fine day of October, we proceed leisurely towards Partick, which lies about half-a-mile to the northward. The air is as mild and genial as the vaunted Indian summer of the far west. Bright snowy masses float in the deep blue sky, and the sunlight has a rich golden tinge, that lends additional lustre to the many-tinted trees which, even in the absence of the slightest breath of wind, are dropping their seared and leafless foliage; while the long rank grasses that fringe the margin of the water are fast assuming that dry skeleton aspect which, despite the spring-like temperature of the season, unerringly indicates that "the summer is past, the harvest is ended,"[2] and that the time of storms is at hand. In the immediate vicinity of Partick, on the western bank of the Kelvin, until within the past few years, there stood a ruinous edifice of no great extent, which was supposed to have been erected as a country residence, at an early date, by one of the bishops of the opulent See of Glasgow. Around the spot a number of fine old trees were scattered, and the scene altogether was just such a one as a dreamy poet or painter would have loved to linger by, peopling the deserted walls with the forms of other days. The appearance of the venerable structure has been preserved by a loving pencil; and a goodly number of years ago a poem of considerable merit was addressed to it by some nameless

---

[1] An inn situated where the Kelvin meets the Clyde (now Pointhouse Quay). It was later used as the offices of the A. & J. Inglis shipyard before being demolished in 1910.
[2] Jeremiah 8.20.

bard in one of the local periodicals. The following verse of the production is all that we have been able to recover from the leaky memory of a friend who committed it to "heart" in his boyhood, and who thinks that it was in a number of the *Bee* or the *Glasgow Magazine* that he must have seen it originally –

> "Lo, Partick Castle, drear and lone,
> Stands like a silent looker-on,
> Where Clyde and Kelvin meet;
> The long rank grass waves o'er its walls;
> No sound heard within its halls,
> Save noise of distant waterfalls,
> Where children lave their feet."

The antiquity of this building, we may mention, has been recently denied, on the authority of certain papers preserved by a descendant of Mr. George Hutcheson, one of the brothers who founded the hospital of that name in the city, and who, according to these papers, also erected the house in question. One of the documents alluded to is a contract with William Miller, mason in Kilwinning, for the erection of the stonework of the aforesaid house, wherein the standard of measurement is pawkily stated to be according to the length of "ye said George's ain fute." In corroboration of this statement also we find in Hamilton of Wishaw's[3] description of Lanarkshire a passage to the following effect: – "Above this, where Kelvin falls into Clyde, is the house of Pertique, a well-built and convenient house, well planted with barren timber and large gardens, which are enclosed with stone walls, and which formerly belonged to George Hutcheson in Glasgow, but now to John Crawford of Myltoun." It would therefore seem that "the Castle," as it was generally called, was not in reality of so ancient a date as was traditionally supposed. It is certain, however, that the proud prelates of Glasgow had for many years a favourite rural residence in the vicinity of Partick; and nothing is more probable than that it was situated at this spot, which in those days must have been

---

[3] William Hamilton (d.1724), Scottish antiquarian and author of *Descriptions of the Sheriffdoms of Lanark and Renfrew*.

invested with a landscape beauty of no ordinary kind. The locality is now occupied by a dyework, while lengthened lines of street are shooting out rapidly in the vicinity, and will soon entirely cover the spot where once flourished the spacious gardens of Pertique.

The village of Partick is romantically situated on the banks of the Kelvin, which at this place rushes dinsomely over a rocky bottom, and is in several places dammed up by artificial barriers for the service of the extensive Corporation Mills. The channel also is here spanned by a time-honoured bridge,[4] which commands a picturesque prospect of the old-fashioned little town, many of the houses of which are evidently of no recent date. It possesses, however, but few architectural features of a remarkable description. Partick altogether has a pleasant half-rural aspect, while the reputed salubrity of its air and its vicinity to the city has rendered it a favourite place of resort on holidays, and on the long summer evenings, with certain classes of our citizens. Numerous handsome villas and cottages also have recently been erected in its environs, principally by thriving business men from Glasgow, which lend it a peculiar air of prosperity and cheerfulness, while the inhabitants generally have an appearance of robust health, which contrasts favourably with that of our urban population.

The Mills of Partick, as is generally known, have for many years belonged to the Incorporation of Bakers in our city, to whom they were granted by the Regent Murray, after the victory of Langside. It is said the Glasgow "baxters" of that day, besides supplying his army with bread while it continued in the neighbourhood, actually sent an armed deputation of their number to assist the Regent in his encounter with the Queen's forces.[5] This party, it seems, did good service on the occasion, and materially aided in the overthrow of the unfortunate Queen's adherents. On his return to the city after this decisive skirmish, Murray publicly expressed his gratitude to the bakers for the important services which they had rendered, when Mathew Fawside, the Deacon, who seems to have estimated properly the value of mere word gratitude, humbly suggested that a gift of the Crown mills at

---

[4] Replaced with an iron rail bridge in 1895 by the Caledonian Railway Company.
[5] For a full account of the Battle of Langside (1568), see pp109 – 110.

"Pertique," by way of acknowledgment, would be highly acceptable to the Incorporation. The Regent, who was naturally in high spirits at the time, acceded to the opportune request, and granted the mills to the sturdy craftsmen, in whose hands and those of their successors they have ever since remained. The establishments, however, have gone on gradually extending their productive powers, as the wants of the community have increased, until, in our own day, they have become of the most stately dimensions, while the Incorporation to whom they belong is one of the most wealthy in the city.

Leaving Partick by what is called the Byres Road, we now proceed, in a northerly direction, for a distance of about a mile, during which nothing calling for special remark comes within our observation, until we arrive at the Great Western Road, immediately in front of the entrance to the Botanic Gardens. We know of no place in the neighbourhood of Glasgow where the lover of nature can more profitably linger for a few hours than in the flowery recesses of this excellent establishment. "From the cedar which groweth on Lebanon to the hyssop on the wall,"[6] all kinds of plants are to be found congregated here. The student will find in its spacious grounds, or on the shelves of its tastefully arranged conservatories, innumerable specimens of the infinitely various vegetable families of the earth. At all times and seasons the attentive observer may find some "thing of beauty"[7] here exhibiting its charms to the eye of day,

"Whether the genial summer warms
        To life and light,
Or winter howls in gusty storms
        The long dark night."[8]

The situation of these gardens is exceedingly well adapted for horticultural purposes, and embraces a variety of fertile slopes, with a fine southern exposure, tastefully arranged into green lawns, which are elegantly intersected by numerous parterres and flower-bordered

---

[6] 1 Kings 4.33
[7] From 'Endymion' (1818) by John Keats.
[8] From 'Lines to William Simpson' (1785) by Robert Burns.

walks. The grounds are screened on all sides by stripes of planting, composed of the principal trees and shrubs of our country, indigenous and exotic. At the base of the hill or brae over which the gardens are spread, is a large pond for the cultivation of aquatic plants, and a rockery, in the crevices of which many specimens of our rarest wild flowers are appropriately located. During the season, these spacious and well-conducted gardens are generally largely attended by the rank and fashion of our city. Nor, thanks to the princely generosity of our townsman, William Campbell, Esq., of Tillichewan,[9] are the humbler classes altogether excluded from a participation in their beauties. By a munificent donation, this gentleman has secured the right of *entrée* to the Botanic Gardens for five days of the Fair week[10] to the working people of Glasgow. On these occasions the grounds present a highly animated and cheerful appearance. Many thousands of respectably attired individuals have each year availed themselves of the privilege thus considerately accorded to them; and it must be highly gratifying to Mr. Campbell, and the friends of the operative population generally, to learn, from the exemplary conduct of these promiscuous crowds, that his munificence has been appreciated in a far higher degree by its recipients than could almost have been anticipated.[11]

At the western extremity of the Botanic Gardens a narrow passage, in popular parlance called the "Kyber Pass,"[12] leads over a green knoll to the valley of the Kelvin at the famous "Pear-tree Well." From the summit of this height an extensive prospect is obtained of the surrounding country, which is of a gently undulating character. Among the more remarkable objects in the landscape, which is bounded by the Campsie and Kilpatrick Hills are the Observatory, where our learned townsman, Professor Nichol,[13] pursues his nocturnal study of the starry heavens; and the Lunatic Asylum at Gartnavel, which stands a

---

[9] 1793 – 1864, businessman and philanthropist.

[10] The Glasgow Fair holiday begins on the third Monday in July.

[11] The Botanic Gardens were acquired by the city of Glasgow and have been available free of charge to the public since 1891.

[12] Filled up sometime in the late 19th century.

[13] John Pringle Nichol, (1804-1859), Professor of Astronomy at the University of Glasgow.

melancholy thing, apart from the noise and bustle of the neighbouring city.[14] This benevolent establishment is indeed most appropriately situated here, in a quiet and secluded place, where ministration to the "mind diseased" is completely undisturbed, as in an urban locality it would necessarily to some extent be by the distractions of discordant external influences. The descent to the river on the northern side of this height passes through a shallow ravine, where many years ago a horrid murder was perpetrated; the very spot, although the scene has undergone considerable alteration, being still remembered and pointed out. It is about midway down the declivity, and was long marked by an immense tree, every vestige of which has now been removed. The victim was a young and beautiful woman, who, from the fact that she had evidently "loved not wisely but too well,"[15] was supposed to have been put to death by her guilty paramour. The body was found shockingly mangled one quiet summer morning lying among the dewy grass and trampled flowers, which in several places were stained with her blood. Great excitement was naturally kindled in the public mind at the time by this atrocious occurrence, but strange to say, in spite of the most vigilant search, no trace of the murderer has ever been discovered; the popular maxim that murder will not hide having been, in this instance, as well as, we are sorry to say, in many others, completely falsified. A poem of considerable merit on this tragical event appeared in a small volume which was published a few years ago by our townsman Mr. James Lemon.[16] At the period of our visit the very spirit of peace seems brooding over the spot, and it is with difficulty that we can associate, even in fancy, such loveliness and quietude with a a tale of blood.

The scenery of the Kelvin in the vicinity of the Pear-tree Well is of the most romantic and beautiful description. The banks are bold, and in many places fringed with masses of foliage to the water-lip; while the rustic bridge, the lonely cottage, and the picturesque mill, seem planted by the very hand of taste, along the meanderings of the

---

[14] Now Gartnavel Royal Hospital, it is still a mental healthcare facility.
[15] From Shakespeare's *Othello* V.ii.
[16] The poem is 'Kelvin Dale' (1845) by James Lemon.

289

rippled and murmuring stream, wherever they are likely to produce a telling effect.[17] A flock of ducks are floating like specks of foam on the brown breast of Kelvin; as we linger on its margin, a loving pair are leaning on the parapet of the bridge, watching the falling leaves, and doubtless whispering those honeyed nothings which only the initiated can appreciate; while a fair-haired boy is launching a mimic bark, to the huge admiration of his little sister, who claps her hands and shouts in the exuberant lightsomeness of her heart, to see it borne rapidly away by the current. Altogether the scene and its accessories present the very choicest of those harmonious combinations of colour and form which the landscape limner loves to gaze upon, and fondly endeavours, in the pride of his skill, to transfer to the living canvas. No wonder it is that Kelvin Grove has long been the favourite haunt of our city lovers, and the favourite theme of our local poets; for nature has indeed strewn its recesses with charms as fresh and beautiful as though it were situated far from the dwellings of men, instead of almost under the wing of our most dinsome and dusky of towns.

The Pear-tree Well issues from the bottom of a steep and thickly wooded bank, which, at this point, rises gracefully from the rocky bed of the streamlet. The crystalline and deliciously cool water is collected into a considerable cavity in the earth; immediately over which three large trees, a plane and two handsome ashes, raise on high their umbrageous heads, while their sturdy roots, in serpentlike convolutions, twine around the watery hollow beneath, as if to defend it from the intrusion of the penetrating noonday sun. Some suppose that it is from this trio of sylvan guardians that the fountain has received its name – and that the "Three-tree," and not the "Pear-tree," Well is its proper denomination. The advocates of the latter theory further remark, that there is no pear-tree in the vicinity, and that consequently the popular name is probably but a corruption of "Three-tree." There is high authority for saying that names are things of slight consequence; but however that may be, we are inclined, in the present

---

[17] All these are gone. The bridge collapsed in the 1880s and was replaced by the Ha'penny Bridge (named for its toll) in 1886. This was washed away by floods in 1994 and replaced again with the present wooden footbridge.

instance, to be conservative of the old name for this favourite well, and to retain it in spite of all attempts at innovation. Whether from langsyne associations or not, we shall not attempt to discover, but Pear-tree Well sounds most musically on our ear and we should be loath to have it suppressed by the word-coinage of any crotchety theorist; and besides, who can tell what kind of trees may have formerly graced the locality? A perfect orchard of the pear tribe may, at some past period, have clothed the banks of Kelvin, for anything that these violators of a time-honoured name – "these men who are given to change"[18] – know to the contrary. No, no! Pear tree Well it has been, and Pear-tree Well to us, at least, it must remain. We had as lief meet an old friend with a new face as an old haunt with a new name.[19]

Having done our devoirs to the spirit of the fountain, by draining a bicker of the translucent water, which, by the way, is slightly impregnated with iron, we sit ourselves down on the bank above, under the ashen tree, when one of two friends with whose company we have been honoured inspired by the half-gelid beverage, bursts suddenly out with –

"Let us haste to Kelvin Grove, bonnie lassie, O."

We of course join heartily in the measure, which has for many years been highly popular in the west of Scotland, and which we naturally enjoy with double zest amid the scenery to which it refers. A musical connoisseur, were he here, might grumble a little at our unskilful execution of the air, which bears the stamp of R. A. Smith's fine genius.[20] It is, nevertheless, entirely to our own satisfaction; and old Kelvin seems to murmur more complacently as his own song goes ringing down the vale. It is well known that this beautiful lyric was composed by Mr. Thomas Lyle,[21] formerly a surgeon in Glasgow, and who is now, in a green old age, after pursuing his vocation in the village of Airth, in Stirlingshire, for many years, once again resident

---

[18] Proverbs 24.21
[19] The spring was culverted in the 1890s when Kirklee Station (now permanently closed) was built by the Caledonian Railway Company.
[20] Robert Archibald Smith (1780–1829), composer.
[21] 1792 – 1859

amongst us. [Dr. Lyle is again (1856) pursuing his vocation in the High Street of Glasgow, a little below the Bell o' the Brae.[22] He holds the office of District Surgeon to the Barony Parochial Board.] The song was originally published in 1820, in the *Harp of Renfrewshire*, a collection of poetical pieces, to which an introductory essay on the poets of the district was contributed by William Motherwell.[23] In the index to that work the name of John Sim[24] is given as that of the author of "Kelvin Grove." Mr. Sim, who had contributed largely to the work, and for a time had even acted as its editor, left Paisley before its completion, for the West Indies, where he shortly afterwards died. In the meantime the song became a general favourite, when Mr. Lyle laid claim to it as his own production, and brought forward evidence of the most convincing nature to that effect. So clearly, indeed, did he establish the fact of his authorship, that a music seller in Edinburgh, who had previously purchased the song from the executors of Mr. Sim, at once entered into a new arrangement with him for the copyright. Mr. Lyle, it seems, was in the habit of corresponding with Mr. Sim on literary matters, and on one occasion sent him "Kelvin Grove," with another song, to be published anonymously in the *Harp of Renfrewshire*. In the meantime Mr. Sim, who had transcribed both the pieces, was called abroad; and after his death, his executors finding the two songs among his papers, and in his handwriting, naturally concluded that they were productions of his own genius, and published them accordingly. In 1827 Mr. Lyle published a small collection of his poetical effusions, and we learn that even in his old age the muse has not entirely deserted him. Let us hope that the good old bard may also find the ever-green verdure of love and sweet content brightening that wintry portion of the path of life towards which his steps must now be tending.

We now proceed up the Kelvin by a somewhat devious path, for the purpose of visiting the aqueduct bridge in the vicinity of

---

[22] The Bell o' the Brae is the steep part of High Street above the junction with George Street and Duke Street.

[23] 1797 – 1835, poet, journalist and compiler of Scottish ballads.

[24] 1797 – 1819, poet and surgeon.

Maryhill. The distance between the two places, according to our computation, may be somewhere about a mile. On the way we pass several mills or bleachworks, situated at intervals along the margin of the river, and which, however useful they may be, and far be it from us to call their utility into question, certainly detract considerably from the picturesque beauty of the scenery. Mr. Lyle, in one of his verses, mentions, among the charms of "Kelvin Grove,"

"That the rose in all her pride
Paints the hollow dingle side,
Where the midnight fairies glide," & c.

We are afraid, however, that the green-coated gentry, who are said to be rather finical in their tastes, must long ago have taken their departure from the locality. Professor Aytoun[25] himself has not a greater horror of everything in the shape of calico than (according to those who are skilled in fairy lore) the leaf-clad subjects of Oberon and Titania. We may therefore reasonably enough conclude that, where printworks, bleachfields, and papermills, not to mention snuff manufactories, &c., continue so abundant on the Kelvin, the "men of peace" must to a man have ere this indignantly emigrated to a more congenial province. Be that as it may, however, there are still many delightful nooks among the banks and braes, through which, as rapidly as it is permitted by dams and other artificial barriers, the streamlet rolls its seaward course. Not the least attractive of these is in the vicinity of Gairbraid House. This handsome edifice is situated on an elevated position on the north bank of the Kelvin, and commands an extensive prospect of the surrounding country.[26] A fine lawn slopes smoothly down in front to the water-edge, which is shaded by a belt of planting; while a shallow glen or dell, in its immediate neighbourhood, has won our especial esteem as the habitat where the snowdrop (*galanthus nivalis*) makes its first appearance near Glasgow, in the

---

[25] William Edmondstoune Aytoun (1813 – 1865), poet and professor of English Literature at the University of Edinburgh.
[26] Garbraid House was demolished in the 1920s. Maryhill, which was built on the former Garbraid estate, is named after Mary Graham (née Garbraid) who feued the land for it in the late 18th century.

early spring months. Our favourite locality, however, for this delicate looking but really hardy little flower, is Castlemilk Glen; there they are to be seen in greater luxuriance and beauty than we have ever observed them elsewhere.

The aqueduct bridge which conveys the Forth and Clyde Canal over the valley of the Kelvin, at this place about 80 feet in depth, is a superb production of architectural skill. The structure is 350 feet in length, 57 feet broad, and 51 from the parapet to the surface of the water. It consists of four arches, each 50 feet wide, by 37 high, and has altogether a most imposing appearance. Mr. Whitworth was the designer of this beautiful edifice, and it was executed under the superintendence of Mr. Gibb, between June, 1787, and June, 1790, at a cost of £8,509.[27] The view of the Kelvin from the summit of the bridge is of the most lovely description, the banks on each side being thickly covered with stately trees, which, bending over the water, here smooth and unruffled, are reflected as in a mirror. The canal in the vicinity of the bridge passes over a considerable incline, and at the period of our visit, a number of vessels are progressing slowly up the watery staircase, moving from lock to lock as gently and securely as on the most placid lake.

The village of Maryhill is in the immediate vicinity of the bridge, from which it is seen in its most favourable aspect. Being nearly, if not altogether, of modern erection, the village has a clean and tidy appearance, and is arranged with considerable regularity. There is a number of public works, such as printfields and establishments for bleaching, in its vicinity, in which the population (a large proportion of whom are of Irish origin) are principally employed. The village itself presents few attractions to the rambler, but the country in its neighbourhood, especially along the valley of the Kelvin, is characterized by a more than ordinary degree of beauty.

Leaving Maryhill and turning eastward, we now proceed by Wyndford along the highway towards Glasgow for about half-a-mile. At this point we turn to the right by the Gairoch Road, which, after a

---

[27] Robert Whitworth (1734 – 1799), English engineer, and William Gibb (1736 – 1791), contractor. This impressive aqueduct is still in use.

brief walk, brings us once more to the Kelvin opposite the Botanic Gardens. Passing the Gairoch Mill, which is finely situated on the margin of the water, we next direct our devious steps along the North Woodside Road, with the intention of returning homeward by that favourite route. As most of our readers are doubtless aware, the scenery on this portion of the Kelvin is possessed of many and various charms, – wood, water, and architectural grace being most effectively and pleasingly intermingled. Wherever the eye is turned it meets a new picture. It is seldom, however, that we have witnessed it under more favourable auspices than on the present occasion, when the searing influences of brown October have tinged the masses of foliage on either hand with a brilliancy of colour unknown at other seasons. The very depth of beauty, however, which the landscape now wears, is suggestive of serious reflection. 'Tis the loveliness of consumption – the herald blush that indicates the silent approach of death, and forcibly reminds us of our own leaf-like mutability.

It is now more years than we care to number since, by the winter evening hearth, we read the narrative of Lieutenant George Spearing,[28] who accidentally fell into an old coal-pit at Woodside, in the year 1769, where he remained undiscovered for seven days and seven nights, when he was happily rescued. The circumstances of the case took a firm hold on our youthful imagination, and it is with something like a feeling of awe that we proceed to visit the spot where the casualty occurred. The pit, after the lapse of so many years, is still open. It is situated within the extensive and romantic grounds of Matthew Montgomerie, Esq. of Kelvinside,[29] about sixty yards or so to the north of what is called the Flint-mill. We may mention, however, that there is little danger of a similar accident occurring now-a-days, as the place is not only secured from intrusion by a high stone wall, but the mouth of the pit is further fenced round with a girdle of stout stabs. [Since this was written the Woodside pit was reopened but at the present time, as we understand, the workings have been again deserted,

---

[28] 1728 – c.1824
[29] 1783 – 1868. Upon Montgomerie's death, Kelvinside House and land were sold and the house was later demolished.

and the dreary prison of the poor lieutenant once more consigned to silence and solitude. Let us hope that the proprietors will not permit it as formerly to remain an unfenced trap.] The narrative of Lieutenant Spearing was originally published in the *Gentleman's Magazine*. We extract the principal features of it, as by this time it must be almost as good as manuscript to the majority of readers:

"On Wednesday, September 13, 1769," says the narrator, who speaks in the first person, "between three and four o'clock, I went into a little wood called North Woodside (situated between two and three miles N. W. of Glasgow), with a design to gather a few hazel nuts.

"I think I could not have been in the wood more than a quarter of an hour, nor have gathered more than ten nuts, before I unfortunately fell into an old coal-pit, exactly seventeen yards deep, which had been made through a solid rock. I was some little time insensible. Upon recovering my recollection, I found myself sitting (nearly as a tailor does at his work), the blood flowing pretty freely from my mouth; and I thought that I had broken a blood-vessel, and consequently had not long to live; but to my great comfort, I soon discovered that the blood proceeded from a wound in my tongue, which I suppose I had bitten in my fall. Looking at my watch, it was ten minutes past four; and getting up I surveyed my limbs, and, to my inexpressible joy, found that not one was broken.

"Night now approached, when it began to rain, not in gentle showers, but in torrents of water, such as is generally experienced at the autumnal equinox. The pit I had fallen into was about five feet in diameter; but not having been working for several years, the subterranean passages were choked up, so that I was exposed to the rain, which continued with very small intermission, till the day of my release; and, indeed, in a very short time, I was completely wet through. In this comfortless condition I endeavoured to take some repose. A forked stick that I found in the pit, and which I placed diagonally to the side of it, served alternately to support my head as a pillow, or my body occasionally, which was much bruised; but in the whole time I remained here I do not think that I ever slept one hour together. Having passed a disagreeable and tedious night, I was somewhat cheered with the appearance of daylight, and the melody of a robin redbreast that had perched directly over the mouth of the pit; and this pretty little warbler continued to visit my quarters every morning during my confinement, which I construed into a happy omen of future deliverance; and I sincerely believe the trust I had in Providence, and the company of this little bird, contributed much to that serenity of mind I constantly enjoyed to the last. At the distance of about 100 yards, in a direct line from the pit, there was a water-mill. The flint-mill was still nearer. I could frequently hear the horses going this road to and from the mill; frequently I heard human voices; and I could distinctly hear the ducks and hens about the mill. I made the best use of my voice on every occasion; but it was to no manner of purpose, for the wind, which was constantly high, blew in a line from the mill to the pit, which easily accounts for what I heard; and, at the same time, my voice was carried the contrary way. I cannot say I suffered much from hunger. After two or three days that appetite ceased, but my thirst was intolerable; and, though it almost constantly rained, yet I could not till the third or fourth day preserve a drop of it, as the earth at the bottom of the pit sucked it up as fast as it ran down. In this distress I sucked my clothes; but from them I could extract but little moisture. The shock I received in the fall, together with the breaking of my ribs, kept me, I imagine, in a continual fever; I cannot otherwise account for my suffering so much more from thirst than I did from hunger. At last I discovered the thigh-bone of a bull (which, I afterwards heard, had fallen into the pit about eighteen years before me) almost covered with the earth. I dug it up, and the large end of it left a cavity that, I suppose, might contain a quart. This the water gradually drained into, but so very slowly, that it was a considerable time before I could dip a nutshell full at a time, which I emptied into the palm of my hand, and so drank it. The water now began to increase pretty fast, so that I was glad to enlarge my reservoir, insomuch that, on the fourth or fifth day I had a sufficient supply; and this water was certainly the preservation of my life.

"At the bottom of the pit there were great quantities of reptiles, such as frogs, toads, large black snails or slugs, &c. These noxious creatures would frequently crawl about me, and often got into my reservoir; nevertheless, I thought it the sweetest water I had ever tasted; and at this distance of time the remembrance of it is so sweet, that were it now possible to obtain any of it, I am perfectly satisfied I could swallow it with avidity. I have frequently taken both frogs and toads out of my neck, where I suppose they took shelter while I slept. The toads I always destroyed, but the frogs I carefully preserved, as I did not know but I might be under the necessity of eating them, which I should not have scrupled to have done had I been very hungry.

"Saturday the 16th there fell but little rain, and I had the satisfaction to hear the voices of some boys in the wood. Immediately I called out with all my might, but it was in vain, though I afterwards learned that they actually heard me; but being prepossessed with an idle story of a wild man being in the wood, they ran away affrighted.

"At length the morning, September 20th, the happy morning for my deliverance, came; a day that, while my memory lasts, I will always celebrate with gratitude to Heaven. Through the brambles and bushes that covered the mouth of the pit I could discover the sun shining bright, and my pretty warbler was chanting his melodious strains, when my attention was roused by a confused noise of human voices, which seemed to be approaching fast towards the pit; immediately I called out, and most agreeably surprised several of my acquaintance, who were in search of me. Many of them are still living in Glasgow, and it is not long since I had the very great satisfaction of entertaining one of them at my apartments. They told me that they had not the most distant hope of finding me alive, but wished to give me a decent burial, should they be so fortunate as to find me. As soon as they heard my voice, they all ran towards the pit, and I could distinguish a well-known voice exclaim, 'Good God! he is still living!' Another of them, though a very honest North Briton, betwixt his surprise and joy, could not help asking me, in the Hibernian style, if I were still living. I told him I was, 'and hearty, too;' and then gave them particular directions how to proceed in getting me out. Fortunately, at that juncture a collier, from a working pit in the neighbourhood, was passing along the road, and hearing an unusual noise in the wood, his curiosity prompted him to learn the occasion. By his assistance and a rope from the mill, I was soon safely landed on *terra firma*. The miller's wife had very kindly brought some milk warm from the cow; but, on my coming into the fresh air, I grew rather faint and could not taste it. Need I be ashamed to acknowledge that the first dictates of my heart prompted me to fall on my knees, and ejaculate a silent thanksgiving to the God of my deliverance, since, at this distant time, I never think of it but the tear of gratitude starts from my eye?"

The poor Lieutenant afterwards suffered severely, however, from ailments contracted during his lengthened exposure. His limbs having been benumbed by cold and want of exercise, injudicious means were taken to restore the circulation, which caused inflammation and ultimately mortification to ensue. On the 2d of May following, all remedies having failed, he had to undergo an amputation of his left leg, after which, fortunately, he rapidly regained his health. Lieutenant Spearing concludes his narrative, written many years after the unfortunate occurrence at Woodside, by stating – "To this day I bless God I do enjoy perfect health, and I have since been the happy father of nine children."

Pursuing our course toward the city, and immediately before emerging into the Great Western Road where it crosses the Kelvin, we pass North Woodside House, which is beautifully situated near a bend of the river, a little to the northward of the bridge.[30] This venerable pile is remarkable as having been the residence, in boyhood, of our distinguished townsman, Sir Thomas Munro,[31] who will long be remembered for his brilliant and highly useful career in India, during which he rose by undoubted merit from the rank of a simple Cadet to the Governorship of Madras. Sir Thomas was born and educated in the city; but during the summer months his parents resided at this place, which then wore a more rural and retired aspect than it does now, when the extending suburbs are threatening speedily to absorb it. The days he spent at Woodside seem to have been in his estimation the happiest

---

[30] This house was demolished in 1869 for the development of a new suburb.
[31] 1761 – 1827

in his life; "youth's morning march"[32] being ever the most delightful portion of our earthly pilgrimage. His biographer, the Rev. Mr. Gleig,[33] says, "Young Munro appeared to enter upon a new state of being as often as he visited Woodside. If he read, it was either seated upon a rustic bench which stood beneath a tall tree in the garden, or perched among the highest branches of the tree itself. If a fit of idleness took him, he indulged it by rambling, sometimes from sunrise to nightfall, among the woods; or he would fish the Kelvin with his brothers or companions, and when weary of that amusement, would refresh himself by swimming in the dam." In after years, when pursuing the "bubble reputation in the cannon's mouth,"[34] he makes frequent allusions in his correspondence to the haunts of his youth. "Were I to go home to-morrow," he says in an epistle to his mother, "one of my first excursions would be to Woodside, to swim down Jackson's mill stream;" and when, in 1808, after an absence of nearly thirty years, he who had gone out to the far East, an unfriended Cadet, returned laden with honours, wealth, and fame, one of the first places he turned his steps to was the Kelvin. In a beautiful letter to his sister, who had invited him to visit her at Ammondel, the following fine passage occurs: – "A solitary walk is almost the only thing in which I have any enjoyment. I have been twice at North Woodside, and though it rained without ceasing on both days, it did not prevent me from rambling up and down the river, from Clayslap to the aqueduct bridge. I stood above an hour at Jackson's dam, looking at the water rushing over – while the rain and withered leaves were descending thick about me; and while I recalled the days that were past, the wind whistling through the trees, and the water tumbling over the dam, had still the same sound as before; but the darkness of the day, and the little smart box perched on the opposite bank, destroyed much of the illusion, and made me feel that former times were gone. I don't know how it is, but when I look back to early years, I always associate sunshine with them. When I

---

[32] From 'The Soldier's Dream' (1804) by Thomas Campbell.
[33] George Robert Gleig (1796 – 1888), army chaplain and writer. This biography was published in 1830.
[34] From Shakespeare's *As You Like It* II.vii.

think of North Woodside, I always think of a fine day, with the sunbeams streaming down upon Kelvin and its woody banks. I mean to devote the first sunny day to another visit to Kelvin, which, whatever you may say, is worth ten such paltry streams as your Ammon." Again and again he visited the spot, bathed in the dam, wandered through the woods, and, it is even said, climbed the aged tree on which he was wont to sit when a boy. Afterwards he returned to India, where still higher honours awaited him, and where he remained in active service until 1819, when he once more returned from the East, and took up his residence for several years in England. We hear of no more visits to the Kelvin, however; and it is supposed that, feeling somewhat shocked by the changes which had been wrought during his lengthened absence, and the melancholy associations which they excited in his mind, he had taken a final farewell of the locality on his second departure to India. In 1826 he received the honour of knighthood, and had the Governorship of Madras, an office of great responsibility, conferred upon him. This distinguished position, however, he was not destined long to enjoy. He died of cholera at a place called Putteecondah,[35] in the East India Company's territories, on the 5th July, in the following year. Among the numerous distinguished warriors and statesmen who have attained distinction in the vast Eastern Empire of Britain, there are few who deserve, or will obtain, more honourable mention on the page of history than Sir Thomas Munro.

Leaving Woodside, near which a spacious crescent has recently been erected, we now proceed toward the city by the Great Western Road. A few minutes' walk brings us to the hospitable house of a friend, where we may as well take leave of our courteous readers, who, by this time, we dare say, are as tired as we ourselves are after our peregrinations along the windings of the classic Kelvin.

---

[35] In Andhra Pradesh, India.

With the appearance of Duntocher and Old Kilpatrick, as seen from the Clyde, the majority of our readers must be perfectly familiar. Passing Dalmuir by the steamer, a fine range of hills is seen stretching from east to west, and approaching the margin of the river immediately previous to its enlargement into the noble proportions of a frith. About half-way up the swelling slopes, and partially concealed amid wooded knolls, a tall chimney or two, and several gigantic factories, mark the site of Duntocher; while a church tower, and a scattered congregation of houses, reposing in the shadow of the hills and in close contiguity to the stream, indicate to the observant passenger that the famous birthplace of Ireland's patron Saint is before him. Those who have only seen these localities, however, from the bosom of the Clyde, can form but a faint conception of the landscape beauties with which they are environed, and must of necessity have entirely overlooked the numerous objects of historical and traditionary interest which are situated in their immediate neighbourhood. Few parishes in Scotland, indeed, command such a rich variety of scenery as Old Kilpatrick, or are invested with more pleasing associations. Forming the boundary, as it were, between the Highlands and Lowlands, it combines the picturesque charms of both in their most striking and attractive aspects. Yet, in these days of "cheap trips" and "pleasure excursions," by river and rail, comparatively few of our holiday wanderers dream of visiting this locality. It has not the enchantment of distance to recommend it to their admiration. It is too near home to be properly appreciated. The crowd must have their shilling's worth of steamer or train, and consequently often "go farther and fare worse;" while delicious snatches of scenery like those in this vicinity are left in a great measure to the solitary enjoyment of such eccentric ramblers as ourselves.

In consequence of the facilities of transit afforded by the ever-passing river steamers, the tract of country between Glasgow and Kilpatrick must be, even to the majority of visitors to the latter, a species of *terra incognita*. We propose, therefore, in accordance with our usual plan, to conduct our readers to that locality by what may not inappropriately be termed the "overland route." There are, of course, more ways than one to Kilpatrick, as there are to most places else. We might have taken, for instance, the low road by Yoker and Dalmuir; or the high road by Garscube and New Kilpatrick. We take neither, however; but evince our characteristic wisdom by steering a judicious middle course, which, although neither the shortest nor the easiest, has the merit of being at the same time the most picturesque and the most original. Leaving the city, then, by Anderston Walk, we make our way towards Partick. It is rather a difficult matter to leave the city in this direction, as she seems determined, in her westward progress, to keep pace with you. In our boyish days there was a "world's end" somewhere about Finnieston, but where the pole may have shifted to now-a-days is beyond our ken. "Our auld respeckit mither"[1] has long passed that once well-known landmark, with her stately streets, crescents, terraces, and squares. What an ogress the old lady must be! gardens and green fields, cottages and mansions, once familiar to our eyes, have disappeared in scores within her capacious maw, and still the cry is "give, give!" There is, in truth, "life in the old jade yet;" she is still justifying her noble motto, and continuing to "flourish".[2]

Passing Sandyford, we turn aside to the right for the purpose of paying a brief visit to the West-end or Kelvin Grove Park. This is a recent acquisition of the municipality, and one which must be considered a decided ornament, as well as a sanitary benefit to the city. The rapid extension of the town in this direction rendered such a breathing space necessary; and if the opportunity had been once neglected, a lasting injury would undoubtedly have been inflicted on the community. The Lord Provost (Stewart), Magistrates, and Council, therefore, acted wisely when, in 1853, the lands of Kelvin Grove and Woodside came into the market, to secure them for the benefit of the public. The original outlay, something like £90,000, was, it is true, a heavy sacrifice, but it was confidently anticipated that a large proportion of the sum would be realized from building feus on certain

---

[1] From 'The Author's Earnest Cry And Prayer' (1786) by Robert Burns.
[2] The motto of Glasgow is "Lord, let Glasgow flourish through the preaching of thy word and praising thy name", usually abbreviated to "Let Glasgow Flourish".

parts of the grounds – an anticipation which time has shown to be perfectly correct. These fine grounds are situated on the eastern bank of the classic Kelvin, which, under a fringe of trees, flows somewhat lazily past the spot. They are in all about forty-two acres in extent, and present an exceedingly agreeable variety of surface. Along the stream there is a stripe of level sward; but from this they slope gradually upwards, in gracefully swelling terraces and banks, to a very considerable height. From a design by Sir Joseph Paxton,[3] the surface is beautifully intersected with walks and carriage drives, turning and twining in every direction – now gliding under stately rows of trees – now meandering amidst blooming borders and gay parterres,[4] and anon winding in the sunshine round terraces of smoothest and freshest green.[5] From the summit, which is now crowned with long ranges of majestic edifices, there is a prospect of great extent and loveliness. At the spectator's feet are the groves and glades of the Park itself, alive with sauntering groups – women and children, men and maidens, in couples, or pacing along in solitary speculation. Here two lovers are seated apart discoursing soft nothings – there a party of wild youths are smoking the fragrant weed, and "laughing consumedly," while yonder, with spectacled nose and arms akimbo, measuring his lonely round, is the professor or preacher pondering what to-morrow, from chair or pulpit, he shall give forth. Looking beyond, we have a long stretch of the Clyde and all its bustle of trade and commerce, with the heights of Kilpatrick and Kilmalcolm rising in the distance. To the southward, over the green slopes and meadows of Renfrewshire, are the braes of Gleniffer – Tannahill's own braes[6] – the Fereneze Braes, Craig of Carnock, Neilston Pad, Ballygeich, where Pollok of the *Course of Time* spent his boyhood and youth,[7] and to the south-east the green-wooded braes of Cathkin and Dychmont. To the northward, again, we have a glimpse of the Campsie and Strathblane Hills, with a

---

[3] 1803 – 1865, head gardener at Chatsworth, designer of London's Crystal Palace, and Liberal MP for Coventry.
[4] formal gardens with enclosed beds
[5] The park has been extended since MacDonald's time.
[6] Robert Tannahill (1774 – 1810), poet who wrote 'The Braes of Gleniffer'.
[7] Robert Pollok (1798 – 1827), poet.

No. XVI. Duntocher and Old Kilpatrick

Highland Ben or two peeping through the gap of the Lennox. From this commanding spot, indeed, may be scanned the principal landscape features within eight or ten miles of Glasgow, with nearly all the towns, and villages, and hamlets, and chateaus included within that range. Thus far we have had nothing but words of praise to bestow upon the Park and its patrons. Before leaving its precincts, however, we must indulge in a word or two of animadversion. The great staircase leading to the uppermost terrace – one of the most spacious and beautiful erections of the kind we have ever witnessed – is stowed away in a corner, where it must be looked for – positively searched after – before it can be seen. Why, in the name of all that is picturesque, was not this grand structure placed under the centre of the towering range which crowns with dignity the brow of the slope? In such a position it would have formed an imposing feature in the landscape of the Park, while in its present situation it is nearly, if not altogether lost. Could this oversight – for such we must consider it – not yet be remedied? Then there is the Kelvin, a perfect common-sewer, redolent of the most unsavoury comparisons. Can nothing be done to cleanse its foul bosom of that perilous stuff which loads the air with unholy odours, and threatens the lieges with fevers and other deadly maladies which are born of miasmatic stench? There was at one time some talk of preventing this pollution, by means of draining and filtration, but hitherto the evil is unmitigated, and every ornament that is added to the grounds, is therefore but an additional enticement to the breathing of unwholesome airs. "Reform it altogether,"[8] say we to the authorities, or at once renounce the credit which you claim as the founders of a new place of recreation for the people.[9] Beautify the grounds as you may, while this evil remains without remead, we can only look upon your efforts in landscape gardening, as the adornment of a lazar-house – the whitening of a sepulchre.[10]

---

[8] From Shakespeare's *Hamlet* III.ii.
[9] The River Kelvin was cleaned up during the late twentieth century, but the staircase, which cost £10,000 and was originally planned for a more prominent spot, is still in this less obvious location.
[10] A reference to Matthew 23.27.

"Then, farewell to Kelvin Grove, bonnie lassie, O;
And adieu to all I love, bonnie lassie, O;
To the river winding clear,
To the fragrant-scented brier,
Even to thee of all most dear, bonnie lassie, O."[11]

But we have yet a lengthened way before us, and must be jogging. Passing Clayslaps, and having stolen a glance at our friend Sandie Baird's beautiful and neatly-arranged beds of pansies, surpassing in their loveliness of hue the "glory of a Solomon,"[12] [Since the period of our ramble Mr. Baird has passed on the stream of emigration to the land of gold, and is now, we have no doubt, worshipping Flora at the antipodes.] we proceed for a mile or so along the high way to Dumbarton, when we turn to the north, near the west-end of Partick, by what is locally denominated the "Craw-road."

An agreeable walk of some half-hour's duration between verdant hedgerows and overhanging trees – during which we pass in succession the mansion of Woodcroft, the auld warld hamlet of Balshagrie,[13] and that most stately but most melancholy edifice, the Lunatic Asylum at Gartnavel[14] brings us to Annisland Toll, where, turning to the left, we pursue our journey in a westerly direction. From the number of coal-pits in this vicinity, it is obvious that the valuable black diamond abounds to an extraordinary degree in the bowels of the land over which we are now treading. Carboniferous districts are generally anything but attractive to the lover of landscape beauty. The country around us, however, is an exception to the rule. Those fine woods to the north-east are portions of the spacious pleasure grounds of Garscube House,[15] the handsome seat of Sir Archibald Ilay

---

[11] From 'Kelvin Grove' (1819) by Thomas Lyle. See p292 for the story of its publication.
[12] A reference to Matthew 6.29 / Luke 12.27.
[13] Both the hamlet and the site of the mansion are now part of Broomhill suburb.
[14] Now Gartnavel Royal Hospital, it is still a mental healthcare facility.
[15] Garscube House was demolished in 1954 and Wolfson Hall of Residence (University of Glasgow) was later built on the site.

Campbell of Succoth, Bart., M.P.;[16] while the dense masses of foliage immediately to the left of our present course, conceal from our view the mansion of Jordanhill,[17] the family seat of Jas. Smith, Esq.,[18] a gentleman who has long been a distinguished ornament of the scientific and literary circles of the west of Scotland.

In former times the Jordanhill estate was held by a family named Crawford, one member of which achieved a name in his country's history by an exploit remarkable alike for coolness and bravery. This individual was Captain John Crawford of Jordanhill,[19] who, in 1571, with a small band of followers, succeeded in taking, by an ingenious stratagem, the Castle of Dumbarton. After the battle of Langside and Queen Mary's flight to England, this strong fortress, then deemed all but impregnable, was held in the interest of the royal exile by the Governor, Lord Fleming, who steadily refused to surrender it to the party then in power. Crawford, who had been a servant of the unfortunate Darnley,[20] and was of course a bitter enemy to the Queen, formed the resolution of seizing this stronghold, and putting her friends to flight. Accordingly, on the occasion alluded to, with a select party of his retainers, he marched towards the castle after night-fall, provided with ropes and scaling-ladders, and having in his company an individual who was familiar with every step upon the rock. Arriving at the castle about midnight, and being completely screened from observation by a dense fog, they commenced operations. After encountering great difficulties and considerable alarm, occasioned by one of the men being seized with a convulsive fit while half-way up the ladder, they at length attained a position on the walls, and, after striking down a sentinel, who was about to give warning of their presence, they rushed upon the sleeping garrison, shouting, "A Darnley! a Darnley!" and easily succeeded in effecting its capture. The assailants did not lose a single man, while so complete was the surprise

---

[16] 1825 – 1866, Member of Parliament for Argyllshire.
[17] Jordanhill House was demolished in 1961 and the Crawfurd Building of the former Jordanhill College of Education was built on the site.
[18] 1782 – 1867, merchant and intellectual.
[19] Actually Thomas Crawford of Jordanhill (1530–1603).
[20] Henry Stewart, Lord Darnley (1546 – 1567).

of the opposite party that they surrendered almost without a blow, and of course their loss was also trifling. The Governor managed to make his escape; but a number of individuals of distinction were made prisoners within the walls of the castle, among whom was Hamilton, Bishop of St. Andrew's,[21] who was immediately tried for participation in the murder of Darnley, and being convicted, was sentenced to be hanged, drawn, and quartered. Benefit of clergy had by this time gone completely out of fashion, and his reverence, who was generally detested, shortly afterwards expiated his crimes on a tree at Stirling. The following wicked Latin couplet is said to have been written on the occasion:

"Vive diu, felix arbor, semperque vireto
Frondibus, ut nobis talia poma feras."[22]

Passing the entrance to Jordanhill, from which a lengthened avenue of stately trees leads to the house, which is effectually concealed from view by its fine sylvan screen, we turn again towards the north by a rough country road to the "Red Town." This is the name given to several ranges of colliers' houses, which are quite as plain, unattractive, and uncomfortable in appearance, as such edifices generally are. We are rather surprised, however, with one adjunct to the Red Town, namely, an extensive and somewhat elegant school. From its capacity one would imagine it was designed to accommodate not only the juvenile but also the adult inhabitants of the village, and probably, indeed, the grown-up natives are fully as much in need of the school master as the rising generation. The moral and intellectual culture of the mining population has hitherto, we are sorry say, been too much neglected. Such an institution as the one alluded to should undoubtedly be attached to every collier village; and we were gratified to learn, from a little fair-haired girl, whom we overtook with a couple of pitchers, returning from the well, that there were "a gey wheen[23] o' scholars in the schule baith on ilka days and Sundays."

---

[21] John Hamilton (1512 – 1571), Archbishop of St Andrews.
[22] Live long, lucky tree, your boughs ever flourishing, that bear us such fruit.
[23] considerable number

No. XVI. Duntocher and Old Kilpatrick

From the Red Town the road gradually ascends to a considerable eminence called Clober, or Cowdonhill, which commands an extensive and beautiful prospect of the surrounding country. On the summit of this elevation, and overshadowed by a girdle of trees, stands the ancient mansion of Cowdon, a dreary, desolate, and wobegone looking edifice. This structure is two storeys in height, and has at one period been of considerable extent. It was in bygone years the seat of a family named Crawford. About the beginning of last century it passed by marriage, with the extensive estates attached to it, into the possession of a certain John Sprewl, who thenceforth adopted the double surname of Sprewl Crawford, From various dates which are still legible on the walls it would appear that the building has undergone extensive alterations at different periods. Over the doorway there is a heraldic carving, much defaced by time, but on which a bird and a star are still observable. On one of the gables, which has lately been rebuilt with the old material, there is a star, with the date 1666; and on the front of the tenement, in a sadly dilapidated condition, is a sun-dial, with the names of John Sprewl and Isabella Crawford inscribed on it, with date 1707.

Strange stories are current in the countryside concerning this "bleak house." A spot is pointed out in the neighbourhood where the grass will not grow, and which, according to tradition, was the scene of some dark deed in days of yore. Couple this fact with the circumstance that a quantity of human bones were, many years ago, found in a portion of the edifice, which was known as "Cowdon's den," and the intelligent reader will have no difficulty in coming to the conclusion that the house must be haunted. Such, according to popular rumour, is indeed the case. People shake their heads when spoken to on the subject, and hint more than they are willing to express. One old lady of the Crawford family, we are informed, having hidden a pot of gold in a niche of the wall during her life, could "get nae rest in her grave" afterwards until she had revealed the secret. A story is also told of a certain wicked laird, a friend and associate of Claverhouse, the persecutor,[24] who was an occasional visitor here. This worthy, on his death-bed, is said to have ordered the servants to keep immense quantities of coals on the fire, that he might have a foretaste of what was awaiting him in the state of existence upon which he was about to enter. Of course such an uncanny end could forebode no good for the future; and it is said the laird is still doomed to revisit, "in his shirt of fire," the glimpses of the moon! If such be really the case (and we are not by any means prepared to prove the reverse), it must certainly gall him sadly, if spirits care for such sublunary things, to witness the decay which has recently befallen his former dwelling. Externally it has indeed a most ghastly and doleful appearance, while the interior, *sic transit gloria mundi*,[25] is inhabited, not by owls and bats, but by several families of colliers. A section of the edifice has also been fitted up as a counting-house and store for a neighbouring colliery. We ask a decent-looking woman, whom we meet at the door of the venerable mansion, if she is not afraid to live in a house which bears such an ominous character. "Atweel no," she replies, "I've leeved here for the last four years, and never saw onything waur than mysel', unless maybe now and then a fou man. I'm thinking," she continues, "the wae drap whisky's the warst speerit that now-a-days enters the auld rickle o' a biggin'."

Before leaving Cowdonhill, we may mention that a curious relic of antiquity was for many generations in the possession of the family. This was a silver spoon, the mouth-piece of which was not less than three inches in diameter, and had the following legend inscribed on it:

"This spoon I leave in legacie
To the maist-mouthed Craufurd after me.
"1480."

At a subsequent date the following limping but pithy lines were also engraven on this gigantic table implement:

---

[24] John Graham of Claverhouse, later Viscount Dundee (1648 – 1689), who opposed the Covenanters.
[25] Thus passes away the glory of the world.

No. XVI. Duntocher and Old Kilpatrick

"This spoon you see
Is left in legacy;
If ony pawn't or sellit,
Cursed let him be."

Descending the brae in a northerly direction, a few minutes' walk brings us to the Forth and Clyde Canal, which we cross a little to the westward, and again proceeding towards the north, are speedily at the famous gate of Garscadden.[26] This place was formerly a favourite resort of holiday ramblers from Glasgow and Paisley, who came for the purpose of inspecting the principal entrance, which is somewhat of an architectural curiosity. The gateway is a massive yet elegant structure, of castellated form, and, being unlike in size and appearance to any edifice of a similar kind in the west of Scotland, it excited in a high degree, on its erection, the wonder of the common people, who formed numerous myths to account for its origin. What these were we need not now rehearse, as the gate has long ceased to be a nine days' wonder, and is but seldom visited. The house and estate of Garscadden are at present in the possession of John Campbell Colquhoun, Esq. of Killermont and Garscadden.[27] In the early part of last century the lairds of Kilpatrick (in which parish we now are) were famous for their devotion to the cup. Like Tam o' Shanter and his cronie, the Souter, they aft "were fou for weeks thegither."[28] Anecdotes of the wild doings in these days are still rife in the parish, and as one of them refers to a former laird of Garscadden, we may as well give it here. A party of these roystering country squires were, it seems, on one occasion engaged as usual in a deep drinking match, when one of the company observed the laird to fall suddenly quiet, while a strange expression passed over his countenance. The observer said nothing regarding the circumstance, however, and the merriment went on for some time as formerly. At length,

---

[26] These gates were demolished in the 1960s following vandalism. The estate is now part of the suburb of Drumchapel.

[27] 1803 – 1870, politician and writer.

[28] From 'Tam o' Shanter' (1791) by Robert Burns.

"In the thrang o' stories tellin',
Shakin' hands and joking queer,"[29]

another individual remarked "Is na' Garscadden looking unca gash the nicht?" "And so he may," said the individual first alluded to, "for he has been, to my knowledge, wi' his Maker during the last half hour; I noticed him slipping awa', puir fallow, but didna like to disturb the conviviality by speaking o't!" It was even so; the poor laird had died "in harness."

About a mile due north from Garscadden House, which is finely embowered in woods and gardens of the most luxuriant growth, rises Castlehill, a gentle but commanding elevation, crowned with a tiara of lofty trees. Towards this point we now wend our way, amid leafy hedgerows dappled with flakes of bloom, and loading the breezes, as they come and go, with sweetest perfume; through daisied pastures studded with picturesque groups of kine; and by corn-fields rippled with verdure, and palpitating, as it were, to the song-bursts of the sky-cleaving lark. Now we pass a comfortable farm-steading, where

"Hens on the midden, ducks in dubs are seen,"[30]

while our unwonted presence is greeted by the house dog's honest but rather unwelcome bark; and anon we are lingering by some lonely patch of planting, reckoning the number of voices that swell its choral hymn, or the number of bloomy eyes that are winking in the fitful radiance that keeps coming and going through its fluttering canopy of leaves. We soon find ourselves on the summit of Castlehill. This spot was, in ancient times, "when wild in woods our noble fathers ran," a station or fort on the celebrated wall with which the Roman invaders endeavoured to check the ceaseless incursions of the unsubdued Caledonians.[31] From its commanding position, and the vast extent of country which it overlooks, this must have been a post of considerable

---

[29] From 'Watty and Meg' (1796) by Alexander Wilson.
[30] From *The Gentle Shepherd* (1725) by Allan Ramsay.
[31] The Antonine Wall, which stretched from Old Kilpatrick to near Bo'ness.

importance to the baffled "masters of the world." "Graham's Dyke," as the immense barrier which then existed between the Forth and Clyde is called in popular parlance, passed immediately over the hill on which we are now stationed. This vast military structure, commenced by Agricola and completed by Antonine, was about twenty-seven miles in length from river to river. It consisted, according to the best authorities, of a great fosse or ditch, averaging forty feet in width, by about twenty in depth, and extending in one unbroken line over hill and plain. On the southern side of the ditch, and within a few feet of its edge, was erected a rampart of mingled stones and earth, about twenty feet in height and twenty-four in thickness at the base. This rampart, or *agger*, was surmounted by a parapet, behind which ran a level platform for the accommodation of the defenders. Within the wall, and generally approximating to it, was a regularly causewayed military road, while it is supposed that not fewer than nineteen forts were erected at various distances along the line. In the lapse of centuries, the traces of this mighty bulwark have become in a great measure obliterated. The plough has passed over the greater portion of its course, and it is only here and there, by slight indentations of the soil, that it can be now discovered. From time to time, however, pieces of rude sculpture, carved stones, urns, and tablets have been discovered along its track – interesting relics of the haughty strangers who, long, long ago, sought dominion in our land. Two inscriptions were dug up many years ago at Castlehill, and are now, to all practical intents and purposes, as effectually interred again in the bowels of the Hunterian Museum. One of these has a number of rude figures, emblematic of a Roman victory over our Caledonian forefathers, carved upon it, with an inscription referring to the completion of a certain portion of the wall. Mr. Stuart, in his *Caledonia Romana*,[32] gives the following translation of the legend inscribed upon it:

"To the Emperor Cæsar Titais Aelius
Hadrianus Antoninus
Augustus Pius, father of his country,

---

[32] 1845, by Robert Stuart.

The Second Legion, Augusta,
(Dedicate this, having executed)
4,666 paces."

The second stone was discovered in 1826 by a neighbouring farmer, and was presented by the proprietor of Castlehill to the Hunterian Museum. It is a votive tablet, and was dedicated "to the eternal field deities of Britain."

On the summit of Castlehill faint outlines of the Roman encampment are still traceable.[33] A belt of trees has been tastefully planted around the spot, while the interior is one unbroken verdant area, save that one lone tree, seemingly by accident, has sprung up near the centre. While we are here a flock of cattle are scattered about the enclosure peacefully chewing their cud, the cushat[34] is cooing among the branches overhead, and the blackbird piping on a leaf-hidden pedestal. It is difficult, indeed, in these times to realize to ourselves the idea that the "pomp and circumstance"[35] of ruthless war have ever marred the scene. Yet here the Roman helmet has gleamed, the Roman sword has clashed, and here man has encountered man in dire and deadly feud. But

"All these are silent now, or only heard
Like mellowed murmurs of the distant sea."[36]

The prospect from Castlehill is of the most magnificent description, and would, to any lover of landscape beauty, amply recompense the journey of a day. To the north is seen the full range of the Kilpatrick Hills from Dumbuck to their western termination. Looking westward over a finely undulating country, adorned with towns, villages, and mansions innumerable, we have the Campsie range from the peak of Dungoyne to Kilsyth. Turning gradually from the south towards the

---

[33] The remains are no longer visible except by means of aerial photography. The stones mentioned are still in the Hunterian Museum.
[34] wood pigeon
[35] From Shakespeare's *Othello* III.iii.
[36] Possibly a misquote for "The stilly murmur of the distant Sea /
Tells us of silence" in 'The Eolian Harp' (1796) by Samuel Taylor Coleridge.

west, we have the valley of the Clyde from Tintoc to Dumbuck spread as in a map before our gaze, with Dychmont, Cathkin, Ballygeich, Neilston Pad, and the Renfrewshire Hills, forming the picturesque outline of the horizon. To attempt a description of a scene so rich and so infinitely varied in its features, would, in truth, but be to exhibit our own utter incapacity: and as self-esteem forbids that we should parade our own deficiencies, we shall content ourselves with quietly recommending the reader to take stick in hand and witness it on his own account, while we make our descent on Duntocher.

Immediately to the north of Castlehill passes the highway from New Kilpatrick to Duntocher, along which, in a westerly direction, we now pursue our course. A pleasant walk of about two miles, principally down hill, brings us to the village of Faifley – a kind of suburb of Duntocher. These villages, with Hardgate, form as it were one irregular and straggling, but cleanly and comfortable looking township. The houses are, for the most part, plain two-storeyed edifices, and in many instances have small gardens attached to them. The population are, in general, either directly or indirectly connected with the extensive factories of Messrs. Dunn & Co. In 1808, when the works at Duntocher first came into the hands of the late William Dunn, Esq.,[37] the village was almost deserted. The former proprietors had lost heart, and everything was in a languishing condition. Mr. Dunn, a man of indomitable energy and perseverance, who had raised himself from a humble rank in society by his industry and shrewdness, speedily infused new life into the concern. The works were gradually extended and improved under his vigilant and enlightened superintendence, until at length they attained a high state of efficiency; and the working population increased from 150, the original number, to upwards of 1,500. By the almost unprecedented success of his manufacturing operations, Mr. Dunn at length achieved a splendid fortune, and died in the possession of one of the finest estates in the west of Scotland. At his decease, a few years ago, the bulk of the property thus

---

[37] 1770 – 1849, industrialist.

accumulated passed into the hands of his surviving brother, Alexander Dunn, Esq.,[38] the present proprietor.

In proportion to its size, Duntocher seems to be amply supplied with the "means and appliances" of religious and intellectual culture. There are no fewer than five places of worship in its immediate neighbourhood, to each of which is attached an educational establishment; while there are several other schools supported by parties unconnected with any local congregation. We understand that there are also several libraries, by means of which the reading portion of the population have, at a moderate rate, their literary requirements abundantly gratified. The situation of the village is highly romantic, and many of the walks in its vicinity are really of the most delightful description. In the background are the beautiful Kilpatrick Hills, scarred with their picturesque glens, down which streamlets are ever tumbling in foam, or stealing gently under the long yellow broom; while immediately below is the fertile valley of the Clyde, with its verdant slopes, its stately mansions, and never-ceasing traffic. The inhabitants generally, as might indeed be expected, have a more robust and healthful aspect than is ordinarily to be seen in less happily situated manufacturing communities.

On a hill of moderate height, which overlooks Duntocher, there existed until recently distinct traces of an extensive Roman encampment or fort. These are now almost obliterated; but from time to time many valuable relics of art, produced by the builders of the great wall – tablets, altars, vases, &c., have been discovered at this interesting locality. Most of these have been deposited for preservation in the Hunterian Museum. Some curious subterranean chambers, supposed to be of Roman origin, were also discovered in the vicinity of the fort in the year 1775. In one of these an earthen jar was found, with a female figure formed of reddish clay, and a few grains of wheat. At the foot of the hill there is a bridge, which is also popularly supposed to have been erected by the Romans, but which, notwithstanding a Latin inscription to that effect, by Lord Blantyre,

---

[38] d.1860. Most of the estate was sold to the Corporation of Glasgow in 1877.

who repaired the structure in 1772, is asserted by long-headed antiquaries to have no more claim to that honour than what may arise from the circumstance that the stones of which it is composed were probably taken from the neighbouring fort. We make no pretensions ourselves to skill in these matters, and shall not presume to express an opinion on the subject. We may mention, however, that when seen from the water-worn channel of the rivulet, the bridge has an ancient and picturesque appearance; and that we should not like to call its antiquity in question where two or three of the Duntocher folks were gathered together. Right or wrong, they are determined to have it a Roman edifice, and would, there is reason to fear, be inclined to deal anything but gently with an obstinate incredulant. Talk ill of Habby Simson at Kilbarchan, inquire for a "bull" at Rutherglen, or a "steeple" at Renfrew;[39] but by all means avoid speculating on the genuineness of the bridge at Duntocher, if you have the least regard for the good-will of the natives.[40]

Leaving Duntocher, we now take our way towards the village of Old Kilpatrick, which is situated on the northern bank of the Clyde, about a mile to the westward. Immediately after our departure from Duntocher, we pass on the left the fine policies of Auchentoshan, the handsome seat of Alexander Dunn, Esq., and a little farther on the mansion and grounds of Mountblow, likewise the property of that gentleman.[41] For beauty of site and extensive command of scenery these stately edifices, which are in close proximity to each other, will certainly bear favourable comparison with any in the lower ward of Clydesdale. In the grounds of Auchentoshan, several faint vestiges of the Roman barrier are traceable; and in the gardens of Mountblow, there is an ancient monumental cross, which is supposed to be of the

---

[39] Habby Simson was the piper of Kilbarchan – see p241. There was once an incident when a bull managed to escape from Rutherglen jail because it was in such disrepair. The old steeple at Renfrew was notoriously tiny – see p278.
[40] Although still called 'Roman Bridge', this bridge was rebuilt in 1943 after it was damaged in the Clydebank Blitz of 1941.
[41] Auchentoshan House was destroyed by bombs during the Clydebank Blitz. Mountblow became a children's home in 1922 and was demolished after the war. The suburb of Mountblow is built on the site.

twelfth century, and is similar to those which have been found at Cantyre[42] and in the Hebrides. This curious relic was used for some time by way of foot-bridge over a neighbouring burn, and was only rescued from that degraded position by the late Mr. Dunn, who had it removed to its present more secure and more honourable site.[43] In consequence of the friction to which it was then subjected, the carving on one side of the cross has been entirely effaced; while that on the other, from lengthened exposure to the weather, has become very obscure. The inscription is perfectly illegible, and two nondescript figures on the upper portion, with a confused kind of ornament, are all that can now be perceived. Time and the elements have indeed taken from it irrecoverably the tale which it was commissioned to unfold. That this interesting relic of a long vanished age may be preserved for a more lengthened period from the destructive influences of "the wind and the rain,"[44] we would venture to suggest to Mr. Dunn that it should be immediately placed under cover.

About half-way between Duntocher and Kilpatrick there is a gentle eminence called Dalnottar, from the brow of which is obtained one of the most lovely and richly variegated prospects imaginable. The Clyde, now swelling into the character of a frith, is seen stretching away into the distance of the Cowal hills, its bosom fretted with numerous ships and steamers plying busily to and fro between the various ports. On one hand is the Kilpatrick range of hills terminating in the rocky height of Dumbuck; while at their base, along the irregular margin of the water, Kilpatrick, Bowling, Dunglass, and the gigantic rock of Dumbarton, are brought at a glance before the gaze of the spectator. On the south side of the river are Erskine House,[45] the seat of Lord Blantyre,[46] and its beautifully wooded banks and braes, with Port-Glasgow and the hills above Greenock in the distance. The scene

---

[42] Now Kintyre.

[43] It was actually Robert Donald, Lord Provost of Glasgow, who rescued the stone in 1793. When the estate was sold, the stone was removed to the Kelvingrove Museum.

[44] From Feste's song in Shakespeare's *Twelfth Night* V.i.

[45] This building is now Mar Hall Hotel.

[46] Charles Walter Stuart, 12th Lord Blantyre (1818 – 1900).

altogether is of the most delicious description, and we need not wonder that it has often tempted the painter into the exercise of his art. Such of our readers as remember the old Theatre Royal, Queen Street, will doubtless recollect the famous drop-scene, taken from this point by the celebrated Naismith,[47] which was so highly appreciated as a work of art that not less a sum than five hundred pounds was offered for it by the manager of one of the London theatres. The prospect from this "coigne of vantage" has frequently been transferred to the canvas since; but we question if it has ever been more faithfully or artistically rendered than in the instance to which we have alluded. Commending the spot to the professional attention of our modern aspirants to landscape honours, we resume once more our downhill course. We may mention at parting, however, that the tasteful little residence on the brow of the hill was occupied for several years by our late highly respected town-clerk, Mr. Reddie,[48] and his family.

The village of Old Kilpatrick is situated on a level space of ground between the base of the adjoining hills and the Clyde. It is of no great extent, and consists principally of a single street, which forms a portion of the highway between Glasgow and Dumbarton. The houses are generally of the plainest architectural description, and several of them are indeed in a half-ruinous condition. There is a number of cosie-looking dwellings about it, however; and, from a pretty extensive application of whitewash, the place has, on the whole, a clean and tidy aspect, while the numerous well-kept gardens about it increase the attractiveness of its appearance, and at the same time augur well for the home comfort of the inhabitants. At the west end of the village stands the parish church, a plain but neat edifice with a handsome tower;[49] and around it, in a spacious church-yard, "the rude forefathers of the hamlet sleep."[50] There are several curious gravestones and monuments in the ground, and one is pointed out to us as that of St. Patrick. There is no inscription on the monument, but

---

[47] Alexander Naysmith (1758–1840), portrait and landscape painter.
[48] James Reddie (1775–1852).
[49] This church, built in 1812 on the site of earlier churches, survives.
[50] From 'An Elegy Written in a Country Church Yard' (1751) by Thomas Gray.

from its appearance it must be of a date long subsequent to the age of the great frog destroyer. This individual is traditionally said to have first seen the light in this vicinity. As in the case of the birth places of other illustrious personages, however, there seems to be some doubt on the subject; and whether "his mother kept a whisky-shop in the town of Enniskillen," as the popular Irish song has it,[51] or whether he came of the "dacent people" of Kilpatrick, it will probably be no easy matter now-a-days to determine. There are two other places of worship besides the Established Church in the village, namely, a small but neat edifice in connection with the Free Church, and an old United Presbyterian meeting house of somewhat dreary appearance.[52] The place altogether, indeed, has rather an "auld warld" air, and has apparently undergone but little alteration for many years.

A short distance west from the village is Chapelhill, a spot which is remarkable as having been the terminating point of the Roman wall. Formerly it was supposed that this immense structure extended to Dunglass Castle, but modern antiquaries, after minute investigation, have become satisfied that it was at this locality that the terminal fort was erected. Many relics of Roman art have been discovered here, and it is even deemed probable that within this elevation a number of subterranean chambers may yet remain uninjured. Two tabular stones were found at the Chapelhill, in the year 1693, by Mr. Hamilton of Orbiston, and presented by him to the University of Glasgow. These stones, from the inscriptions upon them, appear to have been erected by the sixth and twentieth legions of the army, to commemorate the erection of the wall and to perpetuate the memory of the reigning Emperor Antoninus Pius. On one of them is a figure of Victory, with a laurel wreath upon her brow, and an olive branch in her hand. Earthen vases and Roman coins have also been discovered at Chapelhill, which, besides its interesting antiquarian associations, possesses charms of a scenic description which will abundantly repay a visit from the poet or the painter.

---

[51] From 'St Patrick Was a Gentleman' (c.1815) by Henry Bennett, and R Tolekin.
[52] Neither of these churches survives.

No. XVI. Duntocher and Old Kilpatrick

After lingering for several hours in the vicinity of Old Kilpatrick, now speelin' the richly wooded braes, every alteration of position revealing a new picture to our gaze, and anon threading the mazes of some nameless glen or dell, radiant with bloom, and musical with the voices of linnet and of thrush, we return to the "Red Lion" to satisfy those cravings which, in spite of landscape beauty or sentimental association, are continually reminding us of our non-chameleon nature.[53] The poet and the rambler are, alas! alas! even as other men, and must ultimately draw their inspiration from such gross materials as the beef steak and the "tappit hen."[54] Having taken "our ease in our inn" for a brief space, we proceed to the ferry (for Kilpatrick, unfortunately for herself as well as for her visitors, has no wharf), and paying our "three bawbees,"[55] are safely deposited on board one of the river steamers, which, in somewhat less than an hour afterward, is "blowing off" within a few yards of the Glasgow Bridge.

---

[53] Chameleons can do without eating or drinking for several days.

[54] decanter

[55] That is, a penny and a half.

"Bonnie lass, will ye gang wi' me,
Whare moorcocks craw and plovers cry?"

In the course of a "twa-handed crack" which we had with the late celebrated Christopher North, some half-dozen years ago, in his own sanctum, Glo'ster Place, Edinburgh, the "old man eloquent" of Maga,[1] while discoursing lovingly on the scenery of the western districts of Scotland, alluded to that curious natural phenomenon, "the Whangie," in high terms of admiration. In answer to our inquiry as to the nature and locality of this strangely named wonder of the "west countrie" (for, to our chagrin, we were compelled to admit our previous ignorance of its existence), he described it as a deep and rugged cleft or gulley, evidently "of sudden and portentous birth," in the side of the hill at the north eastern termination of the Kilpatrick range, and apparently the production, in a bygone epoch, of some extraordinary terrene convulsion. He descanted rapturously, at the same time, on the wild and grizzly features of the spot, and on the magnificent prospect of mountain and flood which it commanded. Our curiosity thus excited, we shortly afterwards made a pilgrimage to the scene, and, contrary to what usually occurs when wizard fancy anticipates reality, we found that in beauty stern and wild the Whangie itself far exceeded our expectations, while the far-stretching landscape around more than justified the matchless poetic prose in which the author of the *Lights and Shadows*,[2] while seated in his ain muckle chair, had depicted its infinite variety of feature. Since that period we have again and again, on days of sunshine and on days of gloom, visited the locality. Increased familiarity, in spite of the musty old adverse proverb, has only produced additional admiration in our mind; and, craving the company of our courteous reader for a long day of June, we shall once more, with willing steps, wend our way to its craggy precincts.

---

[1] Professor John Wilson (1785 – 1854), who often wrote under the pen name Christopher North. 'Maga' is *Blackwood's Magazine*. MacDonald visited Wilson in 1846.
[2] Wilson's collection of stories and sketches, published 1822.

No. XVII. New Kilpatrick and the Whangie

Taking time by the forelock, we start at an early hour, and emerge to the northward from the mazes of the city by the Garscube Road. The morning is gray and lowering, but as the barometer has been doggedly pointing to rain for the last twenty-four hours, and never a drop falling, we have every reason to expect a day of fair weather. There are gulfs of blue, besides, intersecting the general murkiness of the sky – a capital sign; and, better still, the swallow is describing his airy circles at a very considerable elevation overhead. So we proceed resolutely, strengthened with the reflection that should it even come to the worst, we are neither "saut nor sugar," as the old wives sagely remark, and can bear without melting the pattering of a summer shower. Just as we have got outside the city, we pass a heap of stones by the wayside, which is popularly known as the "Smuggler's Cairn." In the days when illicit distillation was more common than it is at present, it is said that a party of the "wee still" folk, while making a midnight run with the produce of their unlawful labours, were intercepted at this place by a detachment of "gaugers."[3] A severe struggle ensued, in the course of which one of the smugglers was killed. The scene of this tragedy (in which the popular sympathy was, as a matter of course, in favour of the defrauders of the Excise) has ever since been marked by the cairn to which we have alluded; and every person passing the spot is expected to contribute a stone to the heap. At what period this deed of blood occurred we have never been able to learn, but its stony memorial has been in existence for a lengthened period, and even yet manifests no symptoms of diminution. The rapid extension of the city in a north-west direction, however, will probably ere long obliterate this among other more important landmarks.[4]

From this point to Maryhill, the Port-Dundas branch of the Forth and Clyde Canal runs for a considerable distance nearly parallel to the highway; and the traveller, as he jogs along, sees stately vessels which seem to have deserted their "native element," journeying

---

[3] exisemen

[4] The cairn, which has now gone, stood about a quarter of a mile west of Queens Cross (where Garscube Road joins Maryhill Road), near the canal.

overland by his side. To quote once more the venerable author of "The Clyde,"[5]

> "Through Carron's channel, now with Kelvin joined,
> The wondering barks a ready passage find;
> The ships on swelling billows wont to rise,
> On solid mountains climb to scale the skies.
> Old Ocean sees the fleets forsake his floods,
> Sail the firm land, the mountains, and the woods,
> And safely thus conveyed, they dread no more
> Rough northern seas which round the Orkneys roar."

We have become more familiar with the wonders of human industry and skill since the days of good old John Wilson; yet there are few sights more interesting, even in this age of marvels, than the passage of a large vessel up or down the watery staircase of a canal. This process may be witnessed to perfection in the vicinity of Maryhill. We find the canal there, within the compass of a few hundred yards, passing by a viaduct over the highway, next by a succession of locks proceeding down a considerable declivity, and immediately thereafter crossing with a magnificent span the deep valley of the Kelvin. Vessels of various sizes, laden and unladen, are continually passing and repassing at this place, exhibiting the whole machinery of artificial water transit in full operation. The banks of the canal in the neighbourhood are, besides, of the most beautiful description, presenting rather the romantic features of a natural stream than the formal lineaments of a channel made with hands.

The village of Maryhill itself presents but few features of attraction. The houses are, for the most part, of the plainest order; and, with the exception of those in the principal street, are scattered about in the most irregular manner. There are a number of public works in the vicinity also, which, however conducive to its prosperity, certainly do not tend to increase the amenity of the locality. Until recently there was only one church in Maryhill. There are now three; one in

---

[5] John Wilson (1720 – 1789) – not the same John Wilson as 'Christopher North'.

connection with the Establishment, a Free Church, and a Roman Catholic Chapel. These are all neat, but, in an architectural sense, rather unpretending edifices, and none of them contribute materially to the adornment of the village.[6]

Scenes of considerable natural beauty abound in the environs of the village. Among these is Dalsholm, a little to the west, where the Kelvin, issuing from the fine policies of Garscube, rushes over its rocky bed with a soft murmuring sound, bordered on the one side by a bold precipitous bank, and on the other by gently swelling slopes and fertile meads. In some places the water is overhung by a profusion of foliage, while it is fretted into foam at others by projecting channel stones, among which the wagtail and chaffinch are flitting about while we linger on the bridge gazing upon the sweet secluded landscape around. A paper-mill on the margin of the stream, and several cottages on the rising grounds, some of them half-concealed by trees through which the blue smoke is ever curling, lend a human interest to the spot, without detracting materially from its natural loveliness. The farm of Dalsholm is remarkable for an ancient tumulus, which was long known by the appellation of the "Courthill," and was supposed to have formed in bygone times the judgment-seat of some feudal potentate. Some score or so of years ago, the farmer, who probably had but a limited degree of reverence for feudality or its remains, set about removing the "knowe," partly as a cumberer of the ground, and partly with the utilitarian view of applying the soil of which it was composed as a top dressing to a neighbouring field. A small portion of the mound, however, had only been removed when the workmen discovered a narrow flight of steps leading towards the interior of the eminence. Following this subterranean staircase for a few paces, it was found to terminate in a flagstone, on which were strewn a quantity of ashes or cinders. On striking this stone it sounded hollow, when they immediately proceeded to have it removed. On accomplishing this, a small cell or chamber was discovered underneath, lined with stone, and

---

[6] The Church of Scotland building was demolished in the late 20th century. The Free Church building is now a nursery and its steeple has been partly demolished. The Catholic Church was damaged by bombs in WWII and later demolished.

containing a number of curious relics. Among these were the visor of a helmet composed of copper, with the head of a spear, and the blade of a sword, the accoutrements probably of some distinguished warrior of the olden time. Several other articles were also found of a nondescript nature, or so much decayed that the purposes for which they had originally been formed could not be ascertained. No human remains were found in the cavity, nor any inscription to indicate the intention with which the erection had been constructed. Such tumuli are generally regarded by students of the antique, however, as funereal mementoes of departed greatness; and the fact that human bones have frequently been found in them seems to countenance the supposition. In the present instance the dust of mortality had so effectually returned to its kindred dust that not one coherent fragment remained to indicate that "a proud one of the earth"[7] had there been laid at rest. Oblivion, that inexorable creditor, had irrecoverably taken possession of his "pound of flesh."[8] On bringing these things to light, the farmer of Dalsholm desisted from the work of demolition, and a considerable portion of the mound still remains intact for the examination of future antiquaries.[9]

Returning to the highway, from our brief digression to Dalsholm, we resume our northerly course, and, after a pleasant walk of about a mile, arrive at the little village or hamlet of Garscube, which consists of a mill, and some half dozen houses. The road at this point crosses the Kelvin by a commodious bridge, as it flows from the soft sylvan banks of Killermont into the wild magnificence of the Garscube grounds. Unlike the majority of Scottish streams, the Kelvin, in the upper part of its course, is dull, sluggish, and canal-like. Rising in the parish of Kilsyth, it flows in a south-westerly direction, placidly and slow, until it arrives at Garscube, when it completely changes character, and tumbles and dances as merrily as a mountain brook, while its banks become bold, precipitous, and highly picturesque. The

---

[7] From Psalm 31.24 in *New Version of the Psalms of David* (1756) by Thomas Cradock.
[8] From Shakespeare's *The Merchant of Venice* IV.i.
[9] The mound was removed completely when the road was straightened.

Kelvin in both its aspects is seen to great advantage from the spot where we now stand. Above the bridge it is over hung by the umbrageous woods of Killermont, which are reflected as in a mirror on its unruffled surface, while along its margin the long rank marsh grasses, mingled with May flowers and other plants that love alluvial richness of soil, are waving gracefully, and the broad-leaved water-lily is floating lazily on its breast. Passing the bridge, however, the waters seem to become instinct with new life, and murmur sweetly among the channel stones as they pass with a fine sweep into the verdant recesses of the Garscube policies, giving and receiving beauty.

Killermont House, the seat of John Campbell Colquhoun, Esq.,[10] an extensive and elegant mansion, is situated on the Kelvin a short distance above our present position;[11] while Garscube House, the residence of Sir Archibald Campbell, Bart.,[12] a handsome edifice, in the style of the old English manor-house, lies screened in foliage about half-a-mile below.[13] The pleasure grounds surrounding the latter structure are of great extent and beauty, being richly adorned with a profusion of the finest timber, while they embrace a variety of landscape features of the most attractive nature.

Passing on, we soon arrive at Canniesburn, where the road diverges into two branches – one leading by Milngavie to Balfron, &c.; the other, which is our route, forms the highway to Drymen. There is a toll-house and a number of scattered cottages at Canniesburn. One of these is of course, a small shop, the window of which is garnished with the usual display of "parleys,"[14] scones, tape, and the other miscellaneous articles which indicate the habitation of the "Jenny-a'-things" of the village. We are rather amused with the humble signboard of the Canniesburn huckstress. Originally it seems to have borne on its honest front a list of the commodities forming the stock in trade of the

---

[10] 1803 – 1870, writer and politician.
[11] Killermont House is now the clubhouse of Glasgow Golf Club. Its golf course was laid out by the famous golfer Old Tom Morris.
[12] d.1870.
[13] Garscube House was demolished in 1954 and Wolfson Hall of Residence (University of Glasgow) was later built on the site.
[14] That is, parliament cakes – rectangular ginger biscuits.

proprietrix, such as teas, tobacco, &c.; but from some cause or other the various items have been successively effaced, until at present the sole inscription is composed of the somewhat significant words, "JANET MUNRO TO SELL." Had we met with such an ominous announcement in the columns of a Yankee newspaper it might have excited but little astonishment in our mind; but we must confess that seeing it on the front of a Scottish cottage, it rather took us aback. Being otherwise provided for in that line, we did not venture to speir Janet's price. For the benefit of our bachelor friends, we think it proper, however, to give a more extended currency to the notice of sale. Some of them might really do worse than give honest Janet a call. [We cannot say whether a bargain has since been effected or not, but the inviting announcement has recently been obliterated.]

A short distance to the west of Canniesburn we pass a small sheet of water, occupying a low-lying position a little to the left of the highway. This is the Chapelton Loch,[15] which is chiefly remarkable as the habitat of various interesting acquatic plants, in search of which it is occasionally visited by the wandering botanist. The water-hen and snipe frequent the sedgy shallows of this diminutive lochlet, and it is said to contain abundance of fine pike and eels, in pursuit of which the rustic angler may frequently be observed, rod in hand, lingering on its rushy margin. Contenting ourselves with a passing glance from the road at its dark waters, over which the swallows are sporting merrily in the glimpse of sunshine which now breaks from the sky, we speedily find ourselves at the beautiful little "kirk-toun" of New Kilpatrick. This is indeed a lovely locality, and somehow it is ever associated in our mind, since first we gazed upon it on a bright spring day some dozen years ago, with sunshine, and opening leaves, and singing birds. In our memory, to use the words of an old song, "It shines where it stands."[16] We can never think of it under a wintry aspect. Often, amidst the turmoil and din of the city, does our fancy wander to that quiet and secluded church-yard; while in our "mind's ear" we seem to listen to

[15] Also known as St German's Loch, presumably after Germanus, Bishop of the Isle of Man, who was associated with St Patrick.
[16] From the traditional song 'Glenlogie'.

the rustling of the wind among the waving boughs, or the lonesome murmur of the passing burn which ever singeth around the green mansions of the dead.

New Kilpatrick is a very tiny hamlet. We should suppose that there cannot be more than a dozen or so of humble cottages in it altogether, if there are even so many. These, however, have been set down with an admirable irregularity, and with their patches of garden, well stocked with apple trees, gooseberry bushes, and kitchen vegetables, make altogether a most agreeable rural picture. Then there is the burn wimpling along its own little vale of flowers, with generally a group of fair-headed urchins paidlin' about in its waters, pursuing the minnow, the eel, or the beardie,[17] while their gleeful voices fall with a fitful music on the ear. Beyond the burn, but half enclosed by one of its links, is the neat little church, plain, unpretending, but elegant withal, and begirt with a kirk-yard so green and quiet that one could almost wish to lie down in its verdant lap, and be at rest.[18] In the immediate vicinity of the church (on the summit of a gentle declivity sloping down to the margin of the burn, and with a fine spring at its foot)[19] is the manse, a neat little edifice of modern erection, in the English cottage style, presenting, with its well-stocked garden and sheltering trees, an extremely pleasing aspect of elegance and comfort. There is also a handsome parish school in the village, with a diminutive hostelry, and a post-office in miniature.[20] How enviable must be the langsyne recollections of children brought up in such a spot, when compared with those of the unfortunate little ones whose lines of early life have fallen in the noisome purlieus of the city, and whose first impressions of the world have been formed amid far other influences than those of leaves, or flowers, or the sweet voices that haunt the summer trees!

---

[17] stickleback

[18] This church, which was extended in the 1870s and '80s, and largely reconstructed in 1909, is still in use.

[19] The spring was shut up after the village was connected to the Glasgow water supply.

[20] All but the manse had disappeared before 1910.

New Kilpatrick, we may mention, is situated directly on the line of the ancient wall of Antoninus Pius. A little to the eastward of the village a cultivated field is pointed out as the site of an extensive Roman fort. All traces of the works are now obliterated by the plough;[21] but up to a comparatively recent period the outlines of the entrenchments were distinctly visible. The area enclosed within the interior *valla* measured, it is said, about 480 by 330 feet, while the fortifications covered a considerably greater space of ground. The great military way passed through the fort, and vast quantities of the stones of which it was composed have at various times been removed for building purposes by persons in the neighbourhood. One farmer remarked, indeed, that the Roman works "had proved a perfect quarry for the parish." Tradition still points to a spot called the "Bear's Den" as the burial-place of the garrison; and a well, long surrounded by sedges and rushes, the outlet of which has been removed by means of a drain to the edge of the field whereon the rampart stood, was supposed, from certain remains of mason-work found about it, to have ministered to the necessities of the Roman soldiers.[22] Carved stones, fragments of pottery, ancient coins, and other relics of antiquity, have also been found at various periods in the vicinity of New Kilpatrick, indicating the presence at some distant epoch of the self-styled "masters of the world."

Resuming our northerly course, we are speedily on ground where the foot of the conqueror never trod. "Hitherto we came, but no farther,"[23] is the legend of the great wall. If it was a mark of conquest, it was likewise an acknowledgment of weakness.

> "The wave of Forth was joined to Clyde,
> When Rome's broad rampart stretched from tide to tide,
> With bulwarks strong, with towers sublimely crowned,
> While winding tubes conveyed each martial sound.
> To guard the legions from their painted foes,

---

[21] The suburb of Bearsden now stands on this location.
[22] The bathhouse and latrines can still be seen in a housing estate off Roman Road in Bearsden.
[23] A reference to Job 38.11.

No. XVII. New Kilpatrick and the Whangie

By vast unwearied toil the structure rose,
When fierce in arms, the Scot, by Carron's shore,
Resigned for war, the chase and mountain boar,
As the chafed lion, on his homeward way
Returns for vengeance, and forgets his prey."[24]

A beautiful tract of country now lies before us, and our path is amid fertile fields, wide-spreading pastures, and shadowy woods. On one hand we have the Kilpatrick range of hills approaching close to the road; on the other, over wooded knolls and picturesque straths, the romantic Campsie Fells, stretching away to Dungoyne and the "Earl's Seat." Passing in succession the mansions of Mains, Balvie, and Craigton,[25] we approach the eastern shoulder of the Kilpatrick range, with its finely marked terraces of trap,[26] and rich variations of outline. At one corner we observe a numerous series of basaltic columns of perfect prismatic form, and arranged in the most regular order, both in a transverse and vertical direction. It is well known that many geological features of a highly interesting nature are to be found upon the rugged surface of these hills, and that the scientific "stoneknappers" of our city frequently visit their recesses, hammer in hand, in pursuit of their favourite studies. Various botanical rarities are also to be found nestling in their sunny nooks. Among these are the orange-coloured hawkweed (*hieracium aurantiacum*), the long-leaved water hemlock (*cicuta virosa*), the serrated winter green (*pyrola secunda*), and, according to Hopkirk,[27] the woolly yarrow (*Achillœa tomentosa*). Some doubts having been expressed by Hooker[28] as to whether the latter species really existed in this habitat or not, a number of our field botanists, some years since, instituted a most rigorous

---

[24] From 'The Clyde' (1764) by John Wilson.
[25] Mains Castle fell into disrepair but remnants of it are found within Old Mains Farm. Confusingly, Balvie House was renamed Mains House. It was demolished in 1954 and Douglas Academy stands on its grounds. Old Craigton House has been converted into flats.
[26] Any dark igneous rock such as basalt.
[27] Thomas Hopkirk (1785–1841), Scottish botanist. The yarrow had apparently 'escaped' from a garden.
[28] Sir William Jackson Hooker (1785 – 1865), author of *Flora Scotica*.

search for the dubious plant, with the view of securing immortality for themselves by having their names inserted in the next edition of the "Flora." There labours were all in vain, however, as the plant, if it ever really existed there, had either been extirpated, or seemed determined

"To bloom unseen,
And waste its sweetness on the desert air."[29]

Among those who thus ranged the glens and the wild woods so dreary, was an old friend of our own, who, hoping against hope, persevered in his search after all others had given up in despair. Month after month, and season after season, with true botanical patience, he was to be found pursuing his devious course with downcast eyes among the everlasting hills, and still the yellow-flowered yarrow evaded his prying gaze. At length one of his companions, a pawky old carle, determined that his wish should be gratified. He accordingly procured some specimens of the plant from a garden, and hieing to the braes, stuck them into the earth at a spot where the enthusiast was almost certain to pass. The bait at once took – the gudgeon was caught. No one saw the discovery; but a few days thereafter the yarrow-hunter appeared among his associates, shouting, "Eureka! Eureka!" and proudly exhibited to his conscious associates what he fondly fancied the reward of all his toils. He would "write immediately to Sir William;" he would "send him the choicest specimens;" and a happy man indeed was he, as in fancy he saw his own name in "gude black prent," associated for ever with *Achillæa tomentosa* and the Kilpatrick Hills. His triumph, we need scarcely add, was but short-lived. Some busybody informed him of the trick, and at once took the wind out of the bellying sails of his vanity. His disappointment was beyond expression severe. He was never heard to mention the genus *Achillæa* again, and we may add, he never forgave the perpetration of this most cruel of practical jokes.

We now cross the Allander, a dark moss-coloured rivulet, which has its origin a short distance to the left in the "Baker's Loch,"

---

[29] From 'An Elegy Written in a Country Church Yard' (1751) by Thomas Gray.

among the neighbouring moors. This stream, after a winding course of ten miles or so, finds its way into the Kelvin, through the channels of which, in seasons of drought, it furnishes a supply of water to the Partick Mills. The woods of Carbeth-Guthrie are next passed, when we arrive at what may appropriately be denominated the great portal of the Highlands. The Kilpatrick and Campsie ranges, which have been gradually approximating, are here separated by a gap about four miles in breadth, on one side of which, like huge guardians of the pass, tower Dungoyne and the Earl's Seat, and on the other the swelling heights of Auchineden, while immediately in front, over a downward sloping expanse of wild moorland, variegated by clumps of wood and fertile fields, Lochlomond is seen reposing in quiet beauty with its sleeping isles, and the mighty Ben lifts his proud crest to the sky over stormy horizon of rugged peaks and ridges frowning in the distance. We now bid farewell to the highway, and by a rough field path, bordered with heather, tormentil, and a rich profusion of desert vegetation, direct our steps to the beautifully situated and elegant cottage of our friend the gamekeeper of John Wilson, Esq., of Auchineden.[30] Our intrusion on the moor is fiercely resisted, however, by sundry ill-natured peeseweeps,[31] which keep flying round our head with their shrill querulous cries, as if persuaded we have come to justify the old boyish rhyme,

> "Peeweep! peeweep!
> Ye'll harry my nest,
> And awa wi't."

Nothing can be farther from our intention, however; and passing the wee trickling burn, fringed with the bloom of lady's-mantle, broom, and hyacinth, and through the planting, where there is a weeping willow reared from a sprig taken from Napoleon's grave at St. Helena, we soon arrived at the hospitable domicile, a neat little one-storeyed

---

[30] MacDonald wrote a poem called 'Wee Annie o' Auchineden'.
[31] lapwings

edifice, with an outlook which a palace might well envy.[32] A green and sunny spot – an oasis in the bleak waste – is in truth the lodge of Auchineden. The columbine blooms on the very, doorstep, and the "appleringie"[33] almost peeps in at the gable window, while the swallow rears his young in the eaves without fear of molestation, and the wee hedge-sparrow sits on her blue egglets undisturbed within a few yards of the house-end. Such confidence betokens kindness of heart in the inmates of the snowy biggin'. Yet mercy is not unmingled with stern justice. Vermin of all kinds and degrees are here treated with well-merited rigour. The toad that plunders the hen-roost, the sleeky weazel, and the stoat – eggsuckers by habit and repute from time immemorial, — with the hoodie-craw, the bawk,[34] and the owl – all birds of evil omen to the game, – are here sacrificed by our stalwart friend with the shortest possible shrift. Look at these relics of the departed reivers nailed *in terrorem* on the rafters of the kennel, and think what a salvation of innocent partridges and grouse has been effected by their destruction! Of our kind reception in-doors we will not venture to speak. Suffice it to say that we have no occasion to regret "the comforts of the Sautmarket,"[35] and that we shall not soon forget the plain good sense of our host, nor the furthy frankness and welcome-beaming countenance of the gudewife.

Immediately behind the cottage rise the heights, on the opposite side of which the Whangie is situated; and after a reasonable period of rest, and a most unreasonable administration to the cravings of the inner man, we set a stout heart to a steep brae, and proceed on our pilgrimage. Our foot is now upon our native heather, and around us stretches a bleak moor,

---

[32] The cottage has been extended into a two-storey private house while the hunting lodge, Auchineden House, has been converted into six flats.

[33] aromatic wormwood

[34] bat

[35] An expression taken from St Walter Scott's *Rob Roy*. What Bailie Jarvie actually says is: "For accommodations, ane canna expect to carry about the Saut Market at his tail, as a snail does his caup."

No. XVII. New Kilpatrick and the Whangie

"Where pesewepes, plovers, and whaups cry dreary,"[36]

and the tufted cannach[37] waves its snowy crest among the dark brown hags. Now we are startled by the whirr of a rising covey – now a mosscheeper[38] goes fluttering and chirping from our path – and anon our attention is attracted by the beauty of some wilding flower, "born to blush unseen"[39] in the untrodden waste, yet fairer than the fairest bloomers' of the gay parterre.[40] With Robert Nicol we can heartily exclaim, while lingering over the solitary dwelling-places of the peerless grass of Parnassus, the purple orchis, and the blaeberry bush with its red waxen bells, –

> "Beautiful children of the woods and fields!
> That bloom by mountain streamlets 'mid the heather,
> Or into clusters 'neath the hazels gather –
> Or where by hoary rocks you make your bields,
> And sweetly flourish on through summer weather –
> I love ye all!"[41]

Ere reaching the brow of the hill, up which we have been toiling, we cast a backward glance on the landscape we are leaving behind us. The straths of the Blane and the Allander are seen stretching far away, in all their garniture of woods and fields and swelling knolls, with lofty ridges of hills on either side, and the high grounds beyond our own city on the dim horizon. 'Tis indeed a lovely Lowland scene. A few steps farther, however, and we have the Highlands before us. The crown of the eminence is passed, and the grandeur of flood and fell bursts upon our gaze. The transition is magnificent; and the spectator, looking upon "this picture and on that," is in truth at a loss to say which is the most attractive in its peculiar features of loveliness. Descending the farther side of the hill, we soon descry the gray storm-

---

[36] From the song 'Kate Dalrymple (c.1820) by William Watt.
[37] cotton-grass
[38] meadow pippit
[39] From 'An Elegy Written in a Country Church Yard' (1751) by Thomas Gray.
[40] A formal garden with enclosed flowerbeds.
[41] From 'Wild Flowers' (1835) by Robert Nicoll.

beaten rocks of the Whangie. On approaching the spot the first thing that strikes the visitor is an immense confused heap of jagged trap, piled against the hillside, and threatening in various places to topple over, while countless fragments of every size and shape are strewn about in the wildest irregularity, as if a congregation of demons had been, in some past epoch, engaged here in a diabolical stone battle. On closer inspection, however, it is seen that a vast section of the hill has been by some means or other wrenched asunder, leaving a lengthened and deep chasm yawning along the line of separation, and that the shattered appearance of the external surface has been produced by the violence of the convulsion which caused the original disunion. Entering the narrow ravine, we proceed as it were into the bowels of the firm-fixed earth. The passage is tortuous and uneven, the projections of one side corresponding with singular exactness to the hollows on the other. In width the Whangie, as this terrible fissure is called, varies from 24 to 10 feet; its medium depth being about 40 feet, while its length is 346 feet. The external wall, if we may use the term, is fearfully fractured in several places, and on peeping through the crevices and beholding the apparently tottering masses overhanging the steep below, the spectator involuntarily shrinks back as if his touch would send them thundering down. Save a stunted rowan-tree or two, projecting from the rifted summit of the chasm, the Whangie is utterly devoid of sylvan adornment. There are a variety of wild flowers and ferns, however, strewn over its lichened and hoary surface, among which we observe the wood-sorrel and wood-rush both in bloom. Does the presence of these plants indicate that trees at one period grew on the spot? or have they been fostered by the genial shade produced by the impending cliffs. Strange to say, tradition has preserved almost nothing in her budget regarding this remarkable production of nature. When the Highlanders were in the habit of ravaging the Lennox, it is said that cattle were occasionally concealed in its recesses, for which purpose, however, they do not now seem very well adapted. It is also said, traditionally, that after the overthrow of the Highlanders at

Culloden,[42] some of the proscribed Jacobites found shelter from the bloodhounds of Cumberland[43] in this solitary den. Nothing definite, however, is remembered of the event; and the Whangie, like Canning's knife-grinder – we love a congruous comparison – has really "no tale to tell."[44]

On a green declivity below the rocky steep, and contrasting agreeably with its hoary front, there is a delicious spring, cool in the noon of summer as the winter snow. Let us rest ourselves for a "blink" by its verdant margin, and, while quaffing a bicker of its icy crystal, scan the prospect which seems spread for our special delectation.

> "It is the land of beauty and of grandeur,
> Where looks the cottage out on a domain
> The palace cannot boast of. Seas of lakes,
> And hills of forests! Torrents here
> Are bounding floods! And there the tempest roams
> At large, in all the terrors of its glory."[45]

How beautiful is the lake, half in sun and half in shadow, with its scattered islands and its guardian hills, the immense soul-filling Ben, tallest and proudest of the mountain brotherhood! Yon bold promontory marks the pass of Balmaha, associated with memories of Rob Roy and Highland foray; that white speck, begirt with miles of forest, is Buchanan House, the seat of the Montrose dukedom;[46] and this conical bosky hill is Duncruin, a celebrated haunt of the green-coated fairies ere the daylight of modern civilization had driven them for ever away. Now

> "Seek the brake and seek the dell,
> The haunted glen, the swelling river;
> And seek the fountain and the rill

---

[42] 16th April 1746
[43] 'Butcher Cumberland' – Prince William, Duke of Cumberland (1765 – 1721).
[44] From 'The Knife Grinder' (1797) by George Canning.
[45] From 'The Wife: A Tale of Mantua' (1833) by James Sheridan Knowles.
[46] Buchanan Auld House burned down in 1852. Its replacement, Buchanan Castle, fell into ruin in the mid-twentieth century.

But all are gone, and gone for ever."[47]

It would take a summer day, indeed, to read the wide landscape before us – to tell of the towns, the villages, the mansions, and the "moors and mosses many, O,"[48] that the eye at one circling glance commands. It is a scene, in brief, to brood over rather than to describe; so pulling forth our "pocket pistol" (we always carry arms), and borrowing the necessary dilution from the bonnie wee well at our feet, let us, with all the honours and upstanding, devote one lipping cup to the

"Land of the mountain and the flood!"[49]

What a stramash that hearty hurrah has kicked up among the peeseweeps and plovers! There they go in myriads, wheep wheeping, as if they had never heard a cheer at the Whangie well in the whole course of their lives. Yet many a merry scene have these gray cliffs looked down upon. This is a favourite rendezvous, be it known, of the moorland rangers, when, in the golden Autumn afternoons, their work of death is over. Here the sun-browned sportsman, with the produce of his gun and his weary canine companions, loves to rest. Landseer[50] would "gi'e his lugs" to witness the picturesque groups that oft assemble here, while birds and dogs and guns are strewn in rich confusion round, and the echoes of the old Whangie ring to the huntsman's cheery chorus.

But "nae man can tether time or tide,"[51] and we must be moving. We have still a long walk before us, and the clouds are beginning to look sour. That conical hill to the westward is Duncombe, and our intention is to place our foot upon its crest. There is no road, so we must make a royal one for ourselves over the intervening moor, a distance of some three or four miles as the crow flies. Unfortunately, as we are steering our way among the "mosses, slaps, moors, hags, and

---

[47] From 'The Last Fairy' (1845) by William Oliver.
[48] From 'My Nanie, O' (1787) by Robert Burns.
[49] From 'Breathes There the Man' (Canto VI of *The Lay of the Last Minstrel*) (1805) by Sir Walter Scott.
[50] Edwin Landseer (1802 – 1873), painter known for his paintings of animals.
[51] From 'Tam o' Shanter' (1791) by Robert Burns.

stiles," now leaping some marshy tract from rush-tuft to stone, now tripping lightly over some heath-clad hillock, and anon pausing to calculate our saltatory[52] powers on the edge of some yawning gully, an unmistakeable Scotch mist envelops the landscape. Benlomond wraps himself up in his gray plaid, the loch, in sporting phraseology, is "nowhere," and even Duncombe is cloud-capt and frowning. How dreary, bleak, and gruesome the waste has suddenly become! The very flowers are hanging their little heads as if in fear, while the cannach[53] nods disconsolately to the passing blast, and the long grasses are whispering together. Dark as night are the lonely tarns, and the whiteness of the seabird's wing, as it flits athwart the inky water, but deepens the universal gloom. Duncombe, it is too obvious, must for the present remain unscaled. Were we to speel it now, instead of a prospect stretching from Ailsa and Goatfell to Tintoc,[54] we should have our circle of vision "cabined, cribbed, confined,"[55] to the diameter of an ellwand,[56] with the chance of breaking our neck as a reward for our temerity. Pushing by the most direct route, therefore, for Duntocher (and anything but a direct route in all conscience we find it), we arrive, in somewhat more than two hours from the time we leave the Whangie, at that village of cotton-mills and Roman antiquities. Passing thence, without calling a halt, to Old Kilpatrick, we get at once on board the "Eagle,"[57] a genuine Clyde clipper, which speedily gives us our discharge at the Broomielaw, droukit to the skin, and, it must be admitted, pretty considerably "used up."

---

[52] of jumping
[53] cotton grass
[54] Ailsa Craig in the Firth of Clyde, Goatfell on Arran, Tinto in the Southern Uplands.
[55] From Shakespeare's *Macbeth* III.vi.
[56] measuring stick
[57] Built in 1852 by William Denny & Brothers of Dumbarton. Sold in 1862 to run the American blockade during the Civil War.

Most beautiful of the months art thou, O leafy June! To welcome thee, the woods have donned their richest umbrageous robes, the fields their freshest luxuriance of green. Thy path is over flowery meads, and by clear-gushing streams, which mirror as they flow their many-tinted fringes of bloom. Thy genial winds are laden with the fragrance of the bean and the sweet breathings of the opening rose. In the depths of the far blue sky the lark, from earliest morn till eve's faint farewell blush, chants joyously to thee; while the sylvan choristers, in the "gloamin' o' the wood,"[1] rejoice with raptured notes of love thy ever-listening ear; and the low undersong of the bee where the wild thyme grows, makes musical for thee the very silence of the sunny braes. Now is the time to leave the noisome haunts of men

> "To wander by the green burnside,
> And hear its waters croon;"[2]

or to linger by some auld howlet-haunted biggin',[3] and dream of days gone by. Now is the time to steal, for a brief space, from the cark and care of city life, and to revel in the inestimable luxury of nature's loveliness. One long golden day among the woods and fields of sweet companionship with birds and flowers and soothing winds – will do thee more good, O gentle reader! both as a moral and physical being, than a whole cart-load of musty tomes, or any possible quantity of pills and potions. Take staff in hand, therefore, and be persuaded, for once, to come with us on our "journey of a day." It is still early; but the sun, who at this season takes only a brief "nap," has got his honest face above the level of the house top opposite, where a merry band of sparrows are engaged in a dinsome matutinal[4] row. Steering our course towards the north-west suburb of the city – now passing a milkman

---

[1] From 'Jeanie Morrison' (1819) by William Motherwell.

[2] Also from 'Jeanie Morrison'.

[3] That is, owl-haunted. A reference to 'On the Late Captain Grose's Peregrinations through Scotland' (1789) by Robert Burns.

[4] of the morning

engaged with a tittering bevy of servant girls; now a baker's boy, powdered from top to toe and tottering under an enormous superincumbent weight of rolls; now an unkempt housemaid on her knees lustily scrubbing the door-steps; and anon a drowsy-looking artisan proceeding pipe-in-mouth to his labour, and leaving an odorous trail behind in the raw morning air – we soon find ourselves beyond the region of streets, amidst gardens and fields, breathing the untainted air. Maryhill and Garscube being soon left behind, we speedily arrive at Canniesburn, where our ramble, properly speaking, may be said to commence. The road, as we have previously remarked, diverges into two branches at this point; the one to the left leading to New Kilpatrick, &c., the other, which we now pursue, to Milngavie, or "Millguy," as in popular and more euphonious parlance it is generally denominated. A short distance to the north-east of Canniesburn – which we leave by a pleasant path between verdant hedgerows, with finely undulating fields on either side, clad with a luxuriant mantle of waving grain, over which the winds are playing in wavy streams – is Ferguston, a comfortable farm-steading, where the line of the Roman wall crosses the highway. Wherever the plough has passed, all traces of this ancient structure are, of course, obliterated; but on a rising ground in the immediate neighbourhood, a deep indentation, a remnant of the fosse, is still distinctly visible.[5] Gordon, in his *Itinerarium Septrionale*,[6] makes special mention of this interesting footprint of the haughty conqueror; and we may mention, for the edification of our antiquarian friends, that it remains as nearly as may be in the same condition as when that zealous lover of the antique visited the locality. To the uninitiated eye, indeed, it has the appearance of a mere natural hollow or ditch, covered with sward similar to that on the adjoining ground; the mighty structure which the legions of imperial Rome took upwards of a century to erect having been so completely prostrated by time and the elements, that, unless to the lynx-eyed antiquary, not even a wrack

---

[5] The fosse is now mostly built over, but part of the wall's foundation can still be seen in the nearby New Kilpatrick Cemetery.

[6] Alexander Gordon (c.1692 – 1755), antiquary. The title means 'Northern Travel Guide'.

remains. Passing on, we have the fine woods of Kilmardinny to the left, embowering in their wide-stretching shades the handsome mansion of the same name, and a lovely little lochlet, some eight acres in extent, begirt with trees, shrubs, and flowers, and abounding in pike, eel, and perch, for the votary of the "gentle art." The pleasure grounds of Kilmardinny are of very considerable extent, and embrace numerous features of natural and artificial beauty. Away to the right, again, are the spacious policies of Dougalstone, richly timbered, and adorned with a loch which covers an expanse of twenty three Scots acres, and abounds in water-plants, some of which are rare, and in various kinds of fish. The estate of Dougalstone belonged at an early period to a branch of the Montrose family. About the middle of the last century, it passed into the hands of Mr. John Glassford,[7] a merchant prince of our own good city, and one who was pre-eminently distinguished in "his day and generation," by the possession of an enlarged and liberal mind, associated with practical shrewdness and the most active business habits. Smollett, in his humorous novel of *Humphrey Clinker*,[8] makes honourable mention of Mr. Glassford. In that delightful work the assumed writer says, "I conversed also with Mr. G-ssf-d, whom I take to be one of the greatest merchants in Europe. In the last war he is said to have had at one time five-and twenty ships with their cargoes – his own property – and to have traded for above half-a-million sterling a-year." Mr. Glassford, who died in 1783, expended large sums on the adornment of the Dougalstone property, which still retains, in its extensive plantations and shadowy walks, abundant evidences of his taste for the beautiful.[9] Of late years, however, the locality has worn an aspect of neglect and waste, suggestive of an alteration for the worse in the fortunes of the proprietors.[10]

---

[7] 1715 – 1783, one of the most prominent of Glasgow's 'Tobacco Lords'.
[8] *The Expedition of Humphrey Clinker* (1771) by Tobias Smollett.
[9] He also had Dougalston Loch created on his grounds.
[10] Dougalston House was demolished in the 1970s and much of the grounds was converted into Dougalston Golf Course.

The village of Milngavie, which we now reach, has an irregular and somewhat straggling appearance. The houses are for the most part plain two-storeyed edifices, in many instances tastefully whitewashed, and consequently wearing an agreeable air of tidiness and comfort. In and around the village, on the banks of the Allander, are a number of public works, the most extensive of which are the calico printing and cotton-spinning establishments of Messrs. John Black & Co., in which a considerable portion of the population, both adult and juvenile, are employed. The locality altogether, although not by any means particularly attractive in what may be called its pictorial aspect, has a cheerful and prosperous appearance. The spirit and prosperity of Milngavie, indeed, are abundantly evinced by the number of respectable looking shops which it contains in proportion to its size, and also by the fact that it now supports a line of stage-coaches, plying hourly to and from Glasgow. There are two places of worship in the village, one in connection with the Established Church, and the other a United Presbyterian meeting-house. The Free Kirk has also, we understand, a considerable number of adherents among the population; and a still larger proportion are Irish Roman Catholics: the former, we were informed, generally attend the ministrations of the Free Church clergyman at Baldernock, while the latter have their spiritual wants supplied in the Chapel at Duntocher.[11] Nor are the educational requirements of the rising generation unprovided for, as several excellent seminaries sufficiently demonstrate; while, as is the case in most of our manufacturing villages, a public library has been instituted, to satisfy the intellectual cravings of the more enlightened portion of the adult inhabitants.

Leaving Milngavie, after a stay of brief duration, we now proceed, in a north-westerly direction, towards the ancient Castle of Mugdock,[12] which is situated on an elevated spot about two miles from

---

[11] The United Free Church at Baldernock was later transferred to Milgavie. A Catholic Mission to the Irish workers on Mugdock Reservoir was begun in 1856, which later developed into St Joseph's RC Church.
[12] The ruins of the 13th-century Mugdock Castle stand in Mugdock Country Park.

the village. It is now the highest noon of summer, and the ever-varying landscape is bathed in warmest radiance, as

> "The sunshine creeps out ower the crags
> Like ravell'd golden hair."[13]

The wayside is a lengthened study of floral beauty, with its sweet-scented borders steeped in richest poetry. The wild rose is there, reminding us of Burns's odorous comparison for dear deluding woman, –

> "My love is like the red, red rose,
> That's newly blown in June,"[14]

A perpetual feast of nectared sweets, indeed, has the rose ever been to the rhyming race; and whether the beloved cheek is with mantling blushes tinged, or whether in sorrow it has waxed "fair, not pale,"[15] doubt not that the rose, in some one of its varied aspects, will fail to furnish the bard with an appropriate emblem. But hark, the boom of the passing bee! We could almost fancy he is chanting a snatch from glorious Will. "I know a bank where the wild thyme grows,"[16] seems the burden of his lay, and behold the belted minstrel has waxed voiceless in the honeyed crimson. A few steps onward the stately foxglove, with her purple crest of "deid man's bells," nods to the grateful breeze that winnows, as with viewless wings, our glowing brow. The speedwells, too, with their bright blue eyes, are peeping at us from the mossy knolls as we pass; while the silver-weed, the bird's foot-trefoil, the tormentil, and the bonny broom with its yellow tassels – weeds of glorious feature all[17] – are strewn in brightest profusion over every bank and brae. Truly, indeed, has the poet said –

---

[13] From 'We'll a' Go Pu' the Heather' (1835) by Robert Nicoll.

[14] From 'A Red, Red Rose' (1794) by Robert Burns.

[15] From part I of 'Christabel' (1816) by Samuel Taylor Coleridge.

[16] From William Shakespeare's *A Midsummer Night's Dream* II.i.

[17] A reference to From 'Muiopotmos: Or The Fate Of The Butterflie' (1590) by Edmund Spenser.

No. XVIII. Milngavie and Strathblane

"There's flowers along the peasant's path,
That kings micht stoop to pu'," [18]

and among them all there is not a sweeter than the bonnie blue
speedwell, which we thus address in the fullness of our affection,

Oh, I love the little Speedwell
    That cometh with the May,
And glints aboon the fresh green turf
    On every bank and brae;
Bright as a bonnie bairnie's e'e
    It glitters 'mang the dew,
As though 'twere blythe the lark to hear
    'Mang ringing skies o' blue.

The birk may don her kirtle green,
    Saft rustling to the breeze,
And glancing waves of verdure play
    Alang the furrow'd leas;
The broom may busk wi' gowden buds,
    The thorn wi' fragrant snaw,
Yet I've still a look of love for thee,
    Undimm'd amang them a'.

The gowan glints, wi' e'e o' gowd,
    Her pearly fringes through,
And scented sweetness lurks aneath
    The violet's hood of blue;
The starwort waves her siller blooms,
    And winds of roses tell,
Yet a glance of joy I've still for thee,
    Thou peerless blue Speedwell.

When by a loving mother's knee,
    In summers of the past,

---

[18] From 'The Gloamin' Star' (1840) by W.G.

E'er time had dimmed the smile of Hope
　　'Neath Sorrow's withering blast,
I mind the gush of purest joy
　　That on my wee heart fell,
When first I saw thy fairy blooms
　　Lone peeping down the dell.

Nae kindly mother now is mine;
　　Life's morning blush is fled;
And hearts that loved me best on earth
　　Lie loveless 'mang the dead.
Yet sunny dreams illume my soul
　　From Memory's dreary cell,
When laughing summer brings to me
　　The wayside wee Speedwell.

Let smiling Beauty busk her brow
　　Wi' roses aff the brier;
Let gowden lilies glad the swain
　　Wi' dreams of one that's dear;
But frae the bloomy wreath of June,
　　Its langsyne tales to tell,
Gi'e me my ain sweet bosom flower,
　　The bright blue-e'ed Speedwell.[19]

Now we are on the lee side of a wood, and walking among flickering shadows. How delicious the shade of the overhanging boughs, which spread their leafy arms, as if in love, to screen us from the almost vertical radiance of the lord of day!

"The deep, deep pause that ever reigns
At highest noon o'er hills and plains,"[20]

---

[19] 'To the Blue Speedwell' by MacDonald himself.
[20] From 'The Magnificence of Winter' (1820) by Noel Thomas Carrington.

is now only rendered more deep by the cooing of the cushat, the yellowhammer's fitful wail, or the faint dewy trickling of some hidden and tiny rivulet. The drowsiness of nature is really infectious, and with the reader's leave we shall yield ourselves to the soothing influences of the hour, and indulge for a blink among the green brackens in a brief sylvan siesta. "Do you believe in fairies, Mac?" said Allan Cunningham on one occasion to a Celtic friend of ours. "Deet, I'm no ferry shure," was the characteristically cautious reply of the mountaineer; "but do you pelieve in them your nainsel', Mr. Kinnikum?" "I once did," said the burly poet; "and I would to God that I could still, for the woodland and the moor have lost for me a great portion of their romance since my faith in their existence has departed." He then quoted Campbell's beautiful lines,

> "When Science from Creation's face
> Enchantment's veil withdraws,
> What lovely visions then give place
> To cold material laws!"[21]

It is well for us that we were born in an age of Mechanics' Institutions, and of isms and ologies "in number numberless," or we should assuredly have committed an unconscious perjury by swearing that we heard the rustle of a green gown on awakening from our midsummer day's dream, and that we obtained a glance of a rushy cap disappearing among the broom! But we know better now-a-days; so giving our head a philosophical shake, and our eyes a sceptical rub or two, we proceed on our course, without wasting a second thought on the "lovely vision," and soon find ourselves within the spacious enclosures of Mugdock.

The approach to the ancient Castle of Mugdock is beautiful exceedingly. On the northern side of the elegant carriage way – which has been recently improved and extended by our public-spirited townsman, Archibald M'Lellan, Esq.,[22] whose residence adjoins the

---

[21] From 'To the Rainbow' (1821) by Thomas Campbell.
[22] c.1795 – 1854, art collector, councillor and magistrate for whom Glasgow's McLellan Galleries are named.

venerable edifice of the olden time – is a lovely little loch about twenty-five acres in superficial extent. [Mr. M'Lellan has since gone the way of all living.] Around the irregular margin of this fine sheet of water, which is adorned at several points with picturesque groups of trees, a commodious drive has lately been formed, from which several fine views of the castle and the various landscape features of the locality may be obtained. The loch abounds with fish of different species, and is the habitation of numerous aquatic plants, some of which are not by any means common. Among these we observe a profusion of the white water-lily (*nymphœa alba*), covering with its snowy blossoms the surface of a miniature bay, intermingled with the broad, heart-shaped leaves of the yellow water-lily (*nuphar lutea*), and the green tubes of the *equisetœ*, or puddock-pipes, as they are popularly and not inappropriately denominated. The little yellow water-lily (*nuphar pumila*) was also found in Mugdock Loch some years ago by the late George Gardner,[23] a Glasgow botanist, who afterwards obtained considerable distinction by his botanical researches in South America, and who ultimately died superintendent of the botanic gardens at Ceylon. Strange to say, the finding of this plant seems to have formed the turning point in Mr. Gardner's life. He had previously, as a medical student, learned the elements of the science under the late Dr. Rattray of this city,[24] and on discovering the interesting plant alluded to, he was advised to communicate the fact to Sir William Hooker,[25] who was then preparing a new edition of his *British Flora*. The result was a personal interview with Sir William, who was so pleased with the enthusiasm of the young botanist that he persuaded him to devote his attention entirely to his favourite science, and afterwards procured his appointment as a botanical collector in Brazil, where he subsequently achieved numerous and valuable discoveries. On his return from this expedition, Mr. Gardner published an account of his travels and their results, immediately after which he

---

[23] 1810 – 1849

[24] Dr James Rattray, author of *Botanical chart; or, concise introduction to the Linnœan system of botany* (1830).

[25] Sir William Jackson Hooker (1785 – 1865), botanist.

was sent to Ceylon to undertake the management of the botanic gardens established there by the British Government. Shortly after his arrival out, however, he was seized with sudden illness and died, to the deep regret of all who knew him, or could appreciate the value of his services in the cause of science. Probably the *nuphar pumila* is still in existence about the loch, although in our cursory examination we cannot discover its whereabout. We should like to have seen it retaining its place as a memento of the poor young martyr of Flora, whose remains are now mouldering far away in the land of the stranger.

At the south-west end of the loch, towering above a terraced bank, which is adorned with a neat series of flower beds, is the time-worn Castle of Mugdock, towards which we now wend our way. That portion of the edifice which fronts the water having been fitted up as a modern residence,[26] has a fresh and apparently youthful appearance; but immediately behind this rises a stalwart quadrangular tower, lichened and gray, bearing undoubted evidences of antiquity in its narrow windows and loopholes, while numerous architectural remains in various stages of decay are scattered around. This lordly structure, majestic even in its desolation, has obviously been the work of several generations. Certain portions of it are unquestionably of great age, while others are as clearly of comparatively recent origin. Having made our *entrée* by a spacious gateway into the interior court, and received a courteous sanction to our inspection of the ruins, we roam about at will, poking our head into every available nook and cranny, and peopling with the creations of fancy the deserted chambers of the past. Now we stand musing in a vault of gloom over the captive's woes; now we are stooping at an arched doorway, wondering at the thickness of the walls; again we are threading the mazes of a narrow staircase, or pacing the lonely hall, where the swallow has taken up his abode and the winds are free to play; and anon we linger to gaze from the window of the tower on the wide-spread and lovely landscape

---

[26] The 17th-century house within the 14th-century castle was demolished and replaced in 1875 with Mugdock House. This burnt down in 1966. The only remaining intact tower of the castle has been turned into a museum.

below. Overlooking a steep bank on the same platform, and at a short distance to the north of the castle, are the ruins of a small chapel, now roofless and a desolate in the extreme. The walls are rent and shattered, while the rank weeds are waving on the floor and trailing over the prostrate stones where once the altar stood.

> "The lichened walls look grim and cold,
>   That totter all around;
> The carved work of ages old
>   Lies withering on the ground:
> The casement's antique tracery
>   Has wasted in the dew,
> And the night breeze, whistling mournfully,
>   Creeps keen and coldly through."[27]

One of the most beautiful features of Mugdock is its stately "girdle of tall ancestral trees."[28] Overshadowing the little mouldering chapel are several of the most handsome specimens of the ash which we have ever witnessed. They are indeed sylvan giants of loftiest stature and goodliest proportion. Evelyn[29] or Gilpin[30] would made a lengthened pilgrimage willingly, we doubt not, have for the sole purpose of doing homage to such "monarchs of the wood." There are also many fine oaks and elms around the spot; and on the line of the carriage way there is a luxuriant avenue of "green robed senators,"[31] through the dense umbrageousness of which even the vertical radiance of noon sends with difficulty but a few golden beams to fret the sweet mid-day gloaming. The Castle of Mugdock was for many ages a favourite residence of the "gallant Grahams" of Montrose, a family whose name is honourably distinguished in the history of our country, but regarding whose memory, as associated with this their ancient dwelling-place,

---

[27] From 'A Lament' (1834) by C. S. B. Busby.
[28] From 'The Homes of England' (1827) by Felicia Hemans.
[29] John Evelyn (1620 – 1706), diarist and author of *Sylva, or A Discourse of Forest-Trees*.
[30] Rev. William Gilpin (1724 – 1804), artist and travel writer.
[31] From 'Hyperion' (1820) by John Keats.

tradition is all but silent. Not a legend or a ballad of the olden time have we been able to discover concerning Mugdock. When an extraordinary or improbable story is told to the neighbouring peasantry, they generally give expression to their incredulity by the somewhat unintelligible exclamation of "Mugdock Castle's no a pyot's[32] nest yet!" and this, far as we are aware, is the only manner in which this home of a ducal race is mentioned in popular parlance. How different is it with our old Highland or Border keeps, every one of which almost has its legend or its lay! From history, also, we learn but little concerning Mugdock. Almost the only events recorded of it are, that the castle and barony were acquired from Maldwin, Earl of Lennox,[33] in the reign of Alexander the Second,[34] by David de Grahame, in exchange for certain lands in Galloway, and that it became, on the burning of Kincardine Castle, in 1646, the principal residence of the Montrose family. After the restoration, in 1688, and during the heat of the persecution in Scotland, Mugdock was visited by the Earls of Rothes[35] and Middleton,[36] with a number of their associates in the work of spiritual tyranny; and it is stated that sad scenes of revelry and bacchanalian license occurred on the occasion. A wild crew, we doubt not, in their orgies they were; and it may well be supposed that the Covenanters of the neighbourhood would watch with silent horror the lighted windows of the tower wherein the foes of their civil and religious freedom were congregated in the madness of drunken merriment. While lingering in the hall of the time-stained edifice, and endeavouring to realize to our "mind's eye" the picture which may have then presented, we find our musings almost unconsciously assuming the form of the following rude ballad strain, which we fancy would, could, or should have been written by some stern minstrel of the Covenant, and the shortcomings of which will, we fondly hope, induce some more accomplished bard to twine a worthier

---

[32] Magpie
[33] Alternatively Maldouen or Maol Domhnaich. Ruled Lennox 1217 – 1250.
[34] Reigned 1214 – 1249.
[35] John, 7th Earl of Rothes, persecutor of the Covenanters.
[36] John, 1st Earl of Middleton (c. 1608 – 1674), mercenary soldier.

wreath of song in honour of this most beautiful yet altogether songless locality:

THE MIDNIGHT REVEL OF MUGDOCK.

What means yon licht in Mugdock tower,
    Whilk winnock and loophole sma'
Lets oot in gowden shafts that fret
    Mirk midnicht's raven wa'?

What mean these voices of wassail rude,
    On the dank wind's gusty wing?
And why sweeps the frichted howlet[37] forth,
    As the loud, loud lauchters ring?

The baukiebird's[38] flickering hither an' yont
    Round the trumlin' castle wa',
And the ghost-moth jinks ower the lichtit pane,
    Wi' many a rise and fa';

As gin the wee creatures o' glimmer an' gloom
    Made blythe in the demon din
That rings in the hush o' the ebon hours,
    To the gruin' stars aboon.

Then tell me, thou carle of the lyart[39] locks,
    What meaneth this midnicht glee?
Has a bairn been born, a bride been won,
    Or a fae been forced to flee?

Nae howdie, quoth the carle, to the auld keep has gaen,
    Nae sweet winsome bride been won;
Nae wreath o' the laurel the Lennox chief can shaw

---

[37] owl
[38] bat
[39] greying

For deeds that his gude sword has done.

But the tyrants o' Scotland are guests here the nicht,
  At the hearth o' the stern Montrose;[40]
And the bluid-red wine is rowin' fast,
  'Mang the Covenant's deadliest foes.

The grim Yerl o' Rothes in his ermine is there,
  Wi' Middleton, the fause and the fell,
And wan Claverhouse, wi' his mim leddie face,
  And his snake-like e'e o' hell.

Steep in the gore o' the guid and the true,
  The airn-saul'd Dalzell[41] is there,
And Bruce o' the Earlsha',[42] wha aft makes a jest
  O'the widow and the orphan's prayer.

Ay, the curses o' puir Scotland are a' here the nicht
  Fell tools o' a fause, fause king;
That adderling wha warmed in his ain kintra's briest,
  Returns for its fealty a sting.

Sae the red cups o' gowd in the warm bleezin' ha'
  Are circlin' richt fast and free,
As the ill-deedy knaves droon the still sma' voice
  In loud rantin' din and in glee.

But the black ban, I trow, o'the sair-crushed Cargill
  Clings cauld as the lead round ilk heart;
Nor jestin', nor sang, nor the rich gushin' wine,

---

[40] James Graham, 1st Marquess of Montrose, who was both a Covenanter and a royalist.

[41] Sir Thomas Dalyell of The Binns, 1st Baronet (1615–1685), known as Bluidy Tam for his cruelty towards the Covenanters.

[42] Sir Andrew Bruce, 6th Baron of Earlshall (1623 – 1696), known as Bluidy Bruce for cutting of the head and hands of Covenanter Richard Cameron.

Gars the chill gruesome wecht e'er depart.

I've heard, in my day, the weary wail o' dule,
    When the red links of luve grew caul;
But the loud, loud lauch, is a far sadder soun
    That is rung from a wae-weirdit saul.

The hooting o' the owl at the sillar glowrin' mune,
    Or the wraith-bodin' tyke[43] at e'en,
I'd rather bide to hear 'mang the shiv'rin's o' the wud,
    Than the persecutor's mirth, I ween.

Then hie thee awa' through the mirk shades o' nicht,
    Nor seek thou the banquet to share,
That's laid for the bluid-hounds o' base-heartit power,
    'Neath the rooftree o' Mugdock the fair.

Oh! rather lay thy heid in the poor man's beild,
    And be thankfu' whate'er may betide,
Than hanker for the wine-cups in yon ha' o' sin,
    Where the malisons o Heaven maun abide!

There is an echo of considerable local celebrity at Mugdock, the reverberative powers of which are frequently put to the test by visitors. The spot from which the echo is most distinctly heard is a slightly projecting rock, on a verdant declivity, about a hundred yards to the south of the castle. A person standing on this, looking towards the edifice, and speaking pretty loudly, will hear his words, or even short sentences uttered by him, repeated with startling distinctness, as if from some mimic at the old tower. Of course, we give the echo sundry specimens of our vocality, and to its credit we must say that it flings them back with amazing fidelity. Paddy Blake's echo,[44] which, on the question being put to it of "How are you?" invariably answered

---

[43] vicious dog
[44] A reference to a popular Irish ballad of this name.

"Pretty well, I thank you!" was unmistakeably a native of the land of Bulls. The Mugdock one must be as decidedly Scottish, as it answers each question put to it by asking another. If there were any doubt on this subject, however, we might mention, in support of our supposition, that it is quite *au fait* at the Gaelic, as we proved to the entire satisfaction of a cannie bystander, who, after listening in silence for some time to our mutual interrogations in that classic tongue, at length exclaimed, "Od, man, that's curious! wha wad hae thocht that a Lawlan' echo could hae jabbered Gaelic?"

From the vicinity of the castle a variety of beautiful prospects of the surrounding country are obtained, as will readily be believed when we mention that, from one spot alone, the eye embraces a range of scenery extending from Benlomond to Tintoc.[45] There are also some delightful copse woods in the immediate neighbourhood, through which one could stroll about deliciously for days; while the dark watered Allander, a short distance to the west, winds through a sweet vale, presenting a most inviting aspect to the disciples of old Izaak.[46] But we have no time to throw a fly to-day, although we observe with envy the rich brown trout, with their freckles of bright red, rising in all directions. Yon lazy heron, now standing motionless as a stone, and anon, as we pass, flapping his drowsy flight along the stream, knows right well where the speckled prey abounds, and doubtless finds this secluded spot a highly favourable situation for his piscatory operations.

Making our way back to the road, we now proceed in a northerly direction towards the valley of the Blane, which, after passing the richly timbered policies of Craigends Castle,[47] a modern erection in the feudal style, bursts upon our gaze in all its quiet loveliness. The straths of the Allander and the Blane, divided by the Craigallian Braes, lie almost parallel to each other, while the two streams flow in opposite directions. The former having its source

---

[45] Tinto is a hill in the Southern Uplands.
[46] Izaak Walton (1593 – 1683), author of *The Compleat Angler*.
[47] Built in 1816, Craigends Castle was briefly a zoo in the 1950s but is now in ruins. Its stable block is the Mugdock Country Park visitor centre.

among the Kilpatrick Hills, and flowing in a south-east direction, ultimately joins the Kelvin; while the latter, a "high-born stream," has its origin in the Earl's Seat, and after a moorland course of three or four miles, comes leaping down the ravine of Ballagan, from whence, by a winding north west course, it flows into the channel of the Endrick, through which its waters are finally conveyed into the fair bosom of Lochlomond. The "Spout of Ballagan," as the cascade is called which is formed by the Blane in its passage from the summit of the Campsie fells to the valley below, is situated a short distance to the south-east of the village of Strathblane, and forms, with its accessories of rock and wood, a scene of the most wild and romantic beauty. When the stream is swollen with rain, the fall, which is altogether about seventy feet in height, presents a magnificent spectacle, as the water tumbles in foam into the rifted and rocky gorge beneath, with a voice of thunder, as if it were astounded at its own temerity. At this season, of course, from the comparatively meagre supply of water, it is seen to disadvantage, while its wild music is pitched on a much lower key. To compensate for this aqueous deficiency, however, the vegetation around is now most profuse and lovely, while the visitor who is not overly sensitive can ascend in the rugged channel to the very bottom of the cascade. To the geologist the section of the Campsie range exposed at this point presents a study of regular and nearly horizontal stratification of the most interesting nature. This section, which must be about 1,000 feet in depth, exhibits, according to certain authorities, about 230 beds of alternate sandstone, limestone, and argilaceous deposits, ranging in thickness from one or two inches to ten feet.[48] The various strata are in a continual state of disintegration. Portions are detached daily, while the immense heaps of debris lying below, bear witness to the rapidity with which the elements are gradually eating into "the everlasting hills." A short distance from the fall, but within sight and hearing of it, the old Earls of Lennox had in former ages a castle, which has now disappeared, leaving not even a wrack behind. A handsome modern edifice, however, the seat of Graham, Esq., of

---

[48] Geological formations of this type are now called 'Ballagan formations' after this glen.

Ballagan,[49] occupies a prominent position in this romantic locality, of which it commands a variety of delightful views.

Proceeding down the Strath of the Blane the prospect before us is of the most beautiful and varied description. On our right hand is the lofty range of the Campsie Hills, fretted with their terraces of trap,[50] and terminating in the bold heads of Dungoyne and Dunfoyne; while the gentle undulations of the Craigallian table-land rise in their sylvan loveliness on the left, with the wooded peak of Dungoiach in the background. In the sheltered bosom of the valley, at the same time, and on its finely swelling sides, are seen scattered the stately mansions, girt with trees, of the gentry; the comfortable steadings of the farmers; the village with its handsome Gothic church[51] and tidy-looking cottages; and, though last not least, the printworks and bleachfields,[52] with their industrial associations and (as if harmonizing with the scenery around) their half-rural aspect. Altogether we should imagine, to take a slight liberty with Tom Moore,

"There is not in this wide world many valleys so sweet,
As the vale where the Blane and the bright Endrick meet;"[53]

and we can assure the pilgrim of the beautiful who may turn his steps thitherward, that his expectations must be high indeed if he does not find them exceeded by the reality.

Passing through the straggling and exceedingly irregular village, which presents few features calling for special remark, we turn to the left, by a road leading in a westerly direction, towards the highway between Glasgow and Drymen, which it joins at Carbeth. A little farther down the vale of the Blane than this point stands the

---

[49] John Graham, third laird of Ballagan (d.1861). Ballagan House was extended in 1896 and again in the 1970s, when it was converted into flats.

[50] Any dark igneous rock such as basalt.

[51] Strathblane Parish Church was extensively renovated in the 1870s, and still functions as a church.

[52] Demolished in 1910.

[53] From 'The Meeting of the Waters' (1808) by Thomas Moore. The original, which describes part of County Wicklow, reads:
"There is not in the wide world a valley so sweet
As that vale in whose bosom the bright waters meet."

ancient Castle of Duntreath, an extensive and interesting edifice of the olden time.[54] This is a seat of the Edmonstones, a family which boasts an infusion of royal blood. We beg leave to borrow the following brief description of it from the pen of the parish minister:[55]

"The castle is approached from the west through a detached gatehouse, and is rather of a rude construction, built round a quadrangle. The north and east sides are completely in ruins, having been unroofed and left to decay about a century ago. In the former of these sides is the chapel, of which, according to tradition, the gallery once gave way during the service, and several persons were injured. The southern front was never finished. In the south eastern part of it is the 'Dumb Laird's Tower.' The castle is surrounded by a park or policy of moderate extent, but very agreeably varied, and the scenery of the whole unites cultivation and romantic beauty in no common degree." About midway between the little bridge along which the road we have alluded to crosses the Blane and Carbeth, the table-land of Craigallian comes to an abrupt termination in a precipitous and wooded promontory, which is locally denominated "the Pillar Craig." Under the guidance of our friend, Mr Blackwood of the Craigton bleachfield,[56] who, in company with a couple of esteemed Glasgow friends we fortunately discover in the vicinity, we now take leave of the beaten path, and at once plunge into the "woods and wilds"[57] of Craigallian. "The Pillar Craig" is so called from a magnificent range of basaltic columns with which the summit is crowned. These we immediately proceed to inspect, and after scrambling with some difficulty, and occasionally, we are afraid, in rather ungraceful attitudes, up the rugged acclivity, we are certainly abundantly rewarded for our pains by the spectacle which they present to our gaze. Let the reader imagine a steep precipice, thirty or perhaps forty feet in height, composed of immense columns of basalt of hexagonal,

---

[54] Most of Duntreath Castle survives, with some 19th-century additions, and it is still in the hands of the Edmonstone family.
[55] Rev. Hamilton Buchanan (d.1841).
[56] William Blackwood (1824 – 1902), or possibly his brother John (1828 – 1881).
[57] Probably a reference to *The Gipsy Boy: A romance of the woods and wilds* (1845) by Thomas Peckett Prest.

octagonal, and quadrangular forms, and regular in outline as if they had been the work of the chisel rather than the produce of a material law! Most of these are of course in firm juxtaposition with each other, but in various instances the pillars stand erect and almost isolated; while one broken column has fallen from its original position, and projects perpendicularly to a height of four or five feet from the debris below, just as if it had been erected by an antediluvian sculptor to the memory of some distinguished individual among the "world's gray fathers."[58] This ponderous fragment is an octagon, judging by the eye, of about three feet in diameter. Strange to say, this interesting geological formation seems to have been entirely over looked by local students of the sermons which are found in stones.[59] At all events we have seen no notice of it in our somewhat discursive readings, nor has any individual with whom we have conversed on the subject ever heard it mentioned. We therefore consider that we are fully justified in commending the locality to the attention of our philosophical stone-knappers as a virgin field for their future investigation.

Clambering to the woody brow of the eminence, which commands to the northward an extensive and finely varied prospect of the broad range of country sloping picturesquely down to Lochlomond – a glimpse only of which is obtained, however, as the huge Ben almost completely screens it from view – and to the east displays the sweet sheltered strath of the Blane from Ballagan to Dungoyne, with the towering Lennox range beyond, – we now turn our face southward, and proceed along the ridge of Craigallian in a homeward direction. The estate over which we are now treading a devious and truly delightful course is the property of Mr Graham of Fereneze.[60] A considerable portion of its surface is covered with broad belts and clumps of trees; while the intervening spaces consist principally of green pasture-land and white tracts of moor. The whole locality, indeed, has a wild, solitary, and sylvan character – a kind of "Forest of

---

[58] From 'To the Rainbow' (1821) by Thomas Campbell.
[59] A reference to Shakespeare's As You Like It II.i.
[60] John Graham Barns-Graham of Lymekilns and Fereneze (1798 – 1875), Liberal politician.

Arden" aspect; while nooks and glades meet the eye at every turn wherein one could fancy the banished Duke might have held his court, or the melancholy Jaques have fitly lingered to muse on the vanity of all that the busy world is proud of. [61] Now we are crossing the spongy surface of a marsh, where the breeze is playing with the white fairy pennons of the cannach,[62] while it bears along the rich fragrance of the bog-myrtle, or sweet gale; now we are passing a ruined cottage, where the long rank nettles are nodding drearily to each other round the cold hearthstone, and the old ash tree overhanging the shattered walls, seems to wail over departed joys; and anon we are threading the stream-like meanderings of an old field-path, athwart which the grass and the weeds are creeping unchecked, while the rose bushes on either side seem extending their blushing boughs as if they would meet in odorous embrace. At length, after passing through a shadowy wood, with a dense green canopy overhead and a floor of feathery brackens and tall grasses below, we come in sight of Craigallian Loch, lying smooth and silent in a sheltered hollow to the west of the high ground over which, for the last hour, we have been wandering. This beautiful sheet of water is about forty acres in extent. From the undulating and romantic character of the ground in its vicinity, Craigallian Loch presents many charms to the lover of landscape beauty; while the botanist will find its vegetation well worthy of a scrutinizing inspection. It abounds also in fish; and our friend Mr Blackwood, who has the privilege of lashing its waters, speaks enthusiastically of the number and quality of its finny inhabitants. At a short distance to the south-east of the loch is situated the house of Craigallian, a small and plain edifice, bearing the date 1704. It is now inhabited by a farmer and his household, and has rather a dreary and crest-fallen appearance. The garden and neighbouring grounds, which have evidently at one period been arranged in a tasteful and orderly style, are now apparently permitted in a great measure to "hing as they grow." There is an air of the old elegance still clinging about the spot, however; while the

---

[61] Both characters from Shakespeare's *As You Like It*, which is set in the Forest of Arden.

[62] cotton grass

luxuriance of the garden, in which we observe a fine holly thickly studded with its red berries, and the stateliness of the timber in its vicinity, among which is a gigantic yew, indicates plainly enough that "it has seen better days."[63]

Passing onward we soon arrive on the banks of the Allander, which we cross by a picturesque old bridge, and by a westerly route over the fields, in a short time reach the *locale* of Mr. Blackwood, at Craigton. The bleachfield here is finely situated on the banks of a little rivulet, and contains all the means and appliances necessary to the production of snow-white yarns, including, of course, a numerous bevy of active and blooming girls. The study of chemicals or womankind is unfortunately not our *forte*, however, – so, leaving the study of these abstruse matters to a scientific widower who forms one of our company, we proceed to gratify our Oldbuckian[64] propensity for time-honoured biggins by an inspection of the venerable mansion of Craigton, which is in the immediate neighbourhood. This edifice is of considerable extent, but is unpretending in its style of architecture, and presents but few features calling for special remark. Above the principal doorway there is a carved stone bearing a dilapidated coat of arms, in which the only objects we can distinctly decipher are a pair of hands clasped, and a star, with the date 1635. The house is now inhabited by several of the operatives engaged in the bleachfield and their families. It is still in a good state of repair, and seems to be kept by its present occupants in a clean and orderly condition. It must be admitted, however, that it has a somewhat disconsolate appearance, as if it were conscious withal that its former glory had departed.[65] Opposite the western front of the edifice there is a magnificent avenue, formed by two stately double rows of trees, the area of which we should imagine to be about thirty yards in width, and nearly one eighth of a mile in length. The inner rows on either side are composed of tall limes, the foliage of which extends to within a few feet of the ground,

---

[63] This farmhouse had replaced the old house that was demolished in 1850. It was itself replaced in 1883 by the present, far from plain, Craigallian House.

[64] Jonathan Oldbuck is the title character in *The Antiquary* (1816) by Sir Walter Scott.

[65] This house has now been converted into flats.

forming as it were two compact lateral walls of green. The external rows are composed of beeches, the majority of which are of gigantic proportions. The general effect, indeed, of this handsome approach is splendid in the extreme, and albeit a little wayworn, we cannot resist, in our admiration, promenading it to and fro for a considerable time.

A warm welcome and abundance of good cheer await our acceptance in the neat little domicile of our friend of the Craigton field, to which we now proceed. After a delicious interval of rest and refreshment, our host's vehicle is brought to the door, in which, the pony being a crack roadster, we are in a surprisingly brief space of time conveyed along the Drymen road, by Canniesburn and Maryhill, and safely deposited within sound of auld Sanct Mungo's bells.

Old father Time has passed the meridian of another year, and is again steering a downhill course towards the golden season of fruitfulness and falling leaves. The time of singing birds is almost past, and the voice of the turtle has ceased in the land. The flowers of spring and early summer have bloomed and nodded their little hours upon the stage, and now are seen no more.[1] We have the rose by every wayside, the water-lily and the sedge by lochs and streams, the pansy and the wild thyme on bank and brae; but the primrose, the craw-flower, and their sweet sisters of the youthful year, where are they? With the gentle Perdita, in Shakespeare's *Winter's Tale*, we could exclaim,

> "O Proserpina,
> For the flowers now that, frighted, thou lett'st fall
> From Dis's waggon! daffodils,
> That come before the swallow dares, and take
> The winds of March with beauty; violets, dim,
> But sweeter than the lids of Juno's eyes
> Or Cytherea's breath; pale primroses,
> That die unmarried, ere they can behold
> Bright Phoebus in his strength."[2]

We have a special love indeed for the thin-strewn blossoms of spring. Things of beauty are they one and all, as they open amidst the smiles and tears of the opening season, each silver starlet and golden chalice redolent of love, and hope, and joy. But alas! even as it is with all that man is proud of, they come like shadows, so depart,

> "And the flowers that busk a bonnie brae
> Gin anither month lie rotten."[3]

In our admiration of the past, however, let us not be ungrateful for the blessings of the present. The earth is now clad with beauty as

---

[1] A reference to Shakespeare's *Macbeth* V.v.
[2] *The Winter's Tale* IV.iv.
[3] From 'Mary, a Sang' (1822) by Hew Ainslie.

with a garment. Ten thousand radiant blooms are at this moment spreading their dewy petals of varied hue in the rays of yon rising sun, which invites us from our city home, to wander forth again among the rustling fields and shadowy woods. Let us be up then and jogging. Our good oaken staff – itself the gift of a genuine "heart of oak," and our faithful companion in many a devious excursion – seems, as if instinct with life, to leap into our grasp. After a few minutes' walk, we find ourselves passing Port-Dundas, "the harbour on the hill," and emerging to the northward from the urban labyrinth by the Possil Road. The morning air is clear and cool, but the cloudless sky above gives abundant indication that a melting day is before us. A gentle breeze, however, is playing over the spiky fields of wheat, and rustling with a whisper softer even than that of lovers on a moonlit bank, among the graceful pannicles[4] of the oat and the silky awns of the bearded bere. The walk from the city in this direction is exceedingly pleasant. About a mile out we pass Possil House, the residence of our respected sheriff, Sir Archibald Alison, Bart., the learned historian of Europe, and the accomplished essayist and critic of Blackwood.[5] The house is a large and substantial but withal plain edifice, and is surrounded by finely timbered policies of considerable extent.[6] The locality, although within such a short distance of the city, has a quiet and retired aspect, and seems peculiarly adapted for the indulgence of those literary tastes in which the worthy Baronet finds his principal solace during the intervals of professional business. After skirting the enclosures of Possil, the road gradually ascends, through a stretch of fertile and well-cultivated land, covered with luxuriant crops, to the gentle eminence of Hill-end, which commands a most magnificent and far extended prospect to the northward. On the summit of this ridge we call a halt, of course, and do homage to the loveliness of the scene. Spread before the spectator's gaze is the noble territory of the Lennox, with its woods

---

[4] A cluster of branching flowers.
[5] 1792 – 1867, Sheriff of Lanarkshire, who was a frequent contributor to *Blackwood's Magazine*.
[6] The house was demolished in the 1870s. The Saracen Foundry and the new suburb of Possil Park (to house the foundry workers) were built on the grounds.

and fields, and softly-swelling undulations, bounded in the extreme distance by the gray mountains of the Gael, and on either side by the Kilpatrick and Campsie hills.

Proceeding down a pleasant and gently sloping course for a short distance, we soon arrive at Lambhill, on the margin of the Forth and Clyde Canal. There is a delightful walk, of about a mile and a-half in length, west from this point to Maryhill, along the banks of the canal, which here passes amid scenes of considerable beauty. Our present route, however, lies in an opposite direction; so, crossing the water, we turn our face northward, and soon leave Lambhill behind. A little to the right of the road we are now pursuing is Possil Marsh, one of the best botanical stations for many miles round Glasgow. This extensive bog or quagmire is covered with a dense mantle of rank aquatic vegetation, among which are a number of rather uncommon species, such as the mare's-tail (*hippuris vulgaris*); the greater spearwort (*ranunculus lingua*), a splendid plant; the sun-dew (*drocera rotundifolia*), and a rich variety of others. Possil Marsh is indeed a valuable adjunct to the Botanic Gardens of our city. What the one is to exotic the other is to indigenous vegetation. For this reason its plashy brink has been for many years the favourite haunt of the local flower lovers. Here the venerable professor and his boisterous band of students come to apply practically the theoretical instructions of the class-rooms. For hours occasionally they may be seen wandering about, gathering the choicest specimens, prying with microscopic eye into the mysteries of Flora, and conversing with exemplary gravity on the number of stamens or pistils to which a certain class and order are legitimately entitled, or the form of leaf and colour of corolla which mark the distinctions of genera and species. Yet "true it is, and pity 'tis 'tis true,"[7] that many of these scientific gents, who can reckon you Latin names by the hundred, feel not one spark of the deep poetry which dwells in the golden chalices they so mercilessly dissect. Dry as an algebraic formula is their knowledge of the things of beauty which are the subjects of their heartless study.

---

[7] From Shakespeare's *Hamlet* II.ii.

"A primrose by the river brim
A *primula vulgaris* is to them
And it is nothing more."[8]

They "consider the lilies of the field,"[9] indeed, but it is only as materials for their herbaria, while the better lesson which the Great Teacher has gleaned from their unwoven vestures of loveliness finds no sympathetic thrill in their tuneless bosoms. We would not place upon our list of friends, however, the man who owned allegiance to such a Dry-as-dust[10] philosophy.

The margin of the marsh is now in its most luxuriant condition, being indeed one tangled mass of verdure and bloom. Forget-me-nots, bed-straws, and cinque-foil, in rich clusters, creep among the green rushes and horse-tails, forming the most delightful combinations of colour imaginable; while at every few steps the snipe springs up in tortuous flight, and the water-hen is heard fluttering amid the floating leaves, and swallows, peeseweeps[11] and other birds in graceful curves keep hovering around. Insects of brightest hue are also here "in number numberless," sporting with merry hum in the sunny air, and reminding us of Moore's fine simile, –

"The beautiful blue damsel flies,
That flutter'd round the jasmine stems,
Like winged flowers or flying gems."[12]

After lingering for a brief space at this favourite haunt of Flora, we return to the highway, and in a short time arrive at Bemulie,[13] now the site of a comfortable looking farm-house, but formerly an important fort or station on the great wall of Antonine, to which we have previously had occasion to allude. These forts were erected along the entire line of the gigantic rampart between the Forth and Clyde, at

---

[8] A play on lines from part I of 'Peter Bell' (1819) by William Wordsworth.
[9] Matthew 6.28.
[10] A reference to Jonas Dryasdust, a fictional character created by Sir Walter Scott.
[11] lapwings
[12] From 'Paradise and the Peri' (1817) by Thomas Moore.
[13] Usually spelled Balmuildie.

regular distances of about two miles. The camp of New Kilpatrick, the one next to Bemulie in a westerly direction, is, in accordance with this rule, as near as may be, two miles distant, as is also the one to the east at Cadder. All traces of the fort at this place, however, are now obliterated. Not the faintest vestige even remains to mark its whereabout. The plough and the elements have effectually completed the destruction of the ancient strong hold. A little to the east, however, a deep groove on the brow of a green hill still indicates the line of the vallum and military way. [14] Various fragments of Roman art have also been from time to time discovered at Bemulie, or in its immediate vicinity. One of these, a mutilated tablet, dug from the earth towards the close of the seventeenth century, and now deposited in the Hunterian Museum, has been of important service to antiquaries, by furnishing them with a fact necessary to the integrity of our country's history. Up to that time the locality of the several British walls and the names of their builders were matters of dispute. Only one of the Roman historians, Julius Capitolinus, in his life of the Emperor Antoninus Pius,[15] refers to the erection of the Caledonian wall by Lollius Urbicus, legate under that august monarch. For upwards of fourteen centuries this doubtful incidental statement formed the sole basis of modern knowledge regarding the individual who erected the wall. The Bemulie tablet supplied the necessary corroborative link to prove the authenticity of the old writer. Students of the antique consequently fell into raptures on the discovery; and Gordon,[16] who afterwards traced the vestiges of the structure from frith to frith, pronounced the shattered relic "the most invaluable jewel of antiquity that ever was found in the island of Britain since the time of the Romans." What, then, is this historic pearl of great price? It is a rude stone, seventeen inches by ten, with the following abbreviated, and, to the uninitiated, unintelligible inscription upon it:

---

[14] Traces of the ditch and outer mound can still be seen in the fields north-east of the junction of Balmore Road and Balmuildy Road. This important fort predated the Antonine Wall and was later incorporated into it.
[15] Of uncertain date, but possibly 4th century AD. Antoninus Pius reigned 138 – 161.
[16] Alexander Gordon (c.1692 – 1755), antiquary.

P. LEG. II. A.
Q. LOLLIO. VR.
LEG. AVG. PR. PR.

By a rule which we do not profess to understand the Oldbucks[17] of the day extended these mystical hieroglyphics into the following votive inscription by the Second Legion to the Legate Lollius Urbicus: – POSUIT LEGIO SECUNDA AUGUSTI PROPRÆTORI. Others translated the legend as a votive tribute by the legate himself to his august lord and master, the emperor. Where doctors differ who shall presume to decide?[18] We might indeed have been induced to hazard an original reading of our own, but that the memory of "Aiken Drum's lang ladle"[19] forbids us to venture on such dangerous ground. The rigid inductions of a Cuvier,[20] however, by means of which, from the splinter of a bone he could reproduce, as it were, an extinct animal, are not more interesting to the reflective mind than are those by which, from a few stray letters rudely carved on stone, the antiquarian has been enabled to rend the veil of oblivion, and bring into our ken the events of a long vanished era.

Passing Bemulie, where the drowsy kine are peacefully pasturing on the site of the ancient battlements, the road slopes gradually down to the Kelvin, which it crosses by a neat and substantial bridge.[21] The river here is somewhat dull and sluggish in its character,

---

[17] Jonathan Oldbuck is the title character in *The Antiquary* (1816) by Sir Walter Scott.
[18] Current thought is that the tablet originally said:
"IMP[ERATORI] C[AESARI] T[ITO] AEL[IO] HADR[IANO]
ANTONINO AUG[USTO] PIO
P[ATRI] **P[ATRIAE] LEG[IO] II** AUG[USTA] SUB
Q[UINTO] LOLLIO URBICO
LEG[ATO] AUG[USTI] PR[O] PR[AETORE] FEC[IT]"
which means "For the Emperor Caesar Titus Aelius Hadrianus Antoninus Augustus Pius, father of his country, the Second Legion Augusta built this under Quintus Lollius Urbicus, the emperor's propraetorian legate."
[19] From *The Antiquary* (1816) by Sir Walter Scott, in which a character tells a patently false story about some ancient ruins.
[20] Georges Cuvier (1769 – 13 May 1832), developer of paleontology.
[21] This bridge still stands, and dredging of the river in the 20th century revealed that a Roman bridge and later a medieval crossed the Kelvin at about this point,

the channel being encumbered with weedy shallows, and the margin thickly overhung with saughs[22] and reeds of rankest growth. It wears, however, a tangled and somewhat picturesque aspect. The tall bulrushes are nodding gracefully as we linger to scan its features, and the rich yellow of the water-lily imparts a degree of brilliancy to the dark-brown and almost imperceptible current; while a group of cattle, scattered in the shade of a willow clump on the bank presents a picture which a Paul Potter or a Cooper would have loved to paint.[23] Soft green undulations rising on either side at the same time harmonize deliciously with the comparatively rugged water course, and enhance the quiet loveliness of the landscape.

This bridge was the scene of a curious adventure some two score years ago. At that period there lived in yon white cottage which adorns the brow of the hill to the left, a surly old carle who had a bonny daughter, a blythe bouncing lassie of merry eighteen. The old man was reputed to be wealthy – the maid was his sole heiress; and of course, where there was beauty and prospective riches, there was no lack of wooers. To the overtures of such visitants the father showed himself peculiarly averse, nor, truth to tell, did the winsome Mary herself seem at all anxious to change her condition. But "there is a tide in the affairs of women,"[24] and at length the Rose of the Kelvin gave her heart in keeping to a handsome youth from our own good town. As usual, however, the course of true love was ruffled and fretted with difficulties. The sweetheart was poor – the father inexorable. The daughter waxed fairer and more fair – the father more flinty and more cross. In sweet stolen interviews the lovers for some time contrived to meet, notwithstanding parental vigilance, until a discovery occurred during a gloaming walk, after which the hapless Mary was strictly confined to the house. Faithful in the time of trial, her lover continued to haunt the vicinity, in hope of obtaining a glimpse of the form and face which were all the world to him, even the reflection of her figure

---

[22] willows
[23] Paulus Potter (1625 – 1654) and Thomas Sidney Cooper (1803 – 1902), a Dutch and an English painter, both known for their depictions of domestic animals.
[24] Originally "of men", from Shakespeare's *Julius Caesar* IV.iii.

in the gloom of the night against the lighted window, proving to him an exceeding great reward for weary hours of waiting. One dark November night, stormy and wet, he left the city as usual, in a vehicle, for the purpose of visiting the spot. Whether the driver had taken a drop too much, or whether the thick darkness had bewildered him, we cannot say, but on passing this bridge, with the impetus of the declivity from Bemulie, the machine was overturned, and the love-sick swain precipitated into the swollen Kelvin. Jehu,[25] who had by some chance alighted safely on the bridge, instead of looking in the roaring channel for his hapless "fare," ran at once to the cottage of Mary's father and gave the alarm. The old man and his servants immediately rushed in a body, with lanterns, &c., to the scene of the catastrophe, and instituted a minute search in every turn and eddy of the angry stream for the body of the unfortunate gentleman. It was all in vain, however, and after a couple of hours spent in fruitless exertion, they returned to the house, moralizing on the sad fate of the supposed stranger. "Hech, sirs! but he's gotten a sudden ca', puir fallow," said the old maidservant, settling herself by the kitchen fire, "and dootless it'll bring a sair stoun[26] to some heart." Her sympathetic remarks were brought to an abrupt termination by the entrance of her master, who inquired for his daughter Mary. The maid went to the chamber of her young mistress for the purpose of calling her. She was not there, however; while on the floor of the room and on the stair there was a watery track as if from dripping clothes. Great was the alarm of the old man when these suspicious circumstances were announced to him; nor, it may be surmised, was his agitation much abated when a little urchin who acted as boots[27] to the family exclaimed, "Ay, Miss Mary's sweetheart was here, a' plashing wat, and she gaed oot wi' him a gude while since wi' her bonnet and shawl on." It was even so, however; and that very night a "Ruglen wedding"[28] consummated the happiness of the Rose of

---

[25] A reference to the charioteer Jehu son of Nimshi, in 2 Kings 9.20, who drove "furiously".

[26] stunning blow

[27] That is, a low ranking servant.

[28] That is, an elopement.

Kelvin and her "drouket Glasgow chappie." A reconciliation of course speedily ensued, and in after years the gentleman has been heard to say, that the most fortunate event in his life was being tumbled neck and heels in the dark, over a bridge, into the bosom of an angry and turbid spate.

A few minutes' walk over an intervening elevation brings us from the Kelvin to the Allander, where the latter stream seems hastening to its junction with the former in a sweet spot about half-a-mile to the south-east. In the vicinity of the bridge by which we cross the rivulet here, there is a bluff bank of brown sand, which for many years has formed a favourite breeding-place for the sand martin or swallow. The steep breast of the declivity is honeycombed, as it were, with the excavations of the little feathered miners, which, in the season of nidification,[29] keep continually flying to and from their sandy domiciles like bees at a hive. We have often sat for hours watching the motions of this interesting colony, or strolled about the bank culling the floral beauties with which it is so thickly studded. We cannot spare time for such dalliance with Flora to-day, however; so, passing the toll-house,[30] beside which the toll-keeper's little son is couched on the green, where his snowy rabbits are munching the succulent clover, we leave the highway, and by a narrow footpath, ascend the hill. Pausing for a moment on its summit, what a splendid prospect meets our gaze! To the south-west, over a richly-undulating surface, we see the ascending vapours of Sanct Mungo, with Tennant's tall chimney, the monarch of his species, towering proudly through the cloud, with his far-floating plume of smoke.[31] Westward, over woods and fields, the Kilpatrick Hills, with Duncombe, like an immense blue bonnet, rising over their highest brow; to the north, the vast strath of the Lennox, with Milngavie and Dougalstone in the immediate foreground. We have touched on the Roman wall already at various points, but from our

---

[29] nest building

[30] The toll house has been demolished, but the junction at the spot is still known as Allander Toll roundabout.

[31] Chimney of the St Rollox Chemical Works in Sighthill, also known as 'Tennant's stalk'. It was once the largest chemical works in the world. The chimney was demolished in 1922 and the plant closed in the 1960s.

present "coigne of vantage" we can trace its course at a glance for some eight or nine miles, and comprehend more distinctly than hitherto the fitness of its plan. Duntocher, Castlehill, New Kilpatrick, and Bemulie are before us now as if on a map; and we can speculate on their relative positions and the combined operations necessary their defence against the attacks of our indomitable but savage Caledonian fathers.

Descending on the opposite side of the hill you may well ask, gentle reader, what lovely sheet of water, so calm, secluded, and still, now bursts upon our view. That is Bardowie Loch – Bardowie the beautiful; and we ask thee if a glance of it would not more than repay thee for a summer day's journey? Yet there are thousands in our own good town – admirers of nature, too, in a fashionable way, and who travel far in search of the picturesque – who have never dreamed that such a gem exists at their own threshold as it were. With such people the far away bird alone is gifted with glorious plumage. Happier those who, with the gentle poet of "The Task," can say, –

> "Scenes must be beautiful which daily viewed
> Please daily, and whose novelty survives
> Long knowledge and the scrutiny of years."[32]

Bardowie, as you will observe, is a spacious lochlet of about seventy acres in superficial extent, its irregular margin being adorned with picturesque clumps of trees, intersected here and there by patches of fresh green pasture land, while its immediate circumference is girt with a profusion of rank aquatic vegetation. Finely situated on its north-east side, and embowered among foliage, is Bardowie House, an edifice of moderate size, and somewhat timeworn, yet withal wearing an appearance of quiet cosieness and comfort.[33] Yon towering flagstaff on the sloping bank, and yon wreaths of blue smoke curling above the old ancestral trees,[34] lend a human interest to the scene, which would otherwise be dreary as a mountain tarn.[35] But let us descend to the

---

[32] From book 1 of 'The Task' (1785) by William Cowper.
[33] Bardowie Castle, which has a 16th century keep, is still in use as a private dwelling.
[34] A reference to 'The Homes of England' (1827) by Felicia Hemans.
[35] corrie loch

mimic beach. Did you ever witness such splendid specimens of the golden iris, such "stately foxgloves fair to see,"[36] or such fragrant foam-crowned queens of the meadow? We verily believe you never did! Everything vegetable in its nature seems indeed more than ordinarily luxuriant here. And what a rich variety there is! The botanist might wander for days by the rushy margin, and fail to exhaust its treasures. We have ourselves ere now seen an eccentric but enthusiastic band of naturalists engaged for hours in rifling the vegetable and animal productions of this tiny lake, and still some longed-for object escaped their eager scrutiny. A curious group they were, in truth, each engaged in his favourite field of study. Here a sedate entomologist, net in hand, pursuing with ludicrous earnestness the flickering moths and butterflies; there a spectacled philosopher with a long ladle groping lovingly in the water for "powheads,"[37] "scurs,"[38] and other nauseous creeping things; at yonder reedy point an ornithologist rejoicing in the discovery of a water-hen's nest, or blowing, with puffed out cheeks and purple brow, the contents from a snipe's egg; while the flower-gatherers, vasculum[39] in hand, were eagerly scanning the surrounding verdure, and muttering at every step some horrid Latin name. A merry as well as a wise corps they were, and many were the good-natured jokes which from time to time they uttered at the expense of each other's hobbies, while the echoes of the lonely loch resounded with their boisterous cachinnations.[40] Alas! they are scattered far and wide now. Some have fallen into the long sleep; others are "far ayont the wave;"[41] while those that remain but seldom walk together in the old familiar paths.

We must be going, however; and see, as we move, a "fisher heron, watching eels"[42] by yon crescent of golden lilies, takes wing and floats lazily, but with a peculiar gracefulness of flight, across the

---

[36] From 'Elegy on Capt. Matthew Henderson' (1790) by Robert Burns.
[37] tadpoles
[38] freshwater shrimps
[39] A stiff metal container usually used for collecting botanical samples.
[40] loud laughter
[41] From 'A Gude New Year I Wish Ye A'' (1846) by MacDonald himself.
[42] From 'Elegy on Capt. Matthew Henderson' (1790) by Robert Burns.

still waters wherein its moving image is reflected. Now it has alighted on the farther shore, and is once more "quiet as a stone." Passing in a north-east direction by the borders of Dougalstone woods, where we regale ourselves with the piquant but delicious fruit of the wild strawberry, now red and ripe by the wayside, and by the farm-house of Dowan,[43] we soon arrive at the kirk-toun of Baldernock. Strictly speaking, however, Baldernock is neither town, village, clachan, nor hamlet. It consists principally of two churches, an Established[44] and a Free,[45] both unassuming buildings, about a-quarter of a mile or so apart, with the necessary adjuncts of manses, &c., and a few stray cottages dropped here and there as if by chance, and without any apparent relationship to each other. There is an old and diminutive meal-mill[46] in the vicinity, the happer of which at the period of our visit is at rest for want of water; and close to the parish church there is a comfortable public-house, where refreshment of excellent quality for man and beast may be obtained. The rambler who has no special objections to the "dew" may have his wants abundantly supplied in this neat hostel;[47] while the "pledged" may have their hearts' content of nature's brewing at a fine spring which issues from a green bank near the mill.

After a brief interval of rest we bid farewell to Baldernock – which is really a delightful rural locality, with its cosie cottages, well-stocked gardens, umbrageous trees, and wide-extending prospects – and pursue our course towards the north-east. On one hand, we have a thick belt of planting; on the other, a fine undulating stretch of country, arable, woodland, and pastoral, bounded by the Campsie Fells, the Kilpatrick Hills, and the far mountains of the Highlands. Every turn of the road alters the features of the surrounding landscape, and brings

---

[43] Now converted into offices.

[44] There has been a place of worship on this site for c.800 years and at the time of writing, the current building (from 1795) is still a functioning church, although threatened with closure.

[45] The Free Church and its manse are now privately owned.

[46] This corn mill was later converted into a paper mill, and is now a private dwelling, but still has its water wheel.

[47] The Kirkhouse Inn is now a cottage.

new beauties to our ken. The wayside, too, is rife with floral loveliness. This dry stane dike, with its divot covering, is one lengthened flower border. Every crevice has its own minute fern, every gap its own rose-bush. Here is one tall rose-tree, in full bearing, which, in its ambition, has actually taken root on the summit of the wall. The Hindoo Shaster[48] says, "The almond tree is like unto the good man, for if you strike its branches, they send down upon you a shower of scented blossoms." Our own wild rose, you see, teaches the same lesson, for by merely giving it "a gude rough shake," we have been enveloped in rosebuds. Let us endeavour to take the fragrant admonition to heart; but meanwhile, here we are at Craigmadie Wood. Within the dense umbrage before us the lies concealed a stately mansion, which is at present residence of Spens Black, Esq.[49] Our intention, however, is not to trespass on the hospitality of that gentle man, but to inspect the "auld howlet-haunted biggin"[50] of Craigmadie Castle, which is situated on a rising ground in the vicinity of the modern house. By an intricate footpath through the leafy maze, and after several times going astray among the tall ferns and flickering shadows, we at length reach the spot. A mere fragment, shattered and weather worn, is all that now remains of this once lordly mansion. One solitary tower, shorn of its fair proportions, yet sturdy even in decay, is the sole vestige of its former grandeur. The roof and the greater part of the walls have tumbled in, probably centuries ago; yet, under the *debris*, a vaulted dungeon-like chamber continues almost entire. The entrance is choked up with rubbish, but by a narrow loophole in the wall the visitor obtains a peep into its interior, which is gloomy in the extreme. There is little, indeed, to interest the archæologist in this crumbling edifice of the dead; but the poet might find abundant material for the exercise of his muse within its deserted and dreary precincts, and the painter obtain a suggestive snatch of beauty from its not unpicturesque desolation. Nature, we may further mention, has been peculiarly kind to this

---

[48] Hindu scriptures

[49] James Spens Black (1816 – 1867), of John Black & Co calico printers. Craigmaddie House still survives as a private residence.

[50] That is, owl-haunted. From 'On the Late Captain Grose's Peregrinations through Scotland' (1789) by Robert Burns.

mouldering relic of the past. Indeed, we have never seen ruin so richly garbed with vegetation as in this instance. The green ivy hangs dense over certain portions of the structure while every seam and scar is fringed with foliage of the minuter ferns and rock plants. On the summit of the walls a Scotch fir and an ash have taken up their station, like warders, with a wild rose, which is a in bloom at the period of our visit, "scenting the dewy air,"[51] while on a projection below is a broad patch of thyme, crimsoned with blossoms. Little is known of the origin and history of Craigmadie Castle. In the thirteenth century it was in the possession of the ancient family of the Galbraiths of Baldernock, who obtained it in the reign of Alexander II.,[52] with the surrounding barony, from Maldwin, Earl of Lennox.[53] About the beginning of the fourteenth century the possessions of this family passed, by marriage with the heiress, to David Hamilton, son of Lord Hamilton, whose descendants afterwards took the title of Bardowie, and of whom the late Dr. Francis Hamilton[54] was the lineal representative. Regarding the circumstances under which the edifice was permitted to fall into decay history contains no record.[55]

Adjoining Craigmadie Wood to the east, and bearing the same name, is an extensive tract of moorland, wild, rugged, and covered with heather. To this dreary expanse we now proceed, to visit the far-famed "Auld Wives' Lifts."[56] These are situated in the centre of a spacious natural amphitheatre in the middle of the waste, and consist of three immense masses of solid stone, two of which are prismatic in shape and lying side by side, while the third, which is nearly eighteen feet in length by eleven in breadth and seven in thickness, is firmly poised above them, so as to form as it were an immense and somewhat rude altar. According to popular belief this curious structure was

---

[51] From 'Wilt thou think of me?' (1842) by R.H.
[52] Reigned 1214 – 1249.
[53] Alternatively Maldouen or Maol Domhnaich. Ruled Lennox 1217 – 1250.
[54] 1762 – 1829, botanist.
[55] The family removed from Craigmaddie Castle to Bardowie Castle around 1550. The ruins of Craigmaddie castle, which seems to have been built on an Iron Age fort, are still visible.
[56] This stone formation can still be found on Craigmaddie Moor.

formed by the united exertions of three old women, in those days when, through the agency of the enemy of man, certain wrinkled crones were occasionally gifted with supernatural powers, by means of which they could take an aerial midnight jaunt on a bind-weed at pleasure, and work all imaginable kinds of mischief on their unfortunate neighbours. Three of these "weird sisters"[57] on one occasion, it seems, engaged in a trial of strength, in which the victory was to be declared in favour of the individual who should carry a large stone to the greatest distance. One took up her "lift," and bearing it along for some time, dropped it at this place; the second next lifted her ponderous burden, and bore it forward, but by some mischance let it fall close to that of her predecessor; on seeing this, however, the third, who seems to have been a Herculean witch indeed, raised a much larger mass than either, and to show her superiority, hurled it with ease on the top of the two preceding stones. Such is the popular myth, and to this day the natives of Baldernock, Strathblane, and Campsie, to which localities the Titanic auld wives respectively belonged, have occasionally serious bickerings regarding the wreath of victory. Heads have been broken in the dispute, but we understand that, after all, it has never yet been properly decided.

Between the three huge blocks there is a narrow and somewhat tortuous passage, through which every unmarried visitant to the spot, who is not desirous of living a life of single blessedness, is recommended to scramble in a direction contrary to the course of the sun. Parties failing to perform this necessary ceremonial in honour of the *genius loci*,[58] either willingly or through neglect, are understood to have forfeited for ever the favour of Hymen,[59] and even although they should afterwards become benedictines,[60] need never expect to witness a tiny group of olive branches springing up around their table![61] Such, according to the popular creed, are the mysterious influences of the "Auld Wives' Lifts." We need hardly mention further, that when the

---

[57] A reference to Shakespeare's *Macbeth*.
[58] guardian spirit of the place
[59] Greek goddess of marriage
[60] those who marry late
[61] A reference to Psalm 128.3.

lads and lasses of the neighbourhood visit the locality, they invariably submit to the ordeal, or that on such occasions there is abundance of good-humoured raillery and loud-ringing laughter. Antiquaries have a different method of accounting for the origin of the "Auld Wives' Lifts," although even they have their differences of opinion on the subject. By some this gigantic cromlech[62] is supposed to be a Druidical altar, whereon, in a dim prehistoric era, the dark rites of pagan worship may have been celebrated. In support of this theory it is stated that, until a comparatively recent period, the remains of an encircling grove of oak trees were visible on the surrounding heights, which, from their gentle ascending slopes, also seem peculiarly adapted for the accommodation of worshipping crowds, who might assemble to witness the sacrifice of human victims whose blood was shed at the rude shrine of Moloch.[63] From the form and appearance, as well as the situation of this lone structure, indeed, this theory seems to our mind exceedingly probable, and with an inward persuasion of its truthfulness, we experience a gruesome but not altogether disagreeable feeling pervading us as we stand upon the stone of blood, which now, thank Heaven! has forgotten the purpose of its erection. We think of the lines written by Keats,

> "There is a pleasure on the heath
> Where Druids old have been,
> Where mantles gray have rustled by
> And swept the nettles green."[64]

The name of Craigmadie, which in the Celtic, by no strained derivation, means the "Rock of God," seems to us an additional evidence that the structure was erected for purposes connected with worship.[65] The cromlech, according to this view of the matter, has given a name to the moor on which it is situated, a supposition which,

---

[62] Or dolmen – two vertical stones supporting a horizontal one.

[63] A deity to whom the Canaanites offered child sacrifice.

[64] From 'Lines Written in the Highlands after a Visit to Burns's Country' (1818) by John Keats.

[65] Current thought is that Craigmaddie means 'wolf rock'.

to our mind, seems not at all improbable. In his excellent and elaborate work, the *Prehistoric Annals of Scotland*, Mr. Daniel Wilson,[66] lately honorary Secretary of the Society of Antiquaries, but now a resident in Canada, has given an engraving and a brief description of the "Auld Wives' Lifts." This gentleman has adopted the opinion that all cromlechs (and of course this amongst others) are of a monumental nature, and that the cavity between the stones was designed for the reception of human remains. From an inspection of this specimen, and with all due deference to so learned an authority, we can only say that it seems to us exceedingly ill adapted for such a purpose. The chamber, as we have said, is highly irregular in form; in fact, it seems rather an accidental effect than the design of the cromlech that it is there at all. The superior block appears somewhat geometrical in form, especially on its upper surface, but the under surface and the two lower stones are rude and unshapely in the extreme. Regarded as an altar we recognize a certain degree of fitness in the appearance and proportions of the cromlech of Craigmadie, but considered as a sepulchral chamber, it violates all our notions of suitability to the desired end. We may mention that the draughtsman of Mr. Wilson has been unfortunate in the point of view from which his sketch of the "Auld Wives' Lifts" is taken, the orifice being left entirely out of sight. He has also failed to convey an adequate idea of the magnitude of the three masses of which the structure is composed.

Ascending the rising ground in the vicinity we obtain a splendid prospect of the surrounding country. We do not, however, see across the island from sea to sea, as certain parties have done. Nevertheless, the spot is well worthy of a visit for its landscape beauties alone. The vast basin of the Clyde, from Kilpatrick to Dychmont, is stretched to the south-west, at the spectator's feet as it were, with Glasgow, Paisley, and countless other towns, villages, and gentlemen's seats, scattered on its breast; while the line of the horizon is formed by the Gleniffer and Fereneze Braes, Ballygeich, Neilston

---

[66] Sir Daniel Wilson (1816 – 1892), archaeologist and ethnologist. His *Archaeology and Prehistoric Annals of Scotland*, published in 1851, introduced the word 'prehistoric' to the English language.

Pad, and Cathkin. Turning in a north-west direction we have, across the dreary moor, the Campsie Fells, scarred by the Clachan and Fin Glens, and the ravine of Ballagan, with the peak of Dungoyne overhanging the sweet strath of the Blane. But we must make our descent; so, taking a farewell glance at the old altar, lichened and gray, around which the wild birds which our presence has disturbed are already settling eerily, we turn our face towards Balmore, which is situated about three miles to the south-east. It is principally down hill, however, so that we shall accomplish the distance, as Paddy would say, "in less than no time."[67]

As we pursue our downward course the country becomes gradually more and more fertile, until having passed in succession the farms of East and West Blairskaith and Glenorchard,[68] we find ourselves among green English-like lanes, with verdant hedgerows and overshadowing trees, entering the village of Balmore, which is finely situated on the margin of an extensive haugh, bounded to the west by the river Kelvin. Balmore is an excellent specimen of an old-fashioned Scottish clachan. It is of no great extent, nor does it seem at all ambitious to increase its dimensions. We should say indeed, that, judging from appearances, it is "a finished town." The houses are, in the majority of instances, plain and of one-storey, with kail-yards attached to them, and lying east and west of the road, with a strong tendency to avoid anything like orderly arrangement. Most of the tenements are at the same time "theekit"[69] in primitive fashion, while the gables are generally surmounted by "craw-steps" and dwarfish lums, which, like wrinkles on the human face, are indicative of an advanced age. A sprinkling of trees increases the rural aspect of the town. Then there are the usual branches of old world village trade. A gaucy[70] public-house of course there is. The souter's sign, "awee

---

[67] An Irish expression.
[68] East Blairskaith farm is now the premises of a landscape contractor and West Blairskaith farm has been replaced with luxury housing. Glenorchard farm is no longer in existence.
[69] thatched
[70] ample or pleasant

thocht agee,"[71] meets your eye here; there is the beild of the tailor, as you are informed by a homely collocation of ill-formed letters; this, again, by the heterogeneous assemblage of scones, snaps, peeries,[72] bobbins, red herrings, and tape, in the window, must be "the bit shopie of Jenny a' things," an indispensable personage in every small community; while the cart-wheel at, and the horse-shoe on, the door of this biggin', tells in unmistakeable terms where the smiddy is located. The presence of wabsters is also announced, as you pass along, by the jingling of the shuttle. It is at the same time evident, by the number of female faces peering from doors and winnocks, as the stranger moves along, that the gudewives and lasses here are not altogether free from the sin that doth most easily beset their sex in other and more polished localities.

There are two curiosities in Balmore; and what does the reader think these may be? Why, nothing less than a "big tree" and a live poet and novelist. The former of these (to give precedence according to local etiquette), a stately ash, with a trunk thirty-nine feet in height clear of branches, and a fine umbrageous head, is the pride and glory of the village. He would require to be a bold and a stalwart man who dared to utter a hint in disparagement of this sylvan giant within "earshot" of Balmore. [This splendid ash, the finest of which the West of Scotland could boast, was cut down and sold for coach-building purposes during the summer of 1855. This was a most cruel case of "tree murder," as Miss Mitford[73] calls this hateful crime.] Such ceremony would be superfluous, we suspect, in the case of the author. Yet Thomas Hamilton Dickson[74] is no ordinary man, as the reader will readily surmise when we tell him that honest Thomas has produced no fewer than two poetical publications, a historical novel, and an autobiography! We have not the pleasure of an introduction to this village genius; but we are informed that he is buirdly[75] chiel, with

---

[71] a little bit crooked
[72] spinning tops
[73] Mary Russell Mitford (1787 – 1855), author and dramatist.
[74] b. 1803. His self-published autobiography was entitled *Life, Memoirs & Pedigree of Thomas Hamilton Dickson.*
[75] well-built

flowing locks and a good development of cranium; and that when "snoddit up" on a Sunday, with shirt-collar *a la* Byron, he has quite a Christopher-Northish appearance.[76] Mr. Dickson is, as we understand, in somewhat humble circumstances; but, from the autobiography alluded to, it appears that, like St. Patrick, he is "come of decent people,"[77] and can boast a pedigree of which any duke in the country might well be proud. One is quite astonished, indeed, at the number of great men whom he can boast among his progenitors. Since a period considerably prior to the days of Wallace scarcely a great battle has occurred in which the Dicksons have not distinguished themselves by extraordinary feats of "derring-do." We regret to say that the descendant of such a line of heroes has been at length permitted, by an ungrateful country, to sink below the level of Lindley Murray.[78] Yet so it is. We have glanced over the writings, poetical and prose, of Mr. Dickson, and are most unwillingly compelled to admit the sad fact. There is a considerable amount of originality, however, in the *subjects* of his muse, as will be admitted when we mention the titles of two of his pieces. They are as follows: – "Verses on a young lady refusing to accept a ticket to a ball with the author;" and "Lines on a young lady refusing to dance" with the same illustrious individual. These are both, as may be easily supposed, deeply tinged with the pathetic. The second, however, concludes with the following spirited lines:

> "By fury! mock me not again,
> So ruthless at your will;
> Must I endure your proud disdain?
> Yea, no! by Jove, sit still!"

One little gem (gude gear gangs in sma' bouk) is worthy of being transcribed entire. It is headed "Worthlessness," and runs thus,

> "A man without a principle

---

[76] Christopher North was the penname of Professor John Wilson (1785 – 1854), who wrote for *Blackwood's Magazine*.
[77] From 'St Patrick Was a Gentleman' (c.1815) by Henry Bennett, and R Tolekin.
[78] 1745 – 1826, grammarian.

No. XIX. Baldernock and Balmore

Is like a town without a wall,
Or a nation free of people,
Or a horse in an empty stall."

The Hibernianism in this is delightful above measure, and we might cull many such, if time and space permitted, from the inspired pages of the Balmore poet. We must refrain, however; but, before parting with our author, and lest we should do him an unintentional injustice, we must quote one other specimen, which, to tell the truth, occurring where it does, takes us completely by surprise:

"RECOLLECTION.

"She's on my heart, she's in my thoughts,
        At midnight, morn, and noon;
December's snow beholds her there,
        And there the rose of June.

"I never breathe her lovely name
        When wine and mirth go round,
But oh! the gentle moonlit air
        Knows well the silver sound.

"I care not if a thousand hear,
        When other maids I praise;
I would not have her brother by
        When upon her I gaze.

"The dew were from the lily gone,
        The gold had lost its shine,
If any but my love herself
        Could hear me call her mine."

Now, good-bye, Thomas! There is simplicity, tenderness, and truth in these lines; and for their sake we will not even allude to thy "Historical Novel of Clamourtown." Would that thou hadst always written thus! but of course the muse, like other coquettes, will only dance when it pleases herself, – so, good-bye! And now for Cadder. [Alas! alas! for the credit of the Balmore bard, the verses we have just quoted turn out, on subsequent inquiry, to have been the composition of quite a different writer. Honest Thomas has appropriated them, without acknowledgment, from the pages of Miss Jewsbury.][79]

Round the fertile haugh of Balmore, the Kelvin, confined by an artificial embankment, makes a bold and graceful sweep. On one side of the stream are luxuriant crops, extending field beyond field over an alluvial plain; on the other are the umbrageous woods of Cadder, covering hundreds of acres, and enclosing leafy glades and sylvan recesses innumerable. Crossing the haugh in a south-west direction we soon reach the dull and sluggish water, which is here crossed by a picturesque line of large stepping stones. One of these masses is hewn into the form of a tablet, and at the period of our visit a group of serious-looking spectacled individuals are engaged in examining it with profound interest. Lingering for a moment, as they obstruct the passage, we learn from their conversation that they are one and all firmly persuaded that the stone in question is neither more nor less than an ancient Roman landmark. "True," one of them remarks in a pompous sort of tone, "there is no inscription on it, but then exposure to the weather and the rude trampling to which it has been subjected, will easily account for that; whilst its characteristic peculiarities of form, and its vicinity to a Roman station, are at least highly probable evidences of its ancient origin." One of the party, adjusting his spectacles, proposes to take an accurate measurement of the valuable relic; another, who seems an artist, at once commences sketching it; while a third mutters something about a communication to the Antiquarian Society. At this moment a couple of sweethearts from the neighbouring village, taking a gloaming walk, come tripping athwart the Kelvin. Being detained a moment in their passage by the enthusiastic philosophers, as we ourselves have been, the lad carelessly asks what they are looking at. "Why, my good fellow (answers one of the *savans*, with a rich Irish accent), its neyther more nor less, my

---

[79] First published under the title 'A Lover's Ballad' by Maria Jane Jewsbury (1800 – 1833).

jewel, than an ancient Roman tablet, a relic of the Emperor Antoninus Pius, which, by some dreadful and unaccountable misthake, has been tumbled into this dirty wather." On hearing this, the girl, who has been hanging back somewhat bashfully, at once steps forward, asking rather glibly to be shown the object of their adoration. It is of course pointed out to her, when, immediately after glancing at it, she bursts into a most unfeminine guffaw, exclaiming at the same time, at the top of her voice, "Antoninus Pius! A'tweel I wat ye're a set o' fules, far a' sae wise-like as ye leuk. It's naething o' the kin'; for it's jist Redbog's auld cheese-press that I've wrought mony a day mysel', and whilk was cuist aside when they got yon new-fangled machine. Antoninus Pius, quotha!"

Cadder is a lovely little village, consisting of a neat modern Gothic church[80] and a number of cottages, not very many, scattered picturesquely about, and perfectly embowered among trees. The name is said to be derived from a British word[81] signifying "a place beautifully embellished with wood and water," and it must be admitted that it well deserves the name. In the vicinity of the village there are well defined traces of a small Roman camp,[82] which we glance at, *en passant*, but as the sun is now below the horizon, we are compelled to hurry on our way. We soon cross the canal, which passes near the village, and in a few minutes thereafter reach the Glasgow and Kirkintilloch Road, by which, passing through the villages of Bishopbriggs and Springburn, we ultimately make our way into the city, arriving at the "Bell o' the Brae"[83] just as the clocks are "chappin' ten."

[80] Built in 1829 and renovated in 1909, this building is still a working church. A church has stood on this site since at least the 12th century.
[81] *coile dobhair*
[82] All remains of the fort above ground were destroyed by sand quarrying in the 1940s.
[83] The Bell o' the Brae is the steep part of High Street above the junction with George Street and Duke Street.

"As yet the bluebell lingers on the sod
That copes the sheepfold ring; and in the woods
A second blow of many flowers appears
Flowers faintly tinged, and breathing no perfume.
But fruits, not blossoms, form the woodland wreath
That circles Autumn's brow. The ruddy haws
Now clothe the half-leaved thorn, the bramble bends
Beneath its jetty load, the hazel hangs
With auburn branches dipping in the stream." – GRAHAME[1]

The year is fast falling into the sear and yellow leaf.[2] Autumn has laid aside her sickle, and the golden tenants crowd the spacious barn-yard, where smiling plenty with inverted horn bids man expect, with satisfied complacency, the coming of the dark and stormy winter. The happy cattle, free from the herd's control, are out upon the stubble rig, browsing on the rich green undergrowth of succulent clover, which, as every dairymaid can tell, yields the most delicious product in the churn. What a glorious time of it, too, the wild birds have amid the fruit-abounding woods and grain-strewn fields! The mottled throstle revels on the red rowan tree, or amid the blushing haws; and even now the fieldfare, from the far, far north, is hastening over land and sea to share the plenteous banquet of the woods. A merry company, as well as a mischievous, are the sparrows at all times and seasons; but doubly joyous, doubly dinsome, are they now, as in vast gregarious flocks they haunt the unmantled fields. Larks and linnets, gray and green, also swarm upon the grateful meadows; but songless all – save that occasionally some minstrel of the sky breaks forth into a brief chirrup that reminds us of departed spring, and that the lintie,[3] in its flight,

[1] From 'An Autumn Sabbath Walk' (1838) by James Grahame.
[2] A reference to Shakespeare's *Macbeth* V.iii.
[3] linnet

gives utterance to the rich musical titter which erst gladdened our ear amidst the yellow broom of summer. The swallow, which knoweth its appointed hour, still lingers, as if in love, over the breast of loch and stream, or glides in gentlest curves around the edifice where its clay-built shed is clinging to the eaves. Revelling in the abundance of the great mother, all things of earth and air, indeed, from the least even unto the greatest, are filled with cheerfulness and gratitude,

"For wealth hangs in each tangled nook,
In the gloamin' o' the year."[4]

Beautiful, indeed, and full of sweet suggestion is the interval which comes between the close of autumn and the winter's snell approach. The Americans talk with rapture of their "Indian summer," but surely its charms are not more worthy of admiration than are those of the corresponding season in our own clime. It is a genuine September day. During the night there has been a smart touch of frost, a foretaste faint of what is in store for us. This morning, indeed, we can assure you

"That hedge, tower, and tree,
Sae far's we could see,
Were white as the bloom o' the pear."[5]

But the glorious exhalations of the dawn – as Wordsworth might poetically have called the cranreuch[6] – have now disappeared, and the atmosphere is beyond comparison clear, and so bracing that one feels a perfect exhilaration in walking. It is just the sort of day, in short, on which we should like to master the "muckle Ben," or some kindred giant, and place our foot triumphant on his brow. So, making our way through the crowded and bustling streets of our good city, with an esteemed friend on our arm, "a fellow of infinite jest," we soon find ourselves comfortably seated in one of the commodious carriages of

---

[4] From 'Hairst' [harvest] (c.1842) by William Miller.
[5] From 'John Frost' (c.1834) by William Miller.
[6] hoar-frost

"the Edinburgh and Glasgow."[7] A few minutes' waiting brings the appointed hour, when punctual as the clock the signal is given, and behold we are in the bowels of the land, pursuing amid darkness and din our passage through the tunnel. This is soon over, however; and emerging in the sunshine at Cowlairs, we are sweeping through the fine undulating country to the north-east of Glasgow. The fields are bare, but the stubble has a rich russet hue that is extremely refreshing to the eye; while the deep green of the turnip patches, which every now and then flit past, gives an agreeable variety of tint to the ever-changing scene. Now we have a picturesque group of "potato-lifters" busily at work on the blighted furrows, with a lengthened row of half-filled sacks behind them; again we are rushing athwart an unreclaimed track of moorland, where the brown heath retains its primitive sway, and peat ricks are seen at intervals; and anon it is a snug farm-steading, with the usual bein[8] accessories, which for an instant courts our gaze and then is gone. Halting for a moment at Bishopbriggs Station, we are informed by an exceedingly civil and well-informed companion of the rail that the bishops of Glasgow, in ancient times, held extensive landed possessions here, and that the name of the locality was originally "Bishop's Riggs," which appellation has been in course of time corrupted into that by which it is at present known. We think the statement not at all improbable, more especially as we subsequently discover that our informant is quite an adept in the antiquarian line. Indeed, although he had swallowed and thoroughly digested a whole etymological library, he could not have been more at his ease among the jaw-breaking mysteries of Saxon, Celtic, and Danish nomenclature. Bishopbriggs is now a village of considerable extent, but of somewhat unprepossessing appearance, and is inhabited principally by the lower order of Irish, who certainly do not make up for its physical defects by any access of moral loveliness. It will be remembered that it was at this spot that a foul murder was committed on the person of an English ganger or overseer by two Irish labourers,

---

[7] The Edinburgh and Glasgow Railway, which opened to passengers in 1842.
[8] cosy-looking

during the formation of the railway.[9] The deed was perpetrated in the immediate vicinity of that bridge under which we are now passing, and the wretched criminals afterwards suffered the penalty of their dire offence within sight of the scene.

The line now tends gradually towards the east, through a fine fertile district of country, studded with gentlemen's seats, farm-steadings, and occasional coal-pits. Nothing calling for special remark, however, occurs until we arrive at the Kirkintilloch and Campsie Junction, when we diverge from the main trunk towards the north. Anything approaching the character of an event is a thing which is fortunately of extremely rare occurrence on this favourite and beautiful line, and we are deposited all right, after a pleasant run of some half-hour's duration, at the Kirkintilloch Station. Here, true to his trust, in suit of sober black, broadish-brimmed hat, and staff in hand, is our esteemed and venerable friend, Walter Watson,[10] the author of "We've aye been provided for, and sae will we yet," "Jockie's far awa," and many other lyrics which have deservedly attained extensive popularity. [Poor old Walter, one of the best specimens of a gash, kindly-hearted Scotsman that we have ever been privileged to meet, is now, alas! in the place appointed for all living.] We must introduce you, gentle reader, to the ancient bard, who, you will observe, is a gash, decent-looking specimen of the auld warld Scotsman. Walter is now on the lee side of fourscore – the snows of time are on his well-formed head, and the furrows of age on his expressive countenance; but there is a merry twinkle in the old man's eye, and a freshness in his complexion, which still indicate the possession of considerable mental and bodily vigour. Long, long ere the writer of this, or the vast majority of his readers had made their *entrée* on the stage of life, our friend Walter was known as a sweet singer in the land, and even until now he finds a solace in the muse. One of the earliest songs which we remember from the lips of our mother was of Mr. Watson's production, and she

---

[9] Dennis Doolan and Patrick Redding murdered a foreman named John Green, and were executed by hanging in 1841 at the scene of the crime in Bishopbriggs.

[10] 1780 – 1854. A granite obelisk to his memory was erected in 1875 in the graveyard of Chryston, where he was born. In 1853 Hugh MacDonald published a selection of Watson's poems, with a memoir.

had committed it to memory when a "wee, wee lassie." When afterwards we learned that the author of that lay was still in the land of the living, we could scarcely credit the fact, as we had somehow or other associated it with a bygone age of poesy. It was not so in reality, however, although the mistake, under the circumstances, was natural enough. Upwards of fifty years have passed away since the song, "We've aye been provided for," was given to the public, and at once became a "household word" among the Scottish peasantry. Since that period it has retained its popularity, and we doubt not will continue to do so.

Walter Watson was born on the brink of poverty, and as he says himself, has "never been able to wauchle very far up the brae." He has been a weaver, a "Scots Grey,"[11] a stone-knapper, a sign-painter, and many a thing besides, for Walter in a strait could turn his hand to "maistly onything;" but he was kept down throughout, like many another honest and industrious man (and such Walter emphatically is), by what the Scots call a sma' family, but which an Englishman would probably denominate a pretty large one. In the course of nature he is now drawing near the close of his career, and amidst age and the infirmities incident to a more than ordinarily extended span, is now earning his living on the loom, in the village of Duntiblae, near Kirkintilloch. Yet is the old man ever cheerful. He has many friends among his lowly compeers, and the respect in which he is held by them has been manifested in many ways, which must have been alike gratifying to his feelings and ameliorative of his necessities. Let us trust that, as he has sung in the past, he may still be enabled to say in the future,

> "We've aye been provided for,
> And sae will we yet."

But here is the ancient poet (who, by the by, is without his spectacles) on the look-out for us all this time. "Ha, Walter! how are you? I hope we have not kept you waiting?" "Oh, just a wee bit blink,"

---

[11] That is, a soldier with the Royal Scots Greys regiment.

says the old man, warmly shaking our hand; "no worth speaking o'; but I hope ye're weel? and is this your frien' (taking his hand) about whom I've heard you speak? Man, I'm glad to see you, and that ye've gotten sic a bonny day for your bit jauntie." As we proceed into the town, which is situated on a rising ground to the west of the station, and quite adjacent to it, Walter informs us that he had recently been threatened "wi' a bit touch o' the jaundice, but was noo comin' geyan weel roun'." Crossing the Luggie – here a considerable stream – by a somewhat time-honoured bridge,[12] and taking up hill, we are soon in the heart of Kirkintilloch, and surveying its curious auld warld aspects. The streets are narrow and irregular, striking off here and there without harmony of design or the least apparent regard for the rectangular. About the cross there is even a dash of the picturesque – some of the edifices being of considerable antiquity, and reminding us, in their positional peculiarities, of the more antique portions of Habby Simson's native village.[13] Here, for centuries, the town fairs were held; and here stood "the auld cross-stane," until it was overturned and destroyed, about thirty-five years ago, by some mischievous individuals.[14] A friend of ours remembers the venerable octangular pillar, with its "steps and stairs," on which the younkers of the neighbourhood loved to congregate, as their fathers of many generations had probably done before them. The destruction of this ancient relic, indeed, caused quite a sensation in Kirkintilloch, and William Muir, a local poet of no mean celebrity, who seems to have sympathized keenly in the general indignation, composed an elegy on the occasion, from which we shall venture to transcribe the following verses, as to many of our readers they will doubtless be as good as manuscript:

> "When thou was set upo' thy feet,
> To look about to ilka street,
> The bodies thocht thee as complete
>   Frae en' to en'

---

[12] This bridge, built in 1715, was widened and improved in 1881.
[13] Kilbarchan. See p241.
[14] In 1815.

As that braw steeple every whit,
    Poor auld cross-stane!

"Whar now will glowerin' bodies stop
To learn a sale or public roup[15]
O carts and harrows, growing crop?
    In letters plain,
On thee they a' were plastered up,
    Poor auld cross-stane!

"Ye bailies! if ye're worth a bubble,
Spare nae expense, and spare nae trouble
To catch the sacrilegious rabble,
    An' make them fain
Awa' in convict ships to hobble,
    Frae th' auld cross-stane!

"War our auld daddies but to rise,
An' see how laigh, poor thing! thou lies,
They'd curse this borough, ance, twice, thrice,
    Wi' angry grane,
Wha thus let mischief sacrifice
    The auld cross-stane!"

In the vicinity of the cross is the parish church, which was erected as a chapel to the Virgin Mary in 1644.[16] It is a plain but old-fashioned edifice with "craw-stepped" gables, and, like many other things in Kirkintilloch, is somewhat eccentric in appearance. At a considerable elevation on the edge of one of the gables is an antique sun-dial, on which, as an old weaver who comes past as we are inspecting it assures as, "the folk langsyne, before horologes were sae common, could mak' out the time o' day to a minute." It would be no

---

[15] auction
[16] Kirkintilloch Auld Kirk, which was renovated in the 1890s, is now a museum and art gallery.

easy matter to do this now-a-days, as the index is evidently in a "shugly" condition. There are several other places of worship in the town, but architecturally they are not calculated to attract the attention of the stranger. Indeed, it must be admitted that, on the whole, Kirkintilloch presents exceedingly few features of general interest. Near the centre of the town there are a number of handsome shops and out-of-the-way structures, but in the bye streets the houses are of the plainest description, and the monotonous sound of the shuttle, which greets the ear at every turn, however indicative of useful industry it may be, certainly does not tend to enhance their charms, or induce us to linger for any lengthened period in their precincts. As in other manufacturing communities, indeed, the population here have an intelligent and sagacious expression of countenance, and we doubt not that, did time permit, a rich harvest of character might be gleaned among these numerous workshops.

Kirkintilloch is situated on the line of the ancient Roman wall close to one of the forts or peels with which it was studded, and its name is supposed to be derived from a Celtic word Carpentulach, signifying a stronghold at the end of a ridge. Whatever we may think of the etymology, this is certainly in accordance with the local character of the town. We now proceed to visit the Roman Fort, the vestiges of which, at a short distance west of the town, and on the same elevation, are still in an excellent state of preservation.[17] During our devious peregrinations, we have several times, (as our readers will doubtless remember) intersected the course of the gigantic bulwark which the self-styled masters of the world erected between the Friths of Forth and Clyde. We have also described the present condition of a number of the forts or stations. The Kirkintilloch peel, however, has the peculiarity of having been the only one erected outside or to the north of the wall which it was designed to defend. For what purpose this deviation from the ordinary rule was made we cannot now discover, but doubtless there were good reasons for the alteration of plan.

---

[17] Most of the visible remains here are actually of a medieval motte, which was built on the remains of the wall.

The fortifications here seem to have been of extraordinary strength, although nothing remains now to indicate the circumstance, save the fosse or ditch, which continues, after the lapse of so many ages, to mark with great distinctness the extent and form of the original structure. It is of an oblong quadrangular shape, measuring 90 yards in length by 80 in breadth. A vast earthen rampart, from 40 to 50 feet in thickness, originally surmounted the present level platform on all sides, having in front the ditch or moat, which was not less than 30 feet in width, with a corresponding depth. Horsley[18] mentions that in his time the peel presented the appearance of having been fortified by a double wall of hewn stone; and adds that the stones had been strongly cemented with lime, and that many of them were chequered in the manner usual with Roman architects. All vestiges of this mason-work have now disappeared, and save the high mound and the deep ditch, which are covered with a dense verdure, nothing remains to indicate the previous existence of the Roman stronghold. A well, faced with stone, however, still occupies a portion of the fosse; and while we are lingering on the spot, a boy from the neighbouring town comes to fill his "stoups" at the very fountain from whence the soldiers of Antonine may have drawn the same cool and crystal fluid nearly two thousand years ago.[19]

As at other stations on the wall, relics of Roman art have been found from time to time in this locality. About fifty years since a legionary stone, measuring 5 feet in length by about 2½ in breadth, was dug up here. At each end are carvings of eagles' heads and other forms of ornament, while in a central compartment there is an inscription, which has been rendered as follows:

"IMPERATORI CÆSARI TITO AELOI HADRIANO, ANTONINO AUGUSTO PIO PATRO PATRIÆ, VEXILLATIO LEGIONIS SEXTÆ VICTRICIS,

---

[18] Rev John Horsley (1685 – 1732), author of *The Roman Antiquities of Britain*.
[19] Peel Well was replaced by a piped supply of water from the Campsie Fells.

No. XX. Kirkintilloch and Campsie

PERFECIT PER MILLE PASSUS."[20]

This tablet, which is broken in two, is preserved in the Hunterian Museum. Another stone, with bulls' heads sculptured in bold relief, with a number of coins of Domitian, Antoninus Pius, Commodus, and Constantine, with a number of other articles, undoubtedly of Roman origin, were also discovered at this place, and are now deposited in the collection of Mr. John Buchanan of this city.[21] Many years ago, while on this subject we may add, Mr. Stewart, proprietor of the peel,[22] who was then engaged in levelling a portion of the ground, brought to light numerous remains of ancient buildings, and found among them a large bar of lead, marked with Roman characters, which were not sufficiently legible, however, to admit of their being deciphered. Such blocks have been found at many other Roman stations, and there can be little doubt that this was a relic of the proud invaders, who, thus far at least, were for a time masters of our land.

From the summit of the peel, as from the majority of the other Roman stations on the wall, a commanding view of the surrounding country, with its fertile fields, its woods and waters, is obtained. To the west are seen the sites of the various forts between this locality and Kilpatrick; while to the east, over the town, those of Auchindavy, Barhill, &c., are visible. North and north-west are the towering Campsie Fells, the broad and beautiful straths of the Glazert and the Blane, and the Kilpatrick Hills, those everlasting ramparts which Nature seems to have reared for the defence of our country's independence, and from the ridges of which our rude sires looked down defiant on the haughty imperial legions. The Roman intruder has long passed away, and only in faint vestiges, few and far between, are his footprints now discoverable; but the old brown hills remain, unchanged amid the ravages of time and the elements, associated with

---

[20] "A detachment of the Victorious Sixth Legion to the Emperor Caesar Titus Aelius Hadrianus Antoninus Augustus Pius father of his country, having completed […] paces."
[21] 1802-1878, banker and antiquarian.
[22] The peel is now Peel Park, a public park.

heart-stirring memories, which, by exciting in us an honest pride in our native land, form constant incentives to the love of liberty. The period must never arrive when we shall think shame to look on the face of those stern old mountains, for the preservation of which from conquest our fathers so long and so successfully struggled.

Returning into Kirkintilloch, we rest our shanks for a brief space in the house of a friend, and taking advantage of the pause, we may glance for a moment at the history of the town. Few of our Scottish communities can boast so high an antiquity as Kirkintilloch. From the time of the Romans it has probably continued a place of some importance; and so early even as the year 1184 it was erected into a burgh of barony by William the Lion. In 1195, as appears from an ancient document, a certain William, son of Thorald, who then held the manor of Kirkintilloch, granted the church to the monks of Cambus-Kenneth, with half a carucate[23] of land. Afterwards the estates passed into the possession of the Fleming family; and in the third year of the reign of Robert the Second,[24] a charter, dated Arnele,[25] 13th May, grants the "Villa de Kerkentuloch to Gilbert Kenedy, grandson of Malcolm Fleming." James V. in 1526 "ratifies and approvis the charter of new infeftment made by our Soverene Lord to Malcolm Lord Fleming[26], making the touns of Biggar and Kerkentuloch burghis of barony, with the mercat dais in all punctis with arteklis after the form and tenor of the said charter of infeftment." In the year 1672 William Earl of Wigton erected a bridge of three arches over the Luggie at Kirkintilloch. The new bridge was said to be "maist necessary and useful for the saife passage of all persons who travel from Edinbro' and Stirling to Glasgow and Dumbarton;" and the Earl, in consideration of his outlay, was empowered for five years to lift certain dues on all horses and cattle which passed over the structure. In 1745 a detachment of Highlanders, who came over the Campsie

---

[23] A carucate is a piece of land that could be ploughed annually by 8 oxen.
[24] That is, in 1374.
[25] That is, Portencross Castle.
[26] Malcolm, 3rd Lord Fleming (c.1494 – 1547), Lord Chamberlain of Scotland under King James V.

Hills by the Craw Road, were passing quietly through Kirkintilloch to join the Chevalier,[27] when some person imprudently fired a gun from a barn window and killed one of the party. This act of treachery naturally roused the ire of the Celts, who, with drawn swords and the most horrid Gaelic imprecations, demanded the guilty individual to be immediately given up to their vengeance. The authorities were sadly perplexed, being quite unable to find the concealed criminal, and a wild scene of pillage ensued. Everything portable was taken from the houses of the devoted inhabitants, while the hungry Highlanders lived, as the old saying has it, at "heck and manger." Ultimately the kilted marauders were induced to depart by the receipt of a heavy fine. Afterwards, when the Chevalier's army was on its return from England to the north, a rumour broke out in town that the Highlanders were again approaching, when a scene of indescribable panic and confusion occurred, every one making off to some place of concealment with his most valuable goods and chattels. One old man was seen driving away his cow with a chaff bed on its back, while others were observed with the most incongruous burdens. Fortunately, however, the reivers did not again appear; and when better times came the inhabitants were in the habit of laughing at the curious incidents which occurred on the occasion of "the false alarm."

Our course is now northward towards Campsie, with old Walter, who "kens the road brawlie," for our guide. "There is life in the old dog yet," and, in truth, he strikes out at a rate which puts our vaunted pedestrian prowess fairly to the test. On our complimenting him, however, on his agility, he modestly replies, "Na, na! I've seen the day there wasna monie wha could ha'e passed me on the road, but that was langsyne, and ye maunna gar me believe that I'm onything extraordinar in that line noo." "By the by, Mr. Watson," interposes our friend, "what old edifice is that to the left? It has really quite an interesting appearance." "Weel, I'll no say that it hasna," quoth the old man pawkily, "but it's jist an auld washin'-house for a' that!" Of course we look perfectly unconscious, and there is silence on the road for at least five minutes. It is interrupted by old Walter, however, on

---

[27] Bonnie Prince Charlie

our arrival at a bridge, where for a few moments we come to a pause. "This is the Kelvin," he remarked, "and if you'll cast your een doon the water a wee bit you'll see its meeting wi' the Luggie. They're baith geyan grumlie[28] the noo wi' the steepin' o' the lint;[29] but they're twa bonnie waters for a' that – at least they aye seem sae to my auld een."

Following with our eyes the direction of our venerable guide, we see the junction of the Luggie and the Kelvin, about a-quarter of a mile to the westward of the bridge on which we are now standing. It is certainly one of the tamest water-weddings which we have ever been privileged to witness. The hymeneal[30] scene is a level plain, somewhat English in its character, and only redeemed from dullness by the heights of Kirkintilloch, which, with their steeples and houses, really look exceedingly well in the middle distance. Both streams are here grim, sluggish, and melancholy – moving as if they had each the most serious objections to the impending union. "The course of true love never does run smooth"[31] it is said, but here the current is placid as can be. Of course the inference is obvious; and we could almost fancy that this ominous "meeting of the waters" is a fit type of those cold, loveless marriages, which rank and wealth too often make, but that we have an affection for the Kelvin, and know that after the honeymoon is over, he and his mate, "dark but comely," will wax right merry, and dance away through a certain classic grove as if they had never known what it was to be sad. Old Walter, too, will have it that the Luggie is at heart a cheerful stream, and says that in the vicinity of his home it is both romantic and beautiful. "Sae, come awa' lads," he continues, setting down his staff, "and as we move alang I'll even try to lilt ye a wee bit sang which I made shortsyne in its praise." We resume our walk accordingly; and as we thread the hedge-bordered way, half-screened by over-hanging trees, the old bard in a low yet musical voice, croons the following sweet little lyric :

---

[28] cloudy
[29] The soaking of flax, to make linen.
[30] Bridal. Hymen was the Greek god of marriage.
[31] From Shakespeare's *A Midsummer Night's Dream* I.i.

"LUGGIE-SIDE.

"Oh lanely and laigh runs the stream of the Luggie,
Aye boring through glens as it wimples alang,
Whar aft on the hazel, or slaethorn sae scroggie,
The bonnie gray lintie sits liltin' his sang.
The bricht-speckled trout haunts the water o' Luggie,
The fringe on her lip gives him covert to hide,
And gloamin' gets lovers, fu' blythsome and vogie,[32]
To whisper their feelings on sweet Luggie-side.

"The lass that I love has her hame by the Luggie,
She's bonnie and sweet as a lassie can be,
And though her dark e'e has a glance o' the roguy,
I aye think her bosom is faithfu' to me.
Our tryst's coming on, when I'll meet wi' my dearie,
And on the green bank mak' a seat o' my plaid;
We'll no think it lang till we hear chanticleerie[33]
Loud warning us hameward frae sweet Luggie-side.

"It maunna be lang till we're staying thegither
Our meeting's a pleasure, our parting's a pain,
And were she to lea' me and gang wi' anither,
I'd ne'er hae a meeting wi' pleasure again;
Gae wimplin' awa' to the Kelvin, wee Luggie,
And lose yoursels baith in the proud river Clyde,
I'll bode for a hame and haudin' fu' snug, aye
To share wi' my lassie on sweet Luggie-side."

The voice of the singer thus dies away, and is of course echoed
by "a very good song, and very well sung," from his delighted hearers.
Yet are our words of praise anything but of the warmest. We never
could administer the highly-spiced compliment face to face. Nay, we
are apt to doubt the sincerity of the man who can do it. Speak as little

---

[32] light-hearted
[33] cockerel

ill as possible of a person behind his back, and no more good of him than is absolutely necessary in his presence.

But hark! the robin takes up the strain. Yonder he is, perched upon the topmost bough of that tall ash, his breast almost like a withered leaf fluttering in the soft breeze of song. We have praised thee to thy face, sweet minstrel of the autumnal woods, and shall again and again. We love thee wisely but not too well,[34] and it is "out of the fullness of the heart that the mouth speaketh."[35] Thou art a type of the true poet, even of him who "crooneth to himself" amid poverty, and want, and toil. Other birds require the sunshine and the flower to wake their musical utterances, but the drifting flake and the arrowy hail stay not thy song. Thou art, therefore, the image unto our fancy of such bards as the old man now by our side (but who knoweth not our secret communings with thee); and thou art at the same time the image of a class, at the birthplace of a humble member of which we are now arrived; and therefore, for the present, sweet bird, we bid thee once again farewell!

Birdston is a tiny little village or hamlet pleasantly situated about half-way between Kirkintilloch and Campsie. It consists of a small congregation of farm-houses and cottages, intermingled with kail-yards, barn-yards, trees, and hedgerows. The September sun smiles sweetly on it now, with its blue curling wreaths of smoke, its fresh yellow stacks of newly-gathered corn, and its groups of rosy-cheeked bairns. There are flocks of poultry straying among the stubble; flocks of pigeons, white and blue, cleaving the air, or settling on the house-tops; and flocks of swallows far overhead, sporting in the clear azure sky. Is it not in truth a pleasant spot? Well, it was down this quiet little lane, in that cleanly little cot, in this tidy little town, that William Muir, commonly called the Campsie poet, first saw the light, on the 28th of November, 1766; and it was from that door, after a singularly uneventful life of fifty-one years, that he was finally carried to his *other* home, in the clachan kirk-yard, –

[34] A reference to Shakespeare's *Othello* V.ii.
[35] Matthew 12.34.

No. XX. Kirkintilloch and Campsie

"Full many a flower is born to blush unseen."[36]

And it is very probable, gentle reader! that thou hast never previously heard so much even as his name. Nor, after all, does it matter very much. Yet William Muir wrote many poems – some good, a few bad, according to our view, and very many indifferent. Probably a modern critic, who judges only by rule, might find very few of them altogether faultless. Amid the chaff, however, there is a considerable amount of good seed. Muir was a working man, and the composition of poetry was the solace of his leisure hours. It interfered not with his industry, and we doubt not it proved unto him, as to bards of more elevated capacities, "its own exceeding great reward."[37] But it did even more than this: his poetry gave pleasure, and still gives pleasure to his rustic compeers; and, along with his amiability of character, it gained him the warm and lasting friendship of many estimable individuals in his own rank of life. Upwards of thirty years have elapsed since his decease; and we have been both astonished and gratified to find that his memory is still fondly cherished in many bosoms. That he is still best beloved by those who knew him best in life, is the most satisfactory testimony to his worth as a man which can be mentioned over his grave; and that such is indeed the case, we have many reasons for believing. Peace to his ashes! He was one of a class of poets which is almost peculiar to Scotland – a class of which any country might well be proud.

The poems of William Muir were published in 1818 – the year subsequent to his decease – with an introduction and a brief memoir of the author from the pen of John Struthers,[38] himself a poet of no mean repute. The contents of the volume, which must now have been long out of print, are of a somewhat miscellaneous description, and embrace a considerable variety and range of topics. Some of the subjects, indeed, might have been *à priori* supposed beneath or beyond the reach of the muse. Swift[39] boasted that he could write an instructive essay on

---

[36] From 'An Elegy Written in a Country Church Yard' (1751) by Thomas Gray.
[37] From 'Old English Writers and Speakers' (1825) by William Hazlitt.
[38] 1776 – 1853, born in East Kilbride.
[39] Jonathan Swift (1667 – 1745), satirist.

a broomstick; but that is an intellectual feat which certainly cannot for a moment be compared with the composition of a poetical address "To a Rusty Nail." This the genius of Muir actually accomplished; and many of his productions besides are on equally incongruous and impracticable themes, – as, for instance "To my Auld Bachles,"[40] "Verses on a Weasel," "The humble Petition of an old Family Clock," "A Hymn to the Herring," and (evil to him that evil thinks) "An Ode to the Itch!" Unpromising as they may seem, there are some of these subjects treated with considerable happiness and tact. The muse may even handle pitch and not be defiled. Let us hear, in testimony of this truth, a portion of Muir's hymn to the inimitable "Glasgow Magistrate,"[41]

"First of fishes! unto thee
    A grateful hymn I'll sing;
For seldom am I doom'd to see
    A fatten'd ox's wing.
A bleater's limb ne'er on the spit
    Is seen to pipe and fry;
But thee, dear fish, I'm proud to meet,
    And on a brander spy.

"On thee, when hunger's calls assail,
    In solitude I feed,
With simple water from the pail,
    And simple barley-bread.
When thou arriv'st, but newly caught,
    Fresh from the briny wave,
And richly nice and cheaply bought
    Oh, what a feast I have!

"Or, if preserved in native salt
    Thou grace my humble board,

---

[40] shoes
[41] That is, the herring.

No. XX. Kirkintilloch and Campsie

And season'd with the juice of malt,
    I think myself a lord.
In all thy various shapes and forms,
    Thy friendship I invite
Fresh, salt, or red, when most thou charms
    The Welshman's appetite.

"For luxury is but a cheat,
    With wealth's high-flavour'd spice;
Dame Nature asks but simple meat,
    'Tis habit calls for nice.
His palate that will reckon thee
    An insult to his taste,
Will still a wretched mortal be
    With puddings, pies, and paste."

The majority of Muir's productions, however, are of a serious and sentimental cast; many of them also are deeply tinged with despondency. Occasionally, as in the above verses, indeed, we find him cheerful and contented with his humble lot, snapping his fingers in the face of saucy Fortune, and defying her to cast him down; but more frequently he is disconsolate and murmuring. Altogether, we consider the book a true reflex of the author's mind, and feel persuaded that its lights and shadows are truthful depictions of those which in life darkened or illumined the lowly destiny of the man.

We are now entering the beautiful valley of Campsie. The bold brown range of hills on our right seems as if it were approaching nearer and more near unto us. How sharply and distinctly is its picturesque altitudinal outline defined against the dark blue dome of day! Every scar and wrinkle on the rugged brae-face, too, is plainly seen, although the white torrent threads of winter are not yet. Even at this distance we could read a geological lesson, or find a sermon in stone,[42] were we so inclined, in those lofty and well-marked terraces of trap.[43] There are

[42] A reference to Shakespeare's *As You Like It* II.i.
[43] Trap is any dark igneous rock such as basalt.

scientific stone-knappers in abundance about Campsie, however, to whom every nook and cranny of these fells is familiar as a long-trodden path, and meanwhile we will not poach on their manor. Let them "drill and bore the earth"[44] as best they may, our game at present lies on the surface. And see, how beautifully intermingled are the lights and shades on the bosom of the everlasting hills! The landscape is steeped in golden radiance. The day is even like unto that which the old poet has described as

"The bridal of the earth and sky;"[45]

but "the summer has its passing cloud,"[46] and there are deep umbral masses of gloom flitting silent and slow over the crags, and passing ever and ever away. Now the sunbeams are sleeping on the heath,

"Like ravelled golden hair;"[47]

anon the cloud-shadow steals over the spot, like a vast stain; and when we lift up our eyes again, behold the place which knew it once shall know it no more for ever.[48] How full of meaning are the shows and forms of nature! Readest thou not thy own destiny, O man! in the living page before thee? We come like shadows, so depart; and this chase of sunshine and cloud is but a type of that which joy and sorrow, pleasure and pain, are ever pursuing in the world which passeth show within our own bosoms. Art thou in the sun? then bethink thee of the coming shade,

"With a hey ho, the wind and the rain!"[49]

---

[44] From book 3 of 'The Task' (1785) by William Cowper.
[45] From 'Virtue' (1688) by George Herbert.
[46] From *Baldred of the Bass* (1824) by James Miller.
[47] From 'We'll a' Go Pu' the Heather' (1835) by Robert Nicoll.
[48] A reference to Psalm 103.16.
[49] From Feste's song in Shakespeare's *Twelfth Night* V.i.

Is thy present lot in gloom? fear not that it will be always – "joy treadeth on the heels of grief;"[50] and as old Walter has hopefully said,

"When we fell we aye got up again,
And sae will we yet."[51]

Pursuing our course we soon arrive at the village of Milton. The Glazert, in a wild rocky channel, fretted by the floods of ages, here passes athwart the road, and is spanned by a substantial bridge. Kincaid printworks are in the vicinity of the village, and the streamlet is discoloured considerably by the chemical matters thrown out here as well as at Lennoxtown. But what of that? we love our own kind better than the kelpies; and when we look around at the comfortable population teeming in the vale, we should reckon ourselves the merest nincompoop if we uttered the faintest possible sigh over the decay of the picturesque. A pleasant little village seems Milton, as we glance at it *en passant*, which is all that we can do, having still a considerable portion of our day's work before us, and digression is "the sin which doth most easily beset us."[52]

At the base of the Campsie Fells, a short distance north of Glorat House (the seat of the ancient family of Stirling)[53] which is situated to our right amidst its finely timbered policies, are the vestiges of two Caledonian forts. These interesting relics of a long-vanished past are both circular in form, one of them being about 100 yards, and the other about 20 yards in diameter. In a direct line these ancient strongholds are nearly two miles distant from the wall of Antonine, and it has been supposed that they were erected by the Caledonians for the purpose of checking the farther progress of the Roman legions. Our antiquarian friend of the rail, to whom we have previously alluded, scouted, however, this supposition, and said that the conquerors would never have permitted the natives to erect such places of strength so near to their frontier. His opinion was that they were Roman outposts,

---

[50] Apparently a misquote for "Grief's fell train / Still treads upon the heels of Joy" from 'Elegy II' (1770) by Samuel White.
[51] From 'And Sae Will We Yet' by Walter Watson, composed c.1810.
[52] Hebrews 12.1.
[53] Glorat House is still owned by the Stirling family.

for the defence of foraging parties when they had occasion to ravage the enemy's territory On this point we are inclined to differ from him. The very erection of the wall was an acknowledgment of weakness. "Hitherto they could come, but no farther;"[54] and we believe, besides, that they had enough to do in defending their acquisitions up to that line, without venturing to make incursions beyond it. But in addition to this, it is well known that the forts of the Romans were uniformly constructed of a quadrangular shape, while those of the Britons, there is every reason to believe, were always of a circular form. It does not necessarily follow, besides, that these places of strength were actually erected at all during the period of the Roman invasion, or with reference to it. From recent archæological discoveries, indeed, it is rendered exceedingly probable that they are of an age long anterior to the occurrence of that event. It has hitherto been too much the fashion with antiquaries to ascribe everything prehistoric to the Druids or the Romans, forgetting that the country was inhabited long previously to the advent of either, and that the aborigines may also have left their "footprints on the sands of time."[55]

The valley or strath of Campsie possesses many features of the most romantic beauty. It is bounded on the north by the towering and rugged Campsie fells, which rise to an elevation of about 1,500 feet above the level of the sea; and on the south by a gently swelling and fertile ridge, called the South Brae, which in some places attains an altitude of nearly 700 feet. At the west end, towards the opening of Strathblane, the vale is only about half-a-mile in width; but gradually, as it unfolds itself towards the east, it waxes broader and more broad, until it is lost in the spacious plains around and beyond Kirkintilloch. The bosom of the valley is of the most undulating description; now rising into gentle knolls covered with verdure, or plumed with patches and belts of timber; now sinking into water-worn hollows and dells,

"Wi' the burn stealing under the lang yellow broom,"[56]

---

[54] A reference to Job 38.11.
[55] From 'A Psalm of Life' (1838) by Henry Wadsworth Longfellow.
[56] From 'Their Groves o' Sweet Myrtle' (1795) by Robert Burns.

and anon spreading out into fertile meads and sunny slopes, where the cattle in straggling groups are pasturing on the stubbled furrows, or lazily chewing the cud. At various points the seats of the gentry are seen peering above their girdles of foliage, as if keeping "watch and ward" over the scattered farms, which are strewn irregularly here and there, each with its yellow cluster of corn-stacks, its thin clump of ash-trees, and its little curling cloud of blue smoke. The strath, altogether, has a cosie and secluded aspect, which is rendered all the more pleasing by the contrast which its quiet beauty offers to the stern and hoary grandeur of its wild battlement of fells, with their precipitous and scarred sides, their jutting crags, and seemingly tumultuous though still and silent torrents of debris. The signification of the word Campsie has been a puzzle to the etymologists. "Even ministers they ha'e been kenned" to arrive at very different conclusions on this interesting subject. Mr. Lapslie,[57] a former well-known incumbent of the parish, for instance, asserted that the name has been derived from a combination of Celtic words, signifying a crooked strath; while Dr. M'Leod,[58] formerly of Campsie, and now of St. Columba's Church in this city, as positively asseverates that it means "a church in the bosom of a hill." Who shall presume to decide when doctors differ? Another doctor? Well, then, we have Dr. Lee,[59] a third incumbent of the parish, who adheres to Mr. Lapslie's version because, as he says, it is certainly descriptive of the locality, and appears to have existed before any church was erected in this place. We do not know how Dr. Lee became aware of the latter fact, as he has advanced no evidence on the point; but this we know, that Dr. M'Leod is one of the best Gaelic scholars in the country, and on such a subject we should be inclined to back him against any Sassenach from Maidenkirk to the Lennox. Grant the correctness of his etymological deduction, and we shall have no difficulty in supposing a church long prior to the first of which Dr. Lee has any account. Judging from his name, we should suppose the

---

[57] Rev. James Lapslie (1750 – 1824), local historian.
[58] Rev. Dr. Norman MacLeod (1783 – 1862).
[59] Dr. Robert Lee (1804 – 1868), Professor of Biblical Criticism.

present excellent minister, Mr. Munro,[60] to be of Celtic origin, and we should like to hear what construction he puts on the disputed word. Has he a theory of his own? or does he treat such subjects with the contempt of our old friend, Walter, who, in reference to the dispute in question, exclaimed, "Hoot, awa' man, there's nane o' them kens aucht about it mair than you an' me. Sic menseless discussions aye mind me o' the auld rhyme,

> "'Mickle din, an' little woo,
> Quo' the Deil when he clippet the soo.'"[61]

Lennoxtown, which may be called the capital of the strath, is an extensive village of modern erection, and has been in a great measure dependent for its growth and prosperity on the various print-works, bleachfields, and factories in the vicinity. It consists principally of one street, which is of considerable extent, with a few irregular offshoots and detached cottages. The houses are for the most part plain and of two storeys, without the slightest pretensions to architectural beauty. Cleanly, comfortable, and withal commonplace in aspect, Lennoxtown, apart from the splendid scenery in its neighbourhood, presents but few attractions to the visitor. The only structure, indeed, of an imposing appearance is the parish church, a spacious modern Gothic building, with a handsome square tower, erected in 1829. It is finely situated on a gentle but commanding elevation a little to the northward of the main street, where it forms a pleasing feature in the landscape of the vale.[62] Besides this, there are other two places of worship in the village, viz., a United Presbyterian meeting-house, and a Roman Catholic chapel.[63] The religious character of the population, it would thus appear, is not likely to suffer from a deficiency of church accommodation. For the educational requirements of the rising

---

[60] Rev. Thomas Munro (1802 – 1879).

[61] "Lots of noise and little wool," said the Devil when he sheared the sow.

[62] This church building was gutted by fire in 1983 and is still in ruins.

[63] Campsie Parish Church stands on the site of the former United Presbyterian, which was demolished due to subsidence. St Machan's RC Church, opened 1846, is still operating.

generation, Lennoxtown, we understand, also possesses an abundant provision. It has likewise an excellent, and as we were gratified to learn, flourishing Mechanics' Institution, for the intellectual improvement of adults, by means of lectures on science, books, periodicals, &c.

Being abundantly supplied with coal and other minerals, and water, Campsie seems to have been designed by nature, as a commercial gentleman once remarked of another locality, to be the seat of manufactures. As if in furtherance of this intention of the great mother, we accordingly find that it contains a considerable number of public works of various kinds. The most extensive of these is Lennox mill print works, which are situated on the Glazert, immediately adjacent to the village. These were originally established in 1786 on a small scale. In 1805 they came into the hands of Messrs. R. Dalglish, Falconer, & Co., the present enterprising proprietors, under whom they have gradually flourished and extended, until now they have attained the most gigantic proportions, employ an immense number of hands, and produce the most amazing quantities of printed calico. Talk of your feudal barons with their multitudinous retainers! How one of these old iron-coated gentlemen would stare, could he be brought back to witness the "skailing"[64] of Messrs. Dalglish & Co.'s populous works. Kincaid-field and Lilyburn-field also employ numerous workers, and contribute materially to the prosperity of the parish, which is further increased by the extensive chemical works of Messrs. M'Intosh & Co., established in 1806, and also by several bleachworks situated along the winding course of the limpid Glazert. Formerly a considerable number of weavers resided in Lennoxtown and its vicinity, but of late years they have become almost an extinct species, while the monotonous music of the shuttle is now seldom heard. This is a consummation, however, which, all things considered, there is but little reason for the philanthropist to regret.

With an accession of two to the number of our party – one a veteran in the ranks of reform, a pioneer when Liberalism was anything but a joke, the other a genial and an intelligent young friend

----

[64] dispersal of workers

– we now bid Lennoxtown for a time adieu, and proceed by an exceedingly pleasant path towards the western termination of the strath. The sun, in a sky of deepest azure, has crossed by a couple of degrees at least his highest altitude, and is wending slowly down the golden afternoon. Warmed by his mellow radiance, a smile is flickering even on the face of the grim and wrinkled fells which tower majestically to our right, as if the proud and stern-featured old giants were contemplating with pleasure the sweet and silent vale recumbent at their feet. Silent, did we say? then were we in error, for is not the murmur of the playful Glazert even now in our ears, as, under the trembling shadows of her sheltering trees, she steals in fairy links along. Now we have a glance of her rippled breast, while she jinks among her channel-stones as if in play; and anon how demure she seems in this dim recess, where she lingers, a "sleeping beauty," with all her glittering beads of foam upon her dark brown breast. How the leaves and flowers are bending over her, as if in love; while one bold brier, begemmed with blushing berries, stretches forth his fruited arms as if he fain would clasp her in one long embrace, yet fears to make the attempt! "I'm sayin', frien'," quoth a voice at our side, "if ye stan' glow'ring there at naething that way, I rather think ye'll no win up the glen afore the gloamin', sae I fancy we had better be gaun." With a half-muttered apology for our dilatoriness, we accordingly proceed.

The South Brae now begins to clothe itself in a dense mantle of foliage. Nor is its vesture by any means "scrimpit," for acres and acres in richly tinted masses are waving in the breeze around its gaucy[65] breast; and see, rising proudly over the far rustling sea of living green are the lofty turrets of a stately edifice. That is Lennox Castle, the seat of John L. Kincaid Lennox, Esq.,[66] proprietor of extensive estates in the parish of Campsie, and the lineal representative of the three ancient families of Woodhead, Kincaid, and Antermony. He is likewise said to be the legitimate heir to the Lennox peerage. This is a subject, however, on which our limited genealogical knowledge forbids us to descant. The magnificent structure before us, it will be

---

[65] pleasant or healthy-looking
[66] 1802 – 1859

observed, is in the boldest style of Norman architecture, and we may mention that it is after a design by Mr David Hamilton of Glasgow. Its erection was commenced in 1837 and completed in 1841. The site, which is in the immediate vicinity of the spot where formerly stood the old house of Woodhead, is nearly 500 feet above the level of the adjoining valley, of which the castle commands an extensive and picturesque prospect, and to which it communicates a striking feature of architectural beauty.[67] Near the entrance to the spacious policies, and within their bounds, the Glazert winds gracefully through a sweet sylvan portion of its course, and receives two tributary streamlets in its bosom. One of these is the Pu', a somewhat sluggish burn which flows from the south-west along the base of the South Brae, and the Finglen Burn, which comes dancing merrily from the north-west. The meeting of the waters is seen to great advantage from an elegant little bridge a few yards within the gateway, where we linger a few moments to feast our eyes upon the quiet loveliness of the scene. Our contemplations are broken, however, by the sound of approaching hoofs, and glancing round we perceive two ladies on horseback cantering gaily past, with their light veils and gracefully flowing robes floating on the breeze. They form quite a delicious picture, when taken in connection with the surrounding accessories of woodland glade, verdant lawn, and proud baronial towers. "Thae's the leddies o' the castle," says one of our friends, when they are fairly past; "and gude leddies they are, tae," he continued. "Lod, man, they had a' the Sabbath-schule weans o' Campsie up at the castle the ither week, and gied them sic a treat as some o' the puir things never saw before. Nane o' your shabby affairs, but just as mickle as the wee creatures could set their faces tae. That's what I ca' being leddie-like." Having given a hearty assent to the concluding proposition of our friend, accompanied by the expression of a wish that such kindly and considerate condescension were a little more common, we again resume our walk.

A great gap now appears in the lofty fells to the north, the vast sides of which slope steeply down to a dark and narrow ravine, which

---

[67] Lennox Castle later became a hospital for people with learning disabilities. It is now abandoned and was partly destroyed by fire in 2008.

forms the far-famed Campsie Glen. Round the eastern shoulder of this magnificent opening in the lofty ridge, twines the "Craw Road," faintly discernible from our present position; while on the pinnacle of the height, a little projecting heap is seen in relief against the sky. This we know to be "Crichton's Cairn," from having long ago speeled to its summit for the purpose of enjoying the extensive and beautiful prospect which it commands.[68] The majority of cairns have a myth or two attached to them, but no one with which we are acquainted seems to be so liberally provided for in this respect as the specimen before us. Every individual almost to whom we spoke on the subject gave us a different version of the originating affair. According to one, the cairn was erected in memory of a kind of local Hercules named Crichton, who having undertaken for a wager to carry a load of meal to the hill-top, by dint of great exertion accomplished the feat, but fell down dead immediately thereafter; another would have it that Crichton was a famous smuggler, who was overtaken and killed by gaugers[69] on the elevated spot alluded to, and that the cairn was raised to perpetuate remembrance of the bloody deed; while a third asserted, without a moment's hesitation, that the identical Crichton had committed suicide, by hanging himself on that lone peak. The latter, it must be admitted, is the most marvellous story of all; for unless an individual about to "lay hands upon himself," in such a "heaven-kissing"[70] locality, could manage to fling a coil over the horn of the moon, we really cannot see how this horrid purpose could be at all effected, a blaeberry-bush being the nearest approximation to a tree which he would be likely to find. Our friend Walter's story seems the most feasible. It is as follows: – "The way that I've aye heard it explained was this: There was ance a minister in the parish, a won'erfu' strong man, that they ca'd Crichton, that could walk, eatin' a pease-bannock[71] a' the time, frae the manse at the Clachan to the tap o' the hill in twenty

---

[68] Crichton's Cairn and other cairns are still present on the Campsie Fells, where they help with navigation.

[69] excisemen

[70] From Shakespeare's *Hamlet* III.vi.

[71] cake made from pea flour

minutes. Noo, it'll tak' an or'nar body near the double o' that time. And the minister was sae proud o' his speelin' poo'rs that he used often to gang up and study his sermons there; and as he was weel liket by a'body, when he dee't the folk bigget the cairn and ca'd it after him. That's the way I've aye heard it accounted for; but whether it's true or no, I'm sure I dinna ken." In corroboration of this statement, we may mention that a minister named James Crichton was inducted into the parish of Campsie on the 23d of April, 1623. If this was the individual alluded to, however, his elevated study does not seem to have been productive of good fruit, as he was subsequently deposed for what was called "corrupt doctrine." [72]

The clachan of Campsie, at which we now arrive, is about a mile and a-half distant, in a westerly direction, from Lennoxtown, and lies in a romantic situation at the *embouchure* of the Kirkton or Clachan Glen, of which it commands a beautiful and highly suggestive prospect. The clachan consists of a tiny congregation of houses, principally cottages, straggling as it were "at their own free will," and finely interspersed with gardens, trees, and hedgerows. A cosie looking edifice, begirt with foliage, flowers, and fruit, is pointed out to us as the manse,[73] and truly it seems, in the words of the old rhyme, "a pleasant habitation."[74] But even the very humblest of the biggins has an air of beinness and comfort which is pleasing to contemplate; while the blue wreaths of smoke from each "lum-head" are seen in fine relief against the green bosom of the glen, which rises in bosky magnificence beyond. This handsome white house, which seems to look a welcome as we approach, is the clachan inn, where "man and beast," as the old signboards have it, may find abundant provender, with all the means and appliances of creature comforts, on the usual terms of course – of

---

[72] Actually John Crichton. He was translated to Paisley in 1629 and deposed in 1639 as a "professed arminiane and popish champion", although he went on to have a career as a chaplain-major in the army and a Professor of Physic at the University of Glasgow.

[73] This manse became an outhouse to the new manse, which is now a private dwelling.

[74] The rhyme went: "[person's name] is my name, Scotland is my nation; [town's name] is my dwelling-place, a pleasant habitation.

"Drink, pilgrim, drink – drink and pay."

A decent and a civil old gentleman withal is the landlord, Mr. Muir, who is, besides, one of the few remaining contemporaries and early acquaintances of Robert Burns. [Like so many others mentioned in these pages, Mr. Muir has been called hence since the date of our first publication. Thus the links are ever dropping from the circlet of life.] Mr. Muir was born and "brought up" on the farm adjoining Mossgiel, when it was tenanted by the Burns family; and although he has no special tale to tell regarding the ploughman poet, who was then a young man, he remembers seeing him at his daily work in the fields, and occasionally he sat at the same bleezing fireside with him in the winter evenings. It is something even to have rubbed sleeves with Burns. The landlady, too, is a douce, motherly looking woman, and the daughter an elegant and intelligent young lady; so that he must be a particularly fastidious traveller indeed who could not "take his ease" in the clachan inn.

But we are rather forestalling; for with a taste peculiar, we fancy, to ourselves, we generally, unless specially thirsty, visit the church-yard of a place before either inn or ale-house. We accordingly pass Mr. Muir's hospitable door, and first seek the adjoining field of graves. The gate is locked, however, and we must wait for a minute till a deputation, composed of our venerable Lennoxtown friend and old Walter, proceeds to a neighbouring cottage in search of the sexton. The man of spades is not to be found; but in his stead we are speedily introduced to the "second grave digger," who is well known in the locality as "David the Earl," and who approaches, key in hand, laughing and fidgin' fain, in anticipation of the dram which he is about to earn. [The poor Earl has also, we understand, gone to his last rest in the clachan kirk-yard.][75] Davie is a stout robust specimen of the *genus homo*, clad in clay-browned moleskin trousers and jacket, with a broad Kilmarnock bonnet overhanging his tanned features. Poor fellow! his intellect is far, far below the ordinary level of humanity; his lack-lustre eye and frequent gusts of unmeaning laughter indicating but too

---

[75] 'David the Earl' died of cholera in 1854.

414

plainly the fearful vacuity within. "You'll let these gentlemen see the kirk-yard, Davie," says one of our friends, as they drew near the gate where we are standing. "Ay wulla, ay wulla," is the instant reply, in a quick, eager kind of voice; "but wull they gi'e me a dram, dae ye think? wull they gi'e me a dram?" Being assured that all is right on this point, Davie bursts into one of those curious, arid cachinnations[76] which seem to follow every sentence he utters, and at once ushers us into the church-yard.

A lovely spot, indeed, is that in which the Campsie dead are laid. It is enclosed by an irregular up-and-down kind of dike, which accommodates itself to the inequalities of the ground. One corner of the spacious enclosure is occupied by the ruined belfry and a portion of the walls of the old clachan church, forming a prominent feature in the scene which meets our gaze. In the foreground, as we enter, are seen the green undulations of long-departed humanity, intermingled with the red graves of those who have recently passed the dark bourne; while headstones and monumental tablets of varied form and size – some old and moss-grown, some fresh from the chisel – are strewn over and around the area of death in picturesque confusion. Stately trees, not yet in the sear and yellow leaf,[77] but clad in the dark garniture of mid autumn, like sylvan mourners, stand rustling around; while sternly, beyond and above all, rise the swelling sides of the glen – the everlasting hills echoing and re-echoing the voices of many waters.

The literature of the church-yard has always presented a dreary charm to our mind. If there are sermons in stones,[78] those of the grave are certainly the most touching and pathetic. There are no lessons that find their way so directly to the heart as those which are inscribed on the cold roof of that narrow house into the silent chambers of which we must all descend. The clachan kirk-yard is peculiarly rich in this melancholy lore; and we immediately proceed to scan a few of its more prominent pages. Here lies Bell of Antermony, one who travelled in

---

[76] loud laughter
[77] A reference to Shakespeare's *Macbeth* V.iii.
[78] A reference to Shakespeare's *As You Like It* II.i

many lands, and returned to rest in the dust of his native parish.[79] There are laid the remains of an individual who sacrificed his life at the call of duty, – one of that noble band who died, in dark and troublous times, to purchase the religious freedom of their native land. Let us read the inscription on the "martyr's grave;" it contains all that we know of his sad story:

"ERECTED IN MEMORY OF
WILLIAM BOICK,
WHO SUFFERED AT GLASGOW,
JUNE XIV., MDCLXXXIII.,

For his adherence to the Word of God, and Scotland's Covenanted
Work of Reformation.

Underneath this stone doth lie
Dust sacrificed to tyranny,
Yet precious in Immanuel's sight,
Since martyr'd for his kingly right.

Rev. chap. vii., verse 14."

Honour to the memory of the Christian hero! and may Scotland always find such in her hour of need! Passing over the intervening mounds, we find a weatherworn stone, fringed and partially veiled by the long grass, which, after brushing the encroaching verdure aside, we find to bear the following inscription:

"This is the burial-place of the Rev. Mr. John Collins. He was admitted minister of Campsie the 2d of November, 1641, and the tradition is, that he was murdered in returning from Glasgow about Martinmas,[80] 1648."

---

[79] John Bell (1691 – 1780) joined the court of Peter the Great and travelled as court physician on embassies to Persia and China. He wrote about this in *Travels from St Petersburg to various Parts of Asia*, which was published after his death.
[80] Martinmas, the feast of St Martin of Tours, is 11th November.

Thereby hangs a tale, which, from tradition, we may condense thus: – Mr. Collins, minister of Campsie, during the period indicated on his gravestone, had a beautiful and a virtuous wife, the pride of his heart and the light of his home. The laird of Balglass, a small estate in the neighbourhood, conceived a guilty passion for the minister's fair lady; but knowing from her spotless character, that he had no chance of obtaining her affections while her husband lived, he, with the view of obtaining the gratification of his desires, resolved by violence to shorten the days of his unsuspecting pastor. Accordingly, when Mr. Collins was returning in the dark from a meeting of Presbytery at Glasgow, about Martinmas, 1648, he was attacked by Balglass at a place called "Lodgemyloons," near the outskirts of the city, and basely murdered. The body of the minister was found next day and conveyed home, when it was discovered that he had also been robbed of his watch and a small sum of money – a circumstance which tended to mislead the authorities into the belief that the crime had been committed by ordinary highwaymen. No suspicion fell on Balglass; and when some months of mourning had elapsed, he appeared, without exciting remark, as suitor for the hand of the beauteous widow. Ultimately, too, he gained her consent to the union, and after a decent interval they were married – whether happily or not we cannot tell; but the murderer and the innocent cause of his guilt lived thereafter for several years as man and wife. At length the lady, on entering a private room unexpectedly one day, discovered Balglass sitting at a table, on which lay a watch, which she immediately knew to be that of her deceased husband. The fatal truth flashed on her mind as she saw him attempting to hide the evidence of his guilt, and she bitterly accused him on the spot of having murdered the object of her early love. The wretched criminal, conscience-stricken, it is said, answered not a word, but rushing from the apartment, left the house, and was "never heard of more."

While one of our Campsie friends, with suitable gravity of face and voice, furnishes us with the particulars we have thus briefly narrated, we form rather a curious group around the murdered minister's grave. Sitting on a tombstone, paper and pencil in hand, is your humble servant; at our side, and evidently grueing at the contemplation of the bloody deed and its sad consequents, is our facetious friend, all traces of humour banished from his expressive face; leaning on his staff, and scanning the inscription at his feet, stands old Walter, with our second Campsie friend erect beyond him; while Davie, bolt upright at the head of the grave, casts many a longing eye towards the inn, and every now and then rubbing his hands as if in enjoyment, interrupts the speaker with his eldritch laugh, which forms a strange incongruous accompaniment to the tragic narrative. "There's the banes o' a gude story there," quoth old Walter when the speaker had concluded. "And the materials of a good picture," adds another. "But wulla get a dram, div ye think?" chimes in the poor idiot, waxing impatient, and again breaking into his characteristic giggle.

There are many curiously-carved old stones in the clachan kirk-yard, which would amply repay a leisurely inspection to any one who possesses, even in a slight degree, the tastes of Old Mortality,[81] but time and space would fail us, were we to attempt at present to describe a tithe of them. One further specimen only we shall notice. It is one of a pair erected to the memory of individuals belonging to the ancient family of Kincaid. This stone is in excellent preservation considering its age. It is a quadrangular slab, the central portions of which are occupied by the armorial bearings and quarterings of the family, while around the edges is the following inscription: – "Heir lyis ane Honourable man James Kinkaid of that ilk quha Desisit[82] ye 9 of Janvar anno 1606." The other stone is almost a fac-simile of this, but, of course, is to the memory of another personage of the same family.[83] A few yards from these stones, and nearer the centre of the ground, is the grave of William Muir, the Campsie poet, without the slightest memorial to mark his "whereabouts." We have heard, however, that a subscription is at present in progress, and we trust that a sum sufficient to erect a decent tablet to his memory may ere long be procured. The

---

[81] A reference to the 1816 novel of this name by Sir Walter Scott, set during the Covenanter conflict.
[82] who died
[83] These stones were used in 1884 for closing up the Lennox Mausoleum.

working men of Campsie do not lack spirit and we have little doubt that they will cheerfully respond to an appeal in honour of one who was during life an honour to their class. [Since this was penned, a handsome monument has been erected over the grave of the poet.]

The auld kirk, as we have already stated, is now a complete ruin. One gable, containing the belfry, and a portion of the side wall, are all that now remain of the edifice. It has been originally, however, of the most diminutive proportions and the plainest style of church architecture. The beautiful situation in which it is placed, and the interesting associations with which it is entwined, alone render it attractive to the visitor. An old bell suspended in the belfry is only tolled when funerals are taking place in the adjacent ground. "Let the gentlemen hear the bell, Davie," says one of our party, to try the fidelity of our unfortunate companion. "Na, na," he replied, "there's nae burial." Nor could even a promise of the coveted dram bribe him from what he considered his duty. Poor Davie! we have known men with many, many talents as compared with thee, who could not have resisted that bribe.[84]

Leaving the kirk-yard, and having persuaded our senior friends to seek the hospitable shelter of the inn until our return, and having given them strong injunctions to remember "Earl David," we now proceed to thread the mazes of the glen. For this purpose we cross the foaming Glazert by a convenient bridge, and, passing a rustic stile and a small bleachfield on the opposite side, soon find ourselves on a pleasant footpath, amid the flickering shadows of certain tall and stately beeches which stand like sentinels at the entrance of the ravine. These sylvan giants, we may mention, are said to have been planted on the occasion of the union of Scotland and England.[85] The channel of the stream at this place is "beautiful exceedingly;"[86] the brown waters rushing fretfully over a series of shelving rocks, which form, with their intermingling tints, a sort of natural mosaic, and produce a most

---

[84] This bell was later transferred to Oswald School in Lennoxtoun and then to the old kirk in Milton of Campsie, which is now disused.
[85] 1707
[86] From part I of 'Christabel' (1816) by Samuel Taylor Coleridge.

pleasing effect as the slanting sunbeams play amid the dancing wavelets. Advancing a short distance, the Glazert is seen tumbling in foam over a tiny linn, and rushing hurriedly away from the rugged pass down which it has just been precipitated. The path now rises amid tangled steeps and overhanging cliffs, from which the tortured stream is seen far below, turning and twining and roaring, as with frightful velocity it dashes over and around immense masses of rocks which seem determined to retard its downward progress. As we proceed amidst a profusion of ferns and wild flowers, the banks wax more lofty, and become clad with a dense luxuriance of foliage. Now we pass a frail wooden bridge, and are in view of Craigie Linn, which is about fifty feet in height. The water – that of a small tributary to the Glazert – with a kind of hissing din, keeps ever straggling down the face of a dark precipice, in threads of silver whiteness, and falls into a craggy gully below. The recess in which this fairy cascade is situated is wild in the extreme, and were the waters in greater volume, would form a fine picture subject. Scrambling on our way, we arrive at a projecting corner where there is a seat, from which a splendid prospect is obtained of the lower portion of the glen. A deep chasm, bosky and rude, slopes steeply away at our feet; beyond is the wood-fringed and shadowy hollow of the ravine, revealing a spacious landscape in the distance, which is basking quietly in the rich amber radiance of the evening sun, and forming a dazzling contrast to the green gloom in which, amid rocks and trees and roaring waters, we are enveloped.

While lingering at this "coigne of vantage," scanning the picturesque scene before us, our attention is attracted by a fair-haired maiden, coming sauntering up the glen with a baby in her arms and a train of toddling wee things behind her. Across the ricketty bridge she trips, and now a little lassie gives her hand to a tinier brother, and assists him over the ledgeless structure. One false step, and destruction yawns for them in the gulf beneath. They seem perfectly unconcerned, however, and in a minute or two they are at our side. We inquire at the girl if she is not afraid to venture on such a dangerous walk in company with children, and are answered with an "Oh no! the bairns are quite weel acquentit wi' the road, and naething wrang has ever happened to ony o' them." We think, as we see the red hips of the brier overhanging the precipitous banks, and tempting the little hands to pluck, that it is really a marvel "something wrong" has not happened. One of our friends, who like ourselves has bairns at home, seems to be of the same opinion, and fumbling in his pockets, brings forth a handful of "sweeties" and distributes them among the gratified younkers, as if for the purpose of wileing them from the contemplation of the dangerous bushes.

The glen, or ravine, as it might perhaps with great propriety be denominated, now becomes narrower, while the path approaches more nearly to the bed of the stream. A beautiful cascade next meets our gaze, the water in one sheet leaping over a barrier of rock, apparently about fifteen feet in height, with a roar that keeps the echoes in a constant state of activity and the overhanging boughs in a ceaseless tremour. Moving onward and upward, a rustic bridge is seen spanning the gulf, and we soon find ourselves leaning over its ledges enjoying the rich snatches of scenery which it commands. Another fine linn occurs immediately above the structure, which has evidently been erected for the purpose of enabling visitors to inspect the scene from the most advantageous point. The height of this fall is, to appearance, about the same as that which we have just mentioned. It is also of one leap, and the waters are precipitated into a deep, dark pool, which is fretted with foambells that are ever rising in myriads to the surface. In the vicinity of the bridge the path comes to an abrupt termination at the base of a considerable precipice. This is surmounted, however, by a rude kind of staircase, locally denominated "Jacob's ladder," up which we manage to scramble without much difficulty. This is rather an awkward ascent for ladies, however, and many are the youthful pair of lovers who have been brought to a pause here. Ay, if that old tree which overlooks the spot were gifted with a tongue, full many a tale it could assuredly unfold of merry giggling groups, of blushing maids, and of loving words of badinage. As we are not likely to find "tongues in trees,"[87] however, and as no fair encumbrance, unfortunately, is on our hands to-day, we can afford to move lightly on, and a few minutes

---

[87] From Shakespeare's *As You Like It* II.i.

brings us to "Niagara," the last, best fall in the series. This beautiful linn is situated on the brow of the declivity up which we have been toiling. It has a little of the horseshoe character of its vast American prototype, and like it possesses a subaqueous cavity, by means of which the adventurous visitor can pass unscathed beneath the falling torrent. In the bed of the stream, a few yards below the cascade, rises a ponderous mass of trap, surmounted by a patch of verdure pranked with gowans ever "wat wi' dew."[88] Ascending this natural altar, the view is indeed lovely; and while we are revelling in the varied beauties which it unfolds, one of our little band, inspired by the *genius loci*, bursts out into Luther's sublime hymn,[89] in which we all join with a fervour which makes the old gray rocks to ring, and almost drowns, for a time, the hoarse unceasing voices of the cataract. Soon our strain comes to an end, however, and the "never-ending, still-beginning"[90] music of the stream resounds as before to the passing breeze. Ages on ages ere we saw the light has its dreary cadences been heard in this lone spot; and when the place which knows us now shall have forgotten us for ever,[91] still "morning, noon, and night" shall the roar of its troubled waters ascend to the everlasting hills. In the words of the old song,

> "Oh, we have wandered far and wide
> O'er Scotia's land of frith and fell,
> And mony a lovely spot we've seen
> By mountain hoar and flowery dell;"[92]

but never within the same compass have we witnessed anything superior, in wild romantic beauty, to the glen through which we have now passed. Taking its features separately, we know that they can, each and all, be surpassed in many instances; but in combination, as we find them, our experience can produce nothing at all comparable to

---

[88] From 'My Nanie, O' (1787) by Robert Burns.
[89] Probably 'A Mighty Fortress is our God' (1529).
[90] From 'Alexander's Feast' (1697) by John Dryden.
[91] A reference to Psalm 103.16.
[92] From the traditional song Good Night, and Joy Be with You All.

Campsie Glen. If we have any fault, indeed, to find with this unique and favourite haunt of the beautiful, it is that there is too little of it, and that its charms are too soon exhausted. This deficiency may be to some extent supplied, however, by a visit to its twin, the Fin Glen, which lies about half-a mile to the westward. This delightful ravine possesses a greater volume of water than the Clachan Glen, and has two picturesque cascades. They are often talked of as rivals, but under the circumstances "comparisons are odorous," to use the words of old Dogberry,[93] and we prefer to consider them as lovely sisters.

Retracing our steps down the glen, one side of which is now in sun and the other in shade, and we, as has been too often our lot, on the side of gloom, we soon arrive at the inn, where we find our good old friends engaged in a "three handed crack," and not altogether a dry one, with the landlord, Mr. Muir. Nothing loath, of course, we join them, and spend an hour or so right pleasantly. We then return to the hospitable house of our friend at Lennoxtown, where the gudewife gives us a warm reception – pouring into us, indeed, both "canister and grape" (if on such an occasion we may borrow a phrase from poor Tom Hood),[94] in well directed and fast-succeeding discharges. Of course, after doing our best, we are at length compelled to capitulate, and cry aloud *peccavi.*[95]

Our homeward course being over the same ground which we traversed in the early part of the day, we now don our "seven-league boots," with the aid of which we speedily get over the ground, and find ourselves, sometime within the bounds of what are called "elders' hours,"[96] either in or on the Globe at George Square.

---

[93] From Shakespeare's *Much Ado about Nothing* III.v.
[94] From 'Lieutenant Luff' (1800) by Thomas Hood:
      "If wine's a poison, so is Tea,
      Though in another shape:
      What matter whether one is kill'd
      By canister or grape!"
[95] An expression of guilt – literally "I have sinned".
[96] Respectable hours, i.e. by about 10pm.

The name of Wallace, the great Scottish patriot, has ever been held in the highest esteem by the natives of the country for whose independence he fought. Indeed, there is something approaching almost to adoration in the feeling with which the memory of the "Wallace Wight"[1] is universally regarded among the population of Scotland. At the winter ingles, over the length and breadth of the land, when the tale and the song go round the glowing hearth, there is no story so welcome as that which recounts the superhuman exploits of the peerless knight of Elderslie, no lay so acceptable as that which does honour to his prowess. The place of his birth – the hiding-places in which he sought shelter from his foes – and the battlefields on which he fought and bled, are all regarded as hallowed spots of earth by the patriotic peasantry, who point them out with honest pride to the admiration of the stranger. Long pilgrimages, too, are made expressly for the purpose of visiting such scenes. Every one will remember that fine passage in the autobiography of Burns,[2] wherein he describes the effect which the reading of "Blind Harry's History" had upon his youthful mind. "The story of Wallace," he says, "poured a Scottish prejudice into my veins which will boil along there till the flood-gates of life shut in eternal rest." In another place the poet tells us he walked a goodly number of miles on a Sabbath day to visit the Leglen Wood, which, according to the rhymed chronicle alluded to, had on one occasion afforded concealment to the Scottish hero and his companions:

"Syne to the Leglen Wood when it was late,
He made a silent and a safe retreat."[3]

"I explored," he says, "every den and dell where I could suppose my heroic countryman to have lodged, and I recollect (for even then I was a rhymer), that my heart glowed with a wish to be able to make a song

---

[1] Valiant Wallace
[2] An autobiographical letter sent to Dr John Moore in 1787.
[3] From 'The Wallace' (c.1477) by Blind Harry, also known as Henry the Minstrel.

on him in some measure equal to his merits."[4] Tannahill also endeavoured to do honour in song to the memory of Wallace;[5] and Campbell, who was born almost on the very spot where the hero encountered and vanquished the Southrons in our own High Street, composed a dirge of deepest pathos on his melancholy death.[6]

Within the scope of these rambles there are several scenes associated by tradition with the memory of

"Scotia's great but ill-requited chief."[7]

Elderslie, the place of his birth, lies within the compass of a forenoon's walk from the Cross of Glasgow; and one of his battles was fought on "the Bell o' the Brae,"[8] within sight of the same spot. Blantyre Priory, a few miles up the river, is said to have witnessed one of his most remarkable escapes from ruthless Southron hands. At Rutherglen kirk, Sir Aymer de Vallance[9] and the "fause Menteith"[10] planned his capture; and at Robroyston, where we now propose to guide our readers, "the deed of shame" was finally consummated.

The sun of a sweet autumn morning, emerging from its veil of chilly mist, flings its broad streams of yellow radiance, intermingled with the huge gray shadows of the towering lines of building, athwart the place of our rendezvous at "King William."[11] On these "plain stanes"[12] strutted the aristocratic Virginia merchants of other days; in the shadow of that edifice, with military pride erect, marched full oft the "Captain Paton" of Lockhart's inimitable serio-comic muse. Even

---

[4] From a letter to Mrs Frances Dunlop (1786), a descendant of Wallace.
[5] 'The Lament of Wallace after the Battle of Falkirk' (1807) by Robert Tannahill.
[6] 'The Dirge of Wallace' (1841) by Thomas Campbell.
[7] From 'Jean of Lorn; or, The Castle of Gloom' (c.1807) by James Bannantine.
[8] The steep part of High Street above the junction with George Street and Duke Street.
[9] Aymer de Valence, (c. 1275 – 1324) 2nd Earl of Pembroke.
[10] Sir John Menteith of Ruskie (c. 1275 – c. 1329).
[11] The equestrian statue of William of Orange that stood near Glasgow Cross. It now stands in Cathedral Square.
[12] Flagstones that ran from Glasgow Cross to the statue, on which only the merchant lords were allowed to promenade.

now we can almost picture to the mind's eye the genial old martial beau, who "left the Saltmarket in sorrow, grief, and woe."

"His waistcoat, coat, and breeches,
Were all cut off the same web,
Of a beautiful snuff colour,
Or a modest genty drab;
The blue stripe in his stocking
Round his neat trim leg did go,
And his ruffles of the cambric fine
They were whiter than the snow,
Oh! we ne'er shall see the like of Captain Paton no mo'e.

"His hair was curled in order
At the rising of the sun,
In comely rows and buckles smart,
That about his ears did run:
And before there was a toupee
That some inches up did grow;
And behind there was a long queue
That down his back did flow,
Oh! we ne'er shall see the like of Captain Paton no mo'e."[13]

But the Captain has long gone "the way we all must go," and is sleeping the last long sleep in the shadow of the old Cathedral, not in that of the "Ram's-horn Kirk" as the poet imagined. The place where our merchants most did congregate, too, is now deserted by the great ones of the city, who, with the rising fortunes of the community, have gradually moved towards the west. Our modern Bailie Nicol Jarvies[14] are no longer to be found in the classic purlieus of the Saltmarket, which is now entirely resigned to folks o' laigh degree. The glory has in truth departed from this ancient thoroughfare. But here comes our two companions, with stick in hand, prepared for the road; one a clever

---

[13] From 'Captain Paton's Lament' (1819) by John Gibson Lockhart.
[14] Bailie Nicol Jarvie was a character in Sir Walter Scott's *Rob Roy*.

young artist, on a visit from the great metropolis [Mr. William Simpson,[15] who has since achieved distinction as the limner of the Crimean War. His inimitable sketches of the late seat of war, and of its principal events, have won the approbation equally of the soldier and the artist.]; the other an old and dear friend, whose name is associated in our mind with all odorous things,[16] he being familiar with all manner of plants, "from the cedar which groweth on Lebanon, even unto the hyssop which springeth from the wall."[17] By many a flowery, many a leafy tie, are our affections interwoven; and many, many a sweet memory of woods, and fields, and streams, and marshes, have we as common property. Our morning salutations over, we wend our way up the crowded and withal repulsive High Street. Here, to borrow a passage from the "Life Drama" of our young townsman Alexander Smith,[18]

> "We meet sin-bloated faces in the streets,
> And shrink as from a blow."

Sin and misery are indeed to be seen here in loathsome union. Squalid mothers are peeping from closes with wan and filthy little children, whom it is a pain to look upon. Strange glimpses of the city's hidden life are obtained as we pass the noisome vennels; and while we think with pitying horror on the wretched denizens of these dim and dark defiles, we hurry on with grateful feelings, that, however humble our way of life may have been, our lot has hitherto at least been cast in comparatively pure and pleasant places.[19] Yet in several respects this is the most interesting street in the city. In picturesqueness of aspect it has no rival, while it is rife in objects of antiquarian, literary, and historical interest. Every here and there the eye is attracted by those fine old edifices with peaked gables and crowsteps which so gratified

---

[15] 1823 – 1899
[16] Roger Hennedy (1809 – 1876), Professor of Botany at Anderson's University, which later became the University of Strathclyde.
[17] 1 Kings 4.33
[18] 'A Life Drama and Other Poems' (1853).
[19] A reference to Psalm 16.6.

Sir David Wilkie[20] when he visited our city, and which so forcibly recall to mind the grandeur of other days. What a noble old pile is the University, with all its glorious memories of the past! What a host of illustrious names come crowding to our lips as we gaze upon its venerable front, or tread with reverent steps its echoing courts! Divines, philosophers, poets, and statesmen, whose names the world will not willingly let die, have passed and repassed beneath that grim portal.[21] It was in the High Street of Glasgow that Adam Smith gave law to nations; that James Watt made those improvements on the steam-engine which have increased a thousandfold the productive power of man;[22] and it was here the bard of Hope[23] first saw the light of that world which his genius has since so much delighted. "The Bell o' the Brae" has heard the clash of that terrible sword which preserved the independence of Scotland from the yoke of the stranger; and in its vicinity, during the infancy of Queen Mary, the din of civil war ushered destruction to the "gudes and gear" of our fathers. It was at the foot of the New Vennel, near the Infantry Barracks, that the "battle of the Butts,"[24] to which we allude, took place. In this encounter the citizens, under the command of the Earl of Glencairn, were totally routed by the troops of the Regent Cardinal Beaton,[25] and about three hundred of them slain. Immediately after the battle the victors ravaged the town, carrying away everything portable even unto the doors and windows of the houses. This was a sair day for Glasgow, and was long remembered with horror by the inhabitants. It was in the College Green adjoining that Sir Walter Scott, in the novel of *Rob Roy*, represents the

---

[20] Artist, 1785 – 1841. He first visited Glasgow in 1817.

[21] After the Glasgow Improvement Act of 1866, many of the old buildings in High Street were demolished. The university moved to new buildings in Gilmorehill, in the west end, in 1870 and the university buildings on High Street were demolished in 1885.

[22] See pp9 – 10.

[23] Thomas Campbell (1777-1844), who wrote *The Pleasures of Hope*.

[24] In fact it was the first Battle of Glasgow in March 1544 that took place on the High Street. The second Battle of Glasgow (the Battle of the Butts) took place near the shooting butts on Gallowgate in May 1544, about a mile from the boundary of the city.

[25] Cardinal David Beaton (c.1494 – 1546), Archbishop of St Andrews.

cousins Osbaldistone as having met in deadly combat, when the bold outlaw interfered to prevent the effusion of blood.

We must not linger in the city, however, as our peculiar field lies principally beyond its precincts; otherwise materials for an interesting volume might be gleaned in the thoroughfare through which we are passing. Higher yet and higher we ascend, until, leaving Drygate Street and Rottenrow, with their antique edifices fast disappearing in the march of civic improvement, we reach the fine esplanade at the summit, where the grand old Cathedral, stern and gray, stands in solitary dignity like a vast shadow of the olden time. Even here, however, we must not give ourselves pause, but in pursuance of our prescribed route, pass the Royal Infirmary, the Blind Asylum,[26] and that great mineral depot, the basin of the Monkland Canal. At this point our attention is attracted by a monumental tablet in the wall, which skirts the way, erected to commemorate the death of three individuals, who suffered for their adherence to the Solemn League and Covenant[27] in the days of persecution. Although of comparatively recent erection, the inscription is so much defaced that it is scarcely legible. We read it, to the best of our ability, as follows. The metrical portion, it will be seen, is sufficiently rude:

"Behind this stone lyes James Nisbet, who suffered martyrdom at this place, June, 1684; also, James Lawson and Alexander Wood, who suffered martyrdom, October, 24th, 1684, for their adherence to the Word of God and Scotland's covenanted work of Reformation.

Here lye martyrs three
    Of memory,
Who for the covenants did die
    And witness is
'Gainst all these ruffians' perjury.
Against the covenanted cause
Of Christ their Royal King,

---

[26] This public subscription building on Castle Street was replaced in 1881 by the current dramatically Scots baronial building.
[27] A covenant to support Reformed Christianity in Scotland.

The British rulers made such laws,
Declared was Satan's reign –
As Britain lyes in guile, you see,
'Tis asked, O reader! art thou free?

This stone was renewed by the proprietors of the Monkland Navigation April, 1818."

This spot was formerly known as the Howgate-head, and the authorities deemed it prudent to have the three Covenanters above named executed here, which was then some distance out of town (rather than at the cross, where these affairs usually took place), with the view of escaping the maledictions of a sympathizing crowd. The case of James Nisbet was one of a peculiarly painful nature, and may well be supposed to have excited public indignation against the powers that were. According to old Wodrow,[28] who has rescued from oblivion the names of so many of these truly brave men who suffered a painful and ignominious death rather than renounce their faith at the bidding of a corrupt government, Nisbet was a farmer in the parish of Loudon. Although under proscription for his principles he ventured to come to Glasgow to attend the funeral of a friend who had perished on the scaffold. In the church-yard he was recognized and apprehended by a trooper, a cousin-german[29] of his own, who carried him before the authorities. On his trial he manfully declared his approbation of the skirmish at Drumclog[30] and the more serious affair at Bothwell Bridge.[31] In those "killing times" this was reckoned cause sufficient for death, and the brave Covenanter was accordingly sentenced to suffer the extreme penalty of the law. He was offered his life, however, if he would acknowledge the King as head of the Church. This he had the fortitude to refuse, and the sentence was in consequence

---

[28] Robert Wodrow, author or *The History of the Sufferings of the Church of Scotland from the Restoration to the Revolution* (1721–1722).
[29] That is, first cousin.
[30] 1st June 1679
[31] 22nd June 1679. Lawson and Wood both fought in this battle against government forces.

mercilessly carried into effect. His body was interred at the place of execution; and in aftertimes the spot was marked by a rude tablet, which was removed by the Canal Company while their works were in progress, and replaced by the present stone, which is now, as we have remarked, becoming sadly dilapidated.[32]

Turning to the right, we now pursue our way in an eastward direction over Garngad-hill. From the summit of this eminence, looking to the south, there is a very striking view of the Cathedral, with the defile of the Molendinar, spanned by the "Bridge of Sighs," and the swelling declivity of the Necropolis, crowned by the grim and colossal statue of Scotland's great reformer.[33] This is certainly the most commanding position from which the High Church can be viewed, and, with its romantic accessories, it would furnish abundant material for a good picture. Notwithstanding the proximity of the great city, which dims the autumn sky with its canopy of smoke, there is even a dash of wild nature along the glen of the Molendinar, which awakens dreams of the dim and distant era when Sanct Mungo dwelt in its bosky recesses, and

"Drank o' ye Molendinar burn,
When nocht better he could pree."[34]

The sooty trail of the tall chimney, however, is over all; the trees have fallen into an untimely sear, the very herbage on the slopes being sadly discoloured; while the good old patron Sanct, were he coming to life again, would doubtless be painfully surprised at the pollution which has fallen upon his favourite stream, and would be amply justified in doing what the poet wickedly hints he did at any rate,

"He wad drink o'ye streams o' ye wimplin' worm,[35]
And let ye burn rin bye."

---

[32] The monument was redone in granite in 1862. It has been moved many times and can now be found in Cathedral Square. The place where MacDonald saw it is now part of the M8 motorway.

[33] John Knox, whose statue still dominates the Necropolis skyline.

[34] From 'Sanct Mungo' (1838) by Alexander (Sandy) Rodger, satirical poet.

[35] That is, whisky.

The Fir Park and the banks of the Molendinar, as well as a considerable expanse of the surrounding country, were at one time covered by a shadowy tract of forest. A Druidical grove, indeed, is said at an early period to have crowned the brow of the hill, wherein mystic rites unholy were performed by the hoary priests of Baal. At a subsequent period, tradition assigns this gloomy sylvan vale as the scene where Aymer de Vallance and Menteith met by appointment immediately previous to the treacherous seizure of Wallace at Robroyston. If so, the dastard pair must have pursued a route somewhat similar to that upon which we now resume our walk.

For a mile or so in this direction the country possesses but few attractions. Here and there we observe a few mansions which have seen better days, but which generally have now a dreary and deserted aspect. The pestiferous smoke from certain works in the northern quarter of the city, notwithstanding their gigantic chimneys, seems to have thrown a blight over the face of nature. The trees are for the most part shrivelled and sapless, while the very wheat in the fields and the hedgerows by the wayside lack that freshness of verdure, which is so grateful to the eye in regions of greater atmospherical purity. Our botanical friend can scarcely recognize his floral favourites in the dwarfed and discoloured specimens which look up so piteously from the ground; and the man of art, all accustomed as he is to London vegetation, looks askance upon the miserable sylvans which skirt our path. As we advance, however, the complexion of the landscape gradually improves. The ragweed brightens into purer gold, the eyes of the daisy wax clearer and more clear, while the downy locks of the thistle, from a dingy gray, become white as the virgin snow. As we lift up our eyes, too, "behold! the fields are already white unto the harvest;"[36] and hark! the soft trickling notes of the redbreast, sweetly, sadly swelling on the gale the symphony of the waning year.

"This is the little hamlet of Provanmill" is the reply which we make to a question with which our friend Mr. Pencil interrupts our musings, as we approach a few houses scattered on either side of the

---

[36] John 4.35.

way. This tiny township consists principally of a "meal-mill" and a miller's house, with the usual pleasing accompaniments of poultry in capital condition, and rosy-cheeked children frisking about the loan. There is also a cart-wright's establishment, as you may perceive by a glance at these bright-coloured carts without wheels strewn helplessly about on the ground, and these equally gaudy wheels without carts, which are lazily leaning against the wall. Here, too, is a smiddy with Burnewin[37] standing begrimed at the door, on which is nailed a symbolic horseshoe, while a stout country lad stands holding a patient-looking Clydesdale by the halter. A little farther on is the village hostelry, which is of somewhat ancient standing, if we may credit an inscription above the door, which would certainly have driven the late Mr. Lennie, of grammatical celebrity,[38] distracted, if he had ever chanced to come this way. Some local Dick-Tinto[39] has delineated on the signboard a rude portraiture of the house on which it hangs; the said house, in the pride of its heart, on having a covering of slate substituted for its original thatch, being supposed to address the passing stranger in the following mellifluous lines, which we copy *verbatim*, capitals and all:

"I here do Stand one Hundred years
With a Straw covering on
While Many of my friends here met
And enjoyed the time so long;
But now I have been Favoured
By a new friend of mine
To cover my head over with stone
That I may not repine."[40]

Passing Provanmill about fifty yards or so we turn off to the northward by a narrow country road which crosses the Caledonian Railway, on which a train is dashing furiously past as we approach.

---

[37] That is, a blacksmith.
[38] William Lennie (c. 1779 – 1852), author of *The Principles of English Grammar*.
[39] A sign-painter turned portrait-painter in the novel *The Bride of Lammermoor* (1819) by Sir Walter Scott.
[40] This inn became a private dwelling sometime before 1910.

One moment there is a rushing noise in our ears and a lengthened mane of snowy whiteness floating on the air, and the next all is quietness, while the cloudlike train of steam remains a moment white, and then is seen no more. Our flower-loving friend is now in all his glory, poking and prying along the vegetable fringe that skirts the path. Every now and then we are startled by his exclamations of delight, as some specimen of more than ordinary beauty meets his gaze. Nor is his attention devoted altogether to the fair children of Flora. Now he directs our admiring eyes to some richly-tinted moth or butterfly, with coat of many colours, all of whom he seems to know by name; and anon he picks up strange shells with curious markings, and creeping things, which we pretend to admire at his suggestion, although the very sight of them in reality makes us "grue and scunner." Odd fellows, I trow, are these same naturalists, with their "books in the running brooks," "their sermons in stones,"[41] and all that sort of thing. But now our friend has found some extraordinary prize, and calls us loudly to his side, that we may share in his rapture. "What a beauty we have here!" he cries, as we approach; and hastening forward we find in his hand – (what dost thou think, gentle reader? but we need not ask thee, for thou wouldst never guess) – why, as we live, a huge bloated toad! Of course we shrink back in disgust; but that won't satisfy our philosophical friend, who talks contemptuously of ignorant prejudices, and ultimately wins us to his side again, with a quotation from the great dramatist, about the toad, ugly and venomous, having a jewel in his head.[42] We venture at last to gaze with the air of a connoisseur upon the panting *Batrachian*, as we think he calls it, and pretend to see great beauty in the eye of the animal, which he explains is the "jewel"[43] alluded to by the immortal dear-stealer.[44] A full, true, and horribly particular account of the monster's habits and mode of living is next

---

[41] Both from Shakespeare's *As You Like It* II.i.

[42] From the same speech in *As You Like It* II.i.

[43] The jewel is actually bufonite (toadstone) which was previously thought to come from inside a toad's head but is really fossilised teeth from an extinct fish.

[44] Shakespeare is supposed to have poached deer from Sir Thomas Lucy of Charlecote.

inflicted upon us, when the loathsome creature is at length, to our infinite relief, permitted to crawl away.

A short distance beyond the railway bridge, the road passes over a gentle eminence, from which an extensive prospect of the surrounding country is obtained. To the north-west the swelling range of the Kilpatrick Hills is seen stretching away into the distance, with the vale of the Lennox, and, in the gap between the Campsie Fells and the heights of Auchineden, Benlomond towering far away on the horizon. Immediately to the left is the loch of Robroyston, which, to borrow a Hibernianism, is really no loch at all, as its waters have been nearly all drained, and what remains of them is overrun with rank vegetation. This was at one time, however, a considerable sheet of water; and we remember well when it was frequented by bands of juvenile anglers from the city, who came out with rod and line to fish for the pike and the eels which abounded in its weedy depths. A large portion of its ancient basin is now under crop and pasture, and there is every appearance that it will soon be brought entirely under the supremacy of the plough.[45] A fir wood partially surrounds the spot, and gives it a peculiarly dreary appearance, which is heightened by the melancholy murmurings of the breeze in the dusky masses of foliage. As we pass along the eye is delighted with a succession of beautiful autumnal features. Among the tall ferns, which shoot out in luxuriant tufts from beneath the hedgerows, the berries of the trailing bramble are seen in large clusters, varying in hue from the brightest red to the most jetty black, while the blush is waxing deeper on the tawny hips of the wilding rose, and the haws are strewn like drops of blood over the foliage of the thorn.

After a walk of about a mile and a-half from Provanmill, we arrive at the mansion of Robroyston, in the immediate vicinity of which the betrayal of Wallace took place. The modern edifice is of considerable extent, and has a somewhat picturesque aspect, with an air of dreariness which reminds one somewhat of the "moated grange," wherein the hapless Mariana of Tennyson's poem lived with her

---

[45] This area is now part of the suburb of Royston.

sorrow.[46] There is a profusion of fine old trees around the spot, principally of the broad-leaved plane species, which, with their heavy masses of foliage, accord well with the sombre associations of the locality. The garden, too, is wild and tangled, and its walls are over run with a green covering of moss. Luxuriant and beautiful as the spot undoubtedly is, we can almost fancy, while gazing upon it, that a curse clings to its precincts. The road winds round this garden, and at the north-west corner, immediately opposite a neat farm-steading, stood the old cottage in which, according to an unvarying tradition, the Scottish hero was so treacherously captured.[47] This shameful occurrence took place on the night of the 5th August, 1305. For the particulars we are indebted principally to the rhymed chronicle of Blind Harry – a document which, with a considerable admixture of palpable error, contains, we are fully persuaded, a large proportion of truth. According to the venerable minstrel, Sir Aymer de Vallance, who at that period held Bothwell Castle for Edward the usurper,[48] invited Sir John Menteith, the professed friend of Wallace, to a conference at Rutherglen kirk. The meeting took place at the time and place appointed, when the English emissary succeeded in bribing the fause Menteith to betray the great Scottish patriot. Wallace was then lurking in the vicinity of Glasgow, and Menteith, who had a nephew in his service, easily discovered his hiding-place, which was at Robroyston, or Rarbreston, as the minstrel calls the locality.

> "Rarbreston, it was near to the wayside,
> And but one house where Wallace used to bide."

Having obtained intelligence through his spies that the hero was to sleep at this place, Menteith, with sixty of his kinsmen, marched in the darkness, and surrounded the little edifice. The treacherous nephew of a traitorous uncle was set to watch by the confiding Wallace, while he and his trusty servant Keirly slept. We must give what followed in the

---

[46] 'Mariana' (1830) by Alfred, Lord Tennyson.
[47] Both the house and the cottage are now gone.
[48] Edward I of England, reigned 1272 – 1307.

rude but pithy language (modernized by Hamilton of Gilbertfield)[49] of the old chronicler:

"But as he soundly slept, the traitor bold
His uncle met, and like a villain told
That now it was indeed the golden time
For him to perpetrate the wicked crime.
Then all the cursed, vile, and barbarous crew,
Surround the house and honest Keirly slew.
The ruffian servant then to work did fall,
Stole Wallace' sword, his dagger, bow, and all;
To bind him then with cords, the coward byke
Fell on the hero; but he, Samson-like,
Sprung to his feet, and with an oaken stool
Broke one rogue's back, – he had no other tool;
And at a second blow, the glowing wall he stains,
With one vile rascal's mingled blood and brains;
While all that could, wild mingling in the fray,
Closed fierce around him, yelling for their prey."

At length the wily Menteith himself appeared, and pretending friendship, induced Wallace to submit. He was immediately thereafter conveyed to Dumbarton, then in the hands of the invaders, and from thence to England, where, to the everlasting dishonour of Edward's name, he was barbarously put to death. An old barn-like edifice, in which, according to tradition, this disgraceful act in a dark tragedy was enacted, stood, until a comparatively recent period, on the spot we have indicated. Latterly it had fallen into decay, and about thirty years ago, as we have been informed, it was finally demolished. Not the slightest vestige of it now remains to mark the site which it occupied so long.[50] Some fragments of its woodwork, however, have been carefully preserved. At the time when the shattered building was in process of removal, the late Mr. Train,[51] the supervisor, an enthusiastic

---

[49] William Hamilton of Gilbertfield (c.1665 – 1751), poet.
[50] A granite monument was erected in 1900 at the site of the betrayal.
[51] Joseph Train (1779 – 1852).

antiquarian (and who, as is well known, supplied Sir Walter Scott with a considerable portion of the raw material, in the shape of old ballads and legends, which he afterwards wove into his inimitable novels), was fortunately located in the village of Kirkintilloch. On hearing that the house in which Wallace was betrayed was about to be removed, he hastened to the spot, and succeeded in appropriating the oaken rafters of the structure. These he got manufactured into a handsome arm chair, which he presented to the great novelist, who would doubtless receive such a relic with the greatest pleasure. It was finally placed among the auld warld treasures of Abbotsford, where, for aught we know, it still remains.[52]

By a pleasant wood-shaded path we now pursue our way in a somewhat easterly direction. After a brief walk, during which we pass the farms of East and West Lumloch,[53] the attention of our artistic companion is attracted by a picturesque old building which is seen upon an eminence peering over the trees. While we are steering our course towards the spot we fall in with a group of rustic juveniles who are congregated by the wayside. Their brown healthy faces are delightful to look upon, after our passage through the High Street of Glasgow with its pallid crowds of hapless little ones. The merry rogues before us have been away among the woods and lanes gathering blackboyds, with which their fingers and lips are deeply stained, and are now resting themselves in this green nook after their devious health inspiring rambles. What a happy boyhood is theirs, compared with that of the youthful denizens of wynds and vennels, where the sun and the winds are shut out – where the wild bird's song is never heard – and where there are neither leaves, nor flowers, nor fruits, to tempt young feet to stray! Addressing one of the urchins, we ask him the names of the various mansions and farms in the vicinity. To all our questions he returns pertinent answers: that house on the knowe is such a farm, and the tenant is Mr. So and so; while this one at the brae-foot is such another farm, and its inhabitant is Mr. T'otherthing. At length we inquire the name of the ancient structure immediately before us.

---

[52] Indeed it does. Abbotsford House is now a museum.
[53] Although modernised, Wester Lumloch Farm survives.

"That's Cardarroch, an auld gentle house," quoth our informant. "And who lives there?" "Oh, naebody," he replies; and coolly adds, after a brief pause, "just some workin' folk." There is certainly a dash of worldly philosophy in the little rogue's reply. "Workin' folk" and "naebodies" are synonymous terms, we are afraid, in the vocabularies of older heads than his.

William Simpson's watercolour of Cardarroch, from the sketch he made on this ramble.

Cardarroch was the seat of an ancient family named Peters, which is now, we believe, extinct. The house is a queer-looking old structure, with peaked gables, crow steps, narrow windows, and a picturesque old doorway, over which is the date of 1625. It is now occupied by several families of weavers and labourers.[54] Our venerable friend Walter Watson, the weaver poet, lived here for a number of years.[55] The old bard selected this residence for the sake of its retired situation and the beauty of the surrounding scenery. "He was a nice auld fallow," said a brother webster, who still drives the shuttle

---

[54] The house fell into ruin in the late 19th century and is now gone.
[55] 1780 – 1854. In 1853 Hugh MacDonald published a selection of Watson's poems, with a memoir.

in an adjoining out-house; "and mony a time I've heard him lilting ower his ain sangs at his ain fireside, in this auld biggin'; but he lost some o' his bairns afore he gaed awa', and I think he was never sae cheery after that. There was mony a ane ca'd here to see the author of 'We've aye been provided for, and sae will we yet.' Ay, ay," he continued, "Wattie was a decent and a kind-hearted old man." While we are conversing with the honest weaver our friend has taken a faithful sketch of the house, and a pretty little picture it makes, with the wee lame laddie sitting on the door-stone, Mrs. Drummond bending over the washing tub, and a stately cock with his troop of hens strutting proudly in the foreground. Even our friend of the shuttle, who is favoured with a sight of the drawing, allows, with a genuine Scotch chariness of praise, that "It is really geyan near the mark."

Our way is now through corn-fields, tinted with the yellow hues of autumn; by green patches of potatoes and turnips, interrupted occasionally by an expanse of moorland purpled with heather, or a dense clump of firwood like a dark shadow on a smiling face. The contrasts of colour on the landscape are harmonious in the extreme, the effect being heightened by the broken lights from a sky in which gray watery clouds are flitting among the prevailing masses of white and blue. Some of the cloud studies would indeed delight the eye of a Ruskin,[56] who can so well read their hidden meanings; and our enthusiastic friend of the pencil and sketch-book again and again exclaims that "It is a thousand pities such glorious combinations should be permitted to pass away undelineated." Ascending the heights of Auchinloch, a prospect of great extent and beauty opens upon our gaze. The vale of the Lennox lies at our feet, as it were, with all its woods and braes – all its villages, mansions, and farms, laid down as in a map. Below us is Kirkintilloch, with its spire above the trees; and away in its own strath the village of Campsie,[57] with the brown fells sleeping in a Sabbath calm which is only disturbed by the silent march

---

[56] John Ruskin (1819 – 1900), art critic and cloud enthusiast.
[57] Milton of Campsie.

of the cloud-shadows that come and go at their own sweet will.[58] There is something exceedingly affecting to our mind in the deep, deep calm which ever seems to rest among the everlasting hills. In the valley and on the plain man has his home, and the din of his works is ever heard; but away up in these mountain solitudes, where the streams are born, he has no abiding-place. As an awestruck stranger he may visit them, but there they tower in aspect all unaltered since creation's morn, and there unchanged they will stand, in their scornful majesty, when countless generations have come and gone, like the shadows upon their breast!

The little village of Auchinloch is delightfully situated upon the ridge from which we are gazing upon the wide spread landscape below. The name of the place is derived from a pretty extensive loch which once existed in the vicinity, but which was entirely drained by means of a tunnel many years ago, the ancient bed of the waters being now covered by waving grain. The village consists of two parallel rows of one-storeyed cottages, inhabited principally by weavers. The population at present amounts to about 126 individuals. In the centre of the village there is a neat little school-house, which was erected and endowed by a native of the place, who seems to have realized a small fortune as a commercial traveller in England. This we learn from the following quaint inscription upon the wall of the edifice: – "Patrick Baird in Auchinloch, merchant traveller to England, mortified to this charity school, in this the place of his nativity, the sum of three hundred and twenty-five pounds sterling money, and also appointed a charity sermon to be preached at this place, about the 25th of December, yearly. He died October the 20th, 1743, aged seventy years. Built in the year 1745. John Baird, portioner in Auchinloch, gave the ground to build this house on, at the desire of the deceased Patrick Baird, his uncle. He gave also a yard." The sum of fifteen pounds is paid annually to the schoolmaster from the endowment, while the sum of one pound five shillings is devoted to pay some young probationer for preaching the annual sermon, and also to the purchase of prize-books and buns to the

---

[58] A reference to 'Composed Upon Westminster Bridge' (1802) by William Wordsworth.

scholars at Christmas. We understand, however, that the sermon has been dispensed with for several years past. This may be partly owing to the fact that the old church, which formerly stood adjacent to the village, has been for many years demolished. It is certainly nowise creditable, however, to the managers of the trust, that the will of the good old pedlar (for such we suppose was the plain meaning of the phrase "merchant traveller" in those days) has not been religiously carried into effect.[59]

By a somewhat circuitous but withal pleasant country road, we now leave Auchinloch for Chryston, which, according to a farmer whom we accost by the way, is situated to the eastward at a distance of "twa miles and a bittock." The "bittock," however, seems to our experience fully equal in length to any of the preceding miles. This parish was formerly remarkable for the extensive cultivation of flax which was carried on within its boundaries. According to the old Statistical Account, published in 1792, about 200 acres of this crop were sown annually. Since that period this feature in the agricultural statistics of the parish has gradually decreased in importance, until at present there is probably not a tithe of the above amount of acreage devoted to this purpose. On our way we pass one large field on which the "lint is in the bell," and really we have seldom a prettier sight. The fresh green of the graceful stalks, and the faint blue colour of the flowers, as they wave in myriads in the autumnal breeze, are indeed exceedingly grateful to the eye. The cultivation of flax is again recommended, we understand, by agricultural authorities; and as the soil in this quarter seems excellently adapted to produce an abundant crop, perhaps it may once more come into favour with the farmers in the neighbourhood, and home-grown linen again become an article of domestic production. Of course, we do not mean that "the rock and the wee pickle tow,"[60] nor even that the spinning-wheel, should be

---

[59] The school was demolished but there is a Baird Memorial Primary School in Cumbernauld to continue Patrick Baird's legacy. The plaque was moved to a new school in Auchinloch, which is now Auchinloch Hall community centre.

[60] A reference to the song by Alexander Ross (1699 – 1784) about a woman spinning with a drop spindle.

revived, but that, with the aid of machinery, Scottish sarks might be again grown to advantage on Scottish fields.

Chryston, at which we now arrive, is a village of remarkable cleanliness of aspect, the houses being mostly whitewashed, and regularly arranged in parallel rows along both sides of a broad and spacious street. It consists principally of one-storeyed cottages, in many instances covered with thatch, and having kail-yards attached to them. Flowers around the doors and windows are alone wanting to realize the picture of a small English country town. At the west end of the Main Street, by which we make our entrance, there is a neat little Free Church, with a handsome school by its side; while at the eastern extremity there is another church, also of small dimensions, in connection with the Establishment.[61] The population consists principally of weavers, with the sprinkling of cart-wrights, blacksmiths, and agricultural labourers, usually found in rural villages.

Near the east end of the village stands a house of some pretensions, which formerly belonged to a family well known in the neighbourhood as "the Grays of Chryston;" and although the old edifice is now in the possession of strangers, the good name of the Gray family still lingers in the memory of the old inhabitants, like golden clouds in the west when the sun has gone down. During the period of the religious troubles in Scotland, the laird of Chryston cast in his lot with the adherents of the Covenant. His house was ever open to afford shelter to the children of persecution. Often in the darkness of night the poor hunted wanderers of the Covenant – ministers upon whose heads a price was set, and lowly peasants who had been driven from house and home – found refuge beneath the roof of the hospitable Grays. At length suspicion fell upon the good old man. He was dragged from his home to a prison, charged with entertaining Covenanting principles, and with having dared to harbour parties under the ban of the law. On his trial he scorned to deny either his creed or his kindness to the distressed, and he was sentenced to be transported to the plantations of Virginia, and to be sold as a slave. The sentence was

---

[61] The Church of Scotland was replaced with a larger new building in 1877 and was united with the old United Free Church in 1929.

carried into effect, and a few months thereafter he was exposed for sale, with many other victims, in one of the market-places of the colony. While standing downcast in the crowd a rich planter approached, and, after scanning him from head to foot, offered a considerable sum for his purchase. The old man remonstrated with the proposed purchaser for offering so much, saying that, as he "was now frail and feckless, he would prove but an indifferent bargain." The sale was effected, however, and he was conveyed to the house of his new master. On arriving there dinner was on the table, and the master ordered his slave to sit down, and, taking a seat himself, said, after a pause, with trembling voice and tearful eye, "Noo, Mr. Gray, will you ha'e the kindness to ask a blessing as you used to do in auld Chryston?" The venerable man was astonished, but without hesitation complied with the request, pouring forth his heart in unaffected devotion. At the conclusion his master, who had meantime been much affected, stood up, and shaking him warmly by the hand, said, "You'll no' mind me, but I was ance your herd callant at Chryston; and I ha'e never forgotten you nor your kindness to me in the days o' langsyne. Many years ago I cam to this country, and things ha'e gane geyan weel wi' me. This day, when I saw you exposed like a brute beast for sale in the market, my heart was indeed sair, and I resolved, without revealing mysel', to bring you to my hame. Sae here you are, and while I ha'e ye sha'na want." Mr. Gray, we need only further mention, remained in Virginia with his old servant and new master, until the "blast was blawn,"[62] and the perfidious Stuarts were hurled from a throne of which they were unworthy,[63] when he returned to Scotland, and ended his days in peace in the home of his fathers.[64]

---

[62] A reference to 'When Wild War's Deadly Blast Was Blawn' (1793) by Robert Burns.

[63] The Glorious Revolution of 1688 – 1689, when James II was ousted in favour of William of Orange and Mary II.

[64] According to Robert Wodrow's *History of the Sufferings of the Church of Scotland*, James Grey was sent to Jamaica, not Virginia, in 1685. Wodrow does not mention this story about the former parishioner, but says there were "several very remarkable providential deliveries and preservations" of Mr Gray.

No. XXI. Robroyston, Auchinloch, and Chryston

In a cottage nearly opposite the mansion of the Grays was born, in the year 1780, our old friend, Walter Watson, the Chryston poet. Here also the boyhood of the venerable bard was spent; here he courted the Maggie of his song and the mother of his children; and here he first made the acquaintance of the muse. Many of the places in the locality, such as the Braes of Bedlay and the Buthland Burn, are celebrated in his lays. It is now upwards of fifty years since Walter made his *debut* before the public as a song writer, and many of our elderly readers will remember, we have no doubt, that "Sit ye doon, my cronie," and "Jockie's far awa," were popular favourites in their boyish years. A poor man's son, the poet has never, with all his industry, managed to speel the stey brae of Fortune, and now at the patriarchal age of seventy-three he earns his bread upon the loom. Although the snows of winter, however, are now upon the head of the old bard, his heart still retains a considerable portion of the greenness of spring. Nor has the gift of song been altogether withdrawn by the trembling hand of age, as the following spirited verses which he composed the other day will abundantly show. In writing them for us, the poet remarks, "I wadna wish to be in better tift."[65] Long may the ancient minstrel be enabled so to speak!

"SONG."
AIR – 'Last May a braw wooer.'

"I needna lie doon, for my e'e wadna bow,
The din o' the storm maks me eerie;
And doubts comin' in, fill my bosom sae fu',
That dowie and daeless I wearie, I wearie,
That dowie and daeless I wearie

"My lad should ha'e been, for he promised to be,
What way can I be but uneasy?
Will some tocher'd hizzie ha'e ta'en his blythe e'e?
Gude life, I'm jist like to gang crazy, gang crazy,

---

[65] condition

Gude life, I'm jist like to gang crazy.

"The burn will be grit, and the steps ower the head,
The Gude ha'e a care gin he tak' them;
The road's jist as ill for the makin' o'speed
As wearin' and water can mak' them, can mak' them,
As wearin' and water can mak' them.

"A waiting on something we canna forget,
A something that luck may mak' free wi',
Gars Patience look doon, like a bairn in the pet,
And naething looks up we can gree wi', can gree wi',
And naething looks up we can gree wi.

"Ha! here he's himsel', it's his tirl at the door,
And life wi' my lad is returning;
The spate may come doon, and the blast tak' its roar,
I'll keep him till gray in the morning, the morning,
I'll keep him till gray in the morning."

Immediately to the east of Chryston is the fine old house of Bedlay. This stately building stands upon a terrace of gentle elevation, on the margin of a little well-wooded dell, through which a streamlet of diminutive size wimples and wanders at its own sweet will.[66] Bedlay House is of quadrangular form, with two round turrets, like gigantic pepper boxes, at one end, and a rectangular tower at the other. The high-peaked gables are rendered more picturesque by having crow-steps, while the windows are small and narrow. On the eastern gable a coat of arms adorns the wall, with the motto, "For securitie." This edifice formerly belonged to the Earls of Kilmarnock. From their hands it passed into those of a family named Roberton, who retained it

---

[66] A reference to 'Composed Upon Westminster Bridge' (1802) by William Wordsworth.

for several generations, when it fell into the possession of a gentleman named Campbell, whose heirs are the present proprietors.[67]

Bedlay House has, or at least had, the unenviable reputation of being haunted. Who or what the ghost was while in the flesh we have been unable to discover, but that *something* uncannie had been seen or heard about the place is, or we should perhaps say was, very generally believed over the neighbourhood. One old man informed us seriously that it was a bad laird of former days who could not get rest in his grave. "He was a sair trouble to a' about him (quoth our informant) when he was leevin', and I think it's rather too bad that he should get leave to come back and disturb decent folk after he's dead." According to fireside gossip a party of ministers were on one occasion called in to lay the unquiet spirit; and we are assured, on the authority of an old man whose father held the reverend gentlemen's horses while they were engaged in the work, that when they came out of the house afterwards, "the very sweat was pouring down their faces." Whether the holy men succeeded in giving the ghost its quietus, or whether the general spread of knowledge, as is perhaps more likely, has put it to flight, we do not know, but one thing is certain, and that is, that there is now considerable doubts among the people of Chryston with regard to its existence. One gudewife, whom we question on the subject while she is filling her pitcher at Bedlay well, says, – "It's my honest opinion there was mair clash than onything else in the ghost story; and for my part I dinna believe ae word o't." Probably she is right.[68] Our artistic companion, who is charmed with the appearance of the venerable structure, having set himself down, however, to transfer a *fac-simile* of it into his sketch-book, we shall fill up the time till he is done with an anecdote of a former laird and our friend the Chryston poet. The said laird, we may premise, was a somewhat eccentric character; at times he would have cracked freely with the poorest person he met, and at others he was the very impersonation of haughtiness and pride. A rumour having reached the weaver poet that the laird had expressed a favourable opinion of some of his verses, nothing would serve him, in

---

[67] Bedlay Castle is still a private dwelling.
[68] Reports of hauntings at Bedlay Castle continued until at least the 1970s.

the vanity of his heart, but that he should write something new, and present it to the great man in person. Casting about for a subject, he at length came to the conclusion that were he to compose a song, the scene of which was laid on the gentleman's own estate, he would be quite certain of a favourable reception. "The Braes of Bedlay" was accordingly written, and snodding himself up with his Sunday braws, the young poet took the road one evening to the big house. On coming to the door he tirled bravely at the knocker, and was at once ushered into the presence of the laird. In the eyes of the young weaver he looked exceedingly grand, and he almost began to repent his temerity in having ventured into such company. "Well, who are you, and what do you want?" said the laird (who was evidently in one of his bad moods), with a voice of thunder. "My name's Walter Watson," faltered the poet, "and I was wanting you to look at this bit paper." "What paper," said the grandee, "can you have to show me? but let me see it." The manuscript was placed in his hands, and stepping close to the candle, he proceeded to peruse it. "It'll be a' richt noo," thinks his bardship. The laird, reading to himself, had got through with the first verse, when he repeated aloud the last two lines –

"Whar Mary and I meet amang the green bushes,
    That screen us sae weel on the braes o' Bedlay."

"Who is Mary?" quoth he abruptly. "Oh I dinna ken," said the poet, "but Mary's a nice poetical name, and it suited my measure." "And *you* actually wrote this!" added the laird. "Yes," replied the poet, gaining confidence, "you'll see I've put my name to the verses." "Well," vociferated his lairdship, raising himself to his full altitude, "are you not a most impudent fellow, to come here and tell me that you have been breaking my fences and strolling over my grounds without leave? I'm just pestered with such interlopers as you on my property, and now that I have the acknowledgment of the offence under your own hand, I've really a very good mind to prosecute you for trespass! Get away with you to your loom! and if ever I catch either you or your Mary among my green bushes again, depend upon it, I'll make you repent it!" Saying this, he flung the manuscript scornfully at the poet (who stood trembling, half in fear and half in indignation), and, ringing the bell, ordered him at once to be ejected from the house. Alas! poor fellow, he went home that night with an aching heart, and sadly crest-fallen. His song was given to the world, however, and immediately attained a considerable degree of popularity, a great portion of which, we are happy to say, it still retains. The laird has left the land which he so churlishly guarded, and his memory is fast falling into oblivion; while that of Walter Watson, who sung its beauties, will be entwined with the spot for ages. Truly there is a lairdship in genius which is more potent and lasting than that which is associated with rent-rolls and title-deeds! It is but fair to state, however, that the laird and the poet afterwards became good friends, and that the friendship was in many respects beneficial to the humble bard.

Our companion having finished his sketch we now make the best of our way to the highway between Glasgow and Cumbernauld, which we enter upon somewhere in the vicinity of the seventh mile-stone from the city. Let our readers now suppose us, all wearied as we are, to assume our seven-league boots, by means of which, passing Garnkirk, Millerston, Hogganfield, and Bluevale, with telegraphic rapidity, we arrive within the precincts of Sanct Mungo before the gray-mantled gloaming[69] has called forth the stars.

---

[69] A reference to 'Love and Solitude' (1838) by Thomas Pringle.

Index

Ingram Content Group UK Ltd.
Milton Keynes UK
UKHW011257120323
418437UK00001B/54